Messiahs and Messianic
Movements Through 1899

ALSO BY ROLAND H. WORTH, JR.
AND FROM MCFARLAND

Congress Declares War (2004)

Alternative Lives of Jesus: Noncanonical Accounts through the Early Middle Ages (2003)

Biblical Studies on the Internet: A Resource Guide (2002)

World War II Resources on the Internet (2002)

Secret Allies in the Pacific: Covert Intelligence and Code Breaking Cooperation Between the United States, Great Britain, and Other Nations Prior to the Attack on Pearl Harbor (2001)

Church, Monarch and Bible in Sixteenth Century England: The Political Context of Biblical Translation (2000)

Pearl Harbor: Selected Testimonies, Fully Indexed, from the Congressional Hearings (1945–1946) and Prior Investigations of the Events Leading Up to the Attack (1993)

Bible Translations: A History Through Source Documents (1992)

Messiahs and Messianic Movements through 1899

Roland H. Worth, Jr.

McFarland & Company, Inc., Publishers
Jefferson, North Carolina, and London

ISBN 0-7864-2311-0 (softcover : 50# alkaline paper)

Library of Congress Cataloguing-in-Publication data are available

British Library cataloguing data are available

©2005 Roland H. Worth, Jr. All rights reserved

No part of this book may be reproduced or transmitted in any form or by any means, electronic or mechanical, including photocopying or recording, or by any information storage and retrieval system, without permission in writing from the publisher.

Cover photograph ©2005 Corel Corporation

Manufactured in the United States of America

McFarland & Company, Inc., Publishers
Box 611, Jefferson, North Carolina 28640
www.mcfarlandpub.com

To Loretta Worth,
in deepest appreciation for three decades of
loving support and encouragement

Contents

Preface   1
Introduction   3

1. Pre–First Century Messiahs   7
2. First Century Messiahs Outside the Jesus Movement   20
3. Second Century Messiahs   38
4. Messiahs in the Years of Western Europe's Decline (A.D. 200–500)   50
5. Messiahs in the Years of Western Europe's Collapse (A.D. 500–1000)   56
6. Messianic Movements in the Late Middle Ages (1000–1300)   63
7. Jewish Messiahs During the Renaissance and Reformation (1300–1600)   83
8. Gentile Messiahs During the Renaissance and Reformation (1300–1600)   110
9. Jewish Messiahs During the European Colonization of the Americas (1600–1800)   127
10. Gentile Messiahs During the European Colonization of the Americas (1600–1800)   166
11. Messianic Movements During the Birth of the Technological Age (1800–1900)   193

Notes   211
Bibliography   236
Index   249

Preface

This volume primarily sketches the history of messianic claimants in the Near East, Europe, North Africa, and North America. There have been others worthy of attention in Asia, Africa, and South America, but information on these individuals is scarce, and I have not been able to assemble enough reliable information to include them here.

I do not make any claim that the list of messiahs for the regions covered is complete. In a case or two I refer to "anonymous" messiahs—individuals who are known to have existed but whose identities never made it into surviving records. Doubtless there were many more of these. In addition, of those who are known by name, the careers are sometimes so little documented that the individuals barely rise above the level of anonymity. I have felt free to omit a few such cases.

There are many ways to spell some of the ancient (and even the more recent) names used in this text. For example, the second century Bar Kochba can also be spelled Bar Kokhba, Bar Koshba, and Bar Kosiba (and with or without a capital "B"). I have adopted one form of each name for the body of the text, but alternative forms are preserved in any quotations.

Finally, there is the matter of the dates provided for the individuals included here. In some cases I have provided the dates of their life-span, but in other cases—especially when the actual life dates are a matter of conjecture at best—I have settled for the date or period in which they came to public attention.

As in my past religious-historical writings, I owe an immense debt of gratitude to the William Smith Morton Library of the Union Theological Seminary of Richmond, Virginia. Their vast collection of resources has proved an invaluable resource for widely divergent views, giving my work a depth that would otherwise have been impossible.

Introduction

Properly speaking, the word "Messiah" denotes a person who has been anointed as a sign of appointment by God to a specific task of importance.[1] Hence the term can technically be applied to any individual set apart for service by God and can include anyone from religious functionaries (priests) to spiritual teachers (prophets) to political rulers (kings).[2]

Indeed, to be a messiah a person did not necessarily even have to be an Israelite, provided that God was utilizing that person's position, service, and talents to accomplish His will. Hence the Persian king is described in such terms in Isaiah 45:1–2.[3] This text is especially useful in bringing out the correlation between anointing and power: it was a visible sign of God's commitment to act in that person's behalf and to overcome all obstacles to his accomplishing the divinely ordained functions.

It is the political aspect that became uppermost in later biblical and then postbiblical discussion of the term. Hence in this volume I often lay aside that large number of individuals who have only claimed a prophetic office even when their actual practice resulted in them exercising de facto or de jure control over their movements.

The distinction between "messianic" and "prophetic" is very important but easily blurred in actual application.[4] The messianic individual elevates himself (or herself, in a few cases) to a level of authority far beyond that of a religious teacher, a self-proclaimed supernaturally-guided prophet, or the official holder of a church position. The movement comes to be uniquely centered on him, his teachings, and the claim to spiritual and sometimes even temporal authority over all his followers.

It is out of a desire both to limit the scope of this study and to avoid attributing to these individuals a specialness or uniqueness that they themselves did not claim that I exclude those individuals who only claimed to be prophets or revealers of a new revelation for the human race. Some element that elevated the person above this level is necessary to warrant inclusion.

An example of such an element is involvement in creating a "messianic situation"; i.e., one that would be viewed as making possible the appearance of the messiah. Hence the various revolutionaries for national and religious independence in first century Palestine are included even though it is impossible to determine the degree to which all claimed or asserted an explicitly messianic role for themselves. In all cases, however — if their goals had been successful and national independence secured — then there would have been at least the potential for them to evolve into that role or to be encouraged by others to do so. In light of the religio-cultural context of the era, this would seemingly have been the inevitable hope of a significant number of their followers.

Much of the scholarship of the late twentieth century shifted dramatically against assuming a messianic status for these individuals. A more expansive understanding of the concept of the search for a messiah still makes them appropriate and necessary individuals to include, however. Furthermore, even if they avoided making such claims, given the temper of the times and the actions we know they undertook, such could easily have evolved if they had been successful.

The messianic individual or movement may make the religious element central in their claims. Others act as if it is of little concern to them. They become not religious redeemers but secular redeemers of a particular religious or ethnic group. And if they do follow the "religious" approach, they may or may not view themselves as superhuman or supernatural. The concept of Messiah, in practice, has brought forth a wide range of creative reactions in defining the term in the actual lives of those involved.

The individuals may have chosen the role for themselves and convinced others to follow. In another type of case we will find that the movements have basically chosen for themselves a messianic leader. These people were more or less involuntarily co-opted by the group into their new role.

To complicate the picture further, some messianic claimants never develop much of a following. They appear, are mentioned in one or a handful of sources, and disappear without leaving more than a token impact on their own age and those that follow. Yet they qualify for attention because of what they claimed to be rather than for their success, since they reveal the wide variety of individuals attracted to the role and show us how their attitudes, claims, and actions have varied drastically through the centuries.

At the other extreme, some redemptive movements remain exactly that — movements, but not led by messianic individuals. They see the group as accomplishing the Divine reformative mission in this life and do not regard it as essential (at least in the short term) for that special role to be given to or expropriated by any one individual. They successfully exist without any individual assuming that role.

Yet so important is the latter that popular imagination normally equates messianic with an individual's claim and is wary of a group interpretation of the motif. Even so, those seeking earthly temporal or spiritual redemption may well come in either form, and it is unwise to fully reject either approach from consideration, though our main emphasis will be on specific individuals.

Furthermore, depending upon the nature of the group and its theology, even when an individual is the center of attention it may not be because of his personal messianic claims. Some have claimed to be the special, unique forerunner whose role is to prepare the people for the Messiah. Others have claimed the more ambiguous role of simply preparing the people for the imminent appearance of the Messiah — thereby lowering the individual's claimed status by a notch, but with little practical result: he *is* the leader, at least in the interim.

One who claims to be the politico-religious Messiah figure depicted in the Jewish and Christian Scriptures must do so from one of two directions. The traditionalist Jew must assume that he is looking for the first (but not necessarily only) coming of the Messiah. If the claimant embraces a Christian heritage, then he has two basic sets of options available: He can either claim that a physical second coming in a new body and with a new name was for some reason essential, or he can claim that the inner essence of Jesus of Nazareth has been imbued upon him. (This works best with a Gnostic-style theory of the Christ person entering the individual, as ancient gnostics assumed happened with Jesus of Nazareth.) In either case, he must explain why it was necessary for this departure from the traditional norm of a "second coming of the Lord" unless he is fortunate enough to be dealing with individuals willing to accept the fact without an explanation.

The messiahs we examine in this book come from varied backgrounds and are scattered over many centuries. At least one (the emperor Vespasian) was an outright polytheist, but merits inclusion because the scriptural imagery was explicitly applied to him by at least one prominent Jew, Josephus. Yet they all bear witness to the belief that "being with Christ in the sky in the by and by" may represent comforting theology, but that many are willing to bet their lives, economic well-being, and status on being able to gain that kind of access while still in a body of flesh and blood.

We have chosen to conclude this book with the end of the nineteenth century. By limiting myself to this earlier epoch, we can consider the individuals and movements with a degree of objectivity and historical distance that is far more difficult to give more recent ones. Indeed, the passage of time has provided a depth of knowledge and even competing interpretations that are unavailable for more contemporary figures. In contrast, to give recent and contemporary individuals, many who worked with them have simply not written about their experiences and, when they have, are typically concerned with preserving the public relations image presented to the world rather than working out the ramifications of the person and the movement. Indeed, even with the best will possible, this normally requires the passage of years or decades.

In addition, the twentieth century brought with it an essentially new phenomena that could easily require the introduction of a radically different type of material as well — a discussion of anti-Judeo-Christian secular messianic movements, i.e., strictly secular ideologies with messianic goals. I have in mind in particular Communism and fascism (especially in its incarnation as Nazism).[5] Both had their theologies (Marxism–Leninism and *Mein Kampf*, respectively) and both had their Messiahs— Joseph Stalin and Adolf Hitler.

The psychological and social dynamics of all this is quite fascinating. And it raises the unanswerable question — unanswerable until actual events provide the answer — as to whether other new ideological systems will arise that will serve traditionally religious goals but in the name of secular "progress."

Yet such matters are so dramatically different in their very nature and require such a dramatic redefinition of "messianic"— however valid that redefinition actually is— that these and other matters related to the twentieth century are better left for consideration in a different context.

1

Pre–First Century Messiahs

The Biblical Legacy: Latter Suspicions That the Predicted Messiah Had Already Come

King Hezekiah was remembered for his reversal of government policy from one embracing polytheism to one backing monotheism. Accompanied by major efforts to minimize (though not totally eliminate) polytheism, he became the embodiment of the ruler who wished to return the nation to its monotheistic roots. (Many modern scholars actually see the traditional "Mosaical system" of monotheism and worship as coming into existence in that era; both later rabbis and the scriptural text look at them originating many centuries earlier and being revived under this king.) Hence it is not surprising that one segment of later Jewish opinion argued that he had been the intended fulfillment of the messianic strain of the ancient Scriptures.

The illustrious first-century Rabbi Hillel declared, "Israel no longer need expect the Messiah for he was already consumed [he already appeared] in the days of Hezekiah."[1] The view was scorned by other rabbis of his time. A Rabbi Joseph responded, "May the Holy One, Blessed be He, pardon Rabbi Hillel."[2] In other words, he was guilty not only of a totally erroneous interpretation but a sacrilegious one as well.

In another slap at Hillel's view, Rabbi Gidel once spoke of how Israel would ultimately be blessed with the reign of the Messiah. One Rabbi Yosef replied, "This is self-evident. Who else should enjoy them? Perhaps Hileq and Bileq (two imaginary persons) should enjoy them?" The Talmud then added that Gidel was not trying to state a self-evident truism but to repudiate Hillel's teaching about Hezekiah.[3]

Bar Kappara of Sepphoris (either second or third century) was probably reacting to the Hillel hypothesis when he attempted to save the messiah for a later age by arguing that "The Lord wished to make Hezekiah Messiah, but Justice protested and said, 'Master of the Universe, David, King of Israel, who sang so many songs and praises unto thee, Thou didst not make Messiah. Hezekiah, in whose behalf Thou hast already performed so many miracles, and who did not sing praises unto Thee, wilt thou make him Messiah?' Wherefore it was closed."[4] In other words, since Hezekiah had not fully honored God even in the manner of David, how could he be given the status? Some take this to mean that his pride and vanity excluded him from the reward.[5]

A variant of the Hezekiah as Messiah motif is that of describing the Messiah as the "second" Hezekiah in a manner parallel to the more typical view of the Messiah as a kind of "second" David. Rabbi Yohanan ben Zakkai (also of the first century) made this substitution, for example.[6] Here, though, the idea is raised not to exclude a future redeemer figure but to provide a historical parallel or precedent for him. This approach permitted an individual to fully believe in the Messiah while discounting later claimants whose actions could stir up dangerous animosity and overwhelming bloodshed in the nation.

Hezekiah could not have been successful without a significant body of supporters who rallied to the cause of monotheistic reform. Hence it is easy to imagine that at least some of them would suspect that the king's actions qualified him for the messianic role. In light of his earlier following of the polytheistic norm, both he and they may well have felt him unqualified to make such a claim and, if so, this would certainly explain the absence of any scriptural hints suggesting such an interpretation of his life.

But what of other Old Testament kings being cast in that role? Some interpreters of the passages describing Zerubbabel in the book of Zechariah have read them as hinting or indicating that there was at least a limited contemporary hope that he would become the messianic figure.[7] For them to have hoped such would not be unnatural, yet the need to massage the text to come to this conclusion argues that, if it existed at all, it never rose above the level of desire to that of explicit conviction.

Herod the Great (40s–4 B.C.)

Herod was brilliantly successful. Aligning himself with the Romans, he maneuvered and outfought his domestic rival to win the throne. Virtually no sooner had this occurred than the Romans themselves plunged into a bloody civil war. Herod's own preference was his long-term friend and ally Antony. However, thanks to the conniving of Antony's lover, Cleopatra, he was diverted into a minor side war that was being waged at the same time.[8] This was but the latest episode in which she had tried to undermine him, having earlier tried to maneuver his wife's preference for high priest into that position in place of Herod's own.[9]

Recognizing that his preferred alliance was being fatally undermined by Cleopatra, he proceeded to shift sides to Octavian. Although everyone knew full well his prior actions and loyalties and he made no effort to hide them,[10] he was still able to convince Octavian that his allegiance had now shifted.[11] The fact that there was no practical alternative to Herod made Octavian's decision that much easier.[12]

Although Octavian triumphed and Herod retained his power, his family relationships created intense domestic turmoil that repeatedly embittered him. The maneuvering to force a substitute high priest challenged his power, as did the repeated efforts of his wife to increase the influence of her own family and kin. If this were not bad enough, her reported adulteries seemed all too credible and struck at his ego and pride.[13]

Stir into this the fact that his own sister, Salome, repeatedly agitated the situation to make the wife and her kin appear even worse,[14] and it is easy to see how Herod's personality slowly became dominated by an almost uncontrollable rage and anger that could endanger any one he regarded as disloyal. His government, out of both self-interest and family-induced paranoia, became nothing less than a police state with widespread informers and the heavy-handed use of power against enemies both real and imagined. Excessive spending on new and upgraded garrisons provided the military muscle to withstand any but the most dangerous challenge to his power.[15]

Yet he was determined to build a positive legacy as well, and the massive building projects of his reign were numerous. These included public entertainment facilities such as theaters, amphitheaters, and hippodromes.[16] Of course, this carried with it the need to finance periodic public entertainments to be offered in them.[17] By the nature of these places, they were of most appeal, of course, to gentiles and to hellenistically inclined Jews.

Most important of all to the Jewish people themselves was the magnificent new temple that was constructed. In this multi-decade project that was the high point of Herod's building accomplishments, one can see both his boldness of plan and expenditure. Yet one can also see the grave public suspicion that much of the public had of his integrity, religious commitment, and intentions: in order to gain approval for the work it had to be agreed that, before any structure or part of a structure was torn down, the material to build a replacement had to be on the scene and available.[18] In spite of all his power, he recognized that defiance of these demands was only going to fuel suspicion and would keep him from carrying out the single largest project of his reign, so he had no choice but to yield.

He even built entire cities. There was a new Jericho.[19] He rebuilt the city of Samaria.[20] The nation lacked an adequate seaport,[21] so he took an existing small one and transformed it into a good one and named the town Caesarea.[22]

However flattering to his ego, such massive accomplishments could not compensate for the literal pains and anguish of his last ten years of life. Although he had been a vigorous man for decades, bodily ailments began to put him in near-constant pain.[23] His family relationships went from bad to worse and became a well-known public scandal that resulted in the execution of kin he had tolerated for many years. Finally, there was an ill-advised military conflict with the Nabataeans that caused the Roman government to become antagonistic and which required much effort to bring about a reconciliation.[24] The man who could rightly claim to be one of the most outwardly successful rulers of his day soon died with most of the nation hating him, his family in ruins, and his body in agony.

Herod as a Messianic Claimant

The possibility that Herod regarded himself as a messianic figure has been rejected on the ground that a belief in a coming Messiah was at the time only in favor with the apocalyptic fringe of society and that Herod was hardly likely to embrace an idea from such a disreputable source.[25] On the other hand, excess brutality must always be justified on one ground or another in order to maintain one's self-respect. Caligula could convince himself that he was literally a deity, working from the assumptions of his own religious and cultural background. Claiming a Jewish ancestry, instead, what more convenient basis for justifying any and all actions was there than the messianic one?

After all, Herod could view himself as not only a God-ordained ruler, but far more as well — that his rulership over the contemporary equivalent of David's Israel proved himself to be the predicted Messiah who would reestablish a kingdom of outward prosperity and magnificence. In a malevolent personality like Herod's, this carried with it the inherent right to do anything and everything necessary to preserve that kingdom against all potential foes. Literally nothing could be automatically wrong in such a sacred endeavor. How seriously he took such an evaluation is impossible to know, but for him not to have tinkered with it in his mind would have been extraordinary in itself.

In addition, there is at least limited data backing the deduction that he viewed himself as messianic and, at least in some circles, was accepted in such a manner. His construction of the temple and how he went about it ties in perfectly with a messianic self-conception. Furthermore, Herod spared no expense in making the temple as illustrious and beautiful as the human imagination could make it. It was not just an accomplishment of his regime; it was to be the showpiece of his reign.

Although Sean Freyne prefers to limit the implications of the project to being an effort "to bolster his image at home and abroad as a benevolent Hellenistic-style monarch,"[26] this could have been accomplished at far lesser expense and effort if this had been his only goal. Indeed, his refusal to undertake any but a few symbolic major changes in the facility could easily have been portrayed as an effort to support the religious judgment of the temple administrators in their efforts to maintain it in its purity as independently as possible of outside control.

Second, his policies regarding the temple also reflected a desire to maximize its impact upon the Jewish population not just domestically but also in foreign lands. In particular, one can think of how he went into the Diaspora to select high priests. This would solidify the Diaspora's interest in the temple and magnify Herod's central role in appointing these outsiders to its most important post.[27]

There is more concrete evidence of Herod's messiahship as well. Archaeologically, pottery was discovered at the Masada excavations bearing the telling wording, "Regi Herodi Judaic (o)," i.e., claiming Herod as king of the Jews. Not just as king. Not just as a Roman client king. But as king of the Jewish people.[28]

Furthermore, he carried out a foreign policy that would place him in the role of becoming the protector of Jews in other regions, i.e., function as their king as well. Josephus speaks of Herod's bragging of this role when recounting his travels in Asia Minor to the people back in his own country: "Appearing before them, he gave an account of his whole journey and told them about the Jews of Asia, saying that *thanks to him* they would be unmolested in the future."[29]

Finally, in the fourth century Rabbi Nathan cites the messianic proof texts that were used by prior generations to prove that the Hasmoneans, Herod, and then bar Kochba should be regarded as messianic figures. He does so not to endorse the use but to rebuke the use of scriptural passages that turned out to have no relevance to what actually happened[30]:

> This verse pierces me and descends to the very abyss: *For the vision to wait for an appointed time, but at the end it shall speak, and shall not lie; though he tarry wait for him; because he will surely come, it will not tarry* (Hab. 2:3). Not as our Masters, who interpreted the verse, *until a time and times and the dividing of time* (Dan. 7:25); nor as R. Simlai who expounded, *Thou feedest them with the bread of tears; and gives them tears to drink a third time* (Psalms 80:6); nor as R. Akiba who expounded, *Yet once, it is a little while and I will shake the heavens and the earth* (Hag. 2:6); but the first dynasty [the Hasmoneans] shall last seventy years, the second [the Herodians] fifty-two, and the reign of Bar Koziba two and a half years.

Simon (4 B.C.)

While Augustus deliberated as to whether Archelaus or someone else would take Herod's place, he appointed Sabinus as interim governor with the specific duty of protecting the considerable financial assets that Herod had accumulated as ruler. Unfortunately he took this as authority to seize the temple treasury as well. When Passover came, conflict erupted with the pilgrims and the rage was so intense and widespread that Sabinus was compelled to retreat with his forces into the palace of Herod.[31] Like a fuse attached to a keg of gunpowder, the situation degenerated into a series of independent insurrections against Roman power.

There is no indication of coordination between the various rebellions, however.[32] Indeed, the three individuals Josephus identifies as regal claimants (Judas, Simon, and Athronges) existed as rivals not only to the probability of Herod's children taking over, but also to each other as well. Sean Freyne is quite correct when he reasons from such facts that they "raise the question of how seriously we are to take the royal pretensions of any of the contenders, or more importantly, how seriously their claims were taken by people in general."[33] Were they mere scavengers at the dinner table hoping to walk off with the main course or should they be regarded as serious insurgents with a significant possibility of taking their place at that dinner table as host and master? Yet even scavengers can still hope to take advantage of an unstable situation and turn a weak claim into a genuine one.

Even divided, each rebellion was significant in and of itself, but a divided foe is a defeatable foe. If coordination had existed through a mutually acknowledged central leader or group, then the rebellions might have been successful.[34] The Jewish problem was that the Romans were determined to hold onto that part of the world by one means or another. Hence the success might have been only temporary until it could bring adequate forces to bear. On the other hand, one could imagine Rome coming to an "understanding" with a united new regime that provided internal independent government but also guaranteed conformity with Roman foreign policy. Yet the lack of unity forestalled this possibility from being considered.

One of the insurrections of this period was led by Simon, a man whom Josephus describes as a "slave" or "servant" of Herod while he was alive. R.A. Horsley speculates that the description could mean that he was "a lower-level Herodian official but more likely a tenant-farmer on the royal estates east of the Jordan."[35]

According to Josephus, he was a handsome individual and had demonstrated his talents to such a degree that, under Herod, he[36]:

> had had great things committed to his care. This man was elevated at the disorderly state of things, and was so bold as to put a diadem on his head, while a certain number of the people stood by him, and by them he was declared to be a king, and thought himself more worthy of that dignity than any one else. He burnt down the royal palace at Jericho, and plundered what was left in it. He also set fire to many other of the king's houses in several places of the country, and utterly destroyed them, and permitted those that were with him to take what was left in them for a prey; and he would have done greater things, unless care had been taken to repress him immediately; for Gratus, when he had joined himself to some Roman soldiers, took the forces he had with him, and met Simon, and after a great and a long fight, no small part of those that came from Peraea, who were a disordered body of men, and fought rather in a bold than in a skillful manner, were destroyed; and although Simon had saved himself by flying away through a certain valley, yet Gratus overtook him, and cut off his head.

Josephus conceded that the insurrection was so brutally suppressed that it actually inflamed the situation further.[37]

The palaces were invaluable beginning points for several reasons. For one thing, they represented the symbol of past authority. For another they provided valuable possessions that could be looted to the economic benefit of the insurgents.

Simon's assertion of kingship would, at the minimum, be an assertion that he should be regarded as Herod's proper successor. Yet there are several factors arguing that a messianic connotation was inevitably connected with this as well. The event happens not only in a Jewish context but also in one of social unrest in which violence and instability with its inevitable apocalyptic concerns would arise. If the world seems to be (and in this case, was) "falling apart," the king they sought would surely be someone divinely endowed to uniquely set things right. In short, a Messiah.[38]

Athronges (4 B.C.)

Athronges was a shepherd by occupation but enjoyed sufficient charisma and organizational skills to assemble a body of armed supporters in Judea who recognized him as king.[39] Much of his appeal appears to have been his physical stature: tall in height and unusually strong in body, he looked the role of a king.[40]

Unlike the other rebel movements of the time, this one is specifically identified as having had some type of formal organization into separate groups,[41] howbeit under men who were his brothers.[42] This would seem to suggest that most of the rival movements were essentially one-man affairs in which loyalty was strictly to their leader. Furthermore, it argues for a much smaller body of supporters than Anthronges', since a fundamental demand of any numerically substantial body would be the division of it into smaller units for the purpose of effectively utilizing the available manpower.

Athronges and his subordinates freely assaulted Jews who were known to collaborate as well as those who were uncommitted to either side.[43] They assaulted and killed both past and present supporters of Herod as well.[44]

These were easy targets, but they were confident and bold enough to go far beyond this and even attack Roman army supply trains as they moved from place to place.[45] Especially alarming was what happened at the town of Emmaus, which lay some twenty miles from Jerusalem. A Roman military unit, accompanied by assorted Herodian forces, had been out foraging supplies in that region when they were ambushed. Almost half of the Romans were killed, but the Herodian soldiers proved their worth in the crisis by successfully covering their escape.[46]

The humiliating defeat of the Romans did not stop their allies. The Herodian forces then continued their sweep of the countryside without the Roman assistance. Ultimately they tracked down and captured two of Athronges' brothers. The others escaped capture for a good while longer.[47] The severity of this insurrection can be seen in that fact that the evidence is compatible with it lasting as long as two years.[48]

Did Athronges claim to be Messiah or was he embraced as such by his supporters?[49] He certainly put on the crown of a king and, in the Jewish context and in one of revolutionary unrest, the hope that he would play the messianic role seems inescapable. And what people want, the astute leader typically becomes—or attempts to.

It has been objected that there is only a crowning and not an anointing to leadership mentioned by Josephus; followers of this theory believe that this might indicate the lack of messianic connotations to Athronges' assertion of kingship.[50] On the other hand, we would expect such an anointing to come from a priestly source, and it was hardly likely that any major figure would commit himself to such an action until or if he actually gained power over a large section of the country and managed to keep it. Crowning would not likely require an authoritative background because its validity rests with the man receiving the crown, while an anointing finds its validity in the person doing it.

Furthermore, the shepherding background of Athronges fit perfectly with messianic aspirations. The prototype/ideal king of Israel was David, who had come from exactly that environment. Indeed, Jewish history as far back as Abraham had spoken of important figures in their history who sprang from these roots.[51]

Judas, Son of Hezekiah (4 B.C.)

Some have assumed that Hezekiah (and, therefore, Judas as well) was a descendent of Hasmonean nobility, thereby providing him with a genetic/ancestral tie-in with the "rightful" rulers of the land.[52] However this is speculatory at best and there is no real evidence or line of reasoning to back it beyond the fact that this would have provided the people with a reason to support the two men.[53]

He was likely a commoner, but since he was known to be the son of a famous brigand, it is possible that he had gained a following among dissidents prior to his formal bid for power.[54] Josephus refers to his viciousness and unrestrained cruelty as characterizing his rebellion. He speaks of how Judas "became terrible to all men, by tearing and rending those that came near him; and all this in order to raise himself, and out of an ambitious desire of the royal dignity; and he hoped to obtain that as the reward not of his virtuous skill in war, but of his extravagance in doing injuries."[55]

In other words, his strategy was one of making a sufficient terror of himself that the people would accept him as king as the simplest method of ending his attacks.[56] This was an approach that might earn their acquiescence but certainly not their active support. It also undercut the need for acceptance that was required if he was to persevere in opposing the

Romans. In short, it was an approach that may have maximized the short-term gains, but would have been fatal in the long term.

The city of Sepphoris played an important role in the history of the rebellion. Josephus speaks of how many people of the city and area joined Judas in "an assault upon the palace there, and seized upon all the weapons that were laid up in it, and with them armed every one of those that were with him, and carried away what money was left there...."[57] It has been reasonably argued that the ability to amass a large body of supporters in the community argues that Herod's reign had been detrimental to their interests or they would not have thrown their support to the insurgent leader.[58]

According to Josephus, Sepphoris was burned to the ground by the Romans in retaliation for this support. Since archaeological findings provide minimal evidence of extensive burning at this time, some have suspected that Josephus engaged in a considerable exaggeration of what occurred.[59] This need mean nothing more, however, than that his own sources had been in error on the extensiveness of the destruction. (For that matter, he may be reporting the local perception rather than what actually happened.)

The fact that the Romans burned Sepphoris, at least to some degree, would most naturally imply that they knew — or suspected — that a significant body of local support remained for Judas.[60] Of course, there may have been additional reasons as well. For example, they may partly have been involved in "preventive retaliation," going to an extreme against a rebellious town as an object lesson that mere passivity would not be acceptable; anything short of resistance to such usurpers might be taken as grounds for any reaction the Romans deemed appropriate.

By virtue of persistence and the power of a very large force sent out to crush him, the rebellion was successfully squashed.[61] Josephus conspicuously does not describe him in terms of a man who actually was self-crowned or crowned by others. Perhaps the delay indicates that the man was enough of a realist to recognize that the crown should be worn only after it was won rather than before his enemies had actually been defeated.[62]

Menahem the Essene (4 B.C.)

Josephus notes that King Herod had respected and admired the Essenes from the days of his youth. This was due to an incident involving Menahem — whom he only identifies as a member of the group rather than specifically its leader: "This man had once observed Herod, then still a boy, going to his teacher, and greeted him as 'king of the Jews.' Thereupon Herod, who thought that the man either did not know who he was, or was teasing him, reminded him that he was only a private citizen. Menahem gently smiled and slapped him on the backside" and provided the promise that he would, indeed, be king, and gave the warning that the playful smack was symbolic of how one may be on the receiving end of both the blessings and the difficulties of life.[63]

Herod did not take the words very seriously until he actually gained power and then he looked at the prediction as evidence that Menahem possessed the prophetic gift. When he called Menahem before him and plied the Essene for how long he would rule, Menahem evaded the question by speaking only of "twenty or even thirty" years and not providing a specific answer for the king.[64] Although vague, this was quite adequate for Herod and he continued to respect the Essenes throughout his reign. Indeed, part of Herod's desire to see himself in messianic terms (see the earlier discussion of his reign) could well rest upon this "miraculous prediction" that he had received of becoming ruler.

In Israel Knohl's reconstruction of events, he assumes that Menahem was far more than just a member of the Essenes; he was actually the group's leader.[65] During the reign of Herod, his own predictions required his peacefulness, and due to the king's admiration of the group the period was a high point of their public acceptability. Afterwards he felt free to put forth his personal messianic ambitions. The evidence for such a messianic self-evaluation comes from the Mishnah which in a tractate moves immediately from a stern rebuke of dishonoring God to its only discussion of Menahem. The connection would then be that Menahem was claiming for himself honor and status that could properly only belong to God.[66]

This fits perfectly with unjustly claiming messianic standing. Certainly something led to a drastic breach between Menahem and the Pharisees. The Midrash on the Song of Songs simply refers to the days of Menahem and Hillel, when there was a dispute between them and Menahem went out."[67] Knohl takes this to be a formal rabbinic hearing at which Hillel presided[68] and which resulted in his formal rejection.

The Mishnah also speaks of Menahem and Hillel as the two most prominent religious leaders of the period of Herod. But it adds, "Menahem went out, and Shammai came in."[69] The Jerusalem Talmud then deals with the question of what happened to Menahem and provides this answer: "Some say he went from one way of behaving to another and some say he turned round and left; he and eighty pairs of Torah scholars clad in golden *tirki* [armor], whose faces went black as pots because they told them, 'Write on a bull's horns that you have no part in the God of Israel.'"[70]

Whatever role they played in the insurrections after Herod's death is unknown. On the extraordinarily weak evidence of Revelation 11:7-8, Knohl concludes that Menahem was one of the two witnesses killed in the temple by the hostile Romans.[71] On its own merits, this location of his death is certainly possible, since the first Passover after Herod's death was extraordinarily rowdy. Archelaus unleashed cavalry on the crowds and several thousand were killed.[72] While Archelaus journeyed to Rome to gain confirmation of his succession, Roman soldiers were attacked. They responded with a counterattack on facilities on the edge of the temple and a number of individuals were killed in the accompanying fray in and around the temple.[73] In either case, one could imagine Menahem and his armed supporters being among the slain. And if one wishes to concede that he viewed himself as the Messiah, this death represented the crushing of yet another messianic movement.

At least during his lifetime, however, the Essenes and Herod were natural allies—they shared the same enemies. If the usual reconstruction of Essene origins is correct, they were a reaction against a Hasmonean being appointed high priest in place of someone of the traditional Zadokite lineage. Since opposition to Herod's kingship rested in the possibility of substituting a Hasmonean for him, then he also viewed his pivotal opposition as being from the same source as that against the Essenes.[74]

Whatever Menahem may or may not have done after Herod's death, the above reconstruction can also be challenged on the grounds that it represents a considerable exaggeration of Menahem's importance both in regard to Herod and in regard to the Essene movement. Rebecca Gray, for example, argues that "unlike Judas [founder of the 'Fourth Philosophy'], who is pictured surrounded by pupils, Menahem is portrayed as a solitary figure."[75] Furthermore, nothing in Josephus' account of the man suggests that Menahem enjoyed any type of ongoing relationship with the king.[76] Having been called to court once or twice argues respect for the man and not his playing a major, much less pivotal role, in Herod's regime.

Historical Context: Overview of the Crushing of the Insurrectionary Forces

Having examined individual insurgents and their activities, it would be useful to step back for an overview of how the rebellions, as a whole, were suppressed. The Jews remembered it as "the War of Varus." Coming in from Syria with two legions reinforced by auxiliaries, Varus divided his forces into a subjection force to take control of Galilee and placed the remainder in Samaritis (= Samaria, which included the main north-south trade route) in order to assure that the insurgents could neither flee south nor receive reinforcement from Judaea. By this strategy, Judas' units were systematically defeated. Sepphoris had been their headquarters, and when it was seized the resistance fully collapsed.[77]

Next, Varus' forces moved through Samaritis to assure that Roman control of that region would be certain. From the Roman standpoint it was noteworthy that there had been only modest outbreaks within its boundaries and they wished to do nothing to inflame the local population. The Nabataean auxiliary forces, however, remembered their long heritage of hostility with Herod and proceeded to loot two villages. In one case, the excuse was that the village was under the control of one of Herod's subordinates.[78] Ultimately Varus tired of such needless provocations and violation of his instructions and sent the Nabataean units back home.[79]

Partially in revenge for the destruction of a Roman century near Emmaus and also in order to secure a second route southward if he chose to use it, Varus attacked that community and burned it to the ground. This also protected him against the rebels using it as a base to attack him from the rear.[80]

Faced with this methodical wiping out of resistance, Varus was able to move south and seize Jerusalem without having to battle for it.[81] Large-scale revolt was now effectively crushed. On the other hand, two of the Athronges brothers were still in the field, and when Archelaus arrived back from Rome he led his own military force in a successful effort to crush this major remnant of rebellion.[82] Meanwhile, Varus completed the squashing of the other remaining pockets of insurrection in Judea and 2,000 accused rebels received the death penalty—crucifixion.[83]

This left Idumaea to deal with. There a large force of 10,000 soldiers was still refusing to admit the power of Rome or that of any other outsider. When Varus' legionnaires arrived on the border, the insurgents' leaders (including certain of Herod's kin) agreed to negotiations through an intermediary. After these were successfully completed, the leaders were shipped off to Rome. Herod's kin were treated with special severity because Herod's own loyalty made them the people Rome should most have been able to rely on in the region.[84]

2

First Century Messiahs Outside the Jesus Movement

Judas the Galilean (A.D. 6)

Josephus describes Judas' activities in this manner[1]:

> And now Archelaus's part of Judea was reduced into a province, and Coponius, one of the equestrian order among the Romans, was sent as a procurator, having the power of life and death put into his hands by Caesar. Under his administration it was that a certain Galilean, whose name was Judas, prevailed with his countrymen to revolt, and said they were cowards if they would endure to pay a tax to the Romans and would after God submit to mortal men as their lords. This man was a teacher of a peculiar sect of his own, and was not at all like the rest of those their leaders.

Although Judas was assisted in his rebellion by a co-leader — according to the account of Josephus in *Antiquities* (XVIII.1.1) — both in the *Wars* and in the mention in Acts 5:37, Judas is the only individual mentioned, which would indicate that he was the overwhelmingly dominant personality.

Some make this Judas' *second* revolt by identifying him as the same Judas who rebelled after Herod's death in 4 B.C.[2] Since no explicit mention is made of the earlier Judas being killed, it is theoretically possible that they are the same. Yet such a linkage seems improbable because the earlier individual had been an indiscriminately violent man who relied upon force alone to gain his way. In contrast, this Judas apparently devised a distinctive theology to justify his behavior. He was, if you will, an intellectual revolutionary. There is also the not minor problem of how he managed to survive out of sight for a decade without the long arm of Roman law (or plain retaliation from kin of those he killed) reaching out and hauling him before a judicial tribunal. Finally, there is the even more important fact that Josephus was unaware that the two were identical and presents them as if different.[3]

As to the current Judas, the appellation "Galilean" sounds odd at first glance because he was actually from Gamala, a city in Gaulanitis.[4] Although politically not part of Galilee, it did lie to the east of the Sea of Galilee and adjoined it. In regard to its culture it was probably identical. Hence, in nontechnical conversation, people presumably lumped the much smaller area into the place-name of the larger political entity of Galilee.[5] When Josephus was given military authority over Galilee, it included this area; this fact also argues that they were commonly linked together as reflecting a shared community of interest and interrelationships.[6]

Although Josephus refers to the taxation causing the revolt, more precisely it was the census that took place in A.D. 6 that was to establish the basis of the taxation.[7] Since the census that gave birth to his revolt took place in Judea, it follows that this was the site of the insurrection that disturbed the social order.[8] It is quite possible that the very appellation "the Galilean" was added because he was an outsider to that area[9] and this was the largest political entity near where he lived.

Many decades of past policy were being repudiated by Judas because taxes had been paid to Rome since Judea became a province of the Empire in 63 B.C.[10] On the other hand, there was a very old Jewish tradition (referred to in 2 Samuel 24 and 1 Chronicles 21) that was hostile to the very idea of conducting a census of the people. If it was evil for Jews to conduct such a poll, how much more so it was to submit to one performed by an outside occupying power![11]

It has been argued that the root of such anti-census convictions was the notion that assessment implies ownership.[12] If so, the idea of a pagan power exercising such "ownership" of God's people was especially repugnant.

As Josephus describes him in his *Antiquities* (XVIII.1.1.), Judas became the intellectual rationalizer for all Jewish revolutionary movements that came afterwards, including that of the Great Revolt of 66–70. It was not that he created a formal sectarian group, but that he developed a conceptual outlook that religiously justified insurrection.

The fact that this way of thinking is contrasted by Josephus with that of the Pharisees, Sadducees, and Essenes argues that these movements skirted or avoided the revolutionary deductions that Judas advocated.

Some take this a step further and argue that Josephus' parallelism with the other groups requires that some kind of formal movement must have sprung into existence as well. The most important objection to this is that he provides no name for it. The problem of saying that Judas founded the Zealots—the most logical choice due to their later importance—lies in the fact that the group does not appear in Josephus' writings until the beginning of the Great Revolt in A.D. 66: Nor would they have called themselves "Sicarii" (assassins), for this was hardly the kind of positive label that any self-respecting movement would desire.[13] Furthermore, if it was a distinct group why does it disappear from the pages of Josephus' writings thereafter while other groups do not?[14]

Josephus is entirely silent as to the course of the insurrection, and that might well argue for its relative brevity and lack of success. Acts 5:37 provides what little is known about such matters: according to Acts, there were "many people" involved, Judas himself "perished" (presumably he was killed), and the followers were "dispersed," a far milder reaction than the Romans sometimes gave such efforts!

Judas probably viewed his rebellion as a messianic one. He presented the revolt as one that would assure "them happiness and security for what they possessed" and insisted that if such beneficial results were not the goal "God would not otherwise be assisting them" in their meetings and efforts to secure independence.[15] Whether or not he took the ultimate step and considered this as the unique moment in which God would act is unknown and unknowable. Yet it seems unlikely that they would have risked the drastic step of open rebellion unless more than a few of his supporters either embraced or hoped that this was the case. For the leader of such a revolt, there would inevitably have been a messianic tinge added to his credentials as well. At least until it was crushed.

A Samaritan Messiah (A.D. 36)?

Josephus provides this account of how the search for ancient religious relics triggered Pilate's violent intervention[16]:

> But the nation of the Samaritans did not escape without tumults. The man who excited them to it was one who thought lying a thing of little consequence, and who contrived every thing so that the multitude might be pleased; so he bid them to get together upon Mount Gerizzim, which is by them looked upon as the most holy of all mountains, and assured them, that when they were come thither, he would show them those sacred vessels which were laid under that place, because Moses put them there. So they came thither armed, and thought the discourse of the man probable; and as they abode at a cer-

tain village, which was called Tirathaba, they got the rest together to them, and desired to go up the mountain in a great multitude together; but Pilate prevented their going up, by seizing upon file roads with a great band of horsemen and foot-men, who fell upon those that were gotten together in the village; and when it came to an action, some of them they slew, and others of them they put to flight, and took a great many alive, the principal of which, and also the most potent of those that fled away, Pilate ordered to be slain.

The fact that this man "knew" that Mosaic relics were on the mountain argues that he claimed prophetic status, for that is the only way that he could have known where they were buried. (If it had been a matter of public knowledge, they would certainly have already been dug up and the items proudly exhibited.) Most ominous as to his intention was that the people came armed. Common potential weaponry such as walking sticks and daggers would have gone unnoted due to the fact that both travelers and individual citizens often traveled with such items. The fact that the armaments are pointed out and emphasized argues that they were the types of equipment that was perceived as mainly or exclusively intended for the purpose of warfare. Connecting the presence of armed supporters and the recovery of Mosaic relics, it is hard to avoid the supposition that the next item in the prophet's agenda was to assert independence and/or actively move against the Romans to achieve it.

The next step is more conjectural, yet not at all improbable. The fact that the relics were Mosaic in origin could easily indicate that the individual viewed himself as needing them in order to play the role of the new Moses. Some see here a possible indication that this was an action to assure recognition of his prophetic status.[17] On the other hand, Moses was both lawgiver and liberator of the nation from Egyptian captivity. Hence a claim to be a new Moses, if taken in a political sense, could easily be translated into that of a redeemer from Roman political control. That interpretation makes the most sense of Pilate's brutal response to what otherwise was a religious pilgrimage.

Others suspect that Pilate was acting strictly out of political concerns alone.[18] A strictly political fear seems highly unlikely since they were seeking religious paraphernalia; on the other hand, to seek such divine tokens of divine approval — as they might well take it — could provide important psychological support for a messianic or prophetic revolt. Pilate had been governor for enough years to have been well aware of that fact.

One could argue that the individual did not consider himself the messiah because the Samaritans instead anticipated the coming of the *Taheb*, a prophet on the level of Moses (Deuteronomy 18:15–19).[19] However, since this was a concept which popular Samaritan opinion of the first century considered as roughly equivalent to the Jewish anticipation of a Messiah (John 4:25), the end result would be the same.

"Liberation" Leader(s) under Felix

Josephus had a special contempt for these unnamed insurrectionaries. In his *Antiquities* he speaks of how[20]

> These works, that were done by the robbers, filled the city with all sorts of impiety. And now these impostors and deceivers persuaded the multitude to follow them into the wilderness, and pretended that they would exhibit manifest wonders and signs, that should be performed by the providence of God. And many that were prevailed on by them suffered the punishments of their folly; for Felix brought them back, and then punished them.

In his *Wars*, Josephus implicitly concedes that the crushing of these rebels was far from simple and that they enjoyed considerable local successes before being repressed. He notes that "they parted themselves into different bodies, and lay in wait up and down the country, and plundered the houses of the great men, and slew the men themselves, and set the villages on fire; and this till all Judea was filled with the effects of their madness."[21]

Since Josephus refers to only one Roman military response to these men, Rebecca Gray argues that he only has in mind one rebellious movement rather than several independent ones.[22] If so, we would have a very unusual degree of cooperation between rival leaders since, when the Great Revolt occurred in the 60s, he heavily emphasized the inabilities of such men to work together.

The going into the "desert" (wilderness) to carry out these activities would be conceptually equivalent to the Jews of the Exodus generation going into the Sinai "wilderness" as part of their escape from Egypt, their growing in numbers, and ultimate triumph over a new land. A reference to the Exodus precedent is quite possibly in mind.[23] (This is not to deny that the less populated regions were also the most practical place to organize the insurrection(s) with the minimum of direct government observation and interference.) Hence the overtones of a messianic movement were inherent in their behavior and this would have affected the opinion they had of their leader(s). If successful, they would surely have viewed it as proof of the divine approval for their actions and the special—even messianic—status of such men.

Theudas (A.D. 44)

Again, Josephus provides us a concise account of what happened[24]:

> Now it came to pass, while Fadus was procurator of Judea, that a certain magician, whose name was Theudas, persuaded a great part of the people to take their effects with them, and follow him to the river Jordan; for he told them he was a prophet, and that he would, by his own command, divide the river, and afford them an easy passage over it; and many were deluded by his words. However, Fadus did not permit them to make any advantage of his wild attempt, but sent a troop of horsemen out against them; who, falling upon them unexpectedly, slew many of them, and took many of them alive. They also took Theudas alive, and cut off his head, and carried it to Jerusalem.

Why was this man who claimed he could work a miracle considered threatening to the civil order? Probably they reasoned that if he could perform even a partial fake one involving the river, that he would secure such a loyalty that his followers would do anything he might ask of them. In other words, the threat lay not in his making the attempt to cross the Jordan and not even in a partial "success," but in how he might exploit a pseudo-miracle against the Roman power.

Furthermore, the original crossing of the Jordan under Joshua was the beginning of the conquest of the land. Hence it would have been very easy for both supporter and foe alike to interpret the attempted action as the first step in reenacting what had happened so many centuries before. He was to become the liberator of the land—the Messiah, savior of it, if you will.

If they were departing westward, one might conjecture that the prophet hoped to establish an independent territory on the other side, and one could easily see why the Romans would intervene even if the threat were not immediately aimed at Judaea. Alternatively (and this would apply in regard to crossing the river in either direction), the leader of the pilgrimage may have been hoping that if the governor intervened that Yahweh would strike him and his forces down as He had the ancient Pharaoh.

That possibility brings us to the other famous water crossing in Hebrew history. If the action was intended to also echo the exodus from Egypt—the liberating flight of the ancient Hebrews from the ever-vacillating Egyptian Pharaoh—their leader's status would have been parallel to that of Moses, a prototype for the Messiah.[25]

The Red Sea crossing symbolizes their gaining freedom; the Jordan crossing symbolizes their gaining a new and independent land. Either would be appealing to them on both patriotic grounds and past scriptural precedent.[26]

Yet the "exodus" could still have been dispersed and its leaders arrested and the degree of violence held to a minimum. Why wasn't this done?

E. Mary Smallwood suggests two possibilities. One is that the soldiers were acting on their own initiative, in the passion of the moment, rather than following orders. The second possibility is that Fadus ordered it to "vent his spite on the Jews for his discomfiture in a trial of strength with them which Josephus narrates before Theudas' adventure."[27]

Another explanation could be sought in the potential for a Jewish success to aggravate other regional unrest. For example, Aryeh Kasher sees just such a possible local political tie-in between Theudas and area events. He suggests that it "may have been a spin-off of the violent border dispute between the Jews of Peraea and the *polis* of Philadelphia; moreover, Theudas himself may have been a resident of Jewish Peraea. This impression principally arises from the fact that he was active in Peraea, as well as from the proximity of these events to the procurator Cuspius Fadus' brief term of office."[28]

If this correlation of events is valid, it would go far to explain the severity of the action taken against him: As an active participant in such violent and controversial local controversies, the procurator would be especially concerned lest Jewish religious/prophetic claims become linked to the debate and create a volatile escalation of the situation.

The simple fact is that whenever the Romans reacted militarily there was no guarantee of how severe their behavior would be. Some situations cried out for a heavy hand, but most allowed a range of responses. The working assumption seems to have been that if one got oneself in a situation that the Romans considered dangerous, one only had oneself to blame no matter how severe the reaction.

Was There a Theudas Who Led a Different Revolt?

We have already seen that there were two different individuals named Judas who led rebellions. Could this have been the case with two different men named Theudas? This issue is raised because of a Theudas being mentioned as a rebel in Acts 5:37. Rebecca Gray, for example, argues that though the description of his activities is consistent with that found in Josephus the chronology is not: "The speech of Gamaliel is set some ten years before Theudas' appearance (according to Josephus' chronology), and yet speaks of him as a figure from the past; indeed, the speech dates Theudas to the period before Judas the Galilean (6 C.E.)."[29] In short, it is an anachronism.[30]

The strongest argument for making the two men the same individual lies in the fact that Theudas was not a common name and therefore it is unlikely (though not impossible) that two rebel leaders would bear the same name.[31]

Glen Miller makes several effective arguments, however, on behalf of the interpretation that the same man was not intended by Gamaliel. The more significant are, perhaps, these: (1) Josephus depicts the insurrection as so large that 20,000 die, while Gamaliel only mentions 400 supporters; (2) Gamaliel speaks of the followers being dispersed, while Josephus hits hard upon many of them being captured; (3) Gamaliel speaks only of a vague death of the insurrectionist, while Josephus speaks of a more dramatic arrest and beheading.[32]

It seems soundest to contend that the Theudas in Acts 5 refers either to a rebel at the time of Herod the Great's death[33] or one of the unnamed rebels whom Josephus mentions in passing as arising upon various occasions. From Gamaliel's perspective in Jerusalem, it is quite reasonable to suppose that those who stuck in his mind as the most interesting, representative, or significant were not always identical with those viewed as such by Josephus.

An Egyptian Messiah in Palestine (A.D. 50s)

The differences in Josephus' accounts has given risen to much discussion. In *Antiquities* the Egyptian raises a following in Jerusalem while in the *War* he does so in the countryside. The *Antiquities* speak of his traveling from Jerusalem to the Mount of Olives while the *War* speaks of him bringing his followers to the city. Finally, the *Antiquities* speaks of how the city walls would collapse at his word while the *War* speaks of his followers preparing for an attack on the city. The *Antiquities* estimates 600 prisoners and dead in the suppression while the *War* speaks of the bulk of 30,000 falling into Roman hands.[34]

Some of this data can be reconciled by reasonable supposition: For example, the Egyptian could easily have begun his work in Jerusalem (at one of the annual festivals?) and then taken a core of supporters into the countryside where he used that initial group to gain additional supporters.[35] Of course the opposite scenario, of covertly taking supporters into the city, would also work—covertly because a large band of organized supporters could easily attract hostile Roman attention—and then using that core to build up a larger constituency inside the city.

Likewise the matter of the walls of the city collapsing versus the people being armed can easily be read as supplemental data: after the walls fell, his supporters would still need those arms to secure control of the city.[36]

When one tackles the vast discrepancy in casualties and prisoners one is far more perplexed. Did Josephus use a different source when he wrote the larger number? Or did he consciously attempt to "correct" a mistake he had uncovered the second time he told the story? Although he might wish to exaggerate the number involved to justify the Romans' decisive crushing of the movement,[37] one wonders why he would not attempt, for consistency if nothing else, to maintain the same number in both accounts. After all, even 600 is not exactly a minuscule threat if they are armed and know what they are doing!

However one integrates this data into a synthesis, two facts remain especially important: the man was a foreigner (which argues that his charisma and persuasiveness must have been great in order to gain and retain a following) and he claimed to be a prophet (which argues that he claimed to be receiving his instructions directly from God). Furthermore, he was to be a miracle-working prophet: "The walls of Jerusalem would fall down; and he promised them that he would procure them an entrance into the city through those walls, when they were fallen down."[38] Combine this with the fact that he "got together thirty thousand men"[39] and it did not take a genius to recognize that this man planned a revolution. And when a first-century Jew attempted to lead a miraculously-based revolution, it is extremely difficult to do anything but to describe the effort as a messianic one and the leader as a would-be Messiah, redeemer, savior.[40]

Taking the matter from a different standpoint, Jonah Lindering sees two evidences that the man had messianic aspirations. In the first place, "Josephus uses the Greek verb *tyrannein* ('to be sole ruler')" to describe the man's claims.[41] He also argues that the site of the Mount of Olives is significant because in Zechariah 14:4 that is where God intervenes decisively against the enemies of His people.[42] To the extent that Felix was aware of these two points, it would certainly have buttressed his intention to crush what was going on.

From Felix's standpoint, it did not really matter whether the Egyptian could accomplish the disintegration of the walls or not. Even if he could, it was his responsibility as governor to make sure it did not happen. Rather than wait for the prophet to initiate an action of some kind, he grabbed the initiative himself in order to decisively crush his efforts.

Josephus tells us that the man escaped alive and was not captured. Yet the memory of this man remained in the Roman military consciousness. In Acts 21:38, we find a Roman military officer wondering whether

Paul might be that mysterious disappeared revolutionary. Here, though, the number of followers is pictured as 4,000, in contrast with the data of Josephus. Regardless of which number we decide to accept, both Josephus and Acts verify the existence of a strong tradition that a large number of people had been involved.

It has been argued that though "the chronology is right" in Luke and "other details of the account agree with Josephus" that "Luke has misidentified the Egyptian's followers as Sicarii: there is no independent evidence linking the two movements, and we may be sure that Josephus would have made it clear if there were any connection between them."[43]

Yet the Sicarii would have been an obvious source of discontent for the Egyptian to tap into. Indeed, the very oddity of an Egyptian being able to attempt a significant revolt in Judaea makes such an explanation quite reasonable whether Josephus uses the term or not. Even so, the real explanation is probably quite a bit different: the words from Luke are actually his quoting a Roman soldier: to a Roman soldier of that time, any violent opposition was likely to be dismissed as coming from the Sicarii (= assassins) whether it actually did or not.

Simon bar Giora (A.D. 60s)

Initially passed over for a leadership position during the Great Revolt of the 60s, he was given an assignment in a more isolated region. Some might have despaired at this rejection, but he used it as an opportunity to attempt to seize control throughout that region and to build up his forces. Josephus pictures it this way: "There bar Giora attacked the rich and influential freely and only a sustained effort caused him to withdraw; to hinder a renewal, his foes had to establish many internal garrisons to protect the upper classes against his inroads."[44]

In line with Josephus' negative characterization, some have argued that since bar Giora attacked the property and owners of the higher class in Arcabatene early in A.D. 67 — possibly a few months earlier, depending upon the chronology one adopts— he must have been just a brigand. Against this is the fact that he had been earlier recognized as military commander of the region near Arcabatene and the command might well have included authority over that city as well, as or at least he could have interpreted his instructions as such. Hence his assault in 67 may not have been an indication of brigandage but of retaliation against foes in the intra-Jewish power structure.[45]

When faced with effective opposition he took up refuge at Masada with the Sicarii. This also has been introduced as evidence that he was a mere brigand. But his men and the Sicarii were clearly working from different premises, as indicated by both his and their behavior: women and children accompanied his soldiers and they were restricted to a part of Masada not as militarily secure as the part the Sicarii held.[46] Later he did join in their raids, but they refused to adopt his proposal for intervention in the military-political affairs in the populated and most war-torn areas of the nation.[47] In other words, it can reasonably be argued that he and the Sicarii were clearly working from two very different military-political frames of reference.

Leaving Masada, he returned to building up a body of supporters. People recognized his capacity for leadership and emphasis on the inequities of treatment of the people at large, and his support grew ever stronger as he moved on Jerusalem to seize power there after the death of the High Priest.[48]

As Josephus tells the story, bar Giora became the dominant authority inside the city. In exchange for their loyalty, he permitted his forces to do whatever they wanted, whenever they wanted, wherever they wanted, to whoever they wanted: "for he permitted them to do all things that any of them desired to do, while their inclination to plunder was insatiable, as was their zeal in searching the houses of the rich; and for the murdering of the men, and abusing of the women, it was sport to them."[49] They were a law to themselves, and that law was self-indulgence.

This would seem to be a recipe for the disintegration of an army. The fact that it did not fall apart argues that Josephus has exaggerated the commonness of the behavior he so understandably criticizes. Furthermore, at least some of his criticism is severely overdone. Josephus' vigorous condemnation of bar Giora inflicting death on deserters is a conspicuously case where something far more significant than personal excess was at work. As R. A. Horsley argues, "Behind Josephus' bitter condemnation of Simon's execution of deserters is simply the social-political discipline necessary to maintain order among the people under prolonged siege."[50]

Although he was now one of the handful of major political players in the Jerusalem political landscape, he never could achieve the dominance over the entire city that he wished. He did, however, make plain by his behavior that he considered himself far more than just another warlord, however powerful.

Two evidences in particular point to a conscious messianic role in his actions. First, he issued coins with the words "Redemption of Zion" upon them. The inclusion of that word "Redemption" (with its moral and spiritual overtones) strongly suggests the importance of the religious factor in what was going on. And for someone of that nature it would be most natural to interpret his role in the affair as being part of a messianic movement and even as being anointed by God to specifically carry out those purposes.[51]

Secondly, the fact that he entered the temple in a royal robe can easily be interpreted not just as the act of a would-be king entering the temple to worship, but the messianic king entering what was properly his temple.[52]

Since no deduction is ever safe from challenge, it is not surprising that others sometimes look at this differently. Martin Goodman, for example, argues that his attire grew out of other factors and had nothing to do with messianic aspirations[53]:

> The arguments for Simon's messianic pretensions are ... [not] convincing. It is clear that he liked to appear impressive to his followers and to act in a regal fashion, but his white tunics and purple cloak were put on not to win their support but to scare Roman soldiers. The significance of the white clothes is anyway ambiguous: he may have wanted to stress his coming martyrdom rather than his messianic power.

This analysis seems quite faulty. Putting "royal" purple on a rebellious Jew was far more likely to anger a Roman soldier than to intimidate him. It would be deemed an outrageous aspersion that such an upstart would claim a role that rightly belonged only to the emperor in Rome!

Furthermore, why would the wearing of white imply martyrdom? The classical imagery of white is that of purity and it may well have been his way of visually asserting the purity of his intentions and motives, however misguided the Romans considered them to be.

In spite of his leadership role, bar Giora survived the war — to be taken to Rome along with John of Giscala and 700 prisoners to be exhibited in the victory parade through Rome.[54] An impressive physical appearance likely played a role in his selection, since Titus selected prisoners on that basis for the triumph.[55] Yet his selection must also be made to fit Roman social snobbery as well. Martin Goodman argues, with what seems sound reasoning, that for him to have been singled out as a prototype of the Jewish foe and "a worthy enemy that he ... cannot have been a poor bandit but rather a respectable member of the ruling class."[56] Poor men were worthy of contempt and simple enslavement or immediate death; only the "better" class of men could be viewed as fighting equals of Roman soldiers.

John of Giscala (A.D. 60s)

As noted above, John of Giscala was the second sectarian leader of the Great Revolt marked for inclusion in the victory march through Rome,[57] which bears witness to how important the Romans regarded him to be.

Jonah Lindering makes two arguments against the propriety of considering John a messianic claimant. The first is that his coins had on them the words "Freedom of Zion," which provides no direct religious context at all. It is, to him, a strictly political message,[58] yet could political independence avoid carrying with it the possibility that, at the height of their success, the Messiah would appear? Or that John or one of the other leaders would be recognized as such for his role in leading the people to independence? (The other situation which psychologically most called for the appearance of the Messiah, would be, ironically, when the nation was in its lowest and most desperate of conditions.)

A second antimessianic accusation is rooted in Josephus' assertions that he ate improper food and ignored the traditional rules of purity.[59] Taking this at face value, one cannot help but suspect that under the rigors of the Roman siege, the need to provide adequate nourishment resulted in few people observing the stricter rules on such matters. John is hardly likely to have stood out as unique. Furthermore, as we will see in some of the medieval Messiahs, it was not unknown for claimants to the position to set aside such rules partly or entirely.

Josephus' condemnation on such matters must be taken unusually cautiously. He despised the man with a passion, depicting him as a person who lied for the simple pleasure of lying, a brazen hypocrite who acted benevolently unless you got in his way, in which case he would violently destroy you without compunction.[60] The fact that Josephus had trusted him and was personally betrayed[61] did nothing to heighten his reputation in the historian's eyes. In short Josephus had every reason to assume the worst of anything John did and to put the worst possible interpretation upon it.

That John man wanted to be king is clear. Josephus concedes that the man was maneuvering for sole kingship and that this was a major factor in turning men firmly against him who had impeded his plans in the past: They were afraid of his retaliation if he once gained that power.[62] So we have a would-be king in a situation in which the people are fighting a war they believe will vindicate God before the polytheistic world as triumphant over their deities. In such a context, could John's kingly aspirations avoid being, at least in part, a bid for recognition as the redeemer/Messiah given by God to accomplish that purpose?

Menahem (A.D. 60s)

The importance of Menahem lies not only in his ties with the Zealot movement, but also in his bid to become the leader of the entire insurrection against Rome. While the Antonia fortress was being besieged by Eleazar in Jerusalem, Menahem moved to secure the powerful and virtually unassailable palace-fortress complex atop Masada. Utilizing cunning rather than brute strength, his men gained control of it, which carried with it access to the well-stocked arsenal of weapons which were needed to arm the revolutionaries.[63] Taking on the appearance of a triumphal military procession, Menahem returned with his jubilant followers to Jerusalem.[64]

Menahem did not have the heavy equipment needed for a direct assault upon the Antonia, where Agrippa, his own forces, and a body of Roman soldiers were lodged. Instead his men dug a tunnel into the structure and broke through, and Agrippa and his forces surrendered with confidence that they would be permitted to survive.[65] The Romans fought on until they negotiated a safe passage from the city. Menahem betrayed the agreement and slaughtered the Romans. Only their commander was spared, and that on condition of being circumcised.[66]

At this point Menahem made a bold gesture that implied that he considered himself the new king by dressing himself in royal attire and leading both his soldiers and his Jerusalem supporters toward the Temple.[67] At this point he made a fatal mistake. Rather than remaining in the Court of the Gentiles and accepting the praise of the multitudes, he proceeded toward the altar where only the priests were permitted. To do this asserted priestly right and to do so in royal vestments as well clearly implied messianic status as well, for who else would dare do such?

The priests, however, lined up and blocked the way. Rather than permitting him to enter, they began to stone him. At this crucial moment, the supporters of Menahem faltered and did not come to his aid or challenge the opposing priests. Instead, the would-be Messiah died inside the Temple, never quite reaching the altar.[68]

Further evidence of his messianic claims can be found in an ancient tale mentioned in *Lamentations Rabbah* (1:16). This refers to Menahem as messiah and as being born in Bethlehem but identifies his birth as occurring near the end of the Great Revolt at about the time the temple was destroyed.[69] The chronology is clearly wrong, unless the reference is to an otherwise unknown individual who came to influence around the turn of the new century and whose activities and exploits are completely unknown. Since the name is the same and since the Great Revolt is mentioned, it is hard to avoid the conclusion that this is a very garbled version of a birth story concerning the Menahem we are discussing.

Emperor Vespasian as Messiah

Josephus — either out of self-interest in flattering the imperial ego or out of the conviction that he had earned the right on the battlefield — dared take the idea of a world ruler chosen by God and apply it not to a Jew but to the emperor responsible for crushing the Great Revolt. As he tells the story, he had been tormented by dreams of the nation's approaching catastrophe.

There were at least three factors that could have produced these dreams. The first is that, unlike most Jews, he had firsthand experience of Rome itself and had personally known the type of men who were waging war against his land. He was well aware of the resources they could bring to bear. Secondly, he had opposed the revolt at the beginning, and the fact that the war was going badly confirmed him in his initial judgment. Finally, he himself had been unable to hold off the Romans, and if he couldn't do it he saw no reason to believe anyone else could be any more successful. Churning in his unconscious, dreams of defeat and Roman triumph would have come quite naturally.[70]

He saw the dreams, however, not as his inner consciousness at work but as a divine warning that God was now on the side of the Romans. Josephus justified his hiding and surrender on the grounds that he would function as a messenger of God to explain to the Romans what was really happening.[71]

Appearing before Vespasian he confidently predicted that he would gain the royal purple[72]:

> When Josephus heard him give those orders, he said that he had somewhat in his mind that he would willingly say to himself alone. When therefore they were all ordered to withdraw, excepting Titus and two of their friends, he said, "Thou, O Vespasian, thinkest no more than that thou hast taken Josephus himself captive; but I come to thee as a messenger of greater tidings; for had not I been sent by God to thee, I knew what was the law of the Jews in this case? and how it becomes generals to die. Dost thou send me to Nero? For why? Are Nero's successors till they come to thee still alive? *Thou, O Vespasian, art Caesar and emperor, thou, and this thy son.* Bind me now still faster, and keep me for thyself, for thou, O Caesar, are not only lord over me, but over the land and the sea, and all mankind; and certainly I deserve to be kept in closer custody than I now am in, in order to be punished, if I rashly affirm any thing of God."

> When he had said this, Vespasian at present did not believe him, but supposed that Josephus said this as a cunning trick, in order to his own preservation; but in a little time he was convinced, and believed what he said to be true, God himself erecting his expectations, so as to think of obtaining the empire, and by other signs fore-showing his advancement. He also found Josephus to have spoken truth on other occasions [as to future events].

In a different context, Josephus goes even further when he elaborates on this theme. According to him, this kingship prophecy was the true interpretation of the ancient Jewish oracles that spoke of a coming king. Yet they were to be fulfilled not within the Jewish people—as everyone had previously believed—but through their Roman conqueror[73]:

> But now, what did the most [motivate] them in undertaking this war, was an ambiguous oracle that was also found in their sacred writings, how, "about that time, one from their country should become governor of the habitable earth." The Jews took this prediction to belong to themselves in particular, and many of the wise men were thereby deceived in their determination. Now this oracle certainly denoted the government of Vespasian, who was appointed emperor in Judea. However, it is not possible for men to avoid fate, although they see it beforehand. But these men interpreted some of these signals according to their own pleasure, and some of them they utterly despised, until their madness was demonstrated, both by the taking of their city and their own destruction.

Polytheist historians were also aware that the Jews were acting out of the desire to fulfill their ancient writings and establish the long-predicted king in place. Tacitus, for example, writes of the context of the fall of Jerusalem[74]:

> Prodigies had occurred, which this nation, prone to superstition, but hating all religious rites, did not deem it lawful to expiate by offering and sacrifice. There had been seen hosts joining battle in the skies, the fiery gleam of arms, the temple illuminated by a sudden radiance from the clouds. The doors of the inner shrine were suddenly thrown open, and a voice of more than mortal tone was heard to cry that the Gods were departing. At the same instant there was a mighty stir as of departure. Some few put a fearful meaning on these events, *but in most there was a firm persuasion, that in the ancient records of their priests was contained a prediction of how at this very time the East was to grow powerful, and rulers, coming from Judaea, were to acquire universal empire.* These mysterious prophecies had pointed to Vespasian and Titus, but the common people, with the usual blindness of ambition, had interpreted these mighty destinies of themselves, and could not be brought even by disasters to believe the truth.

Suetonius introduces the messianic-kingly prophecy in the context of discussing not the end of the revolt but the motive for it[75]:

> Being in consequence banished not only from intimacy with the emperor but even from his public receptions, [Vespasian] withdrew to a little out-of-the-way town, until a province and an army were offered him while he was in hiding and in fear of his life. *There had spread over all the Orient an old and established belief, that it was fated at that time for men coming from Judaea to rule the world.* This prediction, referring to the emperor of Rome, as afterwards appeared from the event, the people of Judaea took to themselves; accordingly they revolted and after killing their governor, they routed the consular ruler of Syria as well, when he came to the rescue, and took one of his eagles.

Some question whether Josephus made any prophecy at all, arguing that he invented it or backdated when it occurred. On the other hand, it would seem improbable that the true situation was unknown to a large number of people. In that circumstance, the "lie" would lack the essential of a good one: credibility. Furthermore, it also creates the question of why Vespasian retained him rather than killing him or punishing him for his role in the insurrection. Something surely stayed his hand.

Others note that there was much backstage maneuvering prior to Vespasian's bid for power and that Josephus had ties to at least some of the major players.[76] Yet would this not be a cause for him making the "prophecy" at the very time he claimed he did, out of a knowledge of what was being attempted in secret? It could do him no harm and might do him great good.

From Josephus' standpoint, the prophecy was important to protect his own self-respect and public image. Rather than die, he had intentionally set out to survive; captured, he decided to cast his lot with the Romans. Hence it was vitally important to provide a rationale to justify his course. Although praising Vespasian served to potentially ingrate himself with the Romans, it served even more to provide a validation for his reversal in loyalties.[77]

The scriptural text under consideration by Josephus could be Numbers 24:17–19,[78] although passages that speak of a coming world kingdom in Joel 2, for example, would reasonably imply the coming of a new world king as well.

Although it is easy to dismiss Josephus' interpretation of the text as totally self-serving, there were several factors that he could use to convince himself of its legitimacy. First of all, in the Old Testament, foreigners such as Cyrus the Great had served redemptive/messianic roles for the Jewish people.[79] Even though Vespasian was a conqueror and Israel existed under his control, yet Israel was blessed through his interest in them — or so Josephus hoped.

Second of all, the Old Testament provided repeated instances in which the Israelites were bull-headedly convinced of the rightness of their cause even when their plans were far from being in alignment with God's intentions. When this happened, they had been defeated because of their impiety and insurrection, a rebellion not so much against their temporal foe but against their God. Applying this to the current situation, it would have been easy for him to interpret Vespasian as God's agent in both punishing Israel, bringing it to its senses, and, perhaps, even to ultimately help guide its rehabilitation.[80]

One final observation needs to be made: Both Jewish sources (Josephus) and Gentile ones (Suetonius and Tacitus) refer to how the rebellion was carried out and flourished because the participants thought that their long-predicted king (messiah) would appear. In short, the revolution was messianically intended, and any man who claimed kingship during it would be viewed as vying for that messianic role. Hence we must put a messianic connotation — or, at least, messianic intent — on any individual who claimed kingship during these years.

3

Second Century Messiahs

Historical Context: Overview of the Unrest of the Second Decade

In A.D. 115–117 a series of vigorous and, indeed, vicious insurrections — as such things so often are — were launched by Jews in several diverse locations. The exact chronological relations are unknown because of the lack of detailed records about what occurred and exactly when.[1] Hence we cannot be sure whether they were essentially simultaneous,[2] and hence coordinated, or whether the anti-Roman hostility was so intense in these places that word of one revolt quickly inspired imitation in other provinces. Yet so many rebellions coming from the same people in such a short space of time makes the theory of coordination extremely tempting even without hard data to directly support it.

Cyrene in North Africa erupted in a spasm of violence that challenged the ability of the local governments to survive. Pagan religious centers were targeted and roads torn up to hinder movement.[3]

In Cyprus the capital was seized and major damage inflicted upon property and Gentiles in general. Holding Cyprus held the potential for disrupting Roman trade in the Mediterranean and, therefore, was an insurrection that had to be forcefully dealt with not just to reassert power locally but to maintain Roman economic interests in its international trade.[4] So outraged were the locals that a law was passed that any Jew who came to the island — even if shipwrecked — was to be punished by death.[5]

The insurrection in Egypt was intense, prolonged, and especially dangerous. It appears that there was, first, a massive Gentile-Jewish conflict in Alexandria — quite possibly provoked by the Gentile side — and then a little later an eruption of a Jewish insurrection in much of the remainder of the country.[6] Egypt was considered the granary of Rome, so if rebels seized and held either Alexandria or the countryside of the province, the emperor would have been in the humiliating situation of having the "breadbasket" of his capital in enemy hands and might easily have been forced into concessions that would never otherwise have been given.[7]

Even in just-conquered Mesopotamia, there were major Jewish uprisings behind the front lines of the Roman troops, who had thought that those areas were now safely subdued. Rearguard garrisons were routed and the main Roman forces had to return for renewed battle.[8] Making the situation even worse from the standpoint of the occupying forces, the rebellion attracted many Gentiles as well.[9]

Total casualties in the various provinces clearly were in of the hundreds of thousands.[10] Indeed, Cassius Dio estimated that in Cyrene alone, 220,000 Gentiles perished (he makes no estimate of the number of Jews).[11]

Whether Palestine itself erupted has been a matter of intense scholarly debate, with most inclined against it on the grounds of inadequate data. There is some evidence, however, though late in date, that the Cyrenian insurgents moved into both Egypt and then Palestine itself.[12] On the other hand, could major Jewish revolts in four other regions have avoided spilling over into Judaea and Galilee? Be that as it may, the massive revolt in Palestine that we can be absolutely certain of did not erupt until the time of bar Kochba, who abruptly appears on the scene and leads the nation in revolt from A.D. 132 to 135.

Simeon Bar Kochba and the Second Great Revolt (A.D. 132–135)

Bar Kochba as Messiah

Bar Kochba himself did not use the term "messiah" to apply to himself. Rather he prefers *nasi'* (meaning "prince, presiding official"), which stressed the this worldly (rather than supernatural) aspect of his position as leader of the people.[13] Even so, it appears that many contemporary Jews found in him the fulfillment of their messianic aspirations.[14] Crucial in obtaining a widespread support from the devoutly religious was the support of Rabbi Akiba (= Aqiba), one of the most prominent religious figures of the time.[15]

According to the Talmud, he was a seasoned foreign traveler, having repeatedly gone abroad both alone and with other rabbis.[16] Hence he had been exposed to Diaspora thinking and, presumably, directly or indirectly to the way Greeks and Romans thought in these various places.

He endorsed bar Kochba by directly affirming that "this is the King Messiah."[17] The proof (as preserved by one of his students) was found in Numbers 24:17: "[He] expounded the passage, 'There shall go forth a star (K W K B) out of Jacob' as follows: There goes K W Z B A out of Jacob."[18] (The capitalized letters are the transliteration of the Hebrew letters involved; he was making what we today would call a play on words to make his argument.)

According to Eusebius, bar Kochba consciously encouraged others to make the connection between him and the "star" text of Numbers 24. In a derogatory fashion, Eusebius describes him as "a man who was murderous and a bandit, but relied on his name, as if dealing with slaves, and claimed to be a luminary who had come down to them from heaven and was magically enlightening those who were in misery."[19] As Eusebius presents it, the rebel leader took the "star" imagery in a kind of mystical form in which he was the earthly manifestation of a heavenly reality.

If Eusebius is anywhere close to accurate, his description of the man as "murderous and a bandit" almost certainly refers to his prewar activities. As a man who had finely honed war-making skills—even if utilized for thievery—he would also be one who knew the ins and outs of how to face a dangerous foe and survive to fight another day. This could hardly avoid building up his prestige among the rebels and their confidence in his talents. Indeed, it could well explain how he became the leader of the entire revolt: He was the right man, with the right skills, the right experience, and with an ego big enough that he thought he could make the dramatic move from small-time banditry to full-scale revolution. Furthermore, he had had sufficient well-known successes to make his bid for leadership credible.

The amount of rabbinic support he enjoyed has been the subject of disagreement. On the one hand, there are those who believe it was significant,[20] yet on the other hand, some minimize it.[21] For some who refrained from endorsing him, it may have been a matter of elemental prudence: If he failed, his humiliation need not compromise their position in the eyes of the lay public[22] or the Romans. And if he turned out to be successful, they could always have pleaded the need for prudent restraint since so many false claimants had arisen in the past.

At least one rabbi publicly challenged Akiba's enthusiasm. As that cynic responded to Akiba, "Grass will grow out of thy chin, Akiba, before the King Messiah will appear."[23] Whether representative of skepticism of a Messiah appearing at all or of just bar Kochba in particular—the broader rhetoric perhaps being for protection against those who might resent his singling out bar Kochba alone—the end result was the same.

Why did Akiba endorse and then continue to endorse a man who, as we will see, had some terrible faults as a leader and who embodied characteristics far from ideal? Even more seriously, bar Kochba did not have a Davidic ancestry.[24] Since we know that at an earlier period Davidic lineage was considered essential,[25] it follows that the previously accepted prerequisite was now modified (at least to Akiba and many others) into something desirable rather than essential. Presumably the reason for this was the perceived need to find someone immediately who could act rather than wait for the acknowledged idyllic individual to arise.[26]

Rabbi Akiba was almost certainly alive in A.D. 70 when the temple was destroyed, which would have made him elderly by bar Kochba's revolt.[27] Hence his mind may have been clouded by age. Related to this is that if Akiba was as old as often thought, then his only hope of seeing the Messiah was to see him *now*. There simply was not going to be time for the cycle of despair, dejection, rebuilding, frustration, and rebellion to occur again in his lifetime. In other words, his endorsement could have been an act not quite of desperation but close to it.

In this psychological atmosphere, an utilitarian approach would have been tempting. Bar Kochba seemed to be the best available possibility to lead the revolt; Akiba could easily have concluded that one must work with what one has rather than what one prefers. Therefore one embraced him — in spite of all his faults — and put one's faith in God for the rest.[28]

Any initial reservations could easily have been removed on the battlefield. Had not bar Kochba enjoyed a number of significant victories? Had he not even done the seemingly impossible of capturing Jerusalem itself? When the Emperor Hadrian reported on how the war was going to the Senate, did it not lack the normal (and expected!) phrase, "I and the legions are in health"?[29] This was an indirect way of admitting that bar Kochba and his followers had seriously harmed the Roman army.

Bar Kochba and the Acceptability of a Non-Miracle-Working Messiah

One thing Bar Kochba definitely did not claim to be was a miracle worker, nor did his supporters attribute supernatural wonders to him.[30] Hence we might call him the prototype of the "secular" Messiah — one intending to fulfill the political aspirations of his people and who might or might not take its religious aspects seriously, but who did nothing to cultivate a supernatural aura about his personality or leadership. Rabbi Akiba's endorsement of him as Messiah while lacking such manifestations argues strongly that he viewed the messiah in such humanistic terms as well.

Some take this a step further and argue that Akiba's endorsement also implies that a "purely human" messiah was standard in the rabbinic interpretation of that day.[31] That may or may not be true, but the fact that Akiba was the only named rabbi to support the rebel leader could equally well be introduced on behalf of the thesis that the dominant opinion expected far more of the Messiah.

By the time of Maimonides, the precedent of bar Kochba was considered by him as definitive proof that even the real redeemer of the nation need not have such power to back up his claims and actions[32]:

> Let it not enter thy mind that the King Messiah must necessarily perform signs and wonders, display some novelty in the world, revive the dead, or do something similar. It is not so; for Rabbi Akiba was among the greatest of the Sages of the Mishnah, yet he was the armour-bearer [supporter] of Ben Koziba, and acknowledged him as King Messiah. Both he and all the other Sages thought him to be the King Messiah until he was slain for his sins; when he fell in battle it was known that he was not the Messiah. The Sages never demanded of him a sign or miracle.

Maimonides then went on to argue that the true Messiah must meet several tests: (1) be "of the house of David"; (2) "one who meditates upon the Torah"; (3) "occupies himself with the commandments according to the written and the oral law"—thereby automatically ruling out anyone who rejected the rabbinic traditions; (4) had convinced Israel "to go in the ways of the Torah"; (5) had successfully triumphed in "the battles of the Lord" against Israel's enemies. Only "then it might be presumed that he is the Messiah." But more must come as well: "If he has succeeded, if he has built up the sanctuary in its place, if he has gathered the scattered of Israel, behold, then he is surely the Messiah."[33]

In other words, messianic status is post facto. Until the triumphal actions expected and demanded of the Messiah, an individual can only be regarded as a possible claimant. In one sense, this makes perfect sense; in another, however, why should a person align himself or herself with such a possible savior figure when there is no standard to prove that he is such before he accomplishes all his mission? How is he to gain followers? How is he to establish credibility? And why prefer one claimant against another who may appear simultaneously?

Maimonides does not discuss such practical difficulties. If one presses his logic to its seeming culmination, it would have precluded anyone at any time from commitment to a possible Messiah except in the most tentative and abstract manner. And without full commitment and vivid enthusiasm, how was that leader (even if the true Messiah) to have the human resources available to accomplish his mission?

It is of interest that the ancient Christian tradition takes the opposite approach to bar Kochba's claims than that presented by Maimonides. Some translate Eusebius' remarks in his *Church History* significantly differently than the version we examined above: that Bar Kochba was "a murderous brigand who traded on his title and pretended to be a star which had descended from heaven to give light to the oppressed *by miracles* [emphasis added]."[34] This translation transforms bar Kocbha's claims from one of providing mystical enlightenment to one who provided "enlightenment" through his supernatural manifestations of power. This is in keeping with the picture found in Jerome, who claimed that bar Kochba once provided the illusion of being able to breathe fire.[35]

The important thing in the current context is not which portrait of the man is correct, but that the non-miracle-working one took root in the Jewish tradition and provided strong precedent for later Jews who vied for the messianic role but who made little or no effort to provide such substantiation for their claims.

Bar Kochba as Leader

Since in this volume we are far more interested in bar Kochba as an individual rather than in the broader course of events he precipitated, in the remainder of our discussion we will emphasize what ancient sources tell us about the personality, attitudes, and practices of this dynamic leader who successfully defied Rome for several years. The few historical details retained by the earliest Jewish references clearly indicate that bar Kochba had minimal consideration for the religious scruples of the spiritual leadership of his day. He was willing to show outright contempt for them while manifesting a vague spirituality that was sufficient to appeal to many of less strict convictions.

(1) *Only under pressure did he yield to their censure of his creating an elite force of soldiers composed of those willing to engage in self-mutilation.* As the account has it, one Rabbi Yohanan recorded that the forces were organized around "eighty thousand pairs of trumpeters," each team in command of "a number of troops." Presumably the idea was to have both a commander and a replacement immediately at hand in case of his death. Twentieth century experience of military commissars to assure the loyalty of commanders and personnel might make one suspect that bar Kochba had thought of a similar idea, of installing some someone directly

answerable to him in each of these units as the theoretical subordinate. Alternatively, it may have represented simple prudence to have a substitute leader immediately ready to step into the position if necessary.

Be that as it may, Rabbi Yohanan spoke of how the inner core of the army was composed of a huge body of men who had subjected themselves to mutilation: "Ben Kozaeba was there and he had two hundred thousand troops who, as a sign of loyalty, had cut off their little fingers. Sages sent word to him, 'How long are you going to turn Israel into a maimed people?' He said to them, 'How otherwise is it possible to test them?' They replied to him, 'Whoever cannot uproot a cedar of Lebanon while riding on his horse will not be inscribed on your military roll.' "

In a literal sense it was impossible to do both at the same time. Hence they could well have meant the ability to ride a horse and to use its strength to uproot a cedar tree from Lebanon. From the legendary size attributed of these massive trees, even that was highly unlikely. Furthermore, how were they going to move the men there to test their ability? And if they could ride horses this well, were they not better utilized as crude cavalry? The demand sounds suspiciously like a test of wills in which the sages were attempting to halt any further increase in bar Kochba's forces by demanding a test of membership that could never be implemented.

On the other hand, horses were expensive to own and maintain and one would expect them only among the more prosperous elements of the community. Hence this could have been a demand to not only avoid the repulsive standard of recruitment through mutilation, but also to limit future enlistees to the more well-off elements of society. If so, this would shift the composition of the army from an exclusively or mainly lower-class one to one representative of better-off segments of society as well.

One could easily go from this deduction to the conclusion that bar Kochba's army overwhelmingly represented those segments of society with the least to lose in a war. By introducing their societal betters, this would both broaden the basis of support — avoiding the danger that such individuals might feel the need to side with the Romans out of self-interest — and introducing the possibility of greater control over what could easily be the undisciplined rabble that could result from an army of the lower-class alone.

Be that as it may, Rabbi Yohanan does not tell us that the idea was adopted, only that the past policy of mutilation was abandoned. The Rabbi said, "There were two hundred thousand who qualified in one way, and another two hundred thousand who qualified *in another way*," without describing what the test of qualification.[36] The implication of such vague language seems to be that bar Kochba backed down from his own standard of qualification, but did not adopt their suggestion as to how to choose — troops. A sly but effective way of manifesting the appearance of compromise and moderation while still keeping the final decisions firmly in his own hand.

(2) *He even went so far as to explicitly reject any plea for divine help in assuring his victories.* "When he would go forth to battle," an early surviving reminiscence recalls, "he would say, 'Lord of the world! Do not help and do not hinder us! "Hast thou not rejected us, O God? Thou does not go forth, O God, with our armies" ' (Psalms 60:10)."[37]

Such language was hardly likely to bring rejoicing among the rabbis of his day. Yet in making his startling claim, he was not above quoting Scripture to prove the rightness of his stance: Since God's people had proved themselves unworthy, Israel must accomplish its temporal redemption entirely upon its own. Such was his spin upon the biblical text he cites. Yet it would not have required a well-trained rabbi (or even layperson) to have been appalled at the idea of divine neutrality being a noble ideal. Israel was supposed to be God's people; God's neutrality was, therefore, incongruous at best and abhorrent at worst.

Bar Kochba's frame of mind could have grown out of either of two very different lines of reasoning. On the one hand, he could have felt driven to the conclusion that past failures so demonstrated Yahweh's rejection of the land that they had to demonstrate their own reliance upon His temporal promises regardless of whether He became directly involved. It was not a matter of lack of faith in God, but an act of national repentance to prove to Him that they were worthy of His support.

Alternatively, he may have despaired of a divinely established kingdom at all. He may have felt driven to establish an ethnic Jewish kingdom for reasons of group pride and survival rather than as a manifestation of any special group relationship to the divine. In that context, the rejection of divine assistance would manifest a conviction that nationhood must rest in a shared racial heritage rather than in a shared spirituality.

Either way, conspicuously absent is any espousal of the need for national moral-spiritual reformation. John the Baptist had spoken of the need for such repentance to all who would listen to him because of the nearness of God's kingdom (Matthew 3:1–2). To rabbis of bar Kochba's own day, such a moral preparation would certainly have been viewed as desirable and appropriate preparation for such a kingdom in either a spiritual or temporal sense.

The apparent lack of it being on bar Kochba's agenda argues that he had decisively separated the moral-spiritual aspects of his heritage from the nationalistic ones. And, in choosing between the two, he viewed his function as exclusively furthering the latter. This segregation of the two areas of life could hardly have been looked upon with enthusiasm by the spiritual leaders he dealt with and may go far to explain the lack of enthusiasm toward him by many of their number.

Even so, there are at least some suggestions that he was willing to encourage the piety of others regardless of how deep his own may or may not have been. When Sukkot grew near in the final stages of the war, for example, he was still careful to send out a request for the necessary palm branches and other supplies to properly celebrate it.[38]

(3) *His tough-minded policy toward those who tried to avoid service in the anti-Roman cause.* Among the letters written by him and recovered, at least in part, by archaeologists, are two concerning citizens of Tekoa. A number of them had apparently fled to areas farther away from the conflict in order to avoid personal involvement. In one letter, he demanded that they be severely punished and warned of dire repercussions for permitting them to remain unpunished: "Concerning every man of Tekoa who will be found at your place — the houses in which they dwell will be burned and you [too] will be punished."[39] In another, he adopted a different approach (were his manpower needs now even more critical?):"Let all men from Tekoa and other places who are with you, be sent to me without delay. And if you shall not send them, let it be known to you, that you will be punished...."[40]

The recognition that he needed all the human resources he could acquire — and, implicitly, was not obtaining — runs as a common theme in both of these letters. In yet a third, he writes, "From Shimeon ben Kosiba to Yeshua ben Galgoula and to the men of the fort, peace. I take heaven to witness against me that unless you mobilize [destroy?] the Galileans who are with you, every man, I will put fetters on your feet as I did to ben Aphlul."[41] Whether "mobilize" or "destroy" is the actual reading is much disputed since the text is damaged and extremely hard to read.[42] Either way, he clearly wanted strong and immediate action taken concerning the Galileans and suspected that the garrison would not follow his demand unless he verbally threatened them — itself a telling indication of the practical limits of his authority and the limited willingness of many others to obey him.

(4) *Near the end the war, he actually killed Rabbi Eleazar of Modiin, whom he did not trust.*

Each day, while wearing the traditional mourning clothing of sackcloth and ashes, Eleazar would pray that God would not judge the nation harshly. This may well carry the connotation that he feared decisive defeat as being God's imminent judgment of rejection and wished the people to

3. Second Century Messiahs 47

escape it. Certainly, Hadrian regarded him as a potential ally in bringing the conflict to an end and desired to meet with him to bring about a surrender. To accomplish this, a Samaritan offered to sneak into the city as a go-between and determine the rabbi's intentions. Actually the Samaritan (if the rabbinic account can be credited) was playing a double game: Although he successfully entered the city through a drain and successfully approached the rabbi while he was "standing and praying" he only "pretended to whisper something in his ear."

Onlookers saw this, grabbed him, and marched him to bar Kochba. They claimed they saw the two men talking with each other. According to the account, the Samaritan lied and claimed that Rabbi Eleazar planned on surrendering the city. The rabbi denied that the Samaritan had made any such suggestion as well as any agreement to it. Bar Kochba did not believe a word of it. He[43]

> gave a good kick and killed [Eleazar]. Forthwith an echo came forth and proclaimed the following verse: "Woe to my worthless shepherd, who deserts the flock! May the sword smite his arm and his right eye! Let his arm be wholly withered, his right eye utterly blinded! (Zechariah 11:17) You have murdered Rabbi Eleazar of Modiin, the right arm of all Israel, and their right eye. Therefore may the right arm of that man wither, may his right eye be utterly blinded!" Forthwith Betar was taken and Ben Kozeba was killed.

Perhaps the horrifying aspect to this story is not that a violent-tempered war hero would act in this manner — the Old Testament Book of Judges, for example, describes Samson, a "judge" of ancient Israel, as acting in violent outbursts also. To the religious establishment, however, it would be both disturbing and insulting that he did it to one of their own, especially to such a highly respected individual.[44] On the grounds of potential public reaction, it was an equally treacherous action: It defied societal expectation of behavior toward one's relatives. After all, Eleazar was no less than his own uncle.[45]

Hence the circumstantial implications are compelling that this action represented the final and definitive break between the religious leadership of the time and bar Kochba shortly before the final defeat. Be that as it may, the story concedes that the Romans thought that the rabbi wished to surrender and was in a position to accomplish it. Bar Kochba's murderous reaction similarly argues that he considered both options credible and, perhaps, high probabilities.

The odd behavior of the Samaritan makes no sense — sneaking into the city to merely "whisper" to the rabbi, and that in public, would serve no useful purpose unless it was to assure that a surrender could not be arranged. Hence this element of the story may have been an invention or exaggeration so that the surviving religious leadership did not have to bear the local stigma of one of their number attempting to capitulate. It would have been quite easy for them to assume that their leader would not have embraced such an option, especially when coming from a Samaritan source. Since the offer couldn't have been made or received, it simply wasn't.

Bar Kochba perished in the rebellion's end. As for Rabbi Akiba, he was ultimately imprisoned and then brutally executed by the Romans.[46]

Historical Context: Aftershocks — Possible Jewish Revolts Later in the Century

A major war erupted between the Parthians and the Romans during the period 161–165, as they attempted to take advantage of the political instability of their opponent to expand their own boundaries.[47] Since it was in the Parthian interest to stir up rebellions inside the Roman sphere of control to facilitate this effort, it would be far from surprising if they did so either just before they militarily moved or early on.

A reference in the *Historia Augusta* (in its discussion of the life of Antonius Pius, 5, 4) has been interpreted as a reference to this. The text speaks of how the emperor "suppressed through his governors and legates many peoples including the rebellious Jews."[48]

Except for this very vague allusion, there is no clear reference to it in the pagan, Christian, or Jewish traditions from the period. The traditional method of celebrating victory through the issuance of coinage it is also lacking.[49] Hence whatever insurrection occurred is likely to have been of very modest size, both in terms of the number of participants and its duration.[50]

War again erupted between the Parthians and Romans during the period 193–199, and the same geopolitical reasons that would have encouraged their-mischief making in the Roman provinces would have existed at this time as well.[51] Hence the appeal of interpreting in this manner the Latin version of Eusebius' *Chronicle*, which refers to the year 197 as the time of the "Jewish and Samaritan war."[52] Based upon this, other ancient writers said that there was a Roman war against these two groups; others took it to mean that these two ethnic communities were involved in a war with each other.[53]

That both the Jews and the Samaritans would be on the same side in a war with the Romans is not an impossibility, but the degree of inter-

3. Second Century Messiahs

communal resentment was such that it would be both unexpected and quite unusual. Furthermore, during this general period of time there were at least several other mini-wars between rival cities and groups,[54] and a Jewish-Samaritan conflict would fit this pattern.

There may be supporting evidence, however, for a war targeting the Jews in the description of Severus' reign in the *Historia Augusta*. The history speaks of how a public celebration of victory had been authorized: "The senate had decreed to him a triumph over Judaea because of the successes achieved by Severus in Syria."[55] Some take this as a reference to events occurring a few years later than the time we are currently considering.[56] This is possible, but not certain. Even if it does refer to a war in the 190s, we are still left with scant detail and information beyond the fact that a conflict occurred. Yet that in itself would argue that Judaea remained a turbulent province and that under the right religious or political conditions even such a "burnt over district"—destroyed by repeated wars and conflicts—might yet explode again.

4

Messiahs in the Years of Western Europe's Decline (A.D. 200–500)

A Persian Messiah in the Days of Julian

Although the Jews of Palestine would obviously have the most immediate and direct interest in the new temple project of Julian, such a dramatic endeavor (sometimes connected in Jewish thought to the Messiah's coming) could easily encourage redemptive hopes in other parts of the Roman Empire and, indeed, even outside it. The *Martyrium des Simon bar Sabbae* was a Syrian work that described the mistreatment and martyrdoms of Jews. The author claims to have witnessed the last of these toward the end of the first decade of the fifth century,[1] that is only a half-century or slightly more after Julian's failed attempted to rebuild the Jerusalem temple.

Writing of that earlier period, the author discusses how word of the project had stirred up great enthusiasm in Babylonia and Mesopotamia[2]:

> After twenty-four years when Constans and Constantius, the sons of Constantine the Great, had died, Julianus was the ruler of the Romans. And at once when he was a ruler he sacrificed to the idols. In order to stir up the Christians and to convict the words of Christ of falsehood which he prophesied on the devastation of Jerusalem ... he ordered the Jews in his whole Empire to go to Judaea and rebuild Jerusalem and the Temple, and to bring the sacrifices in accordance with the decree of the Law. Many went up actually and started to dig out the ground works of Jerusalem.
>
> Meanwhile there came an imposter to the land of the Persians and proclaimed to the Jews saying, "It is the time of return appointed by the prophets and I have been ordered by God to proclaim to you the return. You shall go up!"

4. Messiahs in the Years of Western Europe's Decline 51

> That imposter came also to Mahoza in Bet Aramaya and deceived myriads of Jews. They left and went out from Mahoza because of the hope of return and they went away three parasangs from the town. However, when the matter was known to Shaput he sent his troops who killed many thousands of them.

That Julian ordered the Jews to go to Palestine en masse is inherently improbable: It would still have been immensely disruptive of the entire empire. Furthermore, many (probably the vast bulk) had deep local roots and would have resented the effort. If emperors could never permanently keep Jews out of Rome (though they occasionally tried), the feasibility of carrying out such a project empire-wide was totally irrational and impractical. Such involuntary dislocations would have stirred up anger and rage among the participants and acted to alienate the Jewish population at a time when Julian so clearly desired to cement their loyalty.

Hence we are almost certainly dealing with the garbled version of what was ordered as it was transformed by word of mouth by the time it arrived in Babylon. In contrast, the reference to a limited number of Jews emigrating to help in rebuilding makes perfect sense: those with the right talents or simply with the wealth to "be on the scene" at the time could hardly find a better excuse or opportunity than the grand project that had been announced.

If the project spurred enthusiasm inside the empire, it is not surprising that it produced significant interest for Jews outside it. According to our text, this was an occasion when it went far beyond this: An unidentified redeemer figure appeared and claimed that he had been divinely appointed to lead the people out of Persia and to Judaea. This vision stirred up "thousands" to follow him. The ruler Shaput violently suppressed the flight, perhaps to keep an economically important segment of his population from leaving to take up residence within the boundaries of a hostile Roman empire.[3] By their deaths the temptation to organize any group to imitate them would be definitively crushed. It was crude and brutal, but surely effective.

Yet the very perceived need to act in this manner argues that the ruler was concerned not only with the immediate problem but also with the precedent that it would set. Whether or not there were literally thousands in the current exodus, he perceived that an unacceptable number would imitate them if he permitted the present group to successfully leave.

Historical Context: The 400s and the Messianic Hope

Italy was invaded by the Visigoths in 410, by the Huns in 452, and by the Vandals in 455. In both 410 and 455, Rome itself was sacked. Roman influence in Africa was undermined by the Vandals in their successful invasion of that continent via Spain in 430. Such repeated and relatively close body blows undermined public confidence and the will to successfully resist.[4]

As Roman Europe passed its prime and found itself faced itself with unprecedented danger of collapse and conquest, Christians in the fourth and fifth centuries interpreted the growing difficulties as an indication that the return of Jesus must be relatively imminent and that the woes of the period were signs of its approach.[5] More immediately, these were a warning that the Antichrist would soon appear, who, in turn, would be vanquished by the returning Jesus.[6]

Among Jews the longing for secular, social, and religious redemption was manifested through a fervent hope for the initial coming of the Messiah. Their conditions were even worse than that of the Christians. In about 425, their religious self-government in Palestine was abolished.[7] The modest number of religious schools still functioning were also closed.[8]

Based upon the biblical analogy of the 400 years in Egypt, many Jews thought that redemption would happen again on the same time scale.[9] Hence in the second century, Rabbi Dosa argued (with Psalms 90:15 and Genesis 15:13 as proof texts), "Know of a surety that your descendants will be sojourners in a land that is not theirs, and will be slaves there and they will be oppressed for four hundred years."[10] With the idea of a "prophetic year" in mind (that is, each day equaling a year and citing Isaiah 63:4 as evidence), Judah ha-Nasi came to essentially the same conclusion by rounding the result off: "If 400 years after the destruction [of Jerusalem] a man says to you 'Buy my field which is worth one thousand dinars, for one dinar,' do not buy it."[11] In other words, the Christ will be coming and the purchase will be worthless.

By such calculations one came to a date late in the 400s.

From the second century, western Jews (at least judging from the surviving writings preserved in Palestine) put their hope for national independence in a Persian victory over the Romans. In the very act of conquering Palestine and the west for themselves, they would be preparing the way for the Messiah. Representative of this stream of thought was Abba bar Kahana, who confidently predicted in the third century, "If you see benches filled with Babylonians in the land of Israel, expect the footsteps of the Messiah."[12]

"Babylonians," of course, refers to the Old Testament–era empire that existed in the same spot. In the second century, they were known as Parthians and as further time passed, they were identified as Persians, thereby causing a shift in language even though the same basic geographical entity is under discussion by the rabbis. Hence the Persians were idealized as a potential tool for Jewish liberation.

A date in the late 400s could also be reached by calculating from the time of creation (in Jewish traditional counting 3761 B.C.).[13] One ancient Jewish tradition argues, "If, 4,231 years after the Creation of the World, a man should say to you, 'Take this field, worth a thousand denars, for one denar,' do not take it" since it would be worthless to you for it would automatically be the Messiah's to distribute to whom he pleased.[14]

A later tradition that uses the style of writing and expression typical of an earlier period — and, therefore, arguing that it originated from a much earlier time than the surviving record of it was penned — speaks of how Rab Hanan bar Tahlifa came across a man who had a manuscript written in Assyrian. Rab Hanan enquired how he came to have it. His answer was, "I hired myself as a mercenary in the Persian army, and I found it among the secret archives of Persia. In it is written: '4,291 years after its creation, the world will be orphaned. As to the years which follow, some of them will witness the wars of the dragons, some the wars of Gog and Magog, and the rest will be the Messianic age; and the Holy One, blessed be He, will not renew His world until after seven thousand years.'"[15] In short, the prerequisites of the messianic age would begin a few decades later than in the previous prediction. (Some believe that there was a manuscript corruption involved in the text and that both speak of 4,231 years, however.)[16]

During the earlier centuries, Babylon had come to replace Palestine as the major center of Jewish religious development and culture, thereby reinforcing these developments. At the very time that religious school after religious school was slowly closed in Palestine, a variety of similar institutions not only existed in Babylon but prospered in spite of occasional periods of persecution.[17] Perhaps because of their better conditions, a messianic passion did not evolve in Babylon as it did in the west. Indeed, if anything, an anti-Messianic mentality was common. Some spoke of not wishing to be alive when the Messiah came and others insisted that all scriptural prophecies had already been completely fulfilled.[18]

These are not the only rabbinic statements which discourage date setting. Another insists, "Seven things are hidden from men. These are the day of death, the day of consolation, the depth of judgment; no man knows what is in the mind of his friend; no man knows which of his business ventures will be profitable, or when the kingdom of the house of David will be restored, or when the sinful kingdom will fall."[19] A different ancient adage said it even more concisely: "Three things come unexpectedly: the Messiah, a lucky find, and a scorpion."[20]

In the mid-and late fifth century, though, adversity came down heavily upon that vibrant Jewish community. In A.D. 469, the Jewish schools were shut down and forced conversions were carried out.[21]

Moses of Crete (Mid–Fifth Century)

Near the end of his writings on church history, Socrates records an account of a religious revival on the island of Crete that had a disastrous result. For over a year one of its members successfully stirred up the hopes of the Jewish community[22]:

> A certain Jewish impostor had the impudence to assert that he was Moses, and had been sent from heaven to lead out the Jews inhabiting that island, and conduct them through the sea: for he said that he was the same person that formerly preserved the Israelites by leading them through the Red Sea. During a whole year therefore he perambulated through the several cities of the island, and persuaded the Jews to confide in his assurances. He moreover bid them renounce their money and other property, pledging himself to guide them through a dry sea into the land of promise. Deluded by such expectations, they neglected business of every kind, despising what they possessed, and permitting any one who chose to take it.

Although often regarded as messianic by later interpreters,[23] he did not explicitly present himself in these terms but as Moses—literally a second Moses. This may, in part, have been a case of adaptation to local circumstances. Residents of Palestine would most naturally picture their ideal in terms of the Davidic-style Messiah who would reestablish an earthly kingdom in the land. Those in a distant country might well find the most promising figure of liberation for them to lie in Moses. One has the factors of distance from Palestine, the seeming impossibility of collective redemption being obtainable, a hostile Roman government, and a huge body of water—which, if it opened as it had for the Biblical Moses—would fully vindicate his claims to be the new Moses redeemer of his people.

One wonders what was to come afterwards. A new law as well? The role of preparer of the people for the Messiah after arriving in Palestine? Or would he view the successful transit of the oceans as divine vindication that he was not only the new Moses but also the Messiah as well?

4. Messiahs in the Years of Western Europe's Decline   55

Indeed, did not the two concepts already function as equivalent in the case of a person who could perform such a wonder?

The surviving documentation gives no concrete evidence of why the Cretan came to the conclusion that the time had arrived for these events to occur. It is known, as already noted, that there had been a considerable amount of messianic speculation that the time the Jews would have to exist without their temple would be equal to the time they had once spent in Egyptian captivity — in other words, roughly 400 years. Hence midcentury would have been to many about the right time to many to look for the appearance of a new Moses-like figure.[24]

Regardless of his long range intentions (assuming he even had consciously arrived at them), what happened next vividly exposed the irrationality of his claims in the most humiliating manner. As Socrates describes it[25]:

> When the day appointed by this deceiver for their departure had arrived, he himself took the lead, and all following with their wives and children, they proceeded until they reached a promontory that overhung the sea, from which he ordered them to fling themselves headlong into it. Those who came first to the precipice did so, and were immediately destroyed, part of them being dashed in pieces against the rocks, and part drowned in the waters: and more would have perished, had not some fishermen and merchants who were Christians providentially happened to be present.
>
> These persons drew out and saved some that were almost drowned, who then in their perilous situation became sensible of the madness of their conduct. The rest they hindered from casting themselves down, by telling them the fate of those who had taken the first leap. When at length the Jews perceived how fearfully they had been duped, they blamed their own indiscreet credulity, and sought to lay hold of the pseudo-Moses in order to put him to death. But they were unable to seize him, for he suddenly disappeared: which induced a general belief that it was some malignant fiend, who had assumed a human form for the destruction of their nation in that place.

They had made fools of themselves in the eyes of themselves and the Gentile population, and a spiritual backlash against their own religion resulted. As Socrates notes, "a great number of Jews who dwelt in Crete were converted to Christianity, through [these] disastrous circumstances."[26]

5

Messiahs in the Years of Western Europe's Collapse (A.D. 500–1000)

Hushil and Nehemiah: Messiahs of the Persian Victory in Palestine (610s)

Messianic hopes had long been identified as most likely to be fulfilled if the Persians triumphed in the Near East. In the early seventh century, these hopes came to fruition. In September 610 the Persians neared Antioch and the Jews attempted, unsuccessfully, to seize the city.[1] In Caesarea of Cappadocia, the local Christian population panicked in 612 and the Jewish community was able to control the gates and let the Persians into their city.[2]

In 614 the Persians were ready to invade Palestine. Although Roman rule had had its severe ups and downs in treatment of the resident Jewish population, Byzantine's policy of forced conversion and ongoing oppression undermined any possibility of a significant pro-Byzantine element among them.[3] Since Persia had long been viewed as a possible source for Israel's political redemption, it is not surprising that such sentiments were encouraged by the nearness of the invading army. Jacob "the Convert" wrote of how he lived at Tiberias during this general period and that a Jewish "priest" had predicted the Messiah's coming in eight years or less.[4]

As reward for throwing their weight on the side of the Persians, the Jews were permitted self-government in the conquered region, including Jerusalem. The Christians considered themselves harshly treated and this was the case; on the other hand, when the shoe had been on the other foot, repression in the other direction had not been uncommon either.[5]

5. Messiahs in the Years of Western Europe's Collapse

The Book of Zerubbabel dates from a little later than these events and indicates that someone named Hushiel did double duty as both a ruler in Jerusalem as well as offering sacrifices. Hence at least a limited revival of temple routine seems to have been carried out.[6] The fact that he carried out both religious and political duties may well suggest that he viewed himself in a messianic role. This period of Jewish self-rule, however, lasted only three years, and the Persians then reversed course and adopted a pro-Christian policy for Palestine.[7]

Those Jews willing to forcibly resist the change rallied around Hushiel's son, Nehemiah, and viewed him as the Messiah.[8] *The Book of Zerubbabel* speaks of how "Shiroy (the son) of the King of Persia went up against Nehemiah and all Israel ... and he pierced Nehemiah through and they exiled Israel into the desert ... and there was woe in Israel such as there had never been the like."[9] This is probably hyperbole for what was the far more limited catastrophe of the exclusion of all Jews from the city of Jerusalem.[10] (It also is evidence of the quite human tendency to label whatever happens to the current generation as the worst that has ever occurred.) Nehemiah himself appears to have been put to death by the Persians at Emmaus.[11]

In light of the destruction of their past hopes, the dream that the Persians would be God's agent in humbling Rome and (unintentionally) preparing the way for the Messiah was now transferred to the Arabs. They would be Yahweh's agent for devastating what remained of Roman, Byzantine, and Persian power and perform the necessary preparatory temporal humbling to make his entry into the world easier and successful.[12]

In the short term, though, it was not a matter of whether there would be severe oppression, but who the oppressor would be. Heraclius led his forces from Constantinople in 622 in a series of wars that decisively defeated the Persians. In 629 Palestine fell and the Jewish leaders met with the emperor in Tiberias to request and receive formal pardon for their past rebellion.[13] The following brief reassertion of Catholic supremacy was destined to last a mere five years. In 634 the Moslems began their invasion and the Byzantines were unable to resist it.[14] In comparison to what they had so recently gone through, the rule of the Islamic victors seemed far preferable,[15] at least in the short term.

Seor of Syria (c. 619)

Seor rose to prominence in about 619 and convinced a number of individuals that he was the Messiah. Recognizing him as one who might stir up unrest, the authorities proceeded to arrest him, which suggests, at the minimum, that he had gained a significant number of followers. This so humiliated him that it apparently forced him to conclude that his messianic claims were delusionary. This can be seen in the fact that he mourned "I have become a laughing stock among the Jews."[16]

An Anonymous Euphrates-Area Messiah (c. 645)

After the Arabs conquered Syria and the Mesopotamian Valley area, they had to face their own Jewish messiahs as had those who ruled the region before them. A Nestorian author describes how an unidentified Jew presented himself at a town on the Euphrates River and proclaimed that the Messiah had come into the world. Seeing his role as anti-Christian, he then burned down three local church edifices. Seeing himself as a revolutionary leader as well, he proceeded to kill the town's leader. This angered the government, which sent a military unit that systematically killed both the rebels and their families. Their leader was then put to death by crucifixion.[17]

The Messiah Serene (c. 720)[18]

He openly proclaimed his status of Messiah and pledged that a national state would be recreated in Palestine after the Chosen People rallied and expelled the Islamists. According to one ancient manuscript from a Jewish critic, a bold miracle would make possible the journey: "He called himself the Messiah and announced that they would be flown to the Promised Land. He commanded them to give away all their possessions so that they would return empty handed."[19] Isaiah 60:8 formed the scriptural precedent for this image of the people returning to their homeland; in that passage, those who returned are pictured as if they were clouds moving through the sky. This text has continued to find its appeal in exactly such a "return" context. As recently as the mass airborne immigration of Soviet Jews to Israel, the text was regarded by some as a prediction of that event.[20]

This Messiah emphasized his right to be a new law giver for his people. In addition, those Jews who were willing to become his followers would be transformed into a new people of God.[21] Natronai ben Nehemiah, writing sometime between 719 and 730, discussed how and whether his followers could be reconciled with normative Judaism. In doing so he discussed the beliefs of Serene and his followers: They had "ceased praying, (ceased) observing the laws concerning ritual slaughter, ceased keeping their wine distinct from the 'wine of (others') oblation,' worked on the second day of festivals, failed to follow the ordinances of the sages as concerns the form of the marriage contract...."[22] In short, they had laid aside much of what was considered contemporary normative Judaism.[23]

Serene's appeal was not limited to one narrow geographic region. Writing in 750, Isador Pacensis spoke of the large number of supporters he gained both in France and in Spain. So motivated were they that they deserted both home and property and traveled on pilgrimage to join him. The local authorities regarded this as adequate grounds on which to seize their abandoned possessions.[24]

The Messiah's reign was brought to an abrupt end by his capture. He then attempted to save his life by arguing to Caliph Yazid II that he was nothing but a con man. He had gone through this elaborate charade simply to deride his fellow Jews. Yazid did not accept this claim and handed him over to those of his own ethnicity to punish.[25]

The leaders of the Jewish community were in no mood to cut him any slack. He was publicly whipped and his possessions were seized. A similar punishment was inflicted upon his most prominent supporters. After pledging not to raise these messianic claims again, he and they were released to attempt to put their lives back together again.[26]

The Messiah Forerunner Abu Isa of Persia (a/k/a Obadiah and Isaac b. Jacob al-Isfahani) (mid to late eighth century)

Although apocalyptic speculation as to the time of the coming of the Messiah provided a wide variety of dates (as in later ages), one focus of speculation centered on the middle of the eighth century.[27] It was about this time that Abu Isa, who lived in Ispahan, made his unexpected and improbable rise to prominence. Educationally of no importance (an illiterate), occupationally occupying only a position of modest significance (a tailor), and in opposition to many powerful rabbis of his day,[28] his success must surely have laid in a combination of the spirit of messianic expectation and his own personal charisma.

His message was a simple one: In the divine plan of things, God had ordained that five specially selected messengers be sent into the world before the sending of the Messiah Himself as the final divine intervention.[29] Four others had preceded Abu Isa in the role of God's special messenger; he was to be the last before the Messiah appeared.[30] It would be Isa's responsibility to bring about national political redemption and produce the political freedom the chosen people had long dreamt of regaining.[31]

Religiously, his beliefs flew in the face of the dominant rabbinic position by acknowledging that both Jesus of Nazareth and Mohammed had been appointed to teach God's will to their own respective peoples. Hence it was useful for Jews to study both the Koran and the four gospels just as they studied their own Scriptures since such investigation would be of ultimate spiritual benefit to them as well.[32] If this were not enough, he firmly rejected the authority of the Talmud,[33] thereby removing it as an authority that could be invoked to ban his innovations.

The group he founded had other distinctive beliefs as well. All divorce was prohibited. Prayer was required seven times daily (citing Psalms 119:164 as the scriptural text requiring it). The group was vegetarian and wine was forbidden to its members.[34]

He gained sufficient support in Persia that he openly rebelled against the ruling caliph. In approximately 755, he was defeated and killed. His followers fled.

This catastrophe came as a shock to them, for they were convinced that he had performed supernatural wonders to vindicate his claim that they would be magically protected from any enemy army. As an unfriendly critic said, apparently not much later than the events,[35]

> Those of the Jews who followed him constituted a large mob. They used to say that he had shown signs and wonders, and they believed that, at the time when they would go into battle over him, he would make a line around his men with a myrtle branch, and he would say to them, "Stand in the midst of this circle and the sword of the enemy will not overtake you." When his enemies approached this circle, they would withdraw, for they would be afraid because of his amulet or because of the charm which he was using.

Many refused to concede that he had died. Some insisted that he had taken refuge in a cave. Others believed that he had disappeared into the desert to take his message to a different audience.[36] According to yet others, Abu Isa was still alive and in hiding, merely waiting to return to public attention at a more opportune future moment.[37]

These various types of individuals formed a movement that was identified by various names: Isawaites, Isunians or Isfahanians.[38] The group's hard core moved en masse to Damascus, where they set down long-term roots.³⁹ In spite of the fact that Isa never reappeared, the group maintained its corporate existence for about two centuries before finally disappearing.⁴⁰

The Prophet/Messiah Yudghan of Hamadan (a/k/a al-Rai, the Shepherd)

Yudghan was a disciple of Abu Isa. With the shattering of his predecessor's plans, Yudghan continued to claim to be a prophetic preparer of the Messiah's way.⁴¹ His followers, however, considered him worthy of being considered the Messiah himself,⁴² a claim that he, too, embraced.⁴³ As the result, they became a group distinct from those who perpetuated the memory of Isa.

This Yudghanite movement (whose members became known as Mushkanites)⁴⁴ also dissented from key rabbinic practices and convictions,⁴⁵ thereby ensuring a breach that would create major difficulties in expanding the scope of their influence. Indeed, according to one ancient writer (al-Shahrastani), Yudghan and his followers "prohibit meat and intoxicating drinks, observe many prayers and fasts, and assert that the Sabbath and holidays are at present no longer obligatory."⁴⁶

Unlike Isa, Yudghan died a natural death. The rebellious instinct in the movement came out again afterwards, however, when another man, Mushka, became the group's leader. In an unsuccessful revolt, he perished at the hands of the government's military forces.⁴⁷

Eldad Ha-Dani: Finder of the Lost Ten Tribes and Preparer of the Coming of the Messiah

Many believed that for the Messiah to come, the so-called lost tribes of Israel had to be found first. Sometime in the second half of the ninth century this happened — or was believed to. Eldad Ha-Dani was the figure who made the discovery. Hence the man who convinced the Jewish people of this — and, indirectly, the Catholic world as well — played an important supporting role in the messianic search even though he did not claim the position for himself.

He claimed to have lived in the part of eastern Africa near modern Ethiopia⁴⁸ in which four of those tribes lived — Asher, Dan, Gad, and Naphtali. He also claimed to have found other remnants in different regions as well.⁴⁹

He spread this joyful tale of discovery extensively in travels through Egypt, Spain and Babylon.[50] The reception within the Jewish community was nearly universally favorable.[51] In turn, these claims became the root of the twelfth-century legend of Prester John.[52]

The Palestinian Messiah Myth of the Mid-Tenth Century

The period 950–1000 was one that produced special interest among date setters for the Messiah's emergence.[53] So intense was this phenomena that rumors of the appearance of the Messiah were reported as far away as Germany. This led to a letter being sent from Worms seeking verification that the Messiah had, indeed, been born.[54] The rabbinic school in Jerusalem responded tartly, insisting that the letter did not even deserve a response. It argued that since the expected visible signs of the Messiah's arrival had not occurred, it was impossible for it to have happened.[55]

In about 960, Hasadi ibn Shaprut, a prominent Jewish leader, wrote more vaguely — not whether the Messiah had come, but whether there was any clear indication of the timing, an enquiry that makes most sense if he had heard of the tales that had reached Germany but wished to avoid embarrassment by openly embracing them.

The king of the Chazars responded that the reason for the delay lay in the moral/spiritual guilt of the people, which postponed the long-sought event.[56] The wording implies that the Messiah's rise had been expected and that an adequate reason had to be sought for its failure. Rather than admit it lay in the erroneous calculations of the rabbinic and other learned speculators, he chose to blame it upon the masses themselves. They had not been pure enough and dedicated enough. This permitted the religious leadership to feel unembarrassed (relatively, at least) and to persevere in its assumption of superior scholarship and spirituality in relation to its followers.

6

Messianic Movements in the Late Middle Ages (1000–1300)

Historical Context: Date Setting at the Beginning of the New Millennium

Although the year 1000 might seem a logical year for major eschatological speculation to center on, it was actually very modest. We read of scattered predictions in Roman Catholic circles for the end of the world to occur in 960, 992, 1000, and 1033 or soon thereafter. But there is no emphasis on the millennium date itself. Rather, what is seen is an ongoing sense that it could be near, a suspicion that could be ignited into temporary passionate concern when specific threatening events or tragedies— such as famines and major wars— plagued the human race.[1] Part of this disinclination to specify the year 1000 lay in the fact that a literalistic interpretation of the "millennium" in Revelation 20 had been rejected by Augustine. Unlike today, most interpreters of the book walked in his path and saw no need to fit such a period into earthly affairs.[2]

The Flying Messiah of "Linon" (Mid to Late 11th Century)

Maimonides is the only one to refer to this individual and he places the man's aborted ministry in "Linon." Generally, historians interpret this as a reference to Lyons in France, but in Hebrew "Linon" was also the name of the important city of Leon, Spain.[3] This figure's appearance has been dated as early as approximately 1060–1070,[4] while others place it in the 1080s.[5]

Some redemptive figures cited Scripture, some cited deductions and calculations based upon Scripture. This one, Maimonides tells us, appealed to miracles: "There arose a man in France and announced that he was the Messiah, and performed signs, according to their opinion, and the French killed him, and many other Jews were slain with him."[6] Whether these executed Jews were active supporters or merely part of the larger Jewish community is not stated, though both types were likely involved. When it comes to arbitrary punishment, "guilt by association" has always seemed more appropriate to most than the requirement of strict proof of association.

The most spectacular of his acts was flying.[7] In an age in which witchcraft beliefs were common and the practitioners of the "dark arts" were believed to have this ability, even the assertion of such a talent was far more likely to arouse dangerous fears and suspicions rather than respect among outsiders.

After his execution, there was a hard core of supporters who refused to accept that he was dead. He was merely in hiding, they insisted.[8]

Historical Context: Messianic Movements during the First Crusade (1096)

It is one of the ironies of medieval history that Catholic and Jewish idealism should both blossom in the year 1096. Catholic Europe had tired of the Arab occupation of Palestine and was determined to recapture the conquered region for their faith. Furthermore, at least among a significant number, there was the conviction that the final climatic battle between good and evil would be fought. For that to occur, they believed, a good Christian people had to be in control of the land in order to play their role in the defeat of the Antichrist and prepare the way for the return of the Lord.

Guibert, Abbot of Nogent, who wrote his account only about 15 years afterwards, described Pope Urban's rationale for the Crusade in just such terms. In a summary of a speech he gave in France, Guibert notes that the Pope argued, among other things, that the Antichrist was about to emerge[9]:

> And if the Antichrist comes upon no Christian there, as today there is scarcely any, there will be no one to resist him, or any whom he might justly move among. According to Daniel and Jerome his interpreter, his tent will be fixed on the Mount of Olives, and he will certainly take

> his seat, as the Apostle teaches, in Jerusalem, "in the temple of God, as though he were God" ... These times, dearest brothers, perhaps will now be fulfilled, when, with the aid of God, the power of the pagans will be pushed back by you, and, with the end of the world already near, even if the nations do not turn to the Lord, because, as the Apostle says, "there must be a falling away from faith."
>
> Nevertheless, first, according to the prophecies, it is necessary, before the coming of the Antichrist in those parts, either through you or through whomever God wills, that the empire of Christianity be renewed, so that the leader of all evil, who will have his throne there, may find some nourishment of faith against which he may fight. Consider, then, that Almighty providence may have destined you for the task of rescuing Jerusalem from such abasement. I ask you to think how your hearts can conceive of the joy of seeing the holy city revived by your efforts, and the oracles, the divine prophecies fulfilled in our own times.

It has been argued that what the Pope had in mind was a well organized, well provisioned, and (by the standards of the day) well trained military force. The popularity of the conquest proposal gripped the imagination of a wide section of the population, however, and produced a much wider desire for immediate and personal involvement in the endeavor. The result was often large, barely controllable conglomerates of zealots that counted enthusiasm and passion as adequate to compensate for any inadequacies they had as a military force.[10]

If Catholics were thinking in messianic terms, so were Jews. A number of Jewish scholars—including those fascinated by the Gematria, the finding of mystic meanings in biblical words and phrases through the calculation of their numerical value when added together—came to the conclusion that this also would be the time when Israel's long hopes would bear joyful fruit.[11]

Initially Jews and Gentiles alike in Byzantium came to a reconciliation as both groups' attention shifted to a shared—yet fundamentally very different—messianic understanding of what the approaching Crusade would produce.[12] The respite was but temporary. Those on the way to the Crusades looked upon the Jews, however, as a foe worthy of extermination. After all, there were very few Jews left in Jerusalem.[13] And the fewer there were anywhere was counted as a blessing.

The cynic might suspect that this faction of the Crusaders knew that they were going to face a battle-worthy foe, so they took pleasure in murdering and massacring individuals whom they knew full well could do little to stop them. Yet just as there was a theological reason for the Crusades (regaining the Islamic conquered lands that once had been considered Christian), there were also theological factors in the anti-Jewish pogroms that destroyed over 4,000 Jews in community after community as Crusaders moved east and into Byzantium.[14]

Through the centuries, Jewish responsibility for the death of Jesus had evolved into collective Jewish responsibility of the entire people, which had evolved into perpetual collective Jewish guilt, which had been made an even greater crime by turning the judicial murder of the prophet-man-God Jesus into outright deicide. Hence the killing of people centuries removed from the original act could be rationalized as not only appropriate but a virtuous deed. Furthermore, it did nothing to discourage such anti-Semitic actions that the Jews could easily be viewed as tacit allies of the Muslim foe.[15]

In France, a contemporary of the events records that when large bands of would-be Crusaders gathered at Rouen, conversation soon turned to taking more immediate action,: "After traversing great distances we desire to attack the enemies of God in the East, although the Jews, of all races the worst foes of God, are before our eyes. That's doing our work backward."[16]

The Jewish account of the contemporary Rabbi Solomon b. Samson records the same kind of rhetoric being utilized that year in Germany as well[17]:

> As they passed through towns where there were Jews they said to one another: "We are going on a distant journey to seek the [Gentile] house of worship [a reference to the Sepulchre of Christ] and to exact vengeance on the Ishmaelites. Yet here are the Jews dwelling in our midst whose forefathers slew him and crucified him without reason. First let us take vengeance on them and destroy them as a people so that the name of Israel shall no longer be remembered, or so that they should be like us and submit to the son of depravity [Jesus]."

Of course, for those Crusaders (of which there were many) who were more interested in bloodletting than in moral principle and who coveted gold far more than ethical excellence, such reasoning provided a mere superficial coating for their own barbarity and greed. The "romantic" sheen that much later generations sometimes placed on the nobility of the European Middle Ages blatantly overlooked the fact that much of that class reflected far more the excesses of minimally controlled power than the search for justice and equity, especially when they were among the weak and powerless. Although only a minority of Crusaders engaged in the anti-Jewish actions, they made up in zeal, venom, and repetition whatever they lacked in pure numbers.[18]

When the Catholic oppression of the Jewish communities came instead of the anticipated redemption, the Jewish messianic interpretation of the age was shifted from one of optimism (liberation is now!) to one of modified pessimism (these were but the birth sorrows of the messianic age that the people must first pass through).[19] The sorrows accompanying the Second Crusade (1145–1147) and the Third (1189–1190) were similarly interpreted.[20] Both interpretations of contemporary history accepted as its premise that the Catholic-Islamic conflict was an indication of the imminency of the Messiah.[21] Their conflicts were the Battle of Gog and Magog spoken of in Ezekiel, and once it was over the Messiah would appear.[22]

In Maimonides' *Ma'amar Kiddush ha-Shem*, he notes that many Jews accepted their forced conversion to Islam because they considered the act irrelevant: The Messiah's appearance was so imminent it would hardly matter because the pretense could quickly be abandoned.[23] Presumably a significant number of Jews coerced into a veneer of Catholicism reasoned, at times, in a similar manner.

Even as late as the seventeenth century, the 1096 date remained an interpretive problem that some felt needed to be explained. At that time, the Polish mystic Nathan Schapiro put the blame for the nonappearance of the Messiah on the sinful transgressions of the Jewish people of that day.[24] The calculators had not failed in their task; the people had.

Menahem of Chazaria (c. 1096)

During or just after the first Crusade,[25] two different men rose to prominence. First was Solomon ben Doudji, who claimed to be the Messiah's "forerunner." He felt a powerful self-interest in the Messiah not only for traditional reasons but because it was his own son, Menahem.[26] Unfortunately, their rise to public attention was just as quick as their disappearance into the sands of lost medieval history.

The Messiah of Ba'kouba, Mesopotamia (c. 1096)

As part of the effect of the First Crusade, the end-times ripples of contemporary thought were felt as far away from Europe as Mesopotamia. This included the city of Ba'kouba, which was located a day's journey away from Baghdad. There ben Chadd openly adopted the messianic label for himself. The caliph promptly resolved the potential embarrassment to his regime by throwing him into prison.[27]

The Announcer of the Messiah: Rabbi Moshe of Fez (c. 1100)

This incident was of special interest to Maimonides because it involved both his father and the town he had lived in. Rabbi Moshe was deeply respected for his piety and knowledge. Furthermore, he seemed to have the prophetic gift, for he enhanced his reputation by a series of accurate predictions of near-term events.[28]

Hence the people were prepared to pay attention when he received a prophetic dream announcing that the Messiah was alive and in the world. Lest he be misunderstood, he carefully cautioned that he himself was not the man.[29] All of Maimonides' father's admonitions, pleas, and argumentation could not alter their acceptance of his claims.[30]

Then things went a drastic step further: Moshe announced that the Messiah would appear before them at Passover eve. Hence they should sell their possessions even at giveaway prices if need be and borrow money with a ten to one return rate. After all, as of Passover there would no longer be the need to repay![31]

Passover came and went, and when the Messiah did not appear, the community faced economic catastrophe. Recognizing that they were never going to get the debt repaid at the promised interest, their Islamic creditors quickly discovered who was behind this foolish scheme and determined to kill him. He wisely bid a swift adieu and headed for Palestine.[32] To add perplexing irony to the story, before he left he gave a series of additional prophecies that turned out to be true.[33] What then had happened to the Messiah?

Tanchelm of Bruges (c. 1110)

Tanchelm began his public career in the minor post of notary for Robert II of Flanders. His religious teaching got him expelled from his hometown of Bruges and he moved out of Flanders entirely and took up residence in Amsterdam. An eloquent speaker who could keep the attention of the masses, he began in about 1110 to wear the robes of a humble monk and to share his reform message with others.[34] It was, however, a scathing and radical denunciation. The priests had so dishonored themselves that none of them were morally worthy to provide the sacraments. Indeed, he depicted the existing church (as an institution) as nothing more than a brothel. In light of such grievous excesses, the masses were clearly not bound to pay their tithes to the church.[35]

The rebuke of the quite visible church excesses was enough to gain him an attentive audience. His rejection of church taxes removed the guilt endured by the poor at not being able to live up to the generosity expected of them.

As his teaching became yet more popular, he drifted from critiquing and condemning the religious establishment to building up his own religious stature. The old habit of the monks was no longer adequate; now he had to dress in garments that were gold colored. Once he had traveled alone; now he traveled with an armed contingent that some claimed numbered in the several thousands.[36]

Nor was it only matters of public appearance that were affected. So were his claims concerning himself. He claimed to be royalty. He claimed to be the Holy Spirit. He claimed to be a deity.[37] In obvious imitation of Jesus, he appointed 12 apostles but, in his own dramatic innovation, included a woman.[38] His followers adored him; some were said to drink his bathwater for the benefits it would provide them.[39]

He faced an intense regional priestly opposition determined to suppress him. He was jailed, but escaped.[40] An attempt to kill him narrowly failed.[41] Finally a hostile priest ended Tanchelm's "reign" in 1115. The messianic figure turned out to be just as susceptible to murder as any other mortal.[42]

It should be noted that all that is known about Tanchelm comes from the mouths of his enemies.[43] Although the stories doubtlessly have a major element of truth at least as regards the ending years of his life (intense opposition tends to feed and inflame whatever "radicalism" a person may harbor within), in the earlier years of his break with orthodoxy one is wise to be far more cautious. After all, he was sufficiently within the pale of orthodoxy to have made a trip to Rome to discuss the rearranging of diocese boundaries so that they might be more efficiently administered and to have been permitted to return unhindered.[44] This was not the type of treatment normally given to one outrageously at odds with contemporary orthodoxy.

Abn Arye: The Messiah of Cordova, Spain (First Decades, 12th Century)[45]

Writing in his *Iggeret Teman* to the Yemenite Jews, Maimonides made passing mention of this "man who boasted that he was the Messiah, and because of him Israel came very near destruction."[46] Maimonides then touched upon the ever-present danger of a backlash against those who supported a false claimant to messianic rulership: if it turns out that he can't back up his assertion, the challenged authorities will always be tempted to come down on those who backed him. Worse, they will be highly tempted to lump together active supporters, passive supporters, and outright opponents.[47] Furthermore, if they have made this kind of challenge to the established order once, what is going to keep them from doing it again? Factor into the mix that the Messiah is from a disliked religio-cultural group within the land and it can easily become a ready-made excuse to strike out against a group the dominant authorities already despise.

In this case — which his father had described to him — the Jewish community had taken vigorous action to avoid the dangerous side-effects that could have occurred. Ibn Aryeh had been tried by the leadership, publicly flogged, and then excluded from the community.[48] Only by such extreme steps were they able to starve off the feared vicious Gentile backlash.[49]

A Palestinian Karaite Messiah (Early 1120s)

At this point one of the major sects of Judaism enters into the picture. The Karaites had appeared as a distinct group in 780. Traditionally, they were viewed as the creative result of the mind of Anan ben David of Babylonia. Although the attribution comes from several centuries later, he seems the most likely creator of the movement.[50] This does not mean that his teaching was regarded as definitive, for later generations felt free to widely depart from what he had written.[51]

The new system was built upon the principle of Scripture alone and the firm rejection of rabbinic and Talmudic tradition.[52] In actual practice, however, it incorporated elements of ancient Samaritan thought as well as ideas derived from Islam.[53] The more radical fringe rejected the authority of both Torah and the oral law.[54]

It began with a rigorous asceticism that would have eventually challenged the ability of the movement to survive — since most people prefer a more "normal" lifestyle — but this was modified over a long period of time in a more realistic direction.[55] Only after its collision with Maimonides did the movement begin to collapse and disintegrate as a viable and distinct movement. By the early fourteenth century, followers had basically been either integrated into Islam or into dominant rabbinic-style Judaism.[56]

In the second decade of the twelfth century, a Messiah arose from this group. We know of him due to the writings of one Obadiah. The Jewish proselyte Obadiah appears to have originated in Normandy, France, and come to Palestine as a Crusader. While there he was converted (1102), and he remained in the land after the crusade was over.[57]

A number of Karaites lived in Palestine at the time, usually in solitary hermit style.[58] In the northern part of the country,[59] Obadiah crossed paths with such an individual by the name of Shlomo.[60]

Shlomo explained that he would be making his messiahship known to the general public in two and a half months and that afterwards he would liberate the land.[61] Obadiah took none of this seriously.[62] After all Shlomo was of Levitic lineage, not Davidic, so how could he possibly fill such a role?[63] How he rationalized the claim is unknown, but Harris Lenowitz has suggested that since one of the biblical images of the messiah is that of priest, Shlomo may have considered Levitical ancestry to be adequate to justify his right to the position.[64]

If the Karaite ever did do anything public, it made so little impact that knowledge of it has vanished.[65] Only in this single written reference is any mention made of the man at all.[66] From the standpoint of cynical realism the time frame of two and a half months was too short for a movement to crystallize around him; it was a matter of either producing the promised national redemption immediately or of being exposed as a false pretender.

Another Messianic Forerunner of Fez, Morocco (1127)

Among those messianic movements with a purported forerunner of the Messiah was the one that appeared in Fez, Morocco, in 1127. In his letter to the Yemen community, attempting to persuade them to fully disavow the local leader of their own regional messianic movement, Maimonides also cited other examples of failed efforts of that nature. He noted that when this man's promise that the Messiah would appear later that year was not fulfilled, major persecutions were suffered by the Jewish community in retaliation for his preaching and teaching.[67]

Abba H. Silver sees two possible facts encouraging the person to make his claim. First there was the popular conviction that the Messiah would finally be disclosed to the world 500 years after Mohammed's birth. More immediately there was a messianic receptiveness at about this time that gave birth to at least one roughly parallel case — Ibn Tumart and the Almohades movement in Islam.[68]

Ibn Alfakar of Spain (1147)

The "forerunner" of Fez was not the only Jew of that century to preach the imminent appearance of the redeemer. Some two decades later, these sentiments were further encouraged by Ibn Alfakar. To his friends and supporters, he seemed to be blessed with remarkable scriptural insight.[69] By his scriptural exegesis he convinced many that the chronology of the future laid out by Daniel required that the messiah soon appear, in the year 1147.

Abraham Ibn Ezra (1092–1167) did not roll over to accommodate the would-be messianic announcer. Instead he insisted in his writings that no one alive could provide a definitely reliable guide to when Daniel's ancient predictions would ultimately be fulfilled.[70] Furthermore, he took tremendous pleasure in ripping to shreds each of the man's individual arguments. So far as he was concerned, he smashed the intellectual facade as definitively as an unsatisfactory vessel is smashed into fragments by a potter.[71]

Maimonides noted the irony that Ibn Alfakar selected the very year that turned out to produce the exact opposite — a major Muslim invasion force entered the country and the Jewish people suffered severely as the result.[72]

Messianic Adventurer: David Alroy (c. 1147)

Of all the figures in these centuries Alroy was both the most well-known and challenging figure[73]: He played the roles of wonder-worker, soldier, and visionary during his rise to fame during the Second Crusade.

Alroy was born in 1147 in the Daghestan, Kurdistan, which adjoins the Black Sea. He was born with the name of Menahem ben Shlomo al-Duji. The self-selection of "David" as his new first name was clearly a desire to link his own desires with the Davidic lineage typically attributed to the Messiah.[74] The last name is likely a misreading of the actual Arabic, but it has become the standard English spelling since Disraeli wrote *The Wondrous Tale of Alroy* in 1839.[75]

The immediate region in which he lived, though ruled by the Muslims, was dominated by those raised in Judaism and those who had converted to it.[76] While David was still a young man, an intellectual known as Efraim teamed up with Alroy's father, Solomon, to make long-term plans to eventually seize Palestine.[77] During this interim, David studied in Baghdad's yeshiva and gained a reputation for his intellectual skills. In addition to his learning in the Torah and Jewish traditions, he studied science, became skilled in Arabic, and was quite proficient in the practice of magic.[78] Clearly he had manifested both skill and talent in a wide spectrum of interests and was never going to be pigeonholed into being a mere "traditional" Jew.

Alroy's father told others that God had sent him as a modern Elijah to prepare the way for his son's messianic victory.[79] With his father's support and that of others, he established a movement that boldly sent out an epistle to all the Jewish communities they could reach: "The time has come in which the Almighty will gather together His people Israel from every country to Jerusalem the holy city."[80] Prior to becoming participants, they were to purify themselves through a strict regimen of prayer and fasting.[81]

Into this was stirred belief in David as the long-awaited Messiah. Although many Jews accepted the messianic claims,[82] most Jews were apparently disturbed by them and his attempts to organize military resistance against the Muslims and attempt a coordinated return to Palestine.[83]

Miracles were attributed to him, but leading religious officials denied that such powers had been exhibited.[84] This raises the problem of whether the purported miracles were invented out of whole cloth or whether any "verifiable" ones were deemed inadequate to justify Alroy's messianic claims. The picture becomes further clouded because the most detailed wonder of Alroy was his supposed ability to hide himself from enemies through invisibility.[85] Is this to be regarded as "miraculous" in the traditional sense of supernatural interposition or as "magical" in nature, which would not involve the supernatural world? And if the latter, could attribution of his alleged wonders to this source have partly fueled the opposition to him?

Initially the Muslim authorities were quite willing to tolerate and even encourage the movement. They traditionally played off local Jews against foreign Christians, and since the Christian kingdoms were equally expansive with the Islamic ones, aid in the ongoing conflict over trade routes was not to be rejected.[86]

They had their agenda, but Alroy's was far different. He centered his attention on his hometown. If this seizure were successful, he theoretically could then move his forces against Edessa and, if triumphant there, to Jerusalem itself.[87] In the short term, the incessant intra-Islamic feuding worked to his advantage.[88] A Muslim dissident movement encouraged his followers in the hope that it would make their own effort to seize the town that much easier.[89]

His strategy for seizing the city was to call into it as many Jews as he could summon from various regions. Word was circulated that he had been arrested by the sultan and had escaped. Using this "success" as a justification, he wrote Jews in areas that might be able to provide armed men asking them to help him in carrying out the plan.[90] Key to the strategy was both numbers and their being able to enter the city with their hidden arms undetected. This strategy proved momentarily successful.[91]

This initial revolt against the Islamic rulers, of course, was designed to be only the opening volley of a much larger campaign. If Alroy gained local victory, he proposed nothing less than what the Christians themselves were proposing, to travel to Palestine and liberate it from its Muslim conquerors.

The Islamic officials, however, ultimately succeeded in capturing the rebel before the scenario went much further. As the Spanish rabbi Shlomo Ibn Verga (1450–1525) later recounted the resulting judicial hearing in his *The Tribe of Judah,* "The king asked him, 'Is it true that you are the messiah?' [He] answered, 'I am the messiah. God has sent me to redeem the people of Israel.' The king responded, 'I will imprison you, and if you free yourself, I will know that you are the messiah, and if not, it will be your punishment, on account of your foolishness, to remain there forever. I will not kill you since you are a fool.'"[92]

After this interview and imprisonment, Alroy somehow managed to escape. Those supporting him were convinced that it was done through the invocation of his magical powers.[93] However he accomplished it, the embarrassment did nothing to generate feelings of sympathy for him from the government.

With his escape, the insurrection continued. The Muslim authorities soon tired of the difficulty they faced in suppressing the rebellion. To deal with it, they began to put pressure on the Jewish population as a whole, warning the religious leadership that retaliation would come down on the heads of even those not directly involved in the conflict.[94] Benjamin of Tudela reported that the efforts of the leaders of the Jewish communities in both Baghdad and Mosul failed in their efforts to convince Alroy to repudiate his messianic claims and actions.[95] Due to this failure, the governor of the region bribed Alroy's father-in-law to murder him.[96]

Such is the most common explanation of his death. For a significantly different description of his demise, we need to turn to the Islamic physician Samuel Ibn Abbas who wrote in 1169 a volume titled *The Silencing of the Jews and the Christians through Rational Argument.* In this account, the local military commander noticed the large number of men coming to his city to see Alroy. He himself had a high opinion of Alroy and initially believed that they had come to show respect for the Jewish scholar. After he discovered that all had come armed, he successfully averted widespread bloodletting by seizing and killing Alroy before any insurrection could be launched.⁹⁷

Writing some two decades after the events, Ibn Abbas was amazed that "the Jews of Amadia hold Alroy even today, in higher esteem than many of their prophets. Many consider him to be the expected Messiah himself, and I have seen many Persian Jews in Khoi, Selmas, Tibriz and Maragha who invoke his name in the most holy of oaths."⁹⁸

The Yemenite Messianic Forerunner of 1172

The Jewish community was in a crunch. The Shiite Muslims often demanded that Jews convert not just to Islam but to their specific variety of it. On the other hand, they had a would-be Messiah who provided a way out of their dilemma if he were truly what he claimed. Hence Rabbi Jacob Ibn Alfayumi, the leader of their community, wrote to Maimonides, the towering Jewish intellect of the day (1135–1204) to seek out his advice.

Maimonides came out vigorously against any effort at date setting. Astrology hadn't provided the needed clue and neither had past interpretation of Scripture. For that matter, he wondered whether it could provide the data to do so: after all, in the final analysis, one could not even definitively establish the exact length of the ancient Egyptian captivity of the Jewish people. And that in spite of the fact that it was discussed at length.⁹⁹ He stressed that the coming of the Messiah was an absolute certainty and that only its timing was an issue. As he worded the sentiment¹⁰⁰:

> It is your duty to know that it is not proper for any man to endeavor to ascertain when the "end" will come; as Daniel explained, "The words are shut up and sealed till the time of the end" (12:9). But some of the learned have indulged in much speculation on this question and imagined they had solved it; as the Prophet foretold, "Many shall run to and fro, and knowledge shall be increased" (12:4)—meaning, the opinions and conjectures on this point will be increased.

Indeed, he suggested that any human speculation was almost certainly going to be wrong since the coming was supposed to be a surprise to the world.¹⁰¹

Although he intellectually recognized the futility of such speculations, even he could not help but wonder whether there might be some evidence after all. In the same letter that quotes Daniel against date setting, he himself wonders whether there might not be a parallel rooted in Scripture that could provide the time. From the days of Creation to the end-time teaching of Balaam in Numbers 23, 2,488 years had passed. By analogy one would take that same figure and apply it as the duration from then until the messianic event predicted in Numbers would be fulfilled. This would yield a date of 4,976 — 1216 in the modern calendar.[102]

The calculation could be an interpolation, yet if one had resorted to that tactic, would it not have been deemed essential to tone down or remove the references to the date being unknowable in order to make the text fully consistent and not to undermine the interloper's own argument? Furthermore, the ancient translations of the text include both remarks, which argues that it was already present in the text they were working from.[103] Finally, if it was an interpolation at all, it must have been an early one; it was hardly likely to have been inserted after the event, for then the passage of time would already have proved the interpretation erroneous.[104] Hence it seems better to regard it as an example of the very human desire to answer the unanswerable — knowing that we can't provide a reliable one, yet our human curiosity and interest may goad us into making the effort. Inconsistent, yes, but quite true to human nature.

Concerned that the Yemenite Jews would continue to tolerate or embrace this supposed forerunner, Maimonides wrote three different essays to them concerning the Messiah in an effort to convince them that the man was thoroughly unreliable. In case they would not listen to reasoned argument, he appealed to their prudence: They were in danger of bringing down the wrath of the government on their heads if they persisted. His warning did little good, and it required just such governmental intervention to shock the man's followers into parting company with him.[105]

In a letter to the Jewish community in Marseilles, France, Maimonides depicted the Yemenite as a well-meaning but unlearned pretender whose unjustified claims endangered all Jews in the region. This individual[106]

> proclaimed himself as the forerunner of the Messiah, paving the way for the latter's coming. He predicted that Messiah will make his appearance in Yemen. As a consequence, a multitude of people, Jews and Arabs, gathered around him in the hills. They listened naively as he deceptively told them: Come with me, let us go out to greet the Messiah for he has sent me unto you to straighten the path before him.
>
> Our brethren of Yemen wrote me a long epistle informing me of his strange behavior and conduct, as well as the innovations he introduced in the prayers and in his mode of discourse. They inquired specifically about some of his miraculous acts which they allegedly witnessed. I deduced from the content of their writing that this man was an impostor, devoid of any understanding, although he pretended to be pious. The rumors about miracles he performed which allegedly were beheld by others, were utterly false and absurd.

When the man was captured and taken before the Arab ruler, he refused to back down about the things he had taught and claimed[107]:

> "Your Majesty, the King, everything I said was authentic in accordance with God's command."
>
> When the King asked him what proof he had, he replied: "If you will decapitate me I shall be resurrected." The King said: "There can be no better proof than that...." The King ordered that a sword be fetched and commanded that he be decapitated at once. When he died (may his death be an atonement for him and all Israel) and thereby was exposed as an impostor, the Jewish community was severely penalized. Heavy financial penalties were invoked upon them, and yet, despite these disabilities, there are still fanatics who believe that this pretender will imminently rise from his grave.

Although claiming only forerunner status, the unidentified Jew clearly intended to form a messianic movement even if he could not claim its ultimate leadership. On the other hand, his dramatic final claim — if executed he would be raised — may well suggest that by that time he had reached the point that his personal claims had merged into one with what he would have attributed to the Messiah himself.

Historical Context: The Thirteenth Century Growth of Catholic and Jewish Mysticism

In the surrounding Catholic world the thirteenth century (and especially the second half) was one of growing spiritual enthusiasm and mysticism. This was the time of Francis of Assisi. It was the time when mystical spirituality became popular both in Italy and adjoining southern France.[108] Joachim of Floris had predicted in the preceding century that the Age of the Holy Spirit would begin in 1260, after a period of successful assault on the church led by the Antichrist.[109] The year 1260 also saw the birth of the Catholic flagellant movement that combined the search for a mystical fulfilling spirituality with the inflicting of pain through bodily whipping upon and by the penitent.[110]

This spiritualizing frame of mind had a distinct echo inside Jewish society. The community was moved to cast aside more-or-less text-driven scriptural exegesis for kabbalistic (i.e., mystical interpretation). In this approach (to those not accepting its premises) the result easily ranged from the speculative to the outrageously irrelevant in treating the texts being examined.[111]

In the later category would come the use of gematria, the determination of the numerical total of a word and its use as the foundation for scriptural interpretation. The most famous example of numerology actually comes from Scripture itself in the Christian tradition in the Book of Revelation. There we read of the "number of the beast" as 666 and the calling for the reader to grasp whose name it stands for. (Traditionally this results in the name of Nero.) Gematria does it far differently: it first begins with a name (for example), adds the numerical value of each letter, arrives at a total, and then proceeds to a deduction rooted not in the text but in that number itself.

Philosophy and a this-world-centered education became more and more disparaged in this time period. In 1305 Solomon ben Adret led a council of 15 rabbis in formally denouncing and repudiating any Jew who dared study philosophy before he turned 25.[112] This carried with it the worldview that philosophy had such little of value to contribute to individual and communal welfare that its study could be beneficially postponed until all the more important work was completed. And from there to ignoring it completely was but a modest step.

Abraham Abulafia (1240–c. 1291)

Abraham Abulafia was born in Saragossa, Spain, in 1240 and at age 20 began a series of wanderings through Greece, Turkey, and the Near East. At the beginning, he had two main goals. One was to find the Sabbath River, which, it was said, only flowed on that one day of the week.[113] The other was to locate the proverbial Ten Lost Tribes of Israel.[114] The Moguls were pushing eastward at that time, and there were more than a few who toyed with the idea that these little-known people were themselves the descendents of those tribes. During Abulafia's stay in Acre, any temptation he may have had to embrace that interpretation was quickly erased.[115]

Traveling then to Greece, he found a wife and, after journeying to Italy with her, began to study both philosophy in general and Maimonides' *Guide of the Perplexed* in particular.[116] After a period there, he completed his trip back to his native Spain and in 1270 began an in-depth study of kabbalistic lore.[117] In the long term, that decision was to prove important to his intellectual development because gradually he began to develop "Prophetic Kabbalah," which involved the use of its techniques to achieve a mystical sense of peace and acceptance with the divine.[118]

His effort to develop his mystical insight did not involve a renunciation of more traditional means; indeed, he wished to merge the two into a synthesis. In the following years he wrote various pamphlets, for example, attempting to merge Maimonides with the Kabbalah.[119]

6. Messianic Movements in the Late Middle Ages 79

In the early 1270s, Abulafia became convinced that God had bestowed upon him a special gift of supernatural insight into spiritual and kabbalistic matters.[120] Out of this grew the conviction that he was to personally play the pivotal role of redeemer of the Promised Land. In spite of this, he never actually advocated a specific program to accomplish that goal.[121] Today we would likely call such a man a dreamer, one who is so confident that his grand construction of the future will emerge triumphant that he never sees the need to lay out a program to accomplish it. It simply will happen. He knows it and that is sufficient.

Such claims bred powerful foes from within Abulafia's own faith community. Solomon Adret, one of the most significant, labeled him as "that scoundrel Abraham who declared himself prophet and Messiah."[122] Abulafia proudly acknowledged being both Christ (and in a literal sense) the Antichrist as well, the latter description being judged as appropriate because of his opposition to Jesus of Nazareth and His teachings.[123]

He also viewed himself as the unique man of his age who could not only claim a traditional Jewish priestly ancestry but even shared the unique priesthood of the much earlier Melchizedek as well, "I am priest on my wife's side, a Levite on my mother's side, and an Israelite on my father's side, and although this may be contrary to logic, it is not so for him who knows the 'mystery of Malkizedek, King of Salem, who brought forth bread and wine, and he was priest of God and most high' (Genesis 14:18)."[124]

Along with his gaining insight into his special relationship with God, he was given a command by God to seek out a meeting with the pope[125]—though he did not carry out that instruction until a decade later. In November 1280, he finally carried out this task that fit so well with his prophetic and messianic claims. In his only personal description of the intended subject matter of the meeting, Abulafia referred to "Judaism in general."[126] This has been taken in various senses.

In the politico-religious sense, the meeting with Pope Nicholas III may have been intended to give the opportunity to plead that the widespread anti–Jewish repressions should be alleviated.[127] On behalf of this scenario, it should be noted that in contemporary Jewish thought this papal mission had clear-cut messianic overtones. Just as Moses had appeared before the Pharaoh to demand freedom for his people, the Messiah would appear before the pope to plead for their freedom.[128]

Some theorize that his goal was more directly spiritual, perhaps to help the pope understand the kabbalistic approach to Judaism in the conviction that it would appeal to his intellect.[129] Others venture that he hoped to simply convert the pope.[130]

Whatever his true goal, it was not to be. The pope received his request at the papal residence north of Rome and firmly rejected it: If Abulafia insisted upon coming in spite of being warned off, he would be put to death. Abulafia decided to go anyway. In a scenario worthy of fiction, he arrived only to discover that the pope had just died, so quickly that there had not even been time for him to make a last confession.[131] Imprisoned for two weeks, Abulafia was unexpectedly released and he left for Sicily.[132]

He explained his incredible escape from burning at the stake in two different ways. He used it as an object lesson in steadfast loyalty to principle even in the face of death.[133] He also cited it as an example of how God had intervened to save his life.[134]

Anger at his ideas and messianic claims spread widely among by his opponents.[135] A number of prominent Sicilian Jews were especially annoyed by these claims and requested the judgment of the most prominent religious authority of Spanish Jewry of the day, Rashba (or, if one prefers his full name, Rabbi Shlomo ben Abraham Ibn Adret).[136] His hostile response was promptly placed in the hands of Abulafia's followers, who were horrified at the intensity of the repudiation. Hoping that it could not be genuine, they showed it to Abulafia, who conceded that it was authentic.[137]

In response, Abulafia wrote a lengthy rebuttal and sent it to an associate of his critic in Spain. In it he vigorously defended himself as well as passionately denouncing the kabbalistic system of Rashba as being far worse than the belief in the Trinity held by the Christians.[138] Hence, either as a debating tactic or out of the genuine concern that Rashba's theological premises were extraordinarily erroneous, he attempted to at least partially shift the question away from his own theological soundness to that of his opponent. Be that as it may, the battle became just as much one over rival forms of Kabbalah as about Abulafia's own personal claims.[139]

By this point Rashba had made discrediting Abulafia one of his highest priorities. He wrote far and wide against both the credibility of his foe as well as that of his religious teachings.[140] The content of Rashba's second response to Abulafia is unknown, but Abulafia did not have much time left in his life and this is probably the only reason he did not respond to it. After he died in about 1291, Rashba spent the remainder of his life boasting of how he had successfully refuted his opponent and kept his theories from gaining a greater audience.[141]

Messianic Forerunner: Abraham, the Spanish Prophet of Avila (1295)

Abraham lived in the city of Avila, Castile, and he suddenly began to receive teachings that he attributed to angels. These were delivered in both dreams and in visions while awake.[142] This apparently illiterate young man then amazed the people by being able to write the teachings down for the benefit of anyone who might wish to read them.[143]

In addition to delivering an inspired text, he was equally guided to write an authoritative commentary on the original work.[144] He called his volume *The Book of Wondrous Wisdom*. The commentary went into prolonged detail on the revelations contained in the original text.[145] Nothing of it, however, has survived to the modern era.[146]

The accomplishment amazed even the skeptically inclined of the community. Respected leaders among them testified both to the lad's lack of book learning as well as the quality of his work.[147]

The dominant Spanish Jewish leader of the day, Rashba (see above), did his best to pour cold water on enthusiasm for Abraham. Faced with credible witnesses of the youth's lack of education and yet his having produced two ably written works, he bluntly rejected the young man's inspiration. On the other hand, Rashba had trouble explaining how Abraham had managed to produce the works attributed to him.[148] Ultimately he fell back upon a priori reading. He argued that the Talmud had established that genuine prophecy required three prerequisites that were clearly lacking in this case: (1) it could only occur in Palestine; (2) it could never be given to an unlearned individual; (3) it could never be given in a period of time in which the people were "unworthy" in God's sight.[149] He urged that further examination be made of the man and his work but argued that there was no way that such an effort would ultimately vindicate him as a prophet.[150]

Abraham dated the Messiah's appearance as due to occur in 1295, and much of the Jewish portion of Avila gathered in the synagogue on the predicted date. Sorrow and bewilderment became the order of the day as it ended and the Messiah had not arrived.[151]

Abraham's visionary work concerning the imminent messianic era should be set within its contemporary framework. The Franciscan Spirituals of that and the following centuries were prone to produce similar works of apocalyptic "prophecy," and there was great hesitation among church authorities in branding any of them as clearly heretical.[152] In part this may reflect scholarly restraint; it almost certainly reflects a contemporary feeling that the world was in such a state that end times speculation was quite reasonable even if a specific individual were erroneous as to a set date.

Indeed, in the very year 1295, friar Pierre Jean Olivi, himself a Franciscan Spiritualist and viewed as saintly and prophetic even beyond his lifetime, wrote of how the time of divine "pruning has come" and how that escape from the coming calamity was only possible through divine assistance.[153]

Another contemporary Catholic gives an even closer parallel to the Jewish prophet. In 1300 Arnaldo de Villanova, a respected doctor highly favorable to the Spiritualist movement, wrote of "a man, almost wholly illiterate ... [who] saw a vision of the future and wrote it down in eloquent Latin and polished style."[154] (The author did not understand the Latin and requested a monk to explain it to him.)[155] Included were prophecies of European wars and of how Palestine would be freed.[156]

Hence, odd as the story of Abraham of Avila — the illiterate literary genius — may seem to our ears, he would not have seemed all that out of place among his Gentile contemporaries of the Catholic faith.

The Syrian Messiah of 1286

Nothing is known of this man's claims, life, or fate beyond the fact that reports of his claiming to be Messiah spread out of Syria into Europe in 1286.[157] He is but another of those "known unknowns" hiding just out of historical reach.

7

Jewish Messiahs During the Renaissance and Reformation (1300–1600)

Historical Context: Jewish and Christian Messianic Speculations during this Period

A number of Jewish calculations of the date of the Messiah's appearance centered on 1358. A different cluster of respected authorities suggested 1403. After both dates passed, a long-term disinclination set in to delve into such speculation at all.[1] Indeed, of the four major known predictors who circulated their findings between 1350 and 1492, one went so far as to project the Messiah into the nineteenth century. One could hardly do more to discourage any sense of imminence of the event![2]

Of those who performed their spiritual mathematics in the late fifteenth or early sixteenth centuries, Isaac Abravanel (1437–1508) deserves special attention. He was a man with an immense knowledge of the literature of both Judaism and contemporary and past Catholicism.[3] By a combination of astrological calculations and scriptural exegesis, he was convinced that the Messiah had been born in 1491.[4] Writing in 1495, he dated the Messiah's public appearance as to occur in either 1502 or 1503. When he brought out a commentary on Zechariah in that time frame, he included the reassuring remark that the appearance "is this year."[5]

If one felt skeptical of his calculations or simply desired confirmation, he reasoned, one should look at the sad state of the world. Did not the social conditions of the day prove that the end time must have arrived? After all, was not the dreaded "French plague" (a form of venereal disease) spreading its havoc far and wide throughout Europe?[6]

In the twentieth and twenty-first century Christian context, one has repeatedly found parallel reasoning: Periods of disease, disaster and calamity have been seen as evidence that the second coming of Jesus must be imminent. An even more horrendous end times scenario is postulated in the premillennial speculation concerning Antichrist, worldwide tribulation and repression, before that second coming.

When the Messiah did not arise, Abravanel recalculated and determined that the true date was 1534. After further reconsideration, he later changed that to 1542.[7]

Oddly enough, there were those who were firmly convinced that date setting was desirable even if the time selected turned out to be wrong. For example, in a sermon delivered in the 1480s, Rabbi Shem Tob of Spain implicitly provides a rationale for this. He argued on the basis of biblical precedent that if people did not believe in the imminence of the event they would repudiate their spiritual heritage[8]:

> The meaning of this important passage is as follows. Although we believe that the redeemer, our Messiah, will indeed come, it was clear that his arrival would be in the distant future. However, if the ignorant masses knew that the Messiah would not come during their lifetime, few of them would remain Jews. They would instead become assimilated to the Gentiles. The ignorant, to whom the salvation of the soul is very remote, serve God only for the hope of living in peace and security. Therefore, if Jacob had revealed this secret about the coming of our Messiah in the distant future, great harm would have ensued.

Whatever value one thought could be attributed to date setting until the messianic event finally occurred, what was the Jew do to keep up his or her spirits and that of the Jewish community in the interim? Those who despaired of date setting faced this problem with special stringency. But for both date setter and date rejecter, one solution to this problem was through the belief that by virtuous behavior one might speed up the divine time table. As his disciple-reporter summed up the concluding words of an early fifteenth century sermon of Rabbi Jacob Segal[9]:

> At the end of the sermon, the rabbi, of blessed memory, returned to the intent of the scriptural lesson. He interpreted the words "And a redeemer will come to Zion" (Isaiah 59:20) to mean that we should pray to God to hasten the redemption. This is the significance of the verse "things concealed belong to the Lord our God" (Deuteronomy 29:28), meaning that messianic dates are hidden with God, for no one knows when the redemption will come. "But things revealed belong to us" (Deuteronomy 29:28) he interpreted to mean that in another sense, messianic dates are revealed to us, insofar as we may pray about them and engage in the study of Torah and the performance of good deeds, so that God will mercifully hasten them. Thus the verse

ends, "to perform all the provisions of this Torah" (Deuteronomy 29:28).

Late fifteenth century Jews certainly needed all the encouragement they could obtain. Many sections of Germany expelled all local Jews in the 1490s. In 1492 came the massive expulsion from Spain; only six years later, their exclusion from Portugal as well occurred. The personal suffering and financial cost of relocation was not all that was involved; the sense of alienation from one's family roots and the need to set down new ones and somehow simultaneously provide for self and family provided intense ongoing pressures. There was little room left for the intellectual pursuits of a more stable time.[10]

The Spanish expulsion was followed in the 1500s with growing restrictions in Italy. The freedom to engage in business was reined in; Hebrew language books had to be submitted for censorship before publication. In Venice the first formal ghetto was created.[11] In this atmosphere of denial and suppression, intellectual traditions of excellence suffered intensely.[12]

In Spain itself there was a psychological backlash that created a further "Jewish problem" for the country's rulers. However much covert Judaism lurked behind the public Catholicism of the *conversios*, who had officially embraced that religion,[13] the expulsion theoretically should have decisively undermined the temptation to "relapse" to their former faith. However, traditional Judaism was not quashed by the expulsion; instead there was an unexpected outburst of enthusiasm for it among these individuals who lived in the Extremadura section of the country. Beginning in 1495, tales circulated that the messianic moment was at hand. In 1500 it burst into the open—even such dangerous theories could not be fully hidden from hostile outside eyes—and the Inquisition went into a near-panic mode as it hastily moved to root out the many individuals who had embraced their Jewish heritage in response to the messianic hope.[14] Although most of the arrests occurred in 1500, continued investigations brought others into the net of the Inquisition as late as 1502.[15]

A few advocates of rededication had rallied many others to their hopes and dreams. The three visionary-prophets were a butcher, Luis Alonso, and two women, Ines of Herrera and Maria Gomez of Chillon. Each developed a significant following at this time.[16]

Kabbalah

If the heavily intellectual, reason-driven traditional rabbinicalism could not handle the situation, it was certainly one in which advocates of kabbalistic emotionalism came into their own. No longer were they a merely tolerated and questionable subspecies of Judaism. They now rose to challenge the traditional approach, and it became credible to believe that its way of thinking would become the new normative Judaism.[17]

Since Kabbalah will repeatedly be referred to in our discussion of a number of messianic individuals (and has already been mentioned), it would be useful to provide a brief introduction to the subject. The term "Kabbalah" literally means "tradition" and first appears in the 1180s and 1190s. The development stage culminated in the work of Moses de Leon of Spain (died 1305) and his *Sefer ha-Zohar* ("Book of Splendor.")[18] This became the essential prerequisite text of virtually anyone seeking to learn and develop the system.

The official myth of its supporters was that Kabbalah originated among the rabbis of the generation following the destruction of the Jerusalem temple in A.D. 70. Hence *Zohar* and earlier works were written in a conscious imitation of the style of presentation and language of the second-century Tannaitic-era rabbis whose writings were preserved via the Talmud. Indeed, the works were attributed to rabbis of this period.[19]

The attributions are certainly erroneous and the claim that the methodology considered kabbalistic actually dates back that far is completely without historic foundation. The distinct symbolism of the system is even missing in works of Jewish mysticism of the early 1100s and it suddenly erupts, as if out of nowhere, in the last decades of that century.[20]

At roughly the same time, certain Gnostic style movements appeared inside Roman Catholicism in the border regions of France near the areas of Spain where the Kabbalah first appeared. Yet there is so much difference between the Albigensian and Cathar ways of thought and those of the Jewish Kabbalah that it seems impossible to propose a direct connection.[21] Indeed, if there was any reliance upon non-Jewish sources, it appears more likely that they came from the "Oriental" world of the day rather than the European.[22]

There was, however, a certain logic and precedent to the appearance of the *Zohar*. It was commonly believed that God had revealed his written will through the Torah of Moses, and that the Oral Law that Moses had not committed to writing was finally preserved in that form in the Talmud. What then was illogical in there being a mystical oral law that was also given to Moses but only committed to the written page in that same time period of early rabbinic writings? Not everyone even at the time bought into this antiquity myth, but few made a public issue of it.[23]

Scripture could be mastered, as could the Talmud, by the human facilities of memorization and intellectual analysis, but the *Zohar* explored mysteries that were beyond the mere intellect and its ability to grasp mere temporal matters. Hence even the obscurities, ambiguities, and strangeness of the *Zohar* enhanced its appeal. These things demonstrated how far the natural mind had to transcend its normal limitations to grasp the ultimate divine truth. On this basis the *Zohar* and the kabbalistic systems that evolved out of it were widely respected deep into the eighteenth century even by those who made no claim to understand them.[24] For that matter, even today it has a strong cadre of advocates.

To the kabbalist, the system explained the hidden mystical realities to the extent that they can be portrayed at all in human language.[25] To those who criticized it, the response was that the critics were taking "literally" what was never meant to be taken in such terms. Hence external critiques, whether of religious or logical origin, could be dismissed as "missing" the truth that the system offered due to an inherently futile insistence upon literalism. The system thereby became immune to all outside criticism and disproof since none but its careful students could possibly hope to accurately comprehend it. It became a self-perpetuated, literally undisprovable system of thought.[26]

Safed became the most important center of Kabbalah study in Palestine beginning in about 1530.[27] It reached its peak of influence from 1540 and into the 1570s and was renowned throughout the Jewish world for its many experts. These leading lights had migrated there from such diverse places as Germany, Poland, and Africa.[28]

Although Safed's population was modest, it was still one of the four largest Jewish communities in the Galilee of its day.[29] Located about twenty miles to the north of the Sea of Galilee, it lay on the main land route into Palestine from Syria. Jewish immigrants coming into the region from the Christian west would normally pass through Syria and, if they did not set down roots there, then pass through Safed on their way to their ultimate destination in Palestine.[30] The area was politically stable and the town enjoyed a far better economy than Jerusalem, due in major part to its thriving textile industry.[31]

Catholic and Orthodox Messianic Hopes

If messianic dreams provided an emotionally useful way out of the current world crisis for Jews, the general world situation was such that Gentiles also were perplexed, worried, and often sought the refuge of the return of their Messiah, Jesus of Nazareth. In 1453 the Turks captured Constantinople, and they continued to nibble persistently at the edges of Christian Europe. Hungary fell in 1547, the Turks ruled the Balkans and all of North Africa as far as Morocco. As far eastward as the Persian border, their armies reigned triumphant.[32]

If these external pressures were not enough, the Christianity of the day splintered. Previously unorthodox and "heretical" movements had been violently suppressed. By the 1500s this approach no longer worked. In Germany, Martin Luther's bold indictment of church corruption and "false doctrine" blithely defended as required orthodoxy gained major support from powerful elements of the German nobility. Papal politics prevented Henry VIII from securing the annulment he would otherwise almost routinely have been granted and drove him to take the English church into organizational independence from Rome. Other nations either fell or were in danger of falling to the new wave of dissidence.

One subsidiary but important element in the growing self-definition of the "Protestant" movements was a consensus that the Antichrist spoken of in Scripture was the papacy itself. It was the mysterious "Babylon" fighting the church in the Book of Revelation. Hence the papacy's defeat was viewed as inevitable and the successes of the religious revolution made many believe that it would likely be imminent.[33]

Furthermore, movements emerged on the theological fringe of the Reformation that carried these sentiments even further. These made even the new "heresies" of Lutheranism, Calvinism, and Anglicanism seem almost praiseworthy in comparison. If this was not enough, the poorest elements of society embraced the radicalism with dangerous enthusiasm. They saw it as an opportunity — in the name of God, no less — to violently vent their anger at the higher classes and governments that had so long abused them. The divine kingdom would either be established by Christ Himself or they would do so on His behalf so it would be ready and waiting for His return.

Shemariah ben Elijah Ikriti of Italy

Born in about 1275 and dying near the middle of the fourteenth century, he attempted to bridge the gap between Karaite Judaism and the dominant rabbinic thought of the day. Later in his life he claimed the status of Messiah. Unfortunately, the sole source of this claim is from an apostate from Judaism and this has resulted in it being seriously challenged.[34] On the other hand, why pick such an extreme claim to vent one's animosity? Remaining a practicing Jew was sufficient to put one under a cloud of doubt in Gentile-dominated Italy. Hence there were plenty of stereotypes available to discredit an enemy rather than invent a charge that was so uncommon in real life that it would have sounded odd even to many opponents of the Jewish community.

Moses Botarel (c. 1393)

Botarel was a Spaniard of varied interests who spanned the years from the fourteenth into the fifteenth centuries. His major interests centered on medicine, philosophy and the magical arts. Indeed, his mastery of contemporary spell casting techniques gained him a reputation as being a skilled sorcerer.[35]

Even so, he devoted much of his attention to the Kabbalah. As he himself declared, "By my head I swear that I did not leave any book treating of this science without first studying it thoroughly."[36] In 1409 he produced a major commentary on the subject that received widespread interest.[37]

A particularly vicious series of persecutions against Jews swept his country in 1391. In his *Berit Menuha*, the prominent philosopher Abraham of Granada interpreted these tragedies as we have seen done in other cases—as signs that the messianic age was about to be given birth.[38]

Quite likely reacting to this wave of repression, in 1393 Botarel openly declared himself Messiah.[39] He claimed that the long-sought messianic age was to begin that same year.[40] Abraham of Granada was so impressed by him that he embraced his cause. Furthermore, the story was spread of his alleged miracles, in particular having survived being thrown into a burning furnace by no less than Spain's own king.[41]

The miracle stories are contained in the letters of Hasdai Cresscas (1340–1410), but their veracity has been challenged on the grounds that he had a track record of rejecting all efforts to calculate when the Messiah would come and he persistently refused to consider the concept a pivotal Jewish belief.[42] In other words, even a sympathetic secondhand account would be unlikely to come from such a person. In addition, a Messiah who lacked such an ability goes back at least as far as bar Kochba, and the "miracle" claims affect the alleged evidence the man could introduce on behalf of himself rather than his messianic claims themselves. Hence the stories likely reflect the gilding of the legend rather than the core of it.

Asher Lemlein (c. 1502)

Lemlein was originally a resident of Germany until he moved to Italy during the period of vigorous anti-Jewish activities in the last years of the fifteenth century. He ultimately set down roots in Istria, a community near Venice, Italy, where he lived and taught between 1500 and 1502.[43] This was a stable environment in which to work since Jews were heavily concentrated in the trading and banking segments of the economy and enjoyed the protection of the local authorities.[44]

He soon announced that the messianic year would be 1502.[45] Within the context of Jewish history, Lemlein is especially interesting because he was the first Ashkenazi Jew to become a prominent and successful advocate of the imminency of the coming of the Messiah.[46] So convincing was he that some enthusiastic Jews went so far as to destroy their Passover ovens: Since the Messiah was coming within a year, they would never again be in need of them.[47]

According to the contemporary historian Joseph Ha-Cohen (1496–1575), Palestinian Jewish leaders proclaimed various special fast days and other observances to ready the people for the event.[48] So typical was this of the popular reaction that a Jewish chronicler of a later generation described 1502 as the "Year of Repentance."[49] This spiritual intensification was so pronounced that in a Christian apologetic work depicting a fictional discussion between a Jew and a Christian, Sebastian Munster (1489–1552) praised its sincerity and intensity.[50]

Yosef Pfefferkorn, a contemporary of the events and, in 1505, a convert to Roman Catholicism, described the events that Lemlein insisted would occur: "A fiery pillar together with a dark cloud was to surround all the Jews, as happened at the time of Pharaoh; also then they would return to Jerusalem, rebuild the temple, and offer sacrifices."[51] As icing on the cake, so to speak, the Christian church would collapse and disintegrate. Since this would be "a sign"[52] that his prediction was to be fulfilled, Lemlein must have viewed the chaos that would result from such a religio-political collapse as making possible the return of his people to their original homeland.

What was to be Lemlein's own role in these events? Was he the forerunner of the Messiah or the Messiah himself? The limited surviving documentation refers to how he spoke of himself as king and how he would lead the people of Israel back to Palestine.[53] In a Jewish context and, especially when involving the inauguration of the messianic age, it is hard to avoid seeing this as a claim of being the Messiah himself.[54] Even so, there is enough ambiguity in his words that some are hesitant to classify the exact nature of his claims,[55] and others deny the messianic connection entirely.[56]

It is, of course, quite possible that the man himself was far more convinced of the fact that he would be ruler and leader of the people than that he was definitely Messiah. He may well have been determined to fulfill what he regarded as his divine commission and leave the possible messianic implications to work themselves out.

As it became clear that his prediction was not going to come to fruition, he disappeared from the public scene.[57] Perhaps he feared the backlash from the discovery that his claims were generated from his fond hopes and imagination rather than grounded in reality. Even so, the enthusiasm did not immediately dissipate[58]; the dream was simply too powerful.

Yet a backlash was virtually inevitable. There is evidence that, when Lemlein died or simply disappeared, the enthusiasm that had once been present was so shattered that a large number of Jews ultimately turned their backs on their traditional faith and became Catholics.[59] Unquestionably, Catholic conversion propaganda considered him a prime example of how, in rejecting Jesus of Nazareth, contemporary Jews had become vulnerable to messianic delusions.[60]

David Reubeni (c. 1490 to post–1535)

Whatever were the inner opinions that he actually believed, outwardly he did the maximum to make himself acceptable to those of all religions and gain their recognition, respect, and, if possible, support. Appearing in Egypt out of Arabia in 1522, he spoke to Islamists as the supposed descendent of Mohammed. To Jews he presented himself as brother of the king of certain of the Jewish "lost tribes": He had come from Khaibar on King Joseph's behalf to bring the scattered Jewish people back to Palestine. To the Christians he came as negotiator to arrange a joint offensive with his brother's armies against the Islamists both in Palestine and elsewhere.[61]

His kind of ecumenical agenda required that he carefully avoid making any explicit and specific messianic claims no matter what interpretations his zealous supporters might read into his words—either with his condolence or active encouragement.[62] For example, when informed that both the Jewish and Islamic communities in Fez were speaking of him in messianic or prophetic terms, he downplayed such efforts.[63] On the other hand, he was not above preparing a lineage that traced his ancestry all the way back to King David[64]—who, not coincidentally, just happened to be the prototype king for the Messiah. It seems best to interpret Reubeni as an individual who was willing to take advantage of this interpretation, even quietly encouraging it upon occasion,[65] while doing all he could to avoid making any claims explicit lest it endanger his goal of gaining support from the Catholic west.

His actual lineage is still uncertain. Some scholars believe that he was an Ashkenazi Jew who originated in Central Europe. Others think he was one of the Falasha Jews who lived in Ethiopia.[66]

Equally speculative is the time of his birth.[67] It is not even certain whether his public name of David Reubeni was his birth name or one he adopted when he decided to undertake his public career: "David" would certainly tie in the man with the traditional prototype of the messiah; "Reubeni" could easily be an allusion to the tribe of Reuben, one of the so-called lost tribes which so intrigued contemporaries.[68]

His physical appearance was described this way by Abraham B. Mordecai Ferizon, a French-born Jewish geographer of the period: "He is of short stature, lean-fleshed, and courageous; he prays frequently, is dark-complexioned, and afflicts himself with fasting. According to the words of the writers, he could fast for six consecutive days and nights. His principal language is the holy tongue [Hebrew], which he speaks almost unintelligibly, like a stammerer."[69]

After traveling in both Egypt and Palestine to publicize his cause, he proceeded to Italy.[70] He made such a powerful impression on the local Jewish community where he first arrived that its members used their connections in Rome to assure that the Jews in that city gave him the attention they were convinced he deserved.[71] So far as they were concerned, his genuineness was unquestionable.

In Rome in 1524, Pope Clement VII even granted him an audience to discuss his goals.[72] Getting to see the pope, not surprisingly, was far from an easy task. To accomplish the goal, he sought the intervention of a powerful Jewish banker who had ongoing relationships with the Roman Curia and who had wide respect in those quarters.[73]

Setting the stage, he next sought to bring to his side a friendly and influential cardinal-adviser to the pope. When he arrived in Rome, a large crowd joined him as he rose to meet with Cardinal Egidio of Viterbo and Joseph Ashkenazi, who had been one of the cardinal's teachers of the Hebrew language and literature.[74] The large and excited crowd was permitted to respectfully stand at a distance but still sufficiently near to overhear the conversation. In spite of the powerful church official he was facing, Reubeni succinctly and ably presented the case for the Christian West to provide him with arms and professionals in gunpowder and its military usages; in exchange, his brother would launch a whole-hearted thrust into Palestine from the South and seize it from the Muslims.[75]

The proposal was, at the minimum, an enticing one. The Catholic west had launched repeated crusades and all had fallen short of delivering a crushing blow that would permanently eliminate the Islamic military danger to Palestine. Whether done by armies of tens of thousands or via

7. Jewish Messiahs During the Renaissance and Reformation 93

dedicated military orders such as the Templars, all had failed to permanently resolve the conflict. In that context, the possibility of a Jewish military triumph to accomplish what others had been unable to could not be automatically dismissed.[76]

Over the next few days, he visited with both Rabbi Ashkenazi and Cardinal Egidio. On the Sabbath evening (Saturday), word was delivered to Reubeni and spread like wildfire throughout the Jewish community: Pope Clement had agreed to meet with him the next day.[77]

Reubeni was accompanied to the meeting by a group of the Jewish leaders and by a large crowd fascinated with what was about to occur. The pope politely received the stranger. Islamic thrusts in the Balkans had made the international and interreligious situation even more dangerous than in the past. Even a failed Jewish crusade in Palestine could do no harm and might even eliminate that expansionism.[78]

Reubeni sought letters of introduction (thereby implicitly providing a papal shield of protection or at least approval) to both the king of France and the Holy Roman Emperor as well as one to present to Prester John, the supposed Christian ruler in Africa.[79] By combining these forces with those of his brother, the Ottomans would be ousted from Palestine.[80] The pope conceded that the concept sounded feasible but noted that the prerequisite for it—peace between France's King Francis I and the Holy Roman Emperor Charles V—was a goal that he had been unable to bring about.[81] Unmentioned was the not insignificant fact that Francis I was currently trying to arrange a treaty with the Ottomans,[82] which was obviously incompatible with launching a war against them.

What was the papacy to get out of this scheme above and beyond the obvious pleasure in seeing the followers of Mohammed ousted from the Holy Land? The version circulated in the Jewish community was reported this way by a contemporary[83]:

> The narrators and prominent Jews who spoke with [Reubeni] declare that this Jew really did ask the pope, the king of the Gentiles, for assistance, that instruments of war (metals for throwing stones) and skilful workers should be given to him, so that he might take them along with him to Arabia Felix to destroy their above-mentioned enemies.
>
> He would give to the pope and his office certain concessions for the benefit of the pope, may his glory be exalted, and in a way to rule over some of the places where there are collectors of wealth, and spices, and simple medicines. The object of this is that these Jews may be united and gathered together to go across and take possession of the Land of Glory and subdue it, for it is an everlasting inheritance into Israel. All this have my eyes seen in truthful letters, and my ears heard from prominent and truthful people.

Other discussions followed this one, but a definitive answer was a long time in arriving. While Reubeni waited for a response, he was widely reported to be acting in a way that either manifested utter confidence or utter recklessness for a Jew in that day and age — indeed, for the Catholics of that era for that matter. A contemporary reported that stories had reached of him of how[84]:

> sometimes prominent men and cardinals of Rome came to visit him in his house, but he thrust them aside, and would not receive them. He rode on a mule in Rome to see the curiosities of the country, and, while on his mule, entered the great temple of St. Peter, even as far as the great altar, refusing to dismount his mule. There were with him about ten Jews running before him, and more than two hundred Christians.

The pope not only tolerated such things but even encouraged the man during this period. On one occasion, he sent his trumpeters to provide a concert for Reubeni at his residence.[85] On another occasion he permitted several Marranos from Portugal to openly return to Judaism — an unprecedented act of generosity toward his foreign visitor.[86]

Clement put the proposals on the back burner for a year, but Reubeni put the time to good use by cultivating friendships among important Jews in Rome and in other parts of Italy.[87] And he built up the grounds on which he could be considered the Messiah. After one prolonged fast, his body rebelled and he gave every indication of being on his deathbed since he could not regain his strength but kept getting worse.

The doctors could provide him with no help. With one he became the comforter, insisting, "I will not die until I have brought Israel to Jerusalem, built the altar, and offered sacrifice there."[88] When he regained his health, such messianic actions that he had promised encouraged the rumor that he was not just a Jewish leader but the Jewish Messiah as well.[89]

The positive reception was common but that did not mean that everyone was ready to cast their lot with his vision of the future. The intra-communal divisions were basically between those of foreign birth and those who could trace their local roots back several generations.[90] What both groups shared in common was a relief from significant external persecution. The liberalism of the time was so pronounced when compared to other European countries that a good number of Jews were enrolled in the local universities and studied for such crafts as doctoring.[91]

Indeed, Pope Clement felt so friendly toward them that he had the rabbi-banker Donzeille (also known as Daniel ben Isaac) draw up an agreement so that the Jews could exercise self-government in affairs affecting

7. Jewish Messiahs During the Renaissance and Reformation

themselves.[92] This progressive environment—for its day and age—made many, apparently the majority, quite content with their current worldly situation. Hence they were quite happy to continue to improve their existing economic and social status rather than run the risks of immigration and war in Palestine.[93]

In spite of such widespread ambivalence or opposition toward his scheme, Reubeni had support among those who counted the most: those Jews who had regular contact with the pope and the Curia. What they lacked in numbers, they far more than compensated for by being well placed and well connected.

Finally, the pope acted, but only with a letter of introduction to the king of Portugal—which was not on the original list of requests.[94] If this idea originated with the pope, it may well be that he thought that the Portuguese could represent an alternative source to back Reubeni's scheme.[95] A contemporary Venetian diplomatic note, however, comments that Reubeni suggested the alternative himself.[96] If so it may be that, having reached one dead end, he was motivated by similar reasoning himself to seek out the best available alternative.

The pope presented Reubeni with an impressive heraldic shield and a generous gift of gold. With these in hand, he left Rome in March 1525. All the way to the seaport of Livorno, both Jews and Gentiles greeted him with the enthusiasm of one who had already successfully carried out his enterprise.[97]

The pope had a vessel ready for him when he arrived at the port. In a gesture of respect, he had even arranged to assure that half the crew was Jewish,[98] a highly appropriate symbolism for the joint Jewish-Christian anti-Islamic Crusade that was being planned.

At first King John III accepted Reubeni at his court with manifest enthusiasm, an incredible act of liberality in a country that had had an extremely active Inquisition seeking religious dissenters.[99] That reception surely encouraged the even more passionate reception that Reubeni received from the Marranos, as contrasted with the enthused (but less intense and widespread) applause he had received in Italy.[100]

Reubeni made such a compelling case to King John III for support for King Joseph's army that John was soon speaking in terms of providing 4,000 cannon plus eight fighting ships. Later John repudiated his preliminary pledge, however.[101]

Even under the best of circumstances, bureaucracies have a way of hindering any ruler's decisions that fly in the face of its preferences. Furthermore, the undercurrent of anti-Jewish sentiment was one that could easily win the day if enough time passed by. And there was reason for letting time pass and to consider other options: there was the not unimportant matter of national priorities. Portugual was already pouring important major resources into trade and exploration. There was Brazil in the New World and the colonization efforts in the Far East. Both already generated important revenue for the government coffers and no one wished to endanger it.[102]

Satisfying as backing the effort to liberate Palestine would be, would it be the best use of the nation's assets? The perpetual clash between idealism and practicality had to be resolved, as did the weighty matter of whether Reubeni could actually be trusted.

The daring tightrope that Reubeni walked was inherently treacherous. After all, there were no armies of his supposed brother King Joseph. This would be transparently obvious and expose him as a fraud when the effort was made to deliver them. Or was this a stratagem for gaining arms on the premise that if he could obtain them the army itself could be conjured up from enthusiastic fellow Jews?

Whatever his ultimate intention, his welcome in Portugal gradually grew weaker among official sources as they became increasingly skeptical of his true intents and motives. Reubeni was accused of trying to convince the Marranos to return to Judaism; the open admission of Solomon Molko that he had returned to his ancestral faith (see below) had been blamed on his influence. That event was the decisive factor in convincing the court that Reubeni could not be trusted and must be expelled.[103]

Back in Italy, he remained in Rome only briefly and then took up residence in Venice.[104] There he was harassed by the government of the Doge, which ultimately ordered him to leave the city under the guise of giving him the "right" to move to a better home.[105]

Later that year of 1530 he was again permitted to meet with Pope Clement. The fact that the pontiff permitted Molko to be present in the meeting as well was remarkable in the context of the time: Here was not only a Jew but also a relapsed Jew who had rejected Catholicism and turned back to Judaism.[106] Such men would normally be jailed or killed, not listened to. Perhaps the Pontiff had heard of the Jewish messianic speculation placing that event in the near future[107] and pure curiosity motivated him. Or perhaps he was so desperate to find a way to oust the Turks from Palestine that he was willing to consider meeting with those he would normally have scorned.

Molko delivered to him predictions of the future. The first would be verifiable locally: A massive flood would hit the city. In October it did just that. Not only was much of Rome underwater, but 300 lives were lost. Remembering the prediction, the pope had sought refuge in Ostia at the first appearance of flood danger.[108] In light of the danger he had escaped, it is not surprising that the Pontiff was deeply impressed.[109]

In 1532 Reubeni wisely or unwisely saw fit for Molko to join him in an effort to convince Emperor Charles V to support their plans for the future of Palestine.[110] It did not help that their enemies in Italian Jewry had successfully thrown in doubt the legitimacy of certain letters he had claimed to once possess but lost. These concerns were passed on to the emperor through third parties and further undermined the emperor's willingness to respectfully receive the two men.[111]

The members of the German Reichstag were meeting in Upper Bavaria at Regensburg at the time,[112] and one of the items on their agenda was the possibility of a new war against the Islamic powers.[113] If they knew of this, it would certainly help explain why they were willing to undertake their mission. If their agenda was adopted, they would be "riding the wave" that was just beginning to take form and if it were rejected, how could the emperor be dangerously hostile to people bearing a proposal that his own Reichstag was considering? Unfortunately for them, the emperor had already made up his mind to oppose the project regardless of who it came from.[114]

Although the duo dressed in their best clothes and made every attempt to appear as if dignified diplomats, Charles refused to have anything to do with them. Instead he had them arrested and put in chains.[115] Tried by the Inquisition, Reubeni was sentenced to imprisonment in Spain and Molko was sentenced to immediately die for having returned to the Judaism of his ancestors.[116]

Oddly enough, the Spanish Inquisition seems to have released Reubeni after he was given over into their hands.[117] About five years passed before he again came to the hostile attention of the authorities, and this time he was put to death.[118] The accusations involved new charges of attempting to convince the Marranos to return to Judaism.[119]

Solomon Molko (c. 1500–1532)

Molko (born Diego Pires) was an uncircumcised member of a family of Marranos in Portugal. Working as a court secretary in that country,[120] he occupied a position of importance in the support staff of the government bureaucracy.[121] Reubeni's mission impressed him deeply. This combined with concern over the oppression of his people, whether theoretical converts to Catholicism or not. Caught between these two strains of thought, he began to have dreams about the future that deeply concerned him.[122]

Reubeni recognized the passionate anti-Judaism present at the royal court and was fully aware of his own vulnerability as an open Jew. Hence he was determined to avoid anything that might be misinterpreted by the king and his ministers. One means of doing this was by keeping the Marranos in an arm's-length relationship, one that worked to protect both him and them.[123]

Obtaining a private audience with Reubeni in 1525, Molko laid out his problem. Sensing in this emotional dreamer a potential danger to his own efforts to present an essentially (or at least predominantly) secular justification for Judeo-Christian cooperation in the liberation of Palestine, he pushed aside Molko's enthusiasm and desire to revert to Judaism.[124] Reubeni advised him that if he was so convinced that such a course was essential, the best thing to do was for him to leave the country.[125]

This rejection was not enough to dilute his enthusiasm, however. Rather than wait until later, he decided to act immediately. Since any doctor who performed a circumcision (and was discovered) was sure to draw the wrath of the Inquisition, that resource was not available to him.[126] So Molko undertook the painful act of self-circumcision to demonstrate his intention to be fully Jewish. This open repudiation of his supposed Catholicism — though actually entered into by his parents and not by his own act[127] — was exactly the type of behavior that could inflame any Spaniard or Portuguese's suspicions of the true convictions of any Marranos. Any defender of it would also be caught in the backlash, so it is not surprising that Reubeni emphatically criticized the man for his action when it became known.[128]

Along with the circumcision, he began to use the name of Solomon Molko in place of his family name of Diego Pires. After his body healed, he began his journey eastward to safer havens within the Ottoman Empire, where he could study Hebrew and gain the knowledge that he had missed in his childhood.[129] These journeys took him to Saloniki, then Adrianople, and finally to Palestine itself.[130]

The result of the rejection by both the people of his homeland and by Reubeni in particular was yet greater self-torment and more intense and powerful dream visions. In them even the voice of God Himself spoke.[131] This pattern of revelatory dreams continued for the remainder of his life. At some point he became deeply interested in the Kabbalah and managed to cram far more knowledge of the subject into his head than one would expect in the few years of his life he had available for the effort.[132] (This is in contrast to Reubeni, who was little concerned with the Kabbalah at all.)[133]

At this point he became not just an interpreter of the Bible, not just

7. Jewish Messiahs During the Renaissance and Reformation

a kabbalistic guided interpreter of Scripture, but a self-proclaimed divinely inspired one as well. As he wrote on one occasion, "Whoever wishes may ask me whatever he wants, to comment on recondite verses and statements, for with the help of God, I am confident that I may answer everyone who asks me in a satisfactory manner sublime things which are sufficient for any intelligent person, which are not written in books, but which I was instructed from heaven."[134]

The depth of his quickly acquired learning fascinated and impressed even those who had far longer exposure to its methodology. As one individual expressed the consensus not long after Molko's death, "[T]here is no one that will deny that he suddenly was imbued with the spirit of this wisdom, the Kabbalah. It was not known from whence it came to him, just that his heart was opened by heaven, as a door of a great hall."[135]

Or as a contemporary put it, "Solomon became very learned in cabalistic lore, and he would utter beautiful and charming words, for the spirit of God spoke in him and His word was on his tongue continually. He would constantly draw beautiful thoughts from the depths of the cabalistic well and would write them down on tablets and send them to his friends in Salonica where they would print them."[136]

In 1529 he published his Hebrew-language sermons under the title *Sefer ha-Mefo'ar*. One of these sermons dated the coming of the Messiah as only a decade in the future (1540).[137] Also his printed spiritual essays became a major means of spreading his kabbalistic interpretation of Scripture.[138] Somewhere along the line in these years he either embraced the Messiah role on his own initiative or did so after much encouragement by others.[139]

Two years earlier, in 1527, Rome had been sacked — its papal connection notwithstanding — by the armies of Charles V and his allies. Pope Clement was imprisoned by them as well. The damage was extensive. As a Venetian described the city in May of that year, "Hell has nothing to compare with the present state of Rome."[140] The people were psychologically devastated; the feeling was pervasive that even worse disaster would follow.

To Molko this catastrophe was the fall of the Christian version of the ancient Edom that the Jews had battled so many centuries before. It could be nothing less than an indication that the Messiah's appearance was imminent.[141] Although others expressed the idea in different terms, the capture of Rome clearly encouraged the end-times interpretation of the era.[142]

And what was to be Molko's role in it? As he saw it, it meant that it was time to return to the west and to Rome in particular. By the final months of 1529, he had reached the ancient city. He arrived poor, hungry, and literally wearing rags. He was observed circulating among the beggars at two of Rome's major bridges as he attempted to gain a better idea of what was being done and said in the city.[143] He begged outside the Vatican for a month, and it has been suggested that he did this not just out of financial necessity but in a conscious fulfillment of a Talmudic story that the Messiah would carry out such an act.[144]

Perhaps the "visions" that came next grew out of his kabbalistic meditations. Perhaps they also grew out of his physically weakened state. In February of 1530, three major visions frightened him as to the future. Rome he saw inundated by a massive flood. His homeland of Portugal he saw struck by a mammoth earthquake. If that were not enough, a new star would appear in the heavens.[145] His sense of responsibility at being given such a supernatural insight drove him to seek an audience with the pontiff.

This was not without precedent. He may have been acting, in part, in conscious imitation of Abraham Abulafia.[146] More recently there had been the papal audiences with Reubeni. Although Molko stressed the visions he had received, it is known (from both Jewish and Catholic contemporaries) that he candidly affirmed his Jewish convictions in their meeting. Something in his character and nature clearly intrigued the pontiff, including Molko's ability to foresee the future.[147]

Learning that Reubeni was in Venice, Molko joined him there. Their views of Israel were so similar that each encouraged the other in his own confidence that he was preparing the way for the bright future of the Jewish people.[148] Sam Waagenaar suggests that in spite of this dynamic interaction there was a fundamental difference in their attitudes: "David's ideas could be said to be of a more practical nature; [Molko's] feelings were more in the visionary realm of prophetic religion."[149] In other words, Reubeni was earth/result centered; Molko theory/vision centered. Looking toward the same results, they had different interests at their core.

Strange as it sounds, Molko now became involved in the bitter dispute over Henry VIII's effort to divorce Catherine of Aragon. Henry's agents had gone to major intellectual centers in many places in Europe in an effort to buttress his case for the divorce. One of the resources they tapped into was two prominent Jews of Venice: Elia Halfon (supported by Molko), came down on one side of the question, and Jacob Mantino on the other. This quickly degenerated into bitter hard feelings on the part of Mantino, a hostility that was to come back to haunt Molko.[150]

Although Reubeni had been ordered out of the city, Molko decided to postpone his own departure from Venice. Yet he did not delay long, for word reached him that his predictions had began to come true. In October 1530 the Tiber flooded on a mammoth and unprecedented scale and his reputation as a seer of the future was confirmed for many.[151] Three hundred had perished, but the pope had remembered Molko's prediction and fled the city while there was still time.[152] When Molko arrived, the scale of the devastation was visibly massive and could have done nothing but confirm him further in his sense of his future destiny.

If the pope became his protector, his conviction that Molko deserved to be protected — practicing Jew or not — was further enhanced by the fulfillment of the two other predictions that he had personally heard from Molko's mouth. In early 1531 a major quake did, indeed, hit Portugal. In the autumn a new "star" did, indeed, appear: later generations knew it as Halley's Comet.[153]

In spite of the pope's friendliness and Molko's success as a seer, Molko was far from free of danger and it came from the Jewish quarter not the Catholic one. Although he had gained great credibility with both the pope and a significant body of Jewish opinion by his successful predictions,[154] powerful elements of the Jewish community were not won over.[155] Mantino had his grudge to settle and utilized his considerable contacts inside the Catholic hierarchy to destroy his foe.[156] In the short term, it soon became clear that the pope had successfully neutralized these efforts.[157]

Seeking a new mode of attack that could not be neutralized, the doctor Mantino obtained some correspondence by Molko. According to the doctor's translation, Molko had made derogatory comments about Roman Catholicism. This was regarded as an unforgivable sin for a lapsed Marrano who had returned to Judaism.[158]

Once the Inquisition's bureaucratic procedure had begun, it had a life of its own that even the pontiff could not control.[159] There were tools of cunning in his arsenal, however, that the Inquisition was unaware of. He had Molko impersonate another individual and thereby escape the clutches of those who would have arrested him.[160] Furthermore, he had another person, a criminal who met Molko's general description, dressed in the man's attire and permitted to wander about.[161] The Inquisition was so rushed in its proceedings to assure that they could not be circumvented that they did not carry out the elemental precaution of confirming that they had the right man, nor did they interrogate him at length to maximize the evidence they had against him. Instead, they seized the lookalike and hurriedly pushed through his prosecution and conviction.

After the burning at the stake was completed, the Inquisitors in charge went to the pope to announce that they had carried out their judgment against the heretic. At that point, the pontiff had a door opened and from the next room came Molko.[162] The shocked Inquisitors had been both humiliated and neutralized. As if to rub further salt in their wounded pride, Clement suggested, "you've made a mistake, now you had better enter into your judgment book that the victim you burned had reviled and cursed his God and King so that no one shall know you have erred, otherwise trouble will follow."[163]

It was quickly evident that the Inquisition was still determined to find some means to lay their hands on Molko once again. Recognizing that there could be but one ultimate end to this if Molko remained in the city, Pope Clement made arrangements to enable the seer to escape before another arrest could be made.[164]

Both Molko and Reubeni now faced a desperate situation. If even papal enthusiasm could not enable them to accomplish their goals, was there any other person left who might be convinced to help them carry out their dreams of Palestinian liberation? There was only one, the emperor Charles. Hence Reubeni and he traveled to Ratisbon in northern Italy in 1532 with the hope of meeting the emperor and enlisting his support in the fight for the Holy Land. By this point, the two very different missions of these men had overlapped and become one in both the mind of the public and their own.[165]

As we saw previously, the journey ultimately landed both men before the Inquisition. Molko himself was burned to death. Perhaps it was merely a tactical move (to discourage further returns to Judaism) or perhaps it was out of a certain admiration for the man himself, but a last-minute pardon was offered on condition that he re-embrace the Catholicism he had scorned. The offer was rejected and he died at the stake.[166]

Luis Dias

Like so many tailors of his day, Dias (a/k/a Ludovico Diaz) was both uneducated and struggling for his very economic survival. His hometown was the seaport of Setubal and it became the setting of his spiritual evolution from ordinary Jew to self-proclaimed prophet to that of Messiah.[167] He did not take advantage of his growing aspirations, however, as a tool to increase his financial status. Yet in spite of his continued poverty he would often have his hand kissed respectfully to show reverence for him and his spiritual efforts.[168] His teaching found an especial interest among the *conversios* (Jewish converts to Catholicism), many of whom embraced his claims.[169]

Having set down roots in Setubal, his movement then spread into Lisbon, where he also gained a large number of additional followers.[170]

The most prominent of these was Francisco Mendes, who served as official doctor for a Roman Catholic bishop.[171]

His arrest occurred only after the authorities learned that he was encouraging the circumcision of the boys of those who had become his disciples. Although an admission of guilt gained him temporary release, his resumption of the practice resulted in a second arrest. This time the death penalty was decreed and it was carried out upon both him and 83 disciples.[172] One report of the time indicates that, after torture, he "confessed" that he had invented the messianic claims as a means of elevating his status in the eyes of others.[173]

Ultimately, more that 200 were punished or executed over a period of years for their adherence to Dias.[174] As late as 1551, a prominent Jewish government official was publicly exposed as having converted back to Judaism due to his encouragement. As in the case of so many others, his major government office did nothing to save him from the death penalty.[175]

Luria of Safed (1534–1572)

Luria was born in 1534 in Jerusalem after his father had emigrated there from Europe — whether his roots had lay in Germany or Poland is uncertain.[176] After his father's death when Luria was age eight, he and his mother became part of an uncle's extended family in Egypt. This relative was fortunate enough to be both an important government official as well as quite wealthy. He freely utilized his status to ensure that Luria would receive the best quality education he could provide for him from the most respected local teachers.[177]

After marrying, Luria began a career as a merchant. Not many years later, he began to be intrigued by mysticism and became preoccupied by the mysteries of the Kabbalah. His obsession with the subject became so pronounced that for seven years he lived alone so that he could devote the maximum time to his pursuit. To assure solitude he even selected an island in the middle of the Nile to live on during those years of intense study.[178]

The leading advocate of the Kabbalah at the time was Moshe Cordovero, and so it is not surprising that Luria's studies concentrated on his writings. Cordovero was not so much a creator of new kabbalistic thought but a brilliant synthesizer of the existing thinking with his own insights and additions.[179] In the early months of 1570 (possibly a little earlier), he made Safed his new home so he could benefit by Cordovero's tutelage.[180]

Cordovero had made the prediction that the person to take his place would be the individual who spoke of seeing a cloud leading the way of his burial procession. When Luria spoke of having witnessed that phenomenon, it assured his initial acceptance into a position of honor.[181]

There is a possibility that Luria may have begun his own private study group while his teaching master was still alive.[182] Regardless of when the group began, it ultimately encompassed at least 35 individuals, and since these are only the known names it is quite likely that some others were involved as well.[183] But not too many—for he and they regarded their group as uniquely the cream of the crop of Kabbalah students and, as such, far above the level of others.[184] Luria's role in the group lasted only about two years, assuming that it began at Cordovero's death in 1570, since his own passing occurred in the summer of 1572.

In spite of this short time frame, his teaching had a powerful impact on his contemporaries and was passed on to later generations under the label of "Lurianic Kabbalah."[185] Although four different disciples preserved, codified, and presented his teaching to the public with their own variants of it,[186] it was the form preserved by Hayyim Vital Calabrese that became identified to later generations as (to extent possible) the true Lurianic form of the Kabbalah.[187]

Luria kept ambiguous and basically out of the public eye his own role in the messianic era. There were repeated stories at the time and after his death, though, that he considered himself the Messiah.[188] The consensus of his students was that if he had lived longer he would have made such claims explicit to the public at large.[189]

At the time, Luria's central emphasis was on the development of his own form of the Kabbalah, and this was deemed so important as to take second place even to messianic aspirations. His inclinations in this direction were reinforced by the fact that the *Zohar*, the foundation book of Kabbalah, predicted that the Messiah would appear in Galilee. The common assumption among those in Safed appears to be that this meant their community in particular.[190]

This preoccupation with kabbalistic theory and mystical practices rather than with actually doing anything to advance his messianic inclinations tells us something about Luria's conception of that position. It seems to presuppose that he viewed his messianic role not as redeemer and not as bringer of his people back to the Holy Land, but as a teacher and advocate of the deeper divine mysteries that he found in the Kabbalah.

As Vital (see below) summed up Luria's teaching, Luria believed that a major method of gaining spiritual insight into the *Zohar* was obtained by a combination of prolonged study and sleep deprivation[191]:

> A person must not indulge in idle conversation; he must rise in the middle of the night and weep on account of our poverty of knowledge.

7. Jewish Messiahs During the Renaissance and Reformation

> He ought to study forty or fifty pages of Zohar each day with the exclusive goal of textual familiarity, without engaging in intensive investigation. He should read the Zohar frequently....
>
> He then told me that while it is true that we applied ourselves extremely diligently, to an extent greater than any of our contemporaries, we did not do as he had done. For how many nights had he remained awake, poring over a single passage of the Zohar? Sometimes he would seclude himself, sit and study only a single passage during the course of six weekday nights. And usually, he would avoid sleeping altogether during these nights.

It seems quite reasonable that such a course would produce a mystical sense of being virtually "out of the body" along with the sensation of "feeling" mystical insights that one could not even express in words. Like the individual who relies on substances such as peyote to accomplish such a result, one must wonder whether that sense of "vision" and "insight" would have been accepted as profound by any nonparticipants if Luria had permitted them to be present and hear his thoughts.

As Luria understood it, the human soul is far from an indivisible entity. Each person's own soul is composed, at least in part, of the soul of some earlier personality or a segment of soul (for lack of a better term) from more than one such individual. Obviously these had an impact on one's own life and decisions, and one of the central purposes of existence is to integrate these fully and completely with one's own unique contribution to the total soul.[192] Because of this transmigration of souls, one has the potential for access to knowledge of events of the past that one has not lived or seen.[193] Presumably, this is the means whereby he could point out unmarked grave sites of important religious leaders of the past and use them to illustrate his teachings.[194]

Of the kabbalists of this era, the most influential was Luria; immediately after him was Vital, not only in his own right but due to his pivotal role in preserving, transmitting, and explaining the earlier man's claims and insights.[195] So closely had the two men worked together and interacted that they rose above teacher and student to the even more creative role of mutual learners. Probably because of this tradition of vigorous interaction and consultation, there are times when statements are attributed to Luria that some believe were actually penned by Vital.[196] It is not a matter of intentional misrepresentation but that the collaboration between the two was so close that they themselves, at times, tended to merge their independent thoughts into a joint creative effort.

Joseph Vital of Safed

Hayyim ben Joseph Vital Calabrese was born in about 1542. Since his father worked in Safed as a scribe, it is likely that this was the city of his son's birth as well.[197] As he told the story, various types of diviners had predicted his future importance[198] and there were even supernatural appearances to others to confirm this certainty.[199] If these stories have even a modest core of historical truth, they surely motivated him to find an area in which he could excel and live up to those anticipations.

Vital became interested in the Kabbalah in his youth, though not initially with the degree of obsession that became the hallmark of Luria. He also sought a wider application of its principles: If Kabbalah could provide crucial spiritual insights for its user, might it not prove crucial in alchemy and the search for earthly wealth as well? Might it not provide tools for improvement of physical health and welfare also?[200]

He also respected the magical techniques of others. As Harris Lenowitz notes, "He remained quite close to seers of different kinds (those who looked into mirrors or oil or water; those who asked dream questions and received answers; chiromancers) in both the Jewish and Moslem communities and often turned to them with questions for them to ask heavenly authorities."[201] Hence he conceived of the possibility of significant (if not total) access to supernatural guidance regardless of radically different theological systems being involved and even though the techniques utilized were very different.

Although Luria had formed his study group by summer of 1570 at the latest, Vital was not one of the original members. Only in the spring of the following year did he become a part of it.[202] The relationship of the two men was far different from tutor/student: Vital appears to have been convinced that he was already Luria's equal in kabbalistic knowledge.[203] Hence, though Luria taught him, he was even more his "groomer," the man who encouraged his development because he recognized Vital's potential to become a messiah.[204]

After Luria's death, his primary intra-group goal was to convince Luria's other disciples to recognize him as the only authoritative explainer of their teacher's doctrine.[205] Some of them openly defied this effort and preserved their own forms of the Lurianic teaching, but none of them became as popular as Vital's formulation of it.[206]

When 1575 arrived, the new year brought with it considerable hope that this would be the time when the Messiah would appear. This may well have been the motive in Vital's convincing 12 fellow students of Luria to become his cadre of supporters.[207] As with many failed predictive dates, when the event did not occur it was "reinterpreted": Merely the *beginning* point, 1575 was the minimal date at which the Messiah would appear. Although this theoretically left the door open for an appearance decades in the future, the group convinced itself that the arrival was far more imminent than long-term.[208]

To consolidate loyalty, Vital demanded a written pledge from each of the 12 members of his group. In exchange for the privilege and right of interacting with him and gaining spiritual insights denied to the non-elite (i.e., everyone else, including fellow kabbalists) they promised to study Luria's doctrine only within their group and to refuse to share any of their conclusions with outsiders.[209]

So elitist were they that Vital vetoed the entry of Moses Alshekh, a rabbi who had been his own instructor earlier in life. Even the rabbi's repeated requests were inadequate to convince him to change his mind.[210] The group itself broke up in 1577 when Vital moved to Jerusalem, and part of the reason for the move may have been tensions with other kabbalistic scholars.[211]

One can sympathize with the desire to obtain full credit for one's work. Yet if the purpose is theoretically to secure great insight into unseen mystical realities, the efforts of Vital to create an isolated group without ties to others must have grated on the nerves of more than a few as being egocentric at best and selfish at worst. Indeed, one wonders how contented his cadre was when he insisted upon them surrendering to him all their personal written notes of Luria's teaching.[212] Since such notes were a quite reasonable way for them to preserve their master's teachings and to serve as the basis for further personal study, one could easily imagine this egotistical demand becoming a major point of conflict if intra-group tensions occurred in other areas.

In all fairness to him, however, he had long contemplated the move to Jerusalem, for he was convinced that only there would he reach his full potential for insight.[213] Hence in 1577 he moved there to undertake rabbinic duties. This indicates that his kabbalistic studies had not eliminated his ability to undertake serious Torah and Talmudic investigation as well. Indeed, he considered himself a halakhic expert because of the study he had undertaken in the subject under Rabbi Joseph Karo, who was considered Safed's foremost specialist in this area.[214] Whether or not he was as good as he thought he was,[215] he provided satisfactory service, and part of that ability to satisfy the synagogue may well have been his careful avoidance of Kabbalah in his public teaching.[216] He also performed rabbinic duties to the satisfaction of the local Jewish community afterwards when he moved to Damascus.[217]

Finally in 1586, Vital moved back to Safed, and he remained there until 1592. Vital's formal ordination as a rabbi did not occur until 1590 in spite of his earlier leadership roles in such places as Jerusalem.[218] The years from 1592 to 1598 are little documented, though there are some indications that he periodically moved from Safed to Jerusalem and back again.[219]

In 1598 he permanently moved to Damascus, which was to be his last home. There he served as the rabbi of the Sicilian synagogue in that city.[220] He was economically pressed during these years in large part because of the small size of the congregation and the inability to gain significant support from other Jews of the city.[221] His physical sufferings made things even worse. Repeatedly he went through periods of temporary blindness.[222]

It did not help his mental well-being that he was the target of long-term criticism by Jacob Abulafia, a rabbi who mocked his messianic claims and played a major role in keeping him from gaining the degree of public acceptance he had hoped for.[223] So intense was Vital's resentment of this man that he became the virtual incarnation of earthly evil in Vital's *Book of Visions*. Indeed, in one place he goes so far as to compare Abulafia with the serpent who destroyed the earthly paradise of the Garden of Eden in Genesis by intellectually subverting Adam and Eve.[224]

Perhaps due to Vital's inability to create a wider base of support, he returned to his earlier technique of selecting a small group whose loyalty he could feel assured of.[225] He died in 1620 and it was left to one of his sons to prepare his works for general circulation.

Unlike Luria, for Vital there was no hesitancy in indicating his own messianic inclinations. In recording his revelatory dreams from God, he describes himself as the "King of Israel" who would rebuild the temple for a third time.[226] Many times in his *Book of Visions* (*Sefer ha-Hezyonot*) he makes clear allusions to such a self-concept.[227] Yet there are other times in his writings when he seems to distinguish between himself and the Messiah[228] as if he were carrying in his mind — in eternal tension — both the ideas of self-identification with the Messiah and distinction from him.

But it was not by personal visions alone that he operated. As he told the story, in 1574 a respected prophet of the time by the name of Abraham Shalom sent word to him of his destiny[229]:

> Tell him in my name that he is Messiah ben Joseph, and that he should go to Jerusalem and dwell there for two years without fail. And in the third year the choice will be in his hand: if he wishes, let him stay there. And after the first year the spirit of the Lord will begin to agitate him, and from then on there will be a conflict about him between the people of Jerusalem and of the Galilee, and the people of Egypt will side with Jerusalem. But with all this, the Galileans will win and make him return to dwell there in Galilee. And there thousands and myriads

7. Jewish Messiahs During the Renaissance and Reformation 109

of Israel will gather around him, and he will rule over them and will teach them Torah. And thereafter I myself shall go there, and I shall be Messiah ben David, and he will be Messiah ben Joseph, if the generation will merit it. And when he goes to Jerusalem let him beware that he should not gather people around him, because this would result in great harm to him, and also because of this reason he would be put in the jailhouse.

The fact that he came from the same study circle as Luria argues that among his followers there was either the strong inclination toward multiple messiahs coming or that a number of individuals would jointly (at least, retrospectively) share in that function.[230] The idea that every new generation would produce a Messiah was one that had existed for a long while; the fact that the Messiah Luria had already died meant that the task had now been passed on to Vital.[231] But it was far more than just the task, it was the very soul or essence of Luria that had now passed into Vital to permit him to perform this function.[232] It was a kind of reincarnation of the inner being,[233] but since Luria and Vital had lived simultaneously it was significantly different from reincarnation in the form in which it would normally be discussed today. Yet, as our quoted text indicates, there was room in his theology for a second Messiah appearing simultaneously as well.

Furthermore, Vital was blessed with the soul of the ancient Rabbi Akiva, a concept that Luria himself stressed to his student.[234] Since this rabbi was considered the embodiment of the Oral Law of the ancient Jews[235] this effectively put him and Vital on the same level as Moses, the author of the written law, and provided Vital "direct" access to that tradition independent of the Talmud or any other source.

Since Vital was Messiah and possessed the key to the secret unwritten will of God, it was natural that he was to play the pivotal role in reestablishing the divine reign on earth. The only problem Vital had was that he lacked a mass movement to accomplish that reality. He died a man who once had dreamed great dreams only to have them collide with the reality of a world that refused to believe him.

8

Gentile Messiahs During the Renaissance and Reformation (1300–1600)

Bartolome Sanchez (1507 to post–1560)

Sanchez was born in a village in Spain in 1507. His problems were fueled by a vision he had in 1550.[1] Although he consulted various priests about its meaning, he was unable to find an explanation that satisfied him, a fact that fed his spiritual discontent.[2]

He then began to share his anger at the Roman Catholic Church and its practices with various acquaintances. Recognizing that he was being imprudent in how many he was speaking with and even more by the passionate intensity of his words, friends pleaded with him for restraint. None could rein him in, however, and he was arrested by the Inquisition for investigation, trial, and punishment. He was candid with his interrogators and revealed that there was something far more basic moving him than traditional opposition to priesthood and specific church abuses of power[3]:

> ... [T]he Messiah that the Inquisition believes in, who came about one thousand and five hundred years ago, that is He, and I confess that He came, and He is the Son of God incarnated in the Virgin Mary; but the *other* Messiah of whom I speak who is coming—the one who is the Elijah—he is the justice God sends on behalf of those whom the Inquisition has killed without cause, and this Elijah and Messiah ... was born fifty-two years ago, more or less, and he is on the earth, and he is born and raised in the village of Cardenete.

Suspecting from this description the identity of the new Messiah, the secretary noted in his account of the interrogation, "When asked to say who is this Elijah and Messiah that he says is born and brought up in the village of Cardenete, he said that he was, and that they don't have to believe him, but here I am, and neither did they believe the Son of God."[4]

After Sanchez's lengthy confinement and repeated interrogations, the Inquisition found itself faced with a difficult dilemma: They suspected that their prisoner was insane rather than heretical but had found no witnesses that would explicitly affirm it.[5] His recantation gave them a way out of their dilemma and permitted them to avoid inflicting the penalty of death. At this point he went from the extreme of claiming to be the Messiah to that of denouncing claims that he had never actually made or been accused of. After, with difficulty, seeming to convince him of the need for truly repenting rather than engaging in further exaggeration, they were convinced of his sincerity and decided it was safe to release him.[6]

He landed before them again when he lost patience with his penance and burned his penitential garments.[7] Imprisoned, he gave alarming evidence that he was relapsing into his Christ illusion: "I am the Son of Man and Elijah, and God orders me to say it, because those who govern the Church are in error."[8] He ultimately reversed himself yet again and repudiated his words.[9] The tribunal saw fit to overlook his messianic claims but punished him for his other actions and again freed him.

Then, a third time, he managed to bring himself to the attention of the religious authorities. During his interrogation and that of others, this time their doubts were fully resolved: They were not dealing with a willful heretic but with a man who was definitely insane. They arranged to send him to a hospital that included the care of the deranged in its work.[10] For its day and age, it was a highly progressive institution that provided as gentle a care of its residents as their condition and behavior permitted.[11] At this point in 1560, the local inquisitors had technically sent the case to their superiors for review, but no further record of it has survived[12] and it is likely that Sanchez lived the remainder of his life institutionalized.

Thomas Muntzer (1488–1525)

In an age when literacy was still uncommon (though, growing less so), Muntzer was a well-educated man. Born in 1488, he studied both Hebrew and Greek and had a wide education in both traditional Catholic theology and philosophy. In the process of accumulating this knowledge, he earned multiple college degrees.[13] As befitted a man who saw his world as equivalent to a temporal exile of suffering and injury, he was especially interested in the three "major prophets" of the Old Testament — so called both because of their longevity and their inherent importance — Ezekiel, Isaiah, and Jeremiah, who dealt with such themes in their own earlier age.[14]

Within a few years of Luther's nailing his theses on the church door, Muntzer had enthusiastically embraced the new theology as well. Even more important was the teaching of Nicklas Storch, a contemporary, who spoke of how the end times were now upon the human race. Also pivotal was Muntzer's doctrine of reconciliation with the divine: By the suffering one endured, one would both become reunited with God but also become virtually as if a deity as well. At that point, one would escape the inhibitions imposed upon mere mortals, reach one's spiritual potential, and become empowered to create the New Jerusalem on earth itself.[15]

Muntzer was a communalist and was convinced that all the property of a town needed to be held for common usage "and should be distributed to each according to his needs, as the occasion required." He was convinced that "[a]ny prince, count, or lord, who did not want to do this, after first being warned about it, should be beheaded or hanged."[16]

His teaching such doctrines caused him to be rejected by the town of Zwickau but he then found Allstedt more amenable. There he both gained a spouse and found his prestige growing rapidly among the miners and peasants as he preached his doctrine of divine judgment and earthly revolution.[17] His open conflict with the secular rulers of the land can be traced to an effort to prohibit outsiders from visiting the town to hear his teaching.[18] There was clearly a major concern that they would either remain there in support of his efforts or carry his ideas back to their home communities. The first could undermine the control of the local authorities and the latter could spread the contagion yet further.

The elector of Saxony called for him to appear in Weimar, share his convictions, and justify his behavior. Radical as the defense he delivered was— there conspicuously not being any room in it for the well-to-do, i.e., men and women like Duke John himself — the immediate response was only a temporary censure: He must cease proclaiming his teachings until a decision could be made.[19]

Government officials were alarmed not only by the contents of his teaching but, even more so, by the violence utilized by his supporters in the League of the Elect in acting against their opponents. The city leaders of Allstedt had appeared at the hearing and washed their hands of any responsibility for these outbursts. At this point, Muntzer decided he had had enough of these unreliable "friends" and began to wander from place to place proclaiming his message.[20]

What turned out to be his most important stop was at the town of

Muhlhausen, where he created his second League of the Elect. Ultimately he outgrew his welcome and was ejected from the town by armed men and the city fathers.[21] He returned to Muhlhausen when the Peasants' Revolt erupted and found the city ready to follow his lead in an open uprising[22] — one that he was more than ready to lead.[23] It was, however, a widespread insurrection and he was leader over only one geographically limited segment of it,[24] though his teachings and example were certainly encouraging to other participants as well.

He was fully confident of their victory. As he wrote to one community considering joining the uprising, "Be of good courage, and trust in God alone. He will give more strength to your small group than you will be able to believe."[25] He cautioned and taught, however, on behalf of organized, controlled revolution rather than the chaos and anarchy that would result from blind striking out at the existing political structure.[26]

When the forces of the rulers confronted the peasants for battle, the princes promised no retaliation against them if they but laid down their arms, returned home, and surrendered Muntzer.[27] Faced with this tempting offer — the opposing forces being far superior in fighting capability — Muntzer frantically lobbied and preached against accepting any accommodation. He assured them (rhetorically or literally in his own mind?) that God would so protect him that he would be able to catch the cannonballs of the enemy and yet be unharmed.[28]

He also invoked messianic self-description to justify himself: "I am the shepherd, David, appointed by the Lord to feed you."[29] On other occasions, he presented himself as the second Daniel, in effect inspired by God to lead the people to a purified earthly kingdom.[30]

At the height of one of his orations, the clouds broke and a rainbow appeared. This was taken as a sign of divine favor since it was the emblem Muntzer had chosen for his banner.[31] Convinced by his language that both he and the peasants were invulnerable to death, they marched enthusiastically into battle.[32] At the first cannon fire, they panicked and were slaughtered by the thousands. Muntzer was afterwards caught hiding and was executed in May of 1525.

Jan Bockelson, the Messiah of Munster

The Anabaptist movement — i.e., advocates of immersion only rather than sprinkling or pouring as its acceptable substitutes — normally had pacifism as one of its key components. Indeed, these two positions were regarded as so subversive of both the secular world (by its repudiation of all war) and the religious one (by its demand that church members become such by a conscious adult act of baptism) that the system was anathema to virtually all political and religious leaders.

In spite of the Reformation, nearly everyone still held to sprinkling even though Martin Luther was far from the only leader to recognize that immersion was either the sole first century practice or was overwhelmingly dominant. Furthermore, political leaders were more than a little nervous about any who would criticize the propriety of warfare since it was so common in their age and could be taken as a rebuke of the leaders' own lack of spirituality. Having challenged orthodoxy on two fundamental issues since the appearance of the movement in about 1523, it is not surprising that it faced severe civil and religious retaliation that included even death of the exposed practitioners.[33]

Some suspect that the extremity of this repression, when combined with their growing conviction that they were living in the end times, caused a significant number to go to the other extreme and embrace social revolution to bring about the promised earthly paradise.[34] If anything, this made the political and religious authorities even more determined to smash and destroy the movement wherever it arose. It was just such Anabaptist activists that played pivotal roles in creating and sustaining the revolution at Munster,[35] one that would embarrass the Reformation movement both internally and in the eyes of its orthodox Roman Catholic opponents.

Munster was, for its day and age, a major city. With a population of between 15,000 and 20,000, it was important in the political and religious affairs of the region,[36] due in large part to the unusual degree of self-government and independence it enjoyed in contrast to other contemporary municipalities.[37] An influx of Anabaptists in the early 1530s left the officials of this Lutheran-run town concerned as to where this would ultimately lead,[38] especially when it became obvious that the immigrants had become so numerous that they were on the verge of having an absolute numerical majority within the town.[39]

Bernard Rothmann, an intellectual and effective propagandist, had already begun agitating against the beliefs of the Catholic minority in the community.[40] He teamed up with Bernard Knipperdolling and they enjoyed pervasive support among the Anabaptists as the town's passions escalated and the community teetered near the edge of a three-way Roman Catholic-Protestant-Anabaptist civil war.[41] Efforts to stabilize the situation by keeping new individuals from entering the city proved ineffective.[42]

Representatives from Jan Matthys entered the city in January of 1534 to announce that he had been ordained by God to be a prophet and to lead the establishment of the millennial earthly kingdom. It would be inaugurated at Munster, they informed both Rothmann and Knipperdolling.[43] This message was reinforced by the arrival of Jan Bockelson (a/k/a Jan van Leiden and John of Leidyn) who arrived a few weeks later and further pleaded the case with the local leaders.[44] The primary base of support was among the lower classes, beginning with the peasants and working upward in the social totem pole to mine workers and weavers.[45]

When Matthys arrived, the support was ready and available. Matthys was the new Enoch and Bockelson was publicly recognized by him as the new Elijah and secondary leader in the movement.[46] Both of these men were good-looking and charismatic and quickly won the hearts of the Anabaptist women of the town. With them as a powerful lobby, few husbands were willing to oppose the new prophets,[47] especially when so much of their message was compatible with their own preferences and hopes.

Both Catholics and traditional Protestants felt unnerved and uncertain of what to do next. The next round of elections gave control of the Great Council of the city into the hands of the Anabaptists.[48] It then became open season on "Romanists," and their churches were ransacked and destroyed. As the month came to a close, all such individuals were forcibly expelled if they had not recanted and been immersed. No exceptions were made for age or gender or even pregnancy.[49]

The hired troops of Bishop von Waldeck by now had the city well surrounded and only a limited number of individuals could furtively edge their way into or out of the city. The excesses being reported made the besiegers even more determined to hold the contagion tightly within its present bounds. On Easter, Matthys/Enoch presided at a massive feast. This clearly was intended as a kind of parallel to Jesus' last supper. The next day he and 20 supporters rushed out to do battle with the besieging foe. Whatever miraculous feat he expected to accomplish that day, it ended with his head on a pike.[50]

Bockelson now proclaimed to the crowds, "God shall raise up unto us another prophet who shall be greater and higher than was even Jan Matthys."[51] Divine revelation, of course, gave that role of new leader to Bockelson himself. The full significance of the "greater and higher" rhetoric virtually required a messianic or divine status (or both) for the new leader.

The pre-new-regime leaders Knipperdolling and Rothmann were not neglected either. The former was designated chief executioner and the latter chief orator.[52] The secular governing Senate was replaced by a council of 12 elders appointed by Bockelson. A new secondary prophet arose in the form of Jan Dusentscheuer, who now occupied much the same status that Bockelson had originally. He went about proclaiming the messiahship of his leader. Bockelson was both saint and prophet. But also, "He will occupy the throne of his father, David, and will carry the scepter till the Lord reclaims it from him."[53]

A little later, the governing elders were requested to yield their authority to him. As part of the transfer, he was formally anointed as ancient kings were. Bockelson took the opportunity to invoke this as evidence that he had been given the authority of a messianic ruler[54]:

> In like manner was David, a humble shepherd, anointed by the prophet, at God's command, as King of Israel. God often acts in this way; and whoever resists the will of God calls down God's wrath upon himself. Now I am given power over all nations of the earth, and the right to use the sword to the confusion of the wicked and in defense of the righteous. So let none in this town stain himself with crime or resist the will of God, or else he shall without delay be put to death with the sword.

He vigorously rejected the few murmurs of protest from the crowd, using messianic language to describe the propriety of his assuming total authority: "Even were you all to oppose me, I should nevertheless become king of the whole earth, and my royalty which begins now in this spot will last forever."[55]

During the following three days, preachers repeated the message that the Old Testament's foretelling of a Messiah had at last been fulfilled. He was now amidst them and leading them and his name was Bockelson.[56] New coins for the city were issued with his image on one side. The other side invoked his supernaturalness by applying to him language adapted from the introductory words of the gospel of John: "The Word was made flesh and lives among us."[57]

The city underwent other dramatic turns in policy. Bockelson's social theory was communistic (communalistic, perhaps, would be more accurate): No longer could any individual own possessions or possess money. It was all to be part of the collective treasury of the community.[58] Hence all money and "excessive" personal possessions (very broadly defined) were to be turned into the city's treasury and meted out according to an individual's need. For anyone in debt to others—and this would have been true of even many of the prosperous of the city—this draconian step was at least partly balanced out by the abolishment of all these financial obligations.[59] And to assure that any existing debt was not resurrected at a later date, it was ordered that all "letters and seals, as well as privileges, registers and all other books and accounts" that recorded such debts be destroyed by burning.[60]

Such communalism obviously created at least modest concern even among those who theoretically would benefit the most. This was new and

8. Gentile Messiahs During the Renaissance and Reformation 117

untried territory; would it really work? Rothmann dealt with this disquiet by reassuring everyone, "You will lack nothing — whether goods, clothing or house and home. You will receive whatever you need. God won't allow you to go wanting. Everything will be common. It belongs to all of us."[61]

When a number of individuals claimed they had no cash to hand over, it was decided the city needed a lesson in proper respect: All those who had been baptized at the time of the mass expulsion were arrested, confined to a church, and told that unless God forgave them they would be executed. After they were humiliated and their will to resist was broken, they were permitted to survive,[62] but the object lesson of full servitude had been made quite clear both to them and everyone else.

Communal meals became obligatory. Polygamy was legalized. This was regarded as a reversion to Old Testament marital norms,[63] though the fact was ignored that even then polygamy was practiced only when economically feasible, and therefore practiced by only a minority of the population. The coercion used to enforce the new system certainly lacked biblical precedent: The new wife could reject the proposal only if she was willing to risk extreme punishment and even death.[64] In all this, there were deep suspicions that Bockelson was acting not out of any ideology or theology but to maximize his own sexual opportunities.[65]

In vivid contrast, in other areas Bockelson imposed an extremely restrictive life code. While he himself openly and proudly wore the best attire available, careful regulations limited the type and number of garments permitted to any man or woman. Even the number of beds and sheets were restricted and everything beyond these numbers confiscated.[66] Yet Bockelson compensated for this by abundant and repeated public feasts with ample food, drink, and dancing.[67] And, it appears, virtually unrestrained sexual license permitted afterwards.[68]

Intellectually, book learning was no longer needed. Possession of books was forbidden, with the sole exception of the Bible.[69] These various extreme practices angered outsiders, who also felt threatened with the disruptive potential for the movement if it spread into their communities and goes far to explain the bitter determination to crush the movement before that could happen.[70]

During these months of growing radicalization, Bishop von Waldeck's men had made repeated efforts to take the city but had been unable to do so.[71] Rather than attempt to exploit their opponents' weakness — or even to escape — Bockelson chose to become self-absorbed in the building up of the regal honors he claimed for himself and his followers.[72]

In October, the bishop sent out an appeal to other princes, arguing that unless Munster were contained and crushed there was simply no way to stop its spread. As the result, 300 cavalry and 3,000 foot soldiers were added to the ranks of the besiegers. Equally important was a combat-tested general who was more experienced in carrying out siege warfare.[73]

In the fall of 1534, the lavish expenditure of stored goods for feasting and celebrating finally had to come to an end. With minimal access to new outside stores, it became a time of drastically reduced rations. With the dawning of 1535 came virtual starvation. When Easter came again, Bockelson appeared in public on few occasions as the physical conditions of both city and residents plummeted to disaster levels.[74]

Surrender terms were given the suffering city, but Bockelson refused to answer them or attempt to negotiate a more generous settlement. He permitted 900 individuals to leave the city, but since surrender had not been agreed to, the surrounding army refused to permit them through their lines. With nothing but grass to eat, they died in the no-man's-land between the city and the waiting foe.[75]

Even at this late stage, there was no indication that the masses were willing to reject their Messiah. A more favorable interpretation would be that they were too cowed by intimidation to rise.[76] After all, previous efforts to oust their lord and king had failed.[77] Probably major elements of both factors existed: Bockelson clung to a large body of support, while those who opposed him had neither the confidence nor the organization to do so effectively.

At this late date, the besiegers were showing no mercy either. Of the many who tried to escape to their lines, all were killed. So when the young Henry Gresbeck took that perilous route in May of 1535, he knew the odds were against him. Driven by desperation and with what both he and his captors conceded was incredible good fortune, he was taken captive alive due to his youth. In exchange for his life, he happily built a model of the city and provided details of its defenses, with an emphasis on where it was most vulnerable.[78]

On June 24 and 25th 1535, judgment day came to Munster. During the night ,a specially selected force of 400 men followed Gresbeck and one or two other fortunate escapees back into the city through secret entrances known to them and, apparently, to few or no others. Although the force was successfully inserted, they were discovered and the battle for the city began earlier than planned. Even so, the bulk of the army was then able to burst through the city's defenses to come to their assistance. Weakened though they were by privation and illness, the defenders still fought a hard and vigorous battle.[79]

As the resistance collapsed around him, Knipperdolling chose the wrong place to hide. The woman whose house he selected traded her safety (the ultimate reward in a situation where precious few prisoners were being taken) and exchanged him for her protection and survival. Bockelson was captured alive and given a slow and painful death after trial in January 1536. Rothmann disappeared entirely. Some were convinced he had died in the widespread carnage, but others believed that he had eluded the besiegers. If so, he was wise enough to keep his identity hidden and no one ever found him.[80]

The excesses connected with Munster had indirect fallout that lasted for more than a century. In the field of religious toleration, the very mention of the term "Munster" was sufficient to create fear of the danger of relatively unrestricted religious expression. If moral excesses and utopian slaughter had resulted when all the reins were removed, might the next time be just as bad or even worse? With that nightmare hanging over the head of even the most religious individuals, the professed goals of supposedly pacifist groups were reacted to with grave suspicion and doubt.[81]

The theological fallout was also profound. Any inclination to take the opportunity of the Reformation reconsideration of established religious truths and use that to encourage the acceptance of an eventual temporal, earthly kingdom of Christ was given a body blow. The concept was now tainted with the (literally) bloody brush of Munster's excesses. The *Second Helvetic Confession* of 1566 summed up the scorn now reserved for such views. It rejected the "Jewish dreams that there will be a golden age on earth before the Day of Judgment, and that the pious, having subdued all their godless enemies, will possess all the kingdoms of the earth."[82] It would take a century for such interpretations to again be viewed as worthy of serious consideration.

David Georg (died 1556)

Georg (or Joris) was the son of a shopkeeper and sometime actor who seems to have named his offspring after the king David whose role he himself had played. His son's initial occupation was that of glass-painter and in pursuit of jobs he seems to have traveled as far as England.[83]

Embracing the Lutheran reformation in its early days, he converted to Anabaptism in 1533 and came into regular contact with some of its leading figures.[84] Rejecting the violent earthly utopianism that disgraced the movement at Munster, he attempted to unite the splintered Anabaptist factions. This was only temporarily successful and one of the few things most of them could agree on was that Georg was not to be followed and that his remedies for healing the divisions were to be rejected.[85]

In the meantime, his own theology moved in an equally extreme but nonviolent direction. He adopted the theory of three dispensations that earlier mystics had sometimes found great pleasure in. First there was the dispensation or era of God, then that which came through Jesus, and finally that provided by the Holy Spirit. In this new and final age, it was Georg who functioned as the divine conduit both of revelation and authority.[86]

As the "Davidists" (as they sometimes were called) expanded in number and influence, they began to draw the unfriendly attention of the religious and political authorities. Beginning in 1539, these authorities repeatedly opposed and attempted to suppress the movement.[87] A number of its members were publicly put to death. Georg himself became a prime target, but he repeatedly managed to escape capture in such extraordinary circumstances that many of his followers became convinced that he possessed the gift of becoming invisible in times of danger.[88]

He gained a temporary reprieve when Philip of Hesse promised him immunity in exchange for embracing the Augsburg Confession.[89] However, he wore out his welcome, and in April of 1544 he and some of his followers moved to Basel. There he adopted a new name — Jan. van Brugge — and covertly began to spread his doctrines via some 200 publications to a growing body of supporters in Holland and nearby areas.[90] Outwardly he became a pillar of orthodoxy (a policy he urged other followers to imitate) and grew quite prosperous. In addition he became well known for his charitable work on behalf of the suffering.[91]

As time passed on, he developed in ever greater detail his theology not only of the divine but of his own relationship to the supernatural world. He insisted that the Holy Spirit had miraculously conceived him and that he was no less than the Christ.[92] As such, he insisted, he fully deserved worship befitting his divine status.[93]

His spouse died on August 22, 1556, but his reputation was not endangered by that. The problem was that he claimed that he himself would never die. That bold assertion received a body blow when he passed away only three days later.[94] He was buried with the usual ceremonies since the public was unaware of his covert double life. In 1559, his disillusioned son-in-law brought information to the authorities, and after an investigation the body was disinterred and burned.[95] This went hand in hand with his available writings being burned as well.[96]

Having earlier come under his influence, Henry Niklaes/Nicholas (see below), carried on the tradition of claiming messiahship.[97]

Henry Niklaes

Within their movement, the Munster fiasco was the final discrediting of the war-making Anabaptist messianic tendency. Whatever other illusions followers might develop as to their true identity and relationship to God, it would no longer be accompanied by a drawing of the sword.[98]

Born in Munster either in 1501 or 1502, Niklaes (sometimes rendered as Nicholas), preferred to be known by his initials, "N.H.," rather than by his full name or first name. He was one of those individuals who was deeply interested in Christianity from his youth.[99] At eight, he was already aware that unless religion produced an improved moral state in a person, it served little value to him.[100] Beginning at nine, he began to have visions that would continue throughout his life.[101]

He was blessed with a good business sense and became a successful merchant as an adult. His marriage was also known to have been a happy one as well.[102] On the negative side of the ledger, in his earlier adult days he was a support of the revolutionary Thomas Muntzer. Afterwards, though, he grew out of this infatuation with violence.[103]

Although a student of Martin Luther, he found the Anabaptist style of thinking far more congenial to his frame of mind,[104] perhaps because it provided more room for the kind of miraculous experiences such as visions that he thought he had enjoyed while young. He believed that through such events and spiritual experiences one enters into a mystical union with deity. In his case, it went far beyond the normal, creating a literal oneness with the divine.[105]

Although embracing immersion for baptism, he placed his form of mysticism as far more important than the niceties of Protestant or Roman Catholic theology. Organizationally he clearly had a love for the Roman power structure, for he created a strong hierarchical structure for his own movement.[106] And it pulled into its rank individuals from both sides of the major religious divide of the day. The secret printer of his literature, for example, was an Antwerp businessman best known for his publication of liturgical material for the Roman church.[107]

Of him and the "Family of Love" movement that he created, a contemporary critic insisted, "They will have this blasphemer, H.N. to be the Son of God, Christ, which was to come in the end of the world to judge the world, and say that the day of judgment is already come, and that H.N. judgeth the world now by his Doctrine."[108]

So far as doctrinal stances went, they rejected the belief in a Trinity in the Godhead and affirmed that the entire human race would ultimately be saved.[109]

In the dual roles of merchant and propagandist, Niklaes sold his goods and taught his gospel in several countries, including England.[110] In England, the name of the group was typically altered to "Familists" and they gained a reputation for sexual libertinism more associated with critics of traditional Christianity than with its defenders.[111] Through the efforts of Christopher Vitell of Southwark, much of the founder's Dutch-language propaganda was translated into English for local circulation.[112]

Claus Ludwig (c. 1550)

Coming from an Anabaptist background, Ludwig secretly created the Community of the Sacred in northern Germany. He claimed to be the returned Christ and that the time of the final war against the hostile surrounding world was imminent.[113]

True communion did not consist of the Eucharist or a Protestantized substitute. Instead, it consisted of the sexual liaison of a man and a woman. Man represented the bread and the woman the wine, and by bringing the two together in such intimate communion they were engaging in the ultimate pious act.[114] Similarly, water baptism was no longer needed; by having sex with a female member of the group a man was automatically inducted into the movement.[115] A woman, however, had to have sex with Ludwig himself to be admitted.[116]

If such claims seemed outrageous, they were counterbalanced by the blessings that were promised. None of the Community of the Saved could perish at the hands of the dreaded plague. None of them could be murdered by enemies. Women could be assured that future childbirth would be painless.[117] If true, these were far from repulsive rewards in an age plagued by needless war in which the masses suffered the most and where death in childbirth was probably the greatest single danger facing an adult woman.

By this theology, sin was transformed from an evil into a good. What the religious world insisted was sin was actually nothing but God's Spirit encouraging them to action.[118] Collective worship included the opportunity to have sexual relations.[119] (The cynic will doubtless be tempted to suspect that this dramatically reduced the problem of nonattendance at church!)

In 1551, it all began to unravel. The first members were discovered, tried, and put to death. Ludwig himself wisely saw fit to vanish from the public scene.[120]

John Moore (1561)

Appearing on the religious landscape of England independent of any organized band of supporters, Moore insisted that he was Christ. In 1561, he was tried, whipped, and thrown in jail in London for these claims.[121]

Some men had less glamorous, but equally implausible "true" identities to lay before the public. Moore's traveling companion at the time was one William Jeffrey, who claimed to be Peter the apostle and was similarly punished.[122]

Nor was Moore the only "Jesus" who appeared in London that April. An unidentified individual from another part of England was arrested and thrown into the stocks for making similar claims.[123]

John White (1586)

In the county of Essex, England, this local minister proclaimed to his congregation and outsiders that he was the "King of Kings." It was his God-ordained role to lead God's people to Jerusalem and regain control of it for them.[124] His schemes, not unexpectedly, went nowhere.

William Hacket: Messiah of London (1591)

William Hacket was a former servant who became a maltmaker. He lacked any formal education and was illiterate as well.[125] Even so, he was able to find a well-to-do widow whom he so impressed that they married. The relationship did not work well because his uncontrolled spending soon plunged them into poverty.[126]

In spite of these intellectual, financial, and social limitations, he became convinced that he had prophetic ability and could perform miracles.[127] At first he merely accepted his closest follower's claims that he was equal to Jesus Christ[128]; as time went by, he even more dramatically began to claim that he was Jesus Christ.[129] No peaceful Christ was this man, for he was known to have a vile rage and was reported to have gone so far as to literally bite off the nose of a person he hated.[130]

This unlikely candidate for messiahship portrayed a self-confidence that impressed others, however. According to observers, "his manner of praying" was such that it seemed "as it were speaking [to] God face to face."[131] No wonder, perhaps, that he was heard to pray, "Father, I know thou lovest me equal with thyself."[132]

He had visited several English towns with his message and had been soundly rejected in each.[133] In London, he attracted the loyalty of Edmund Copinger (or Coppinger) and Henry Ardington (sometimes spelled Arthington) and appointed them to be his prophets. Coppinger was to literally "seal" supporters on their foreheads in order to show that they had professed the new messiah. As such, he functioned as "prophet of mercy." In contrast, Ardington was to be the hellfire-and-damnation proclaimer of prophetic wrath and punishment. He was to be the prophet of punishment.[134]

Entering the impoverished Cheapside section of the city of London, Hacket boldly preached that the bishop of Canterbury had committed treason against God and that the queen no longer deserved to be such.[135] He sent out Copinger and Ardington to proclaim him as the Christ returned to judge the world and who was even at that hour dwelling in a local inn. He was invulnerable; no human being could put him to death.[136] This attracted intense interest but not much in mass loyalty. Even so, when they returned to Hackett, Arthington enthusiastically proclaimed, "Behold the King of the Earth."[137]

With or without a large following, these men were deemed a potential threat to the political and social order of England. Hence the two prophets along with their messiah were promptly arrested and jailed.[138]

Some of Elizabeth's advisers were, oddly enough, intrigued by these men in spite of their radical message.[139] The more important matter, they all recognized, was how to deal with them. One camp feared that London could be facing a Munster-style situation unless the men were promptly executed and the potential revolt nipped in the bud. Another camp dismissed them as insane and insisted that there was no real danger.[140]

The queen became preoccupied by the matter and she was not one to run needless risk. She conspicuously did not bring heresy charges against Hacket; since he denied the validity of her rule, she had him tried for treason instead.[141] Specifically, he was charged with "maliciously and treacherously compassing, imagining, devising, and intending the deprivation and deposing of our Sovereign Lady Elizabeth." Furthermore, he had symbolically killed the monarch by poking "an iron instrument into that part" of her picture "that did represent the breast and heart."[142]

He went to his death convinced that God not only could but *must* rescue him. On the very scaffold itself, he roared out to God, "Oh thou God of Heaven, come down and save me, or else I'll rent Thy throne asunder."[143] He was unable to escape death on earth, and one must assume that he was equally unsuccessful in wreaking vengeance on God afterwards.

When it came to Copinger, Elizabeth was content with long-term

8. Gentile Messiahs During the Renaissance and Reformation 125

incarceration. In retaliation for the punishment, he refused to eat and ultimately died of his self-imposed starvation.[144] Actually, he did not think it was going to end that way. He was still so convinced that Hacket was genuine that he claimed that God would miraculously remove the bolts from any chains that held him.[145] God didn't.

Ardington may have faltered in faith but certainly not in prudence. Seeing what was in store for the other two, he repudiated his work for Hacket and was permitted to escape both death and confinement. Indeed, no less than the earl of Cumberland provided him with a stipend through the remainder of his life. He then wrote widely and far less controversially than he had spoken during his brief period of public notoriety.[146] Ardington, though, never did accept personal responsibility for having embraced Hacket; instead he insisted that he had been the victim of wicked witchcraft.[147]

At the time, the case was a major sensation. Part of this was because anyone challenging Elizabeth's authority was on the guaranteed road to self-destruction. Above and beyond this, the incident became a useful tool in the religious squabbles of contemporary England. The fact was that both Ardington and Copinger were Puritans, and Hacket had had ties with a number of others in the movement. These ties, however, were vastly exaggerated as to their importance but still proved a useful tool in spreading guilt by association.[148] Indeed, some have suggested that the successful exploitation of this issue was one of the significant factors that contributed to the setback in influence that the Puritan faction was currently undergoing.[149]

Queen Elizabeth of England as Messiah

In addition to the traditional excesses of pro-royal rhetoric typical of the age, that exalting Elizabeth took on a heavily religious aspect as well due to her pivotal importance in saving the nation from the Catholic restoration under "Bloody Mary," her predecessor. It was further encouraged by the hopes of the large Puritan element in the Church of England that she would be the agent through which their hoped-for reforms would be established.

For some, Elizabeth's role was vaguely expressed in their rhetoric and writings. The translators of the Geneva Bible spoke in the dedication of their work that they expected that "God should bring to pass some wonderful work by your grace to the universal comfort of His church."[150] Thomas Becon saw her as "noble conqueror of Antichrist."[151] But who is the conqueror of Antichrist but Christ Himself? Hence the rhetoric edged up to messianic claims without making them explicit.

The only writer of the time who seemed ready to openly cross that line was James Sandford. He spoke of "some diviner thing in her Majesty, than in the Kings and Queens of other countries" and of the wonderful new world that her reign would produce.[152] He was considerably out of the religious mainstream of his day, but his assertion of a kind of divinity seems only a more open use of the ideas found in more cautious form in men such as Becon.

Yet the line could become extremely thin if one chose to take the language quite literally. For example, John Almyer had been an exile during Mary's reign and then returned to London when Elizabeth gained the throne and ultimately became bishop of the city. As he once wrote, it was England that set the stage for the current religious revolution by producing the reformer Wycliffe, who "begat Husse, who begat Luther, who begat the truth. What greater honor could you or I have, then that it pleased Christ *as it were in a second birth to be born again of men* among you?" (emphasis added). Elizabeth was, in short, "God's chosen instrument" to establish His will on earth.[153]

9

Jewish Messiahs During the European Colonization of the Americas (1600–1800)

Although colonization by the Spanish in Mexico and South America had begun earlier, by 1600 the settlements had set down sufficient roots to assure their long-term survival. Just a little later, the English began their own major colonization efforts in the new world. Hence 1600 serves as a useful approximate date to chronologically divide our study of Messiahs and messianic movements.

Historical Context: The Apocalyptic Milieu of Europe (c. 1648–1670)

The preceding thirty or so years had exhibited so much brutality and abuse that despair was a natural reaction. There was little or nothing to suggest that the tide had turned in the in the direction of peace, stability, and prosperity. Even the staunchest rationalists and deniers of the supernatural were hard pressed to deny the attraction of a supernatural deliverance of the world from its turmoils, for the hand of man had clearly failed to do so.

The Thirty Years' War, however, finally ended in 1648. The seemingly endless hatreds of the combatants and the refusal of all parties to let the conflict come to an end saw the population of the affected areas reduced from about 16 million to six million. Five out of six towns were ravaged, burned, or razed during the war. Most simply ceased to exist for the duration.[1]

During those decades, it had been natural for Gentiles to wonder whether their world was not coming to an end through the ceaseless conflict. Although Jews were on the sidelines of the combat and richer moneylenders among them presumably profited from the financing they provided (if they were astute enough to have lent to the winning side!), most were as impoverished by the multidecade conflict as their neighbors.[2] In addition, they endured the usual insult of wearing a yellow badge that would identify their ethnicity and mark them as part of a despised minority.[3] If this were not enough, economic competition between Gentile Germans and Jews resulted in repeated riots by envious guilds and merchants.[4] These external pressures were quite sufficient for the ravaged Jewish communities to look for a messianic solution. Religious literature picturing 1648, as that grand year was widely distributed and discussed — and believed.[5]

Though that year did not bring with it the Messiah, at least it brought relief from the years of war. Yet if 1648 and the Treaty of Westphalia marked a return to prudence upon the part of the Germans, it was immediately Poland's turn to face vast devastation and destruction. The period of Polish unity that survived almost two centuries had begun to crack in 1572. In 1648, what had been a bad situation turned disastrous with the Cossack Rebellion. This brought both Cossacks and Tartars in huge numbers first into the Ukraine and then into Poland as well. The invaders viewed the literal elimination of both Poles and Jews as both desirable and their goal.

In the bloody battles of 1648 and 1649, they made a large dent in accomplishing that purpose. Jews alone suffered between 100,000[6] and 300,000 murdered.[7] Refugees spread far and wide the story of these atrocities and the destruction of 300 of their communities.[8] Even in an age when extreme cruelty was far too often the norm rather than the abnormal, this bloodlust was hard to exceed. The contemporary Nathan Nata Hanover wrote in a book published in 1653 that what happened went far beyond the usual "four forms of death, by trial, stoning, burning and strangulation" to far worse atrocities.[9] In addition,[10]

> Of some they removed their skins and the flesh, they threw to the dogs; some they cut off their arms and legs and cast them on the wayside to be driven over by carriages and horses; on some they inflicted many wounds but not enough for them to die, and threw them out so that they would not die soon and would convulse in their blood until their spirit would depart from them; and many they buried alive; ... they cut up many children like fish; ... some [women], they cut their stomachs, and put a live cat in them and sewed up the stomach, and

cut off their hands so that they could not tear out the live cat; ... and they speared children on sticks and burned them on the fire and brought them to their mothers to be eaten by them....

In 1654, both Russian and Swedish armies invaded and made the situation even worse. For the first time, Polish Jews began to place messianic hopes at the center of their dreams.[11] After what they had been through, Gentile Poles, of course, were far from hostile to such dreams as well.

In a far different country, beginning around 1640, a two-front war was waged within Britain: Parliament demanded its rights and the king insisted upon his supremacy, while the Anglican Church attempted to maintain its orthodoxy (watered-down "Romanism" to its opponents) Puritans demanded a far more thorough organizational and doctrinal reformation. These conflicts tended to be pictured in terms not merely of politics or of prudence but of right versus wrong and of the triumph of good or evil. With so much believed to be at stake, much of the Protestant community was willing to at least consider whether the current turmoil was leading up to the return of Jesus, and a significant minority became obsessed with it.[12]

The turmoils in Europe increased the credibility of the scenario since world chaos was virtually universally interpreted as a sign of the end times. As the 1647 English pamphlet *Doomes-Day* reminded its readers, Daniel 12:1 had spoken of a period of unprecedented woes. It pointed to the current international conflicts and asked what other period of history could the text possibly refer to? When had there *ever* been a more blood-filled era?[13]

Natural disease and messianic claimants could also cause an outburst of interest in end-times speculation. The famous diarist Samuel Pepys on February 13, 1666, spoke of how "the plague is increased this week, and in many places else about the town [of London], and at Chatham and elsewhere."[14] On the 16th he refers to "the plague time" that had afflicted London. With a clear sigh of relief, he noted on March 1, "Blessed be God! A good Bill this week we have; being but 237 [dead] in all, and 42 of the plague, and of them but six in the City [London]: though my Lord Brouncker says, that these six are most of them in new parishes, where they were not the last week."[15]

In the middle of this, he heard of the messianic speculation about Sabbatai Zevi (see the quotation in the discussion of this figure below). Hence it is not surprising to find his interest in ultimate matters stirred and his seeking out reading matter on the subject. In his entry of the 18th he observed how he "took coach, and home, calling by the way at my bookseller's for a book writ about twenty years ago in prophecy of this year coming on, 1666, explaining it to be the mark of the beast."[16] This was Francis Potter's *An Interpretation of the Number 666.*[17] He did not have an intense interest in the book because it was only on November 10 that he completed it. He commented in his diary of that date about how he had "read an hour to make an end of Potter's Discourse of the Number 666, which I like all along, but his close is most excellent; and, whether it be right or wrong, is mighty ingenious."[18]

His interest in the date was likely enhanced because of its emphasis in much contemporary politico-religious thought as well: The most common date for the earthly millennium of Jesus to be established was 1666, according to the thinking of the Fifth Monarchy Men of England (see below).[19] In light of Pepys' own very mixed moral record, he may well have viewed this possibility with considerable apprehension, especially when finding that the same date was being brandied about among Jews as well.

Mothers of the Messiah in Mexico (1640s)

When the Inquisition investigated alleged secret Jews in Mexico in the late 1640s, they discovered that there was a widespread conviction that the Messiah would be born from one of two families—either that of Simon Vaez Sevilla or that of Tomas Trevino de Sobremonte.[20] The kin of these two families had grown to a significant number, so the Messiah theoretically could be born to any of a number of the female members.

Two in particular attracted the attention of the Inquisition, though punitive action was taken against them all. The first was Doña Juana Enriquez. Even the investigators had to concede that she was so goodhearted and generous in her charity and in her personal observance of her religion that she led the kind of life that among Roman Catholics had led women to be canonized.[21] This did not, however, prevent her from being whipped to make her see the errors of her way.[22]

The second woman to stand out in the eyes of the Inquisition was Ines Pereira. In her case her family had developed a virtual cult, a kind of Judaized version of the veneration of the Virgin Mary. As the Inquisition account has it, starting when Ines was seven her kin were convinced[23]

> that this young Jewess would give birth to the Messiah. [One relative] convinced his sons and daughters of this and thus compelled them to keep the law of Moses. This is also why, in her young years, they dressed her with a tunic of violet. They would place her in the middle of the drawing room and surround her with burning candles. They worshipped her and adored her as a person from whom would be born their redeemer and chief.

Two other women who were similarly venerated within the family confines were Maria Gomez and Blanca Juarez.[24] That so many would appear in such a narrow frame of time bears witness to the powerful impact of the messianic dream within these families.

Sabbatai Zevi (1626–1676)[25]

Youth and Intellectual Achievements

Sabbatai's father was Mordecai Zevi, a poor poultry merchant originally from Greece. Seeking to economically improve himself, he moved to Smyrna. During a war between Venice and Turkey — one which other Western governments refused to join in — Mordecai became the local representative for both English and Dutch traders and used these connections to become a prosperous and well-to-do merchant.[26] Desiring to provide his son with the best available education, he arranged to have tutors come and educate him in all matters Jewish, with a heavy emphasis on the Talmud.[27]

By age fifteen, Sabbatai Zevi had become extremely knowledgeable in the Talmud as well as more recent rabbinic literature and had gained considerable local recognition for his intellectual accomplishments.[28] On his own, he struck out to master the Kabbalah and did so with considerable success,[29] with a dominant emphasis on its Lurianic form.[30] This independent study, of course, meant that the interpretation he evolved was overwhelmingly the result of personal study rather than learning from others or, more importantly, without the interaction of authoritative teachers who might modify or alter his personal conclusions. He felt himself sufficiently versed in the subject that he then recruited a group of fellow students who examined the subject under his tutelage and encouragement.[31]

In his mature years, he was the image of a man who both could and deserved to have high aspirations. As one close student of Italian Jewry remarks, "According to various etchings that exist, his appearance mixed the features of an Eastern potentate and a Dutch aristocrat, with well-trimmed beard, wavy moustache, starched lace collar and Rembrandt-like beret."[32] His handsome appearance was reinforced by an impressive singing voice that reveled in both the religious and secular songs of his day.[33]

The Man and His Personality

The years 1642–1648 exhibited the two opposing tendencies that existed throughout his life: periods of emotional emptiness that resulted in his withdrawing from society to wrestle with his problems and, at the other extreme, periods of enthusiastic public zeal that annoyed and angered his coreligionists since they resulted in actions that violated the normal religious traditions.[34] In modern terminology, many would describe him as a maniac-depressive.[35] One contemporary follower of Zevi provided this description of the intensity of his leader's depression when it came upon him[36]:

> It is said of Sabbatai Zevi that for fifteen years he has been bowed down by the following affliction: he is pursued by a sense of depression which leaves him no quiet moment and does not even permit him to read, without his being able to say what is the nature of this sadness which has come upon him. Thus he endures it until the depression departs from the spirit, when he returns with great joy to his studies. And for many years already he has suffered from this illness, and no doctor has found a remedy for it, but it is one of the sufferings which are inflicted by heaven.

When these moods overwhelmed him, he even seemed repelled by his own exuberant claims that had seemed completely justified and appropriate in his more optimistic periods. At the bottom of one of these mood swings, he was reported to have written a note that included the despairing words, "Thus speaketh the utter fool."[37]

With a man who so clearly exhibited indications of a lack of control over his emotions and actions, one must ponder how he managed not to discredit himself among his followers. Robert N. Levine suggests that it demonstrates the power of the messianic dream: When people are oppressed for a lengthy period of time, they are willing to embrace even an individual who would normally be rejected out of hand.[38]

Since they continued to embrace him, the problem arises of how his supporters rationalized his violations of traditional Jewish religious norms. Jacob Katz contends that such behavior actually tapped into a vein of Jewish thought that had always been available to messianic claimants[39]:

> The traditional messianic doctrine itself authorized the abrogation of tradition in days to come. The annulment of tradition by the Messiah would represent its fulfillment rather than its repudiation through the abandonment of its basis. At the moment of action, the revelation of the Messiah gave an impetus to the Jews' preparedness for crisis as a single, catastrophic change. What the faithful looked forward to was not a gradual social change but a complete new order of things—in both the material and spiritual sense.

Looking at it from a different standpoint, the restrictions were viewed as necessary for the spiritually immature; since the Messiah's followers had moved on to a new level of insight, they did not need to concern themselves with such matters.[40] The behavior that would otherwise be proof of their sinfulness became evidence, instead, of their spiritual superiority over the traditionalist.[41]

The First Bid for Messianic Status

If a significant element of Christian apocalyptic interpretation was inclined toward 1666 as the messianic year, Jews tended toward 1648.[42] In particular, there was a text in the *Zohar*, which was the core document of Kabbalah, that mentioned 1648 as the pivotal year for the Messiah's coming.[43] But there were other equally promising words in the *Zohar* as well. The resurrection, for example would occur "in the year 408 [that is, 1648] of the sixth millennium, they that lie in the dust will arise...."[44] The resurrection part had not occurred but might not the *Zohar* be right in regard to the messianic aspect? Because of Zevi's acquaintance with the work, such thoughts would have been inescapable.

Presumably, Zevi was consciously or unconsciously attempting to fulfill the prediction when he made his bold move for messianic status in 1648; when he renewed it with enthusiasm in 1665–1666, he was utilizing a date more popular among Christians but one many Jews would have been aware of as well.[45] Another factor in embracing the first date lay in a profound psychological revulsion at the widespread anti-Jewish pogroms of 1648 and the fervent desire to redeem his fellow Jews out of them.[46]

In the fully developed Sabbatian scheme of things (which evolved over a period of time) there were two Messiahs that God would send. The identity of the second was never fully resolved. What could be agreed on was that the Messiah to descend from Joseph was Zevi.[47]

Yet what evidence could be introduced to prove his messiahship? His being born on the same date as the Jewish temple had been destroyed in A.D. 70 met one traditional evidence of legitimacy.[48]

Another evidence lay in his ability to gain insight into spiritual matters without the assistance of others, a trait that was manifested even in youth. As one early biography of him made the linkage, "He learned everything from himself, for he was one of the four to arrive at the knowledge of their creator by themselves, as it is stated in the midrash; these are Abraham, Hezekiah, Job, and the Messiah...."[49]

A third area of evidence would have been bold, public miracles. In 1648, Zevi found himself frustrated and the subject of considerable personal embarrassment over this matter. He would quote texts that he took as creating precedent for humans flying off into the sky and turn to his onlookers and challenge them as to whether they had seen the amazing, supernatural levitation he had just performed. When they responded they had not, he fervently condemned their lack of spirituality — while they went away convinced that they could safely ignore his rebukes.[50]

His 1648 pronunciation of the Tetragrammaton was quite inflammatory. In speaking of the proper name of God, the substitute "Adonai" was always used. This was because the individual was traditionally prohibited from utilizing the actual term in the biblical texts. According to the Mishnah, anyone who dares to speak the actual name "loses his right to the world to come."[51] However, it also speaks of the true name being utilized in "the world to come" and since, this expression was used, upon occasion, to describe the messianic age, Zevi's use could be invoked as proof positive that the messianic era had finally arrived.[52] Such reasoning failed to satisfy the vast majority. To them, his conduct was clearly sacrilege.

As the result of such behavior, he was ultimately expelled from the community. There was little to hinder it. His support at the time and in following years was so minimal[53] that it can be described as virtually nonexistent.[54] This makes even more amazing his later success in gaining a large international following that went from Africa, through the Near East, through Europe, and even into England. However many people wanted a redeemer, there was clearly nothing in his charisma, actions, or knowledge at that stage that caused significant numbers of individuals to embrace him.

Rejected in Smyrna, he moved to Salonika in Greece, which was a major Jewish center. There he continued to advocate his personal claims and vision of the Jewish future. The people were impressed by his emphasis on the Kabbalah and its promises of redemption from exile and return to Palestine.[55] To provide a living symbol of this he once went about the city holding a fish in a basket. As he explained to enquirers, the fish symbolized Pisces and it was under that zodiac sign that the people would escape captivity.[56]

That aspect of his message had a natural appeal, but it could not ultimately be disentangled from his claims about his personal status in the eyes of God. His actions became, if anything, even more bizarre and self-discrediting to anyone inclined in such a direction. He reaffirmed his messianic role, for example, by engaging in a marriage ceremony — with the Torah.[57] However symbolic of loyalty and fealty this was intended to be, the local religious authorities were indignant at the mockery.[58] They dismissed this as the latest action of an unstable man.[59] Worse, as that of a sacrilegious madman. As the result, the local religious authorities moved to expel him from both their faith community and town in retaliation.[60]

A Woman Destined to Be the Messiah's Mate

Next for Zevi was a sojourn in Constantinople where his behavior and claims resulted in yet another excommunication.[61] In addition, he received a vigorous flogging to show what the local authorities thought of him and his claims.[62]

Wherever he went he was rejected. At Cairo the religious authorities spurned him.[63] At Jerusalem the rabbinical establishment opposed him, excommunicated him, and ordered him from the city.[64] After this record of unbroken rejection, the pivotal event occurred: In 1665 he heard of Nathan of Gaza and made it a point to meet him (see below).[65]

Between 1648 and the outburst of enthusiasm around him in 1666, he had been periodically adding to his earlier claims of being God's agent by adding new aspects to his teaching. In 1658, for example, he spoke of the coming of a replacement Torah and how it was to be manifested in rituals not previously practiced. Ethically this new Torah permitted one to properly defend certain actions that had been previously dismissed as unquestionably evil — now they were not to viewed as indications of one's own weakness, but as outright holy deeds that ultimately honor God.[66]

During these years, his relationship with women was a rather odd one. He married two different women, yet consummated neither relationship and promptly dissolved each of them with a divorce.[67]

And then there was the third wife, a woman as convinced of her own divinely ordained destiny as Zevi was of his own. A factor that should never be underestimated in encouraging Zevi's messianic self-conception — and willingness to hold to it in spite of mockery from 1662 onwards — was the presence of this wife, who fully embraced his belief.

Sarah was born in Poland and her family perished in the vicious fighting that went on there in the 1640s. She made her way to Holland and then to Livorno, Italy, and survived on whatever forms of work she could find.[68] She gained a reputation as morally dissolute,[69] which may say as much (or more) about the trying economic circumstances she lived under as about her basic moral inclinations. If her freewheeling sexual escapades did not do enough to undermine her acceptance in traditional religious society, her practice of magic and fortune telling would have compromised it even further.[70]

Somewhere in her wanderings in Italy, she had a prophetic dream in which she was informed that when the Messiah appeared she was destined to be his mate.[71] If one seeks a psychological interpretation, this may well have been, at least in part, a desire to redeem her life from its past excesses and to bring meaning into it. She took news of Zevi and his claims as a sign that this destiny was about to be fulfilled. Traveling to Cairo, she met the man, impressed him and they were married in 1662.[72] At this point, Zevi's success became a matter not just of his own dreams but of that of his spouse as well. The marriage itself was literally an act of faith on her part: After all, he had already been twice married and, almost as quickly, divorced each spouse.

The Second Bid for Messianic Status

Now Nathan of Gaza enters the picture to promote Zevi's popularity to the level Zevi had long dreamt of. Nathan's reputation for what the twentieth century would have called psychological counseling from a spiritual perspective brought Zevi before this widely respected sage.[73] Through his counsel, Zevi hoped to purge himself of the inner anguish and torment that had so often plagued him[74] by discovering their causes and becoming fully in tune with his Jewish heritage.[75]

Nathan saw the solution to Zevi's difficulties in his fully and enthusiastically embracing his messianic destiny. After all, had not Nathan seen a vision in which Zevi's name had been shown as that of the Messiah?[76] The psychological and social roots of that vision and the identification it made can only be guessed at. Could Nathan have absorbed so many reports of Zevi's claims and concepts that they merged into his belief that now was the time for the appearance of the Messiah? The two fitted together like hand in glove due to the lack of viable competitors for the claim.

Only at Nathan's urging did Zevi make his new bold public affirmation of messiahship on May 31, 1665.[77] In the modern idiom, Nathan put steel in Zevi's backbone and provided the necessary incentive, encouragement, and impetus to embrace the role that he had previously accepted but then often held at arm's distance.

Nathan functioned as prophet for the movement and predicted that when the following year (1666) ended, the actual messianic reign would begin.[78] In the meantime, Zevi appointed 12 disciples to be his key followers, one for each of Israel's traditional 12 tribes.[79]

He returned to Smyrna, the site of his first public humiliation, and this time the bulk of Jews reacted to the claims and actions with festivities and dancing.[80] Local rabbinic authorities felt far more ambivalent about the claims they were hearing and the enthusiastic behavior that embraced their previously banished foe.[81] Nathan's presence assured them that the exuberance was at least partly balanced by public displays of sorrow for sin.[82] So great was the response in the short term that even business came to a temporary stop.[83]

Enthusiasm for His Messianic Claims: Support and Possible Underlying Reasons

The enthusiasm rapidly spread from Smyrna. Some estimate that an outright majority of the Jewish population throughout Europe eventually embraced his claims.[84] Others prefer to speak in terms of it being a mass movement[85] or assert that "hundreds of thousands" of Jews of all social classes embraced him.[86] Hearing his story secondhand may well have helped. In this form, they were safely immune from observing his drastic mood swings and behavior that challenged contemporary Jewish ritual norms.[87]

This enthusiasm spread as far as Britain. In Samuel Pepy's diary entry of February 19 he refers to how it had become a topic of conversation and even betting[88]:

> I am told for certain, what I have heard once or twice already, of a Jew in town, that in the name of the rest do offer to give any man 10 pounds, to be paid 100 pounds, if a certain person now at Smyrna be within these two years owned by all the Princes of the East, and particularly the grand Signor, as the King of the world, in the same manner we do the King of England here, and that this man is the true Messiah. One named a friend of his that had received ten pieces in gold upon this score, and says that the Jew hath disposed of 1100 pounds in this manner, which is very strange; and certainly this year of 1666 will be a year of great action; but what the consequences of it will be, God knows!

An English propaganda tract of early 1666, supposedly written by the French ambassador stationed at Constantinople, can serve as an example of the stories that were widely circulated about Zevi[89]:

> Now that I may add this to your joy, I would have you take it for certain, our Jews yesterday received from Alcaire, Livorn and Venice, so many letters, and of so great credit, that all of them publickly in their Synagogues do now believe, that the Tribes of Ruben, Gad and the half of Manasseh are come to Gaza, as the Prophet Nathan foretold. And that at Smyrna, King Sabbathai Zevi, doth now publickly shew himself abroad, and professeth himself to be King of the Jews.
> For hitherto, for a time he lay incognito, until by signs and many wonders, he had demonstrated he did act in the name of God, and not in his own. Among which signs whereby he proved himself to be sent of God, is, That he foretold the sudden death of some men, and the very day thereof. And that he premonished men of an obscure dark-

ness, with a marvelous showre of Hail, And especially he commanded a Fire to be made in a publick place, in the presence of many beholders; as well of Christians, as of Turks, and Jews; and entered into the fire twice or thrice, without any hurt to his Garments, or to an hair of his head: with these, and the like prodigious signs he hath now gained so great authority to himself; that he is not afraid to go in the streets of the City in kingly manner, with a great Retinue of Attendants. Yea, moreover the King said; he is suddenly to go to Constantinople, And that in the month of June next, The Redemption of Israel will be published throughout the whole world.

A number of factors appear to have contributed to Zevi's success. One that has been heavily stressed is the fact that, just as in the case of his first bid for messianic status in the 1640s, the one in the period 1665–1666 also occurred at a time when one can postulate a direct correlation between external maltreatment of Jews and his re-embracing the Messiah role. Especially in Poland, the Poles and the Polish Jews had suffered immensely in recent decades.[90] Yet other areas also lived in awareness that these dangers might unexpectedly erupt where they were as well, and the messianic event would provide them a way to escape this danger. This certainly acted as kindling in those many places that Zevi had never traveled to but where huge numbers embraced him.[91]

Albert I. Baumgarten wisely suggests that though this is certainly one major incentive for such movements it is far from the only one. For example, they can grow out of a dramatically favorable event — such as an imminent terrible tragedy for a people, city, or nation suddenly becoming transformed into a victory — which sets off exuberant hopes that such a "miraculous" transformation must be a foreshadowing of the glorious triumph for God's people that lies inevitably ahead. In other words, tragedy may motivate millennialism, but triumph in spite of or after disaster may equally well do so. Baumgarten suggests the popularity of the Fifth Monarchy men in seventeenth century Britain (see next chapter) as a prime example of this type of enthusiasm. After the hoped-for (but never assured) victory and execution of the king, anything and everything seemed possible in a way it never had before.[92]

The Jewish problem, however, was the opposite of the Protestant one in Britain; the Fifth Monarchists had to interpret their successes. Jews had to interpret their calamities. Both sought a way out of it through the imminent divine kingdom, and in Zevi a large proportion of the Jewish population became convinced it would be established.

The pivotal difference between that time and two decades before was the widespread propaganda campaign that furthered his claims. This was led by the prophet Nathan, who effectively argued both in person and via the printed word that Zevi was the long-awaited redeemer.[93] The fact that he was able to make his propaganda credible in spite of having to promote an emotionally unstable individual speaks vastly not only of his personal faith in Zevi but also for his ability to find appealing rationalizations for behavior that was inexplicable — inexcusable even — to those who were hostile.

It is not to be denied that in certain subsets of the population there were additional incentives for embracing Zevi. Those kabbalistically centered (especially in its Lurianic form) may well have found Zevi's embracing of it as encouragement for their allegiance.[94] That this element of proof played a major role, though, has been vigorously challenged.[95]

More convincing is the significance of the marranos in forming a core subset of supporters. A number of the communities where support for Zevi was most conspicuous are known to have had a significant percentage of these individuals.[96] The correlation works best in Catholic and Muslim areas of Europe and less so in the Muslim Near East and North Africa. In those areas the interpretive problem is further complicated by a lack of the detailed data concerning the movement that is often available from European sources.[97]

His reception was just as profound in places directly affected by outbreaks of violence as in those where hostility was minimal and the extremes known by first-and secondhand reports.[98] Hence some would argue that it was simply one of those periods when a broad consensus had been reached that now was the appropriate time for redemption.[99] This phenomena certainly does occur in regard to other religious matters: for reasons that one can never fully understand, a kind of consensus evolves that now (as compared to the past or future) is the appropriate time for some action or change that is deemed essential. Some come to the conclusion for one reason and others for yet another, with the unifying factor being the conclusion and not the means whereby they came to it.

The Messianic Dream Is Put to the Test

Things came to a head in early 1666 when Zevi left by ship from Smyrna for a journey to Constantinople. Unfortunately for the messianic aspirant, a number of factors now converged to cost him his liberty.

From the standpoint of his supporters, there was the general conviction that, with God's assistance, he would literally remove the crown from the Sultan and proceed to rule as God's regent on earth. Nathan of Gaza's propaganda machine was working so effectively that Zevi's aspirations were widely known,[100] which meant that they were known by the Turkish government as well. If taken seriously, he intended nothing less than the regime's overthrow. Furthermore, no matter how much one discounted this possibility as delusional, business activity by the vitally important Jewish segment of the economy had slowed dramatically due to preoccupation with Zevi and his plans. Hence the man posed both a potential religious revolutionary threat as well as an even more immediate economic one.[101]

When the ship was intercepted in February 1666, Zevi was chained and brought ashore to be imprisoned at Gallipoli. The authorities treated him with unusual leniency, even though anyone viewed as a revolutionary was normally put to death as quickly as feasible. Instead of facing this penalty, his followers were given regular access to him during the following months.[102] Admittedly, bribery assisted in this,[103] yet it is inconceivable that even bribery could have obtained this leeway if he had been regarded as a serious security threat.

The imprisonment posed an immediate theological problem: How could it possibly have been permitted to occur? This, Zevi explained, was necessary suffering so that the sins of the people might be fully expunged. True, the process had already begun through what the people collectively had already endured; but it would be completed through his own anguish.[104]

Furthermore, Zevi attempted to use his prison time to neutralize any doubts by building up the confidence of those many supporters who came to visit him. Indeed, some came from as far as Poland. To them all, he gave a similar message of reassurance: God would soon act against the oppressors of His people.[105] Since this could easily be construed as meaning that he still intended a revolution against the Sultan, it did nothing to reassure the government and assured that the man would have to be formally tried.[106]

He was next moved to Adrianople. There he became badly sick, and only the skilled intervention of the personal physician of the Grand Vizier — an Islamic convert from Judaism — enabled him to pull through.[107] In September 1666 came the dramatic appearance of the "Messiah" before his judge. He had prepared for the trial with confidence. Nathan had spread word that Zevi would be able to convince the ruler to abdicate. Then Zevi would utilize the existing army to attack Israel's enemies and permit the regathering of the people to their ancestral homeland.[108]

Abdication was never in the works, of course, but Zevi's reputation and charisma was such that one could well imagine the sultan seriously considering whether he could use this man as an excuse for an attack upon the European Catholics and Orthodox.[109] On the other hand, even the possibility of this more limited option was destroyed by one of Zevi's periodic mood swings from optimism to uncertainty and trepidation.

Originally, he planned on the meeting with the sultan wearing a green belt even though this color was forbidden to Jews. It was, however, one worn by a man of importance, and obviously the Messiah would wear it. When his followers saw that in the last hours prior to the hearing he was overcome by fear of doing what he had promised, they became alarmed at what would come out of the scheduled meeting.[110]

At the hearing, he was challenged to prove that he was the Messiah by such a public act that no one could question its genuineness. An English traveler of that period, Nathaniel Crouch, described what happened in his *A Journey to Jerusalem* (Hartford, 1796). First Zevi demanded a translator, and after this delaying tactic was fulfilled,[111]

> The grand seignior would not be put off without a miracle, and it must be one of his own choice; which was that Sabatai should be stripped naked, and set as a mark to his archers: if the arrows pierced not his body, then he would believe him to be the Messiah. But Sabbatai not having faith to stand so sharp a trial, renounced all his title to kingdoms and governments, alledging that he was an ordinary "chocham" [learned man], and a poor Jew, as others were, and had nothing of privilege or virtue above the rest. But the grand seignior not being fully satisfied with this plain confession, declared, that having given public scandal to the professors of the Mehometan religion, and done dishonor to his sovereign authority by pretending to draw such a considerable portion from him as the land of Palestine; his treason and crime were not to be extirpated but by a conversion to the Mehometan faith, which if he refused, the stake was ready at the gate of the Seraglio to impale him.
> Sabbatai ... replied with much chearfulness that he was contented to turn a Turk, and that it was not of force, but of choice, having been a long time desirous of so glorious profession; he esteemed himself much honored, that he had an opportunity to own it first in the presence of the grand seignior.

Revi adopted for himself the name Mehmed Effendi.

How did he rationalize his startling action? He claimed he had "been a long time desirous" of making that step. At first, that sounds like a very self-serving falsehood to justify repudiation of his basic convictions. On the other hand, there is evidence that he believed he had received a revelatory instruction to convert as retribution for the failure of the Jewish community to adequately comprehend the nature of the Deity.[112] However satisfactory that may have been to him, the underlying reasoning is likely to strike the modern reader as more along the line of "cutting off your nose to spite your face" or, more precisely, "to spite your Jewish community's face."

In public correspondence to fellow Jews, he insisted upon his sincerity: "My brothers, know ... that the True One, which only I have known for many generations and for which I have toiled, wanted me to enter Islam with all my heart."[113]

When Nathan traveled to Italy a year after Zevi's conversion, he had a new "spin" on how Turkish assistance would be obtained for the liberation of the Palestinian homeland: Instead of the sultan bestowing his authority upon Zevi, Zevi would use his influence upon the sultan to obtain his support for the Jewish cause. The specific means would be through the power of his singing and the respect it would draw from the Islamic ruler.[114] This revisionist scenario was built upon the acknowledged fact that Zevi was known to have an impressive singing voice[115] and may have been an allusion to the Old Testament account of the beneficial impact the singing of the youthful David had upon Saul, the king of that earlier day.

With the encouragement of Nathan and others, followers found ways to justify what had happened. Some were content to believe that it was simply God at work in another of His mysterious ways. Even during his preconversion days, Nathan had rationalized the extreme behavior of Zevi as his ultimately successful wrestling with the demonic.[116] Just as each individual Jew must undergo his or her battle with temptation, so must the Messiah. Indeed, for those using gematria, their interpretation of the mystical meaning of numbers was invaluable. *Moshiah* (Messiah) had the same numerical total of 358 as *nachash* (serpent). Hence the two must be intertwined in conflict until the ultimate triumph of good.[117]

Indeed, the greater the sin the less room a person had to hide from the responsibility for his sin. This would ultimately produce freedom from sin.[118] Hence, some reasoned, one had to sink as low as one could. For the Messiah of the Jews, what could be lower than to convert to the alien religion of Islam?[119] His conversion thus was not a matter that might be forgiven as mere human weakness under horrendous pressure but as a perquisite for fully living up to the role of his office.[120]

There were two types of defenders of Zevi's apostasy. One faction considered it a necessary part of his messianic role that his followers should emulate; the other faction conceded that it was essential for Zevi but for others to imitate his example would be to arrogate to themselves a role that was properly reserved only for him.[121] Abraham Cardozo, another messiah (see below), was one of those who wrote at length defending Zevi's apostasy while denying it was right for other Jews to imitate his example.[122]

The authorities recognized the prestige that his conversion could bring to Islam, so Zevi was permitted to live freely in Adrianople and was even given the title "keeper of the palace gates."[123] Despite his professions of pleasure on becoming a Muslim and embracing of certain of its outward forms, his correspondence with foreign and domestic Jews continued and he was a regular attendee at synagogue services.[124] Well-financed enemies of his within Judaism finally resorted to bribery. Through a highly placed officer of the Turkish government, a campaign was launched to spread word that Zevi was creating reverse conversions, convincing Muslims to embrace Judaism. These charges failed to convince the Sultan.[125]

On the other hand, the governing authorities accepted the charge that he was observed publicly wearing Jewish attire and even phylacteries instead of the garments expected of a Muslim.[126] Perhaps this was the straw that broke the camel's back or perhaps they had simply had enough of this strange enthusiast who had been such a disruptive force to the realm. In punishment, Zevi was sent to Albania, where he dwelt in their fortress at Duleigo (in the 20th century, part of Yugoslavia) until his death in September 1676.[127]

Nathan of Gaza: Prophet of the Messiah

Although we have briefly discussed the role of Nathan in the career of Sabbatai Zevi, he also deserves specific attention in his own right. His full name was Abraham Nathan ben Elisha Hayyim Ashkenazi. From Polish stock, his father had brought the family to Jerusalem.

Nathan viewed himself as the new Elijah whose purpose was to prepare the way of the Messiah.[128] Nathan's doctrine of the Messiah was that of one who would bloodlessly triumph over Israel's enemies.[129] He also rebuked those who demanded miracles to back up these claims, arguing that they were unneeded and their insistence upon such would bring them divine condemnation.[130] After he embraced Zevi's claims, he argued that to the extent that they would have a "miracle" at all, it would be in the form of Muslims and others accepting his messiahship.[131]

The disavowal of miracles, however, did not stop the widespread circulation of such stories concerning deeds allegedly done by or connected with Zevi.[132] In modern terminology, this permitted "deniability": His popularity grew due to the stories, but anything particularly outlandish could be repudiated if challenged since the need of miracles had been denied from the beginning.

At times, Nathan's mind had played with the possibility that it was his own destined role to be the Messiah.[133] What ultimately moved him in a different direction was a public ecstatic experience. Near Pentecost in

1665, he went into one of his trance states during the synagogue service and began to utter various remarks that made little or no sense to listeners. Coming out of the trance, Nathan interpreted his own words and what he had seen in the trance as meaning that he had been given prophetic status by God and that the Messiah was Zevi.[134]

Nathan's teachings on such occasions were claimed to be the result of the supernatural revelations given to him. Those seeking temporal explanations of the phenomena can point to what may be called his emotional-intellectual "pump priming" to create visionary experiences. One technique to encourage disassociation from the surrounding world was to engage in a prolonged period of abstinence from food and association from others, i.e., social and physical isolation, which opens one to the triumph of nonphysical experiences generated by the mind. To further stimulate his intellect, he utilized forms of meditation in favor in the kabbalistic community: He centered his mind at length on the secret meaning of words, phrases, and numbers in an effort o connect his inner being with the supernatural world.[135]

Yet Nathan always remained very traditional in many ways. For example, he demanded both repentance and proof of it: Had one fasted? What had one's behavior demonstrated to prove that the power of the flesh had been tamed? Such were his demands.[136] Likewise, in regard to the traditional religious rituals of the day, these were fully (even rigorously) practiced and encouraged by him at the same time Zevi felt free to permit a more liberal approach.[137]

After his messiah's conversion to Islam and the Turks' crushing public display of Sabbatian sentiments, Nathan lived the life of a fugitive until 1680, when he died a natural death while still on the run.[138] Yet Zevi's actions had not disillusioned him: In order to bear the sins of the nation he had to undergo this "conversion." He had to sink as far into sin as he could go. Hence it was all part of God's ultimate redemptive plan for the human race.[139]

Why couldn't Nathan grasp that his hopes had gone fatally awry? Robert N. Levine probably has it right when he suggests that "to fail to reinterpret each painful twist in the road in a way that validated his messianic dream would have been to admit that his life's work had failed and that he too had perpetuated a cruel hoax on the Jewish people. Perhaps that was more than Nathan and his core followers ever could face up to."[140]

A complementary explanation is that Nathan rooted messianic status not in behavior but in spiritual insight. In this approach, that is the essential difference between the Messiah and the rest of the human race as well. Behavior becomes not irrelevant, but almost so in comparison with the central importance of his spiritual perception. If that is present, the rest need concern one but little.

Nathan described this concept when he argued that the Messiah "reaches the understanding of the greatness of God, for this is the quintessence of the Messiah. And if he does not do so then he is not the Messiah. Even if he displays all the signs and wonders in the world, God forbid that one should believe in him, for he is a prophet to idolatry."[141]

This led him to openly rebuke those who demanded outward evidence for acceptance of Zevi. "Due to our numerous sins, the majority of the community of Israel remains far from the truth. Not being familiar with the secret lore, they pridefully and mockingly say, 'What have we seen to make us believe in the Messiah?'"[142] Indeed, Nathan argued that one of the prime proofs that Jesus of Nazareth was a pseudo-Messiah was His rooting His claims upon the miracles He worked. The Jews of his day, therefore, who expected such outward wonders were working from just as erroneous a premise as the Christians.[143]

Moshe Idel rightly regarded Nathan's attitude toward external evidence as an elitist stance because it assumed the essentiality of a knowledge of Kabbalah that only a minority possessed and which most had neither the time or inclination to master.[144] If the Messiah's behavior were verifiable by the proper interpretation of the Kabbalah, that settled the matter once and for all no matter what actions the man had taken. It was the ultimate proof that could never be obtained from miracles or any other source. Such sentiments kept Nathan steadfast to his death, but did nothing to keep the bulk of Jews from moving away from the once-popular embodiment of their dreams and hopes.

Abraham Miguel Cardozo (1626–1706)

Cardozo was born into a family that was ethnically Jewish but officially converted to Roman Catholicism. As the result, he received an extensive religious education in both Catholicism (publicly) and Judaism (in private).[145] At the same time, he received a secular training in medicine so he could financially support himself.[146] He formally returned to the faith of his ancestors in 1649.

The only physical description of him comes from an enemy who mocks him for his love of wine and good food and as a man who would be "fondling a woman with one hand and a pastry with the other."[147] In short, he was a man who loved life and its pleasures, if one prefers a favorable interpretation, or a self-indulgent and self-centered man, if one prefers an unfriendly interpretation.

His journey as a Jew and mystic was a long one that would take him down many hard and difficult roads and cause him to endure much rejection and scorn, both from outsiders who spurned his Judaism and from his own co-religionists who scorned his kabbalistic theories and messianic convictions. It can be said to have begun when he first came to know his ethnic backgroumd. "When I was six years old," he writes, "my parents made known to me that I was a Jew. When I was twelve … I took to reading the [Old Testament] Scriptures in Latin, despite the tremendous danger that this entails everywhere in Spain."[148] In those early years, he developed the habit of wandering the countryside, attempting to reason his way into the mysteries of God's nature and being.[149]

Finally, both Cardozo and his older brother gave up on their homeland and moved to Venice. There he underwent further extensive study in the Torah and the ancient supplemental Jewish works interpreting and explaining it.[150]

By 1663 he had moved to Tripoli and, at about that time, is known to have become a polygamist by taking a second wife. The number of his wives had grown to four by at least 1674. Although this was out of step with the monogamous demands of contemporary Jews in France and Germany, the rule was not regarded as obligatory by either Sephardic Jews or those living in Muslim lands. Even so, few others seem to have taken advantage of their theoretical right to take multiple wives.[151]

This period in Tripoli was one of prosperity for him. As a respected physician, he was able to afford servants, slaves, and horses. Just as important for the intellectual side of himself, he had ample time to pursue his spiritual studies.[152]

In Tripoli he began receiving both dreams and visions that moved him to embrace Zevi's theology and claims.[153] In one of them, he saw the words that in the year 5425 in the Jewish calendar the Messiah would appear (which would overlap the European years of 1664 and 1665).[154] Soon after 1666 had begun (one year later than he had originally anticipated), he became convinced that the appearance of a huge starlike object in the sky would provide visual confirmation that the Messiah had come. On May 15, 1666, it finally happened. He reported, "It was the size of the moon; people saw it shining with a clear, brilliant light."[155] His frustration must have been immense as he received these reports from eyewitnesses, for he himself was enduring a major bout of eye problems and was bedridden.[156]

During Zevi's life, Cardozo appeared to be the third most important

9. Jewish Messiahs During the European Colonization 147

leader in the movement, ranking only behind Nathan of Gaza and Zevi himself.[157] Yet even then he was very much his own man and followed his own course. He conspicuously declined to propagandize for Zevi after his lapse into Islam or to personally move with him during those years. These inactions have caused some to come to the conclusion that Cardozo's role in the movement has often been overrated.[158] Perhaps a fairer evaluation is that he was not one of the diehard loyalists who refused to ever admit the failure of his hopes, which argues nothing against his importance in the preconversion years of Zevi.

In 1672 a revolution broke out in Tripoli against Osman Pasha who died during the siege of his palace after a brief bout of severe illness. He was attended by a doctor whose identity is uncertain but who may have been Cardozo. There were suspicions of poisoning, and Cardozo's own writings (from decades later) leave the impression that he wished others to believe — without quite directly saying it — that he himself had played a role in the ruler's demise. Such a role in the widely desired death would certainly explain the mufti's subsequent banning of any violence against this outsider who had been a regal physician.[159] Even so, prudence suggested it was time to go elsewhere, and he moved to Tunis the following year.

In Tunis his zeal for Zevi was well known and there were divided feelings as to how to treat him. The Jewish community sought advice from Venice and the rabbis there insisted that Cardozo had to be banned. Officially, he was banned but, embarrassingly, the bar was ignored by many members of the community. Some foe, however, bribed key city officials and he was ordered to leave.[160]

Cardozo initially wished to return to Italy, so he decided to take up residence in Leghorn, Italy. The Jewish community officials, with only partial success, attempted to keep both him and his family confined to the facility for lepers. When that failed as a long-term solution, they managed to get him sent to Turkey.[161]

Arriving in Izmir, Turkey, in 1675, he attempted to set down roots there. By 1679 or 1680, his unconventional religious convictions had so annoyed the leading figures in the Jewish community that they were able to have him expelled from the town. In one sense, he hated having to endure this, for he had been able to develop a close-knit group of followers. Though numbering perhaps only two dozen men, they stood by him through the remainder of his life in spite of the expulsion. On the family level, the stay was a horrendous disaster. In 1678 plague hit. By the end of the summer, one of Cardozo's wives and 11 of his children had perished at its hands. Two other children had also died due to other causes equally tragic.[162]

Next he moved to Constantinople, where he found a wealthy supporter of Zevi, Solomon Galimidi, who soon transferred his loyalties to Cardozo. The Jewish community, once generally enthusiastic about Zevi, had become thoroughly disillusioned and was determined to make life difficult for anyone who continued to support him.[163] Galimidi provided vital psychological and financial support to counterbalance this barrage of opposition.

During the summer and autumn months of 1681 Cardozo repeatedly taught that the final redemption of Israel would occur at Passover of the next year. The story made the rounds that, like Zevi earlier, he had ordered the fasts in honor of the temple's destruction to be skipped since the messianic dreams would burst forth in full fruition the following year. The rabbinic officials in Constantinople refused to believe his denials, officially ousted him from the Jewish community, and made it plain that discovering his dead body would not bother them in the least.[164] In short, he was being thrown to the wolves and the religious leadership had made it plain they were neither going to protect him nor care if anything bad happened to him.

In light of the stringent passions his teachings had aroused, he moved to the city of Rodosto. It was there, as 1681 drew to a close, that he learned that Zevi's spouse was on the way to the city—with every intention of marrying him. Cardozo stalled, wishing to postpone the marriage until after the messianic Passover. Feeling thoroughly rejected, she returned to Adrianople. This interlude did work to Cardozo's theological benefit, however, because her words of praise were taken as endorsement of his claim to be messiah.[165]

Confident that his predictions of Israel's redemption would occur, he returned to Constantinople for the Passover of April 22, 1682. This would be the day when his work would be vindicated. This would be the day that his revelatory role in the divine scheme of things would be validated.

The next day he was faced, not with crowds of jubilant hero-worshippers, but with the need of explaining how his predictions had been so totally wrong. Emotionally crushed and unable to comprehend what had gone wrong, he was faced with rumors that there was a plot to murder him: He had plagued the community long enough and it was time to permanently remove this false prophet and disturber of the civic peace.[166]

Recognizing the need for prudence, he soon packed his bags and left. The remainder of his life was basically filled with rejection, repeated bouts of personal and family illness, and a grim effort to financially survive. Sometimes he was able to obtain help from others, but his primary means of support was via his medical experience, though occasionally he had to fall back on his fortune-teller capabilities.[167] In some places, the Jewish leaders refused to let him become part of their community; in others, he was temporarily admitted, only to be rejected for his heretical practices and doctrine. Even his efforts to go to Jerusalem were successfully blocked by the local Jewish authorities before he got further than Jaffa.[168]

In these final years, even he had to recant his illusions. "I am no Messiah," he confessed upon one occasion.[169] On another occasion, he added to his recantation, "If I believe that I am Messiah, may God never forgive me. And may I have no share in the God of Israel, in this world or the next."[170]

His death in 1706 kept him from the temptation of reversing himself yet again. Or did it? The very book in which he invoked upon himself divine punishment if he claimed to be Messiah is a volume that begins by him calling himself *mem-bet-aleph*, the very initials that Cardozo took to represent "Messiah ben Ephraim."[171] Furthermore, the messianic figure in Zechariah 12:10 is described as one who has been "pierced." And Cardozo deliberately provoked a deadly quarrel with a relative who he knew liked to use a knife as a weapon—and was pierced to death with it.[172] It was as if even in the very act of dying, he could not quite bring himself to fully abandon his hopes and dreams of being a Messiah sent by God.

Cardozo's Theology

Cardozo wrote extensively and composed more than 60 works dealing with the nature of God. To him, understanding the true nature of deity represented the essence of religious faith and insight.[173] In taking this approach, he represents a distinctly different theological emphasis than that of Nathan of Gaza. As Yehuda Leibes observes, "Cardozo's mystery of divinity may, and perhaps must, be defined abstractly, whereas for Nathan the feeling aspects—faith and love—were more important than intellectual knowledge for the relation between the believers, God, and the Messiah."[174]

Individuals might differ as to how they conceived of the Messiah: Nathan of Gaza considered him divine.[175] To Cardozo, this was totally irrelevant because it was far more important to grasp the true nature of God. As he wrote in one letter, "Now, on the question of the Messiah or of redemption believe whatever you wish. But regarding God, blessed be He, be careful lest Yom Tov Romano and others like him take you away from our faith."[176]

He adopted the two-messiah doctrine and claimed that he was the one descended from Joseph rather than David.[177] This did not involve a rejection of Zevi's messianic role, just the assertion that both men would play that role. Indeed, at first Cardozo considered himself the secondary redemptive figure; only years after Zevi's lapse into Islam and extended further thought on the matter did Cardozo come to the conclusion that his own messianic status was the superior one. The basis for that superiority, not surprisingly, was his insight into the true nature of God, a subject that Zevi seemed willing to forgo, to the frustration and annoyance of Cardozo.[178]

His view of the messianic triumph was far different from that of most others. It would not be a time of the Jews collectively returning to Palestine but of their living freely and peacefully wherever they wished. He wrote, "When the Redeemer comes, the Jews will still be living among the Gentiles even after their salvation is accomplished. But they will not be dead men, as they had been previously. Through their redemption they will experience happiness, enjoy dignity and honor."[179]

He also claimed that the dead came in spirit form to speak with him, as did angels. Indeed, he claimed the power to compel them to appear. Although he was suspected of this at least as early as 1669, he vigorously denied such allegations. It has been noted, however, that in making the oath he invoked a name for God that Cardozo was not using at the time. Since he did not believe in God (under the name invoked) the oath may only have been a misleading pretense to escape condemnation by others. Within the next decade, however, all pretense had disappeared and he became quite proud of his ability to summon the dead.[180]

Third man in the Zevi movement, co-messiah with Zevi, speaker to the dead: Cardozo accumulated more than enough reasons for traditionalists to scorn him and, as we saw, suffered severely for such claims.

Yakov Querido (a/k/a Filosof)

In 1683, whether by previous encouragement, personal hopes, or adroit seizure of the moment of opportunity, Zevi's last wife (Yocheved) informed all who would listen that the soul of her deceased spouse now dwelt in her brother, Yakov.[181] As Zevi's spouse told the story, she and her brother had dwelt in isolation for three entire days and nights. In that period, her brother had died, Zevi had returned and made her pregnant, she had carried the baby to term and given birth, and he had grown to 15 years of age. And that baby now had the form and appearance of her brother. Indeed, it was now only superficially her brother; it was really Zevi's son.[182]

Yakov adopted the name Querido ("the beloved") as his surname, and strange stories of "light beings" making their appearance enhanced his reputation among former supporters of Zevi.[183] Because of his claims and the strange phenomena that his disciples were convinced had appeared, he became the recognized leader of the Sabbatian faction in Salonika.[184]

The process of Zevi converting to Islam had taken years. In the case of Querido, it was a matter of months before he fully followed that course.[185] He carried with him some 400 followers, and they became known as the sect of Donmeh.[186]

Yehoshua Heshel Tzoref (1633–c. 1700)

Working primarily in Poland and Lithuania, Tzoref was a jeweler by trade and had received a minimal education. After Zevi's death, he claimed to be the Messiah from Joseph and that it was his divinely assigned role to rule until Zevi returned from death to resume his own role as the Davidic Messiah. In the short term, he was the dominant Sabbatian leader in his region, and Jews came from far and wide to listen to his teaching and predictions of the future.[187] He was regionally significant but his support went no further.

Hayim ben Shlomo (c.1650–c. 1717)

Given the name Malakh ("the angel") by his followers, Shlomo studied Sabbatian thought in his native Poland and in Italy and Turkey as well. He was cofounder of the Society of the Pious that undertook a major collective pilgrimage to Palestine in 1700, and much of this Sabbatian movement accepted him as its director upon the death of its chief organizer. Finally, returning to Poland, he played an important role in popularizing the theology of Zevi and thereby preparing the way for Jacob Frank's rise to importance (see below).[188]

To the extent that he made a clearly messianic claim, it was that of an interim one, who would pass his authority back when Zevi reappeared. Because of the ambiguity in his claims, some have been cautious in attributing to him the self-perception of Messiah.[189] Against this doubt must be balanced the fact that many accepted his leadership of at least a faction of the Sabbatian movement. Why do so in contrast to others who did make explicit messianic claims unless his claim to authority was perceived as at least equal or superior to theirs? Hence the internal logic of the leadership position he claimed in the Zevi movement argues the likelihood that he was accepted as de facto Messiah whether or not he formally made such a claim.

Mordecai Eisenstadt

In the late 1600s, Eisenstadt became a respected preacher of repentance among Italian Jews. With this traditionally positive role went the far more controversial claim of being the Messiah, a self-description that was enthusiastically received in both Modena and Reggio, Italy.[190] In other areas, he gained significant disciples, such as Hungary, Moravia, and Bohemia.[191]

He embraced the two–Messiah doctrine, claiming that Zevi had been only the Messiah of Ephraim. He himself was the Davidic Messiah, befitting the facts of the case as well as the fact that he had come from impoverished background.[192]

His claims engendered such a strong reaction that his foes took the initiative in bringing him to the attention of the Inquisition in the knowledge that they would act against him. Before they could do so, however, he fled the country entirely.[193] It is said that after his return to Bohemia and, later, to Poland that he totally lost contact with reality and was recognized as thoroughly insane.[194]

Yehuda Leib Prossnitz (1670–1730)[195]

Living and working mainly in Moravia, he worked as a peddler until both Luria and Zevi began making appearances to him. Attracted to Sabbatianism by both its doctrine and these appearances, he began to preach its message to others. Though he successfully gained converts, neither his zeal nor his teachings were appreciated by the religious hierarchy of several of the towns he worked in and they formally rejected both.[196] If these early convictions were not sufficiently radical to upset the Jewish religious mainstream, he also crossed the path of a group of Sabbatians from Salonika and became convinced that he was the Messiah to descend from Joseph.[197]

His critics were convinced he was an outright fraud. Upon one occasion, he invited those favorably inclined to visit him in his hovel. While he waited behind a thin curtain, the visible light of God shone from behind it where he stood. Through its sheerness the visitors could see him dressed in white with the letters of the Tetragrammaton written on his chest. One of those present was skeptical enough to jerk down the curtain, and he discovered that the Shekinah was not the presence of God but a combination of alcohol and turpentine that Prossnitz had lit.[198] Such was the version his foes circulated, but it did little to abort his acceptance among Sabbatians, though it appears to have proved fatal to any effort to expand his acceptance beyond that base.[199]

Barukhia Russo (died c. 1720)

As with various other claimants to Zevi's leadership position, Russo was also given a new name, that of Senor Santo ("Holy Lord"). This he meant quite literally, since he claimed to be divine as well as Messiah and even accepted the title of Elohei Israel ("God of Israel").[200]

According to his teachings, God created this world but takes no ongoing interest in it.[201] (Rather like the deist concept on the matter.) Perhaps of even greater provocation to traditionalist thinkers among his people was the claim that there are two Torahs and that they are in contradiction. The physical Torah (Genesis through Deuteronomy) condemns many things as sin, but these prohibitions can be safely set aside because the ultimate Torah that God had not seen fit to previously share with humanity demands many of those acts.[202] These included both ritualistic changes (eating of nonkosher food, for example), as well as sexual license both outside the family (adultery and orgies) and inside it (including incest).[203]

Moshe Hayim Luzzatto (1707–1747)

Born in Italy, he was brought up in Judaism and received a well-grounded secular education as well. An accomplished playwright and poet, he was one of the outstanding Jewish intellectuals of his age.[204]

He created a Holy Society to share in his studies of the Kabbalah and he embraced the group's conviction that he was God's Messiah.[205] Repeatedly rejected by various governing Jewish religious tribunals, he temporarily backed off from some of his claims but never more than temporarily.[206]

On a more conventional level, he was and is regarded as one of the most authoritative and valuable kabbalists of his time. His volume *Derech HaShem* ("The Way of God") continues to be studied as one of the preeminent presentations of the so-called Oral Torah that Moses himself never committed to writing.²⁰⁷ His work on Jewish ethics is also considered of modern as well as historical value.²⁰⁸

Jacob Leibovicz Frank (c. 1726–1791) and the Frankist Movement

Frank was born in about 1726 under the name of Jacob ben Judah Leib in Podolia, a region that has shifted between Ukraine and Poland through the centuries. After moving to Bucharest, he supported himself by becoming a local merchant and also by taking needed goods into other regional markets. Local business clearly bored him and he came to manifest a preference for long business trips that took him to faraway regions.²⁰⁹ One of these resulted in an extended stay in Smyrna. There he engaged in studies of the *Zohar* and was introduced to the stories about Zevi and enthusiastically embraced his cause.²¹⁰

Over a period of time, he gained increased stature through his repeat visits to places such as Smyrna and the grave site of Nathan of Gaza. On at least some of these visits, he was accompanied by respected rabbis of the Sabbatian movement. Hence it was not an unnatural progression for him to become recognized as its Polish leader.²¹¹ The local Sabbatian groups were so small and widely dispersed that it may well have been more his recognition that they needed leadership than any conscious decision on their part to bestow it upon him.²¹² The loyalty to him was also encouraged by the growing belief that he literally possessed the same divine essence which had earlier resided in Zevi.²¹³

In 1755, while Frank was on a visit with fellow Sabbatians in the city of Lanskroun, hostile Jewish opponents observed the religious rites he was conducting. They claimed it was nothing short of an orgy and brought charges against him with the government. Although those traveling with him were forced to remain jailed, he himself was viewed as being a Turkish citizen and was soon released and left the country.²¹⁴ Claiming to be Turkish and having to abandon those who had supported him created no inner guilt: The theology he was developing classified such an act as guiltless because it was viewed as essential.²¹⁵

Traditional Jews remained outraged. A formal religious investigation was launched at Satanow which condemned the Sabbatians on both doctrinal and moral grounds. This result was ultimately passed upwards to a major religious convocation and a general writ of excommunication was drafted for Frank and all his followers.²¹⁶

At the urging of Frank, his local followers requested that Bishop Dem-

9. Jewish Messiahs During the European Colonization   155

bowski of Kamieniec-Podolski keep the traditionalists from persecuting them. As part of this strategy, they urged that a formal debate be held before the Catholic bishop to judge the merits of the disputes.[217]

Nine subjects were debated in the series of meetings in 1756 and 1757. One was the long-standing blood libel that "Christian blood" should be used in Jewish rituals. Another argued that the Talmud was in blatant contradiction to and repudiated the teaching of the Torah. (For that matter, the Frankists were convinced that in any apparent conflict between the Talmud and the Kabbalah, the Talmud also had to be in the wrong.)[218]

A third was that after the Messiah appeared, the Jewish people would not enjoy any special status. All the subjects were worded in such a manner as if to imply (without directly saying such) that Frank and his followers agreed with Catholicism and opposed Judaism.[219] This earned the favor of the religious authorities, put themselves in the best light, and diverted attention from those religious and moral subjects on which they were quite vulnerable in both Jewish and Catholic eyes.

The Frankists performed very well in this series of debates and clearly came out as the winners of the discussions.[220] Hence, when the Bishop issued his decision, he came down firmly on their behalf. The traditionalist Jews were faced with various punishments, including the destruction of their copies of the Talmud.[221] Authorized searchers entered the homes of individuals who were suspected of possessing copies. There was every indication that a full-blown persecution was imminent as well.[222]

The upper hand of Frank lasted only until the bishop died, mere weeks after these actions had been authorized. Afterwards the traditionalist Jewish community made life so difficult for the dissidents that many migrated to Turkey.[223] The long arm of his well-financed enemies reached even there. Credible rumors began to spread that large gifts were being bestowed on the sultan in order to gain influence that could ultimately be used against Frank. Hence he deemed this an expedient time to convert to Islam,[224] a course followed by his compatriots who had joined him there.[225]

Those who remained behind did not give up hope. They repeatedly petitioned both government and church officials for the freedom to openly practice their convictions. King August III ruled in their favor in 1758, and a large number of those who had left for safer places returned. One of these was Frank himself.[226] After returning home, he consolidated under his wing a cross-section of Sabbatian supporters who had previously remained independent of him.[227]

At first, he began to drop hints that baptism and adopting Christianity might well be the proper course for them in the future.[228] He was careful in when and how he presented this radical step: "Gradually I began to tell others of the truth about the Christian faith and the need for baptism."[229]

At the same time that he was preparing his followers for conversion, his supporters engaged in a second set of church-approved debates over religious matters beginning on July 17, 1759. In the earlier debates, there was at least the appearance of the two groups of Jews having a shared theology and that the dispute was over its proper and true interpretation. This time no such effort was made. Instead, the clear rhetorical strategy of the Frankists was to distance themselves from traditionalist Jews and to stir up Roman Catholic animosity against these opponents.[230]

This effectively diverted at least some of the attention away from exactly what the relationship of the Frankists would be to Roman Catholicism. When Catholic leaders became wary of their semi-Catholicism-at-a-distance, Frank and his backers petitioned for formal admission into the church, as a self-governing body within the authority of the Roman Catholic Church. This bid at semi-independence was rejected and formal baptism demanded. For Frank, this occurred in September of 1759.[231]

Even after converting to Roman Catholicism, the movement did not fall apart. Jewish followers in eastern Europe tended to follow the example of their leader, while those farther west tended to shun it. By the end of the year after his own baptism, more than 500 members of the movement had imitated him.[232]

Even so, official suspicions did not disappear. Members' first loyalty seemed to be to Frank and not to the church. Furthermore, there were alarming tales that Frank considered himself the most recent incarnation of Deity,[233] the kind of assertion that was guaranteed to rattle the nerves of the church establishment. The fact that interrogated members acknowledged him as the contemporary Messiah did nothing to reassure them either.[234] The element of deception further sharpened the anger at discovering that, in the earlier debates over the Messiah's coming in sinless form in the flesh, the Messiah being defended was actually Frank and not Jesus.[235]

The new discoveries now reached critical mass, and Frank was arrested and imprisoned.[236] In February 1760 he was tried and exiled to a fortress at Czestochowa. In one sense, he was quite fortunate in his place of imprisonment since the guard staff consisted of only 80 men plus officers, all of whom were sent there in place of outright retirement from duty. The terms of his imprisonment were relatively generous. He was given the privilege of wandering throughout the prison and receiving the religious works he desired. He was also permitted to write to family members and outsiders.[237]

Meanwhile, the movement went underground while discreet visits

9. Jewish Messiahs During the European Colonization 157

were made to him in prison. Time lightened church worries, and the low profile of the movement members further discouraged negative attention coming their way at the hands of the church. In 1762 it was decided that the severity of his imprisonment could be further lightened. Part of this involved his wife joining him and a group of disciples being permitted to take up residence nearby.[238]

In June 1765 Frank initiated a scheme to transfer his group's loyalties from the Roman Catholic Church to the Russian Orthodox.[239] Becoming aware of the scheme, a group of Jewish opponents was sent in 1767 in a bid to starve off any Russian recognition, an action that might lead them to pressure the Poles for his release. They hit hard on his lack of spiritual commitment to any system of belief except whatever would benefit him the most in the short term: "Don't you see these instigators are acting dishonestly? They are already to receive their fifth religion! First, they were Jews, then Turks, afterwards Sabbatians, followed by their acceptance of Catholicism. Now, they want to gain the release of their leader by trying to turn to [Russian] orthodoxy."[240]

After hearing their side of the case and further considering the matter, the Russians refused to embrace Frank's scheme. When the Russians captured the place of his imprisonment in 1773, however, he was still promptly freed.[241]

After intermediate stays in various other localities, in 1775 both he and his daughter took up residence in Vienna, where he gained popularity in Gentile circles. In that city's context, he was viewed as an effective propagandist for Christianity.[242] Yet, again, things were not quite what they seemed. Although he outwardly lived the life of a practicing Catholic, he introduced into his worship unorthodox customs from the "Oriental" world of his day.[243]

In these post-release years, the strength of the Frankist movement shifted from Poland into Moravia and, even later, into Germany.[244] Perhaps recognizing this shift, Frank himself chose to move to Offenbach (near Frankfurt, Germany), where the prosperity he had accumulated permitted him to live on the level of a contemporary nobleman.[245] His popularity had not waned, and he regularly received pilgrims from throughout Europe and beyond until his death in December 1791.[246]

It has traditionally been thought that the later generations of those who followed Frank through his religious evolution and into Catholicism later enjoyed a disproportionate influence on their communities. By about 1850, it was believed that a clear majority of the lawyers in Prague could trace their lineage (if they were candid) back to disciples of Frank.[247] In the 1990s he continued to be a figurehead for praise or condemnation in

Poland. Jews pointed to Adam Mickiewicz — the most popular Polish poet of the past — as coming from a Frankist heritage. On the other side of the coins, Gentile Poles happily denounced politicians they did not like as having rejected their Catholicism and walking in the footsteps of Frankist imitation Catholicism.[248]

Theology of Frank and His Movement

His followers boasted of their opposition to the Talmud and of their love for the mystical writings of the *Zohar*. Hence they felt the name "Zoharists" described their loyalties much better than any other label.[249]

In their meetings, behavior easily degenerated. Inflamed by a heavy dose of music and dancing, their aroused emotions found no evil in sensual behavior that violated the sexual norms in which they had been raised.[250] Frank, at least in the fully developed form of his thinking, found nothing wrong in this. It was part of his divine mission to release mankind from all moral inhibitions: "This much I tell you: Christ, as you know, said that he had come to redeem the world from the hands of the devil, but I have come to redeem it from all the laws and customs that have ever existed. It is my task to annihilate all this so that the Good God can reveal Himself."[251]

Indeed, only by going to excess could one lay the foundation for gaining genuine spiritual insight: "No man can climb a mountain until he has first descended to its foot. Therefore we must descend and be cast down to the bottom rung, for only then can we climb to the infinite. This is the mystic principle of Jacob's Ladder, which I have seen and which is shaped like a V."[252]

Hence it is not surprising that the kind of Christianity to which he gravitated was one in which all law and restrictions ceased to exist.[253] In order to rise to the heights of true holiness, one had to first descend to the depths of extreme excess in sexual matters. The more repugnant the acts, the greater the ascent. Yet for evil to have redeeming value it still had to be hidden evil, carefully kept out of the attention of outsiders.[254] This also, of course, protected against retribution and prosecution.

Nor was this the only unusual aspect of his Christian religion that would have been startling to the orthodox. He considered Jesus of Nazareth the mere outward form; the inward being had been Frank himself![255] Nor was he going to permit his followers to be amalgamated into mainstream Catholicism; they were forbidden to marry Gentiles and were to keep all relationships with them at a minimum.[256]

As to God's kingdom, he believed that a horrendous war would occur and that part of the aftermath would be the establishment of a new divine kingdom on earth. Not in Palestine—as so many before and since have thought—but in his own homeland.[257]

Eva Frank: The Messiah's Mother

The nature of Frank's doctrine of the supernatural involved the existence of God, but that God was not the creator of the tangible universe. Evil created our world and blocked human access to the Deity and vice versa. Hence it was Frank's role to remove that gap by becoming the divine human who bridged the gap between the divine and the mortal.[258] This provided for the male element in Deity.

The female element was embodied in his wife. When she died, that part of Deity then took its place in his daughter, Eva, and she played the role of the divine female human previously occupied by her mother.[259] In developing this concept, Frank seems consciously to have adopted traditional Catholic veneration of the Virgin Mary in its most extreme forms and taken it even further. Indeed, he utilized the term "Matronita" ("the Lady") to describe her in her importance and grandeur.[260]

Looking at it from a different perspective, there was a third supernatural being involved as well: The one who began it all (Zevi) was regarded as the ultimate deity while Frank in particular was God over the Jews. The child to be born by Eva would also be a deity,[261] forming a kind of Jewish trinity between the three. Apparently, the paternity of the messianic child was to be left in the hands of chance. She freely slept with many men, and coitus with her was regarded as an inherently praiseworthy act that carried no permanent obligations on either party.[262] Presumably to increase her prestige, when she and her father lived in Vienna, he spread the tale that she was an illegitimate daughter of the Romanov rulers of Russia.[263]

After her father's death, the issue of the leadership of the group inevitably arose. Although Franz Thomas von Schoenfeld apparently had the opportunity to take the post, he declined it. After this, a triumvirate of the three children of Frank (Eva and her two brothers Josef and Rochus) took control.[264]

Oddly enough—or, in light of the various drastic shifts in his theological direction, wisely enough—systematic efforts were made to preserve Frank's teachings only after his death. It was at this time that a collection of his teachings was finally prepared, as was a detailed account of his life.[265]

The movement was clearly in decline, however. The Frank children simply did not have the combination of charisma, organizational power, and wisdom necessary to maintain the vibrancy of the group.[266] By 1803 the three were barely able to provide for themselves, and nearly all the disciples in their town of Offenbach had wandered off. By 1810 the two brothers died and in 1816 Eva followed them.[267]

Soon afterwards, a final official conference was held and the group disbanded.[268] Most adherents slowly melted into the mainstream of Polish Catholicism during this period of the movement's disintegration.[269] Even so, small communities labored on and one such group is known to have moved together to the United States in the period 1848–1849.[270]

Hasidism as a Messianic Theology: Israel Baal Shem Tov (the Besht) (c. 1700–1760) and the Movement He Created

History is full of historical ironies. In the current context, the irony is that Hasidism rose in the same Podolia as the Frankist movement.[271] Similarly parallel is that during its founders' lifetime the strength of both movements never went above a few thousand in the region of their birth.[272] Furthermore, dissident movements that occur simultaneously will always have at least some conceptual parallels — parallels that will often be vastly exaggerated by their critics — and stories of other similarities will often be given credence even when based upon rumor and innuendo. Both Zevi and the Besht made their love for the Kabbalah a major element in their convictions.[273] They both found joy in the pleasures of life and, creatively interpreted, one could move on to use these and other matters to prove a dangerous linkage in their basic mind frame and attitudes.

Justified or not, this guilt by association with Zevi and the Frankist movement provided a major contemporary rationale for rejecting Hasidism. Zevi had proved a horrendous embarrassment both to the Jewish community and to cynical outsiders. It made most Jews deeply wary of any further tendency toward radical religious innovation.

In marked contrast with Frank, however, after the Besht's death, Hasidism began to grow dramatically until a large percentage of eastern European Jews embraced it.[274] Even in areas where it was not clearly dominant, a large minority embraced it.[275]

The story of the life of Israel Baal Shem Tov (better known as the Besht) was first published a half-century after his death in a volume entitled *In Praise of the Besht*. Although this provides much information, later scholars have found it extremely challenging to determine where the history ends and the myths take over.[276]

One highlight of his early years appears to have been a desire to be alone, to seek solitude for meditation and thinking. Indeed, legends later said that it was in the midst of one such forest sojourn that he received the divine revelation of those "truths" that were the foundation of his future spiritual development.

Even though he never had much formal education, he was still considered adequately prepared to work as a teacher's assistant, primarily assuring that the children safely reached school each day.[277] The income from this he supplemented in his early years as a woodcutter.[278] He then moved on to become a synagogue sexton.[279] In his spare time in this early period of his adulthood, he spent as much of his free time as feasible in an intense study of the Kabbalah.[280]

After he married, he worked in the clay and lime pits, and these products were then sold by his wife.[281] Unfortunately, his wife soon died. Later he remarried, and eventually his economic situation improved enough so that he and his wife were able to open an inn.[282] This business effort failed, and then the Besht became an itinerant traveling teacher and moralizer.[283] Perhaps it was his experience as an elementary educator that led him to his regularly use short illustrative stories and tales to illustrate spiritual, moral, and practical aspects of life.[284]

He built his reputation as a Ba'al Shem ("Master of the Name"), that is, an individual who invoked the various biblical, traditional, and esoteric names of God in order to heal and cast out demons.[285] This did not mean that he dismissed temporal means of healing; he regarded the two approaches as going hand in hand to produce the desired result. Especially important so far as temporal aids to healing was the effective and creative utilization of herbal remedies, of which he became an acknowledged master.[286] So good was he at his combination of divine invokings and herbal cures that his title was expanded to Ba'al Shem Tov ("Master of the Good Name").[287]

His "miraculous" cures attracted some to the movement. Later followers, though, carefully emphasized that such successes should never be permitted to obscure his central role of teacher and explainer of the divine.[288]

Nearly all such practitioners were cure-centered individuals. The Besht stood out because from the beginning of his public work during the 1730s, he violated the norm of what a later generation would call "nondenominationalism," i.e., the practice of his craft without appeal to some special set of teachings that he was propagating. Indeed, he was one of the few who combined healing with the teaching of specific spiritual "truths" and, even more impressively, began to win significant numbers to embrace them.[289]

The view of most of the early significant figures in the movement (and, therefore, presumably his own) was that everyone, theoretically, could join in mystical union with the Deity. On the other hand, there was a vast qualitative difference in that obtained by spiritual leaders as contrasted with the lesser success of their followers. Hence the true depths of the union could only be obtained indirectly, through careful adherence and loyalty to this select few.[290]

The depth and intensity of that human-divine conjunction could be magnified not only through traditional practices (such as Torah study and personal prayer) but also through normal everyday acts as varied as having a meal and having sex with one's spouse. What made the difference was the conscious desire to be united with the divine by such actions.[291] He refused to develop this concept to permit excess and immoral behavior; instead, his followers were encouraged toward a spirituality of joy in all the activities that honorable men and women would normally engage in.[292]

If one wished to use Christian terminology, one might well speak in terms of a "gospel of joy."[293] The movement was regarded, in contrast to the orthodox restraint of its day, as liberal in its attitude toward the innocent pleasures of life.[294] This alienation from the religious mainstream was strengthened by the conviction that purity of soul and religious intent was far more important and useful than mere Talmudic book-learning.[295] Not that the Besht despised the Torah in any fashion; he just thought it needed to be kept in its proper perspective. As he put it, "I came into the world to show another way, to cultivate the love of God, of Israel, and of the Torah, and there is no need for fasting and mortification."[296]

His biblical proof text for his positive and even jubilant attitude toward life was Isaiah 6:13, which speaks of the world around us being full of God's glory. Hence everything good in it should be recognized as reflecting that divine glory. To give a very inter human application of this emphasis, he once reminded his listeners, "Don't deny that a girl is beautiful. Just be sure that your recognition of her beauty brings you back to its source — God."[297]

With this went a further development of kabbalistic thinking.[298] One aspect of this was the effort of his followers to develop mystical union with the supernatural through what they called "attachment to the letters" of the Torah. As Stephen Sharot describes it: "One contemplated and meditated on each letter until they lost their contours, and their concreteness dissolved; then the divine attributes became visible, and the soul cleaved to God. Since the letters of the Hebrew alphabet were endowed with creative power, Hasidic prayer could participate in and assist the process of divine unification."[299]

Can early Hasidism be regarded as a messianic movement? This has been a topic of vigorous debate, with scholars arguing both sides of the matter.[300] Perhaps the clearest evidence that it was such can be seen in a dream the Besht recounted in one of his letters. In it he entered the heavenly temple and asked the Messiah point-blank when the promise of His coming would be fulfilled. He received the response, "By this you shall know: When your teaching — which I have taught you — has been revealed and spread in the world and the waters from your well have been scattered about."[301]

In short, the Besht and his teachings would prepare the world for the coming of the Messiah. The movement that spread it, therefore, constituted a messianic one in which the movement (rather than just its leader) served as a kind of collective "John the Baptist" preparatory role. The other side of the coin, though, is that the dream answer actually discouraged the Besht because he knew it would take an extremely long time for his message to gain that kind of widespread attention.[302] Whether one would date the coming of the Messiah in the near or short term, however, would not seem to have any impact on the movement's role in preparing the way for it whenever it occurred.

Nahman of Bratslav: Preparer for the Messiah (1772–1810)

Nahman manifested strong spiritual leanings from childhood, spending much time in secret prayer and attempting to bring his sexual urges under control, an effort he conceded was only successful after many years of struggle.[303] He married at 14 and, as was customary, moved into his father-in-law's residence. In the following years, his spiritual interests were so effectively shared with others that he attracted a significant following. Although he hesitated to bid for open recognition as a spiritual leader because he had seen such men repeatedly abuse their power, he finally concluded that he had the obligation to exercise his spiritual talents to the fullest.[304]

Hence Nahman became the zaddik (spiritual leader) for a group of Hasidic Jews in the late eighteenth and early nineteenth centuries.[305] He contended that every generation had one zaddik who performed the contemporary role of Moses and functioned as the pivotally important intermediary between the human race and God. According to him, in his generation he had been given that heavy responsibility.[306]

This claim ran into a problem: many said they had difficulty understanding his teaching. If his listeners had trouble understanding him, he explained, the blame was purely their own. Because of his unique status as God's agent, the simple fact was that no one could hope to fully comprehend him and his wisdom.[307]

On the practical level, he had a very different set of emphases than the bulk of contemporary rabbis. He had no objection to the serious study of the Torah or the Talmud; indeed, he thought such study was quite desirable.[308] Likewise, he was quite content with the religious forms of the contemporary synagogue. Yet he was convinced that such things too often became a substitute for true spiritual growth. In rebuke of this attitude, he said that, "All that I have achieved, I have achieved not through study, but through prayer."[309] If that were not enough, he described one Talmudist of his day as "a man who through sheer study of the Law has no time to think about God."[310]

Furthermore, any inclination to asceticism and the rejection of the honorable pleasures of this life was to be firmly rejected: "Whoever maintains that this life is worthless is in error: it is worth a great deal; only one must know how to use it properly."[311]

He argued that it was his role to bring about the salvation of the men and women of his day from the curse of sin — especially sexual sin.[312] The role of the zaddik had traditionally been interpreted as helping to accomplish this, but Nahman emphasized it to a degree not found in others.[313] As an early disciple of his recorded,[314]

> I heard that when he was in Lipovits he said to his disciples: "In what way can you repent? Would all of your combined strength and all your days suffice to repair even a small bit of the damage you have done? But I do penance for you, and God gives me the power to repair all that you have damaged (so long as you desist from conscious sin)."

Although Nahman sometimes lapsed into language equating himself with the Messiah,[315] he usually retained a clear distinction between the two.[316] This seems best expressed as a wavering in his own mind as to which best expressed his personal role in the divine plan of things. Indeed, it appears that both he and his disciples destroyed or censored his writings on this theme, deeming them inappropriate for open and explicit discussion where outsiders would have the material available.[317]

Although Nahman qualified to be messiah that did not mean that he alone could make that claim. At some point after having fathered a son, he announced the child as the promised Messiah.³¹⁸ His hopes in this direction were shattered when the boy died while still an infant.³¹⁹ It still did not shake his conviction of his own important role,³²⁰ but it did mark the point at which his messianic emphasis began to flicker and dramatically diminish.³²¹

Yet at another time he implied that the Messiah would be the product of the marriage of his daughter Sarah with Isaac Leib Dubrovner.³²² It was as if, by one means or another, he and his family would produce the Messiah; it was only a matter of how and when.

After he died, those loyal to his memory insisted that he would one day return in order to complete the defeat of evil that he had only begun during his lifetime.³²³ So intense was the loyalty to him that following generations refused to formally replace him as their rebbe, permanently reserving to him that unique status³²⁴ — a fact that in and of itself argues that his contemporaries viewed him in messianic or, at the minimum, near messianic terms.

Those outside of his movement remember him most for his absorbing short stories of injustice and danger. In them there are lost princesses denied their rightful kingdom and infants of unimportant families who have been substituted for the children of important individuals. The tales speak of the efforts to right such wrongs and, in some cases, the issue is left unresolved,³²⁵ as if to say that in real life not all injustices can be rectified. Involving both traditional fairy-tale elements and ones borrowed from contemporary folklore, they work on two levels, providing immediate entertainment to the reader but also, on a deeper level, often delivering moral/spiritual lessons for those looking for them.³²⁶ Indeed, these functioned virtually as a kind of contemporary new Scriptures, enlightening the hearer as to the intents and purposes of the original ones.³²⁷

10

Gentile Messiahs During the European Colonization of the Americas (1600–1800)

Edward Wightman (1612)

Born in Staffordshire, Wightman married in 1593 and fathered seven children. For a livelihood he became a mercer and it proved a successful outlet for his skills. In the spiritual arena, he came to the conclusion that infant baptism was scripturally unjustified and became not only what the era considered a "Baptist" but even a Baptist minister.[1]

His desire to defend his beliefs and convince others of their legitimacy resulted in his sending a petition to the king explaining and justifying these matters.[2] Rather than resulting in any change on King James' part, it brought the obscure merchant to the hostile king's attention and resulted in 11 charges of heresy being lodged against him.[3]

His trial was so heavily attended that, at one point, the hearings had to be moved to a more spacious facility to accommodate all those who wished to attend.[4] The trial record summed up his religious convictions (it appears, quite accurately and without misrepresentation) and included convictions such as these[5]:

- "That there is not the Trinity of persons (the Father, the Son, and the Holy Ghost) in the unity of the deity."
- "That Jesus Christ is not the true natural Son of God, perfect God and of the same substance, eternity and Majesty with the Father in respect of his Godhead."

10. Gentile Messiahs During the European Colonization 167

- "That Jesus Christ is only man and a mere creature and not both God and man in one person."
- "That Christ our Savior took not human flesh of the substance of the virgin Mary his mother."
- "Of the sin of blasphemy against the Holy Ghost, which shall never be pardoned in this life nor in the life to come, are meant of yourself [i.e., Wightman]."
- "That the soul doth sleep in the sleep of the first death as well as the body and is mortal as touching the sleep of the first death, at the body is. And that the soul of our savior Jesus Christ did sleep in that sleep of death as well as his body."

So far as prophetic status, he claimed to be the prophet that Malachi 4:5 says would be raised up by God,[6] a prediction that the New Testament applies to John the Baptist. Worse, he took Deuteronomy 18:18's promise of a new prophet like Moses and applied that prediction to himself,[7] a text that the New Testament applied to Christ (Acts 3:22; 7:37). Finally, the Comforter that Jesus promised in John 15:26 was fulfilled in him, he insisted.[8] Hence accepting his teaching was essential to one's salvation.[9] Unfortunately, this text was traditionally interpreted as a reference to the Holy Spirit and third person in the Trinity. Taking passages applied to both Jesus and the Holy Spirit was inevitably going to be viewed as blasphemy and, if taken seriously, as an indication that Wightman was claiming supernatural status as well

He was convicted of these dissident beliefs in December 1611[10] and the execution warrant listed 16 specific items of alleged heretical beliefs he had been found guilty of.[11]

Wightman's execution in 1612 made him a prominent footnote in the religious history of England: He was the last Englishman ever to be sent to the stake for doctrinal deviancy.[12] (This is a little misleading, for a few later individuals were, indeed, executed, but none by this specific method.)[13] His execution was a botched and embarrassing affair to those involved. The sheriff thought he heard Wightman hollering out a retraction of his beliefs and he ordered the execution stopped. When a few weeks passed and it was clear that he continued to teach the same things and refused to sign the required document of recantation, the sentence was again attempted, and this time completed, on April 11, 1612.[14]

Because of his claim to be a Baptist, he has sometimes been remembered as a martyr in the cause of religious liberty for daring to defy the established church's inflexible demand for sprinkling and childhood baptism.[15] For those who believe in church succession (i.e., the belief that one can trace the modern Baptist movement back to the first century through specific individuals and/or previous and differently named groups), there is more than one genealogy proposed. The Welch lineage traces itself through the Midlands Association of Baptists, of which Wightman was a member.[16]

What is often forgotten are the other charges made against him, most or all of which he clearly accepted, and which involved theological conclusions that few Baptists today would feel comfortable with and whose exponents they would not wish to have as a member.[17] Some of the charges were quite possibly overstated (a not untypical strategy for blackening the reputation of a doctrinal deviant) and even at the time there were those who were convinced that even if they were all valid, he was clearly insane rather than a heretic.[18]

William Franklin (late 1640s)

For most of his life, this rope-maker was respected as honest in business, dedicated to his family, and devoutly religious.[19] While pursuing his trade just outside London in the mid-1640s, several members of his family died and he himself suffered a life-threatening illness. Then he began to speak in literally unknown tongues. This might have been viewed as merely eccentric if had not also begun to act in an entirely new manner toward his family. He had not really fathered his supposed children, he insisted. He wasn't actually married to his supposed wife, though they had lived together for many years as such. And then there were the beatings he started to give this alleged nonwife, a brutality thoroughly out of keeping with his past behavior.[20]

Into this tumultuous domestic situation came one Mary Gadbury. Seven years previously, her husband had deserted her in preference for one of their servants. She willingly listened to Franklin's visions and voices, and they thoroughly enchanted her.[21] Her faith was tried but temporarily when he insisted that he was Jesus Christ. Furthermore, his past marriage was inherently invalid: It had been in his untransformed body of sin. Since he had undergone the transformation to something greater, such relationships were now totally irrelevant to his behavior and conduct.[22] This freed him to follow his God-ordained future role with Mary: She was to be literally the Bride of the Lamb,[23] taking the description of the church in the Book of Revelation in its relationship to Jesus and applying it to himself.

She accepted and traveled with him as his wife as he taught his divine revelations and recruited disciples. She began having visionary experiences herself as well. Both her own religious experiences and those of Franklin attracted disciples, and soon they had a small group of reliable supporters.[24] At least one Church of England minister, William Woodward, was so impressed by Franklin while the man lodged with him that he openly endorsed Franklin's claims.[25] Franklin and Gadbury were often provided housing and food by local disciples. But there were limits to the practicality of such a means of support, and he periodically returned to London to take a job and replenish his coffers.[26]

In addition to his direct supernatural claims, he asserted that God had provided him additional revelations. One, for example, proclaimed, "I have made an end of sin and transgression for me and my people."[27] Unfortunately, its actual meaning to him and his followers is uncertain,[28] though one natural interpretation would be that it meant that through Franklin sin and evil would be atoned for and removed.

In or about 1646, Franklin went through a stage in which he felt abandoned by God. His physician thought the solution for this spiritual depression was quite down to earth: blood-letting.[29] Whether that was the cause of his recovered confidence is unknown, but he was soon going about once again proclaiming his doctrinal beliefs.

The oddity of his religious claims was guaranteed to attract public legal note sooner or later. But what brought actual action against him and Mary lay not in his doctrines but in his relationship with Mary: What was he doing living in a relationship with a woman not his legal wife?[30] As the result, in January of 1649, he was brought to trial in Winchester. In an effort to save himself, he conceded that his claims had been false and insisted that it was because he had yielded to the temptation of the Devil. In vivid contrast, Mary could not bring herself to repudiate the visions and ecstatic experiences she had undergone nor to repudiate her faith in Franklin.[31]

Convicted on charges of adultery, both were sent on to London for sentencing and imprisonment. The woman's case especially annoyed the judges and, after a week in jail and a whipping, she recanted her adherence to Franklin as Christ. She absolutely refused to admit there had ever been any sexual relationship between the two. The judges literally laughed in her face at the denial.[32]

Considerable public pressure was building up for leniency, however. Large numbers of individuals visited them in jail and spoke with the judges to seek mercy.[33]

In light of his public goodwill and his recantation, Franklin was permitted to present a bond for his good conduct.[34] In light of Mary's stubborn refusal to admit the true sexual relationship the judges were convinced had existed, they made her serve a full year in jail.[35]

The pamphlet *Pseudochristus* appeared in May of 1650 and described in detail the life of Franklin. Anger at the supposed Messiah likely caused the drafting and presentation to Parliament of the Blasphemy Act to cover such individuals.[36] This proposal was written broadly enough to apply to men as diverse as atheists and those who denied the existence of heaven or hell as literal places in which the dead would exist. Others ran afoul for insulting Christianity in general. Claiming that one would trade a large container of beer for all the religions in the world did not go over well with judges, nor did the unwise fellow who announced he would rather be in bed with the woman he desired than go to paradise after he died.[37] Of course, it could also be used as a tool of repression against messianic claimants who had become a public nuisance as well. This was the apparent direct cause of the act being drafted and adopted.

King Charles as Messiah (1644)

The long-going breach between Parliament and King Charles finally erupted into civil war and led to his execution. In a historically amazingly short period of time, dominant religious opinion had been transformed from the "divine right of kings" to the "divine right to execute kings." English rulers had grudgingly and often unwillingly been subject to varying degrees of restraint and modified policies due to popular pressure and, specifically, Parliamentarian pressure. For the first time, the right was demanded and exercised to violently remove and execute a king who had drifted too far from the will of the majority of the English population.

Yet Charles had his core of supporters, as all rulers did. One of these was a poor laborer by the name of Roland (others record it as Reynold) Bateman. He came to public attention during the summer of 1644 after declaring himself to be "Abel the Righteous" and taught that he would be arrested, put to death, and rise from the dead.[38]

He had been involuntarily forced into the new Parliamentarian army and quickly deserted it. He was caught in Essex, and the local Assize demanded to know why he had done this.[39] He explained that his flight was due to a deep religious conscience and recognition that the king had a theological importance that even his most passionate supporters would have hesitated to claim. The army, he explained, by pressing him into military service "did compel God to go against God. And that the young child that is conceived in King Charles and himself, both united in one, is the

King of Heaven and ... that when he shall be put to death then King Charles will come home and not before." In addition, no one had an adequate "knowledge of the Scripture, but King Charles and himself and three Lords. And ... when he ... is put to death after three days he shall rise again and then whom he will he will save and whom he will he will damn."[40]

John Robins of London: God in the Flesh (c. 1650)

After Cromwell's Protectorate was established, among the religious radicals who sprang up was one John Robins. He preached that his mission was to gain 144,000 faithful followers. Afterwards a miracle would take them to Palestine and they would survive in their new homeland by supernaturally granted manna.[41] Robins was a tee-totaler in an age when drinking was virtually universal, and he insisted that this course was one that his 144,000-man army had to embrace — or, at least, that small part of that number that he managed to gather — in order to prepare themselves for the rigors and responsibility of their holy crusade to liberate the promised land. As to food, he began to insist that they were to literally survive on bread alone.[42]

On the other hand, there were certain advantages to be gained from these sacrifices. Beyond divine approval and the assurance of abundant food in their new homeland (a not unimportant promise in an age of widespread poverty), there were more immediate rights as well. For example, one had the right to leave one's spouse and take a new one, as one might think best.[43]

Furthermore, John was none other than God the father (hence the biblical Adam's creator),[44] his pregnant wife was the Virgin Mary, and their child, quite naturally in such a formulation, was to be Christ.[45] Some argue that the identification of them as God, Mary, and Christ came from his supporters rather than Robins himself and that all he publicly professed was his mission to lead the liberation of Jerusalem.[46] Yet if he limited himself in this manner, he seems to have undertaken no firm action to squash the tales that mangled his reputation among outsiders— at least not before he was imprisoned.

Their home in London was finally visited by the authorities and Robins, his wife, and 10 supporters were arrested.[47] Imprisoned, Robins backed off from his deityship claims.[48] In contrast, a large proportion of his supporters loudly and persistently refused to do so.[49]

Some followers quietly drifted away from the movement as Robins' hopes failed to materialize. Others left it embittered. Lodowick Muggleton, for example, did not remain in the movement for long. As he started developing his own body of disciples, he wrote a letter to Robins denouncing his claims.[50] Indeed, as time went by he became convinced that Robins was not only not God but actually "the last great Antichrist."[51]

Robins is often labeled a Ranter[52] but this seems more because of certain similarities in belief and his outlandish claims rather than to any actual connection with such groups. In other words, there is the strong tendency today to think of the Ranters in terms of being a movement rather than as a more formal and organized church or sect. They were men and women moving in a similar conceptual world rather than being organizationally tied together in a distinct religious body.[53]

The Quaker Christ: James Nayler (c. 1617–1660)[54]

Although a man known for his gentleness, such was the temper and the perceived needs of the day that he volunteered at age 25 for military duty and served for seven years in the Parliamentary army during its conflicts with the Royalists.[55] His ability was rewarded with his promotion to the position of quartermaster and he was respected for his character and conduct throughout those years.[56]

Unfortunately, he contracted a serious case of tuberculosis and was forced to leave the army. Returning home, he again took up farming and his health gradually returned.[57]

That first winter home, in 1651, marked a turning point in his life, for he met George Fox and became convinced of his doctrine of the "inner light" that could reveal God's will and shape one's life.[58] While plowing one day, Nayler heard God's voice commanding him to leave the farm immediately and begin preaching God's message. Obeying the command to leave without extra garments and without even informing his family, he proceeded to travel, teaching the Quaker doctrine.[59]

Due to the manifest success of his ministry he is considered cofounder of the Quaker movement along with George Fox, now better remembered.[60] Indeed, Nayler had a better education than Fox and initially matched him in popularity.[61]

Nayler was arrested twice for minor offenses, but this did nothing to hinder his teaching ministry. Some creative mind noted that the Elizabethan law against "wandering persons"—legislation which targeted beggars—was actually written broadly enough to encompass itinerant ministers of the Quaker or any other stripe who seemed to potentially endanger the public order. In spite of harassment with this as its legal pretext, he continued his preaching until it brought him to London and regular contact with Fox.[62]

So enchanted were women followers by his message that some became convinced that Nayler was far more than mortal. Fox warned him against yielding to their ego-building entrapments.[63] Martha Simmons was one of the louder voices encouraging just such an interpretation of his true nature. Condemned in writing by other Quakers for her enthusiasm, she insisted that Nayler embrace it. Staying for three days in the home of her and her husband, he wrestled in prayer over what to believe and do. On the one hand, he felt drawn to the elevation of his status that such women were proclaiming; on the other hand, he felt as if that mysterious "inner light" was flickering at the same time.[64]

Although Simmons' behavior was excessive even by Quaker standards, it must be remembered that the modern staid and formal, restrained form of that religion only came later. In its early stages it was a highly emotional system in which people literally did shake and quake as they gathered together in their religious services.[65]

Nayler dealt with his mental confusion by fleeing to Bristol. Learning he was there, Simmons followed him there and embarrassed the other Quakers by her display of worship at Nayler's feet.[66] Yet a small faction insisted on standing steadfastly by her side, joining her in their enthusiasm,[67] and their persistence began to wear away his resistance.

In the public mind, the abiding image of Nayler was the day he attempted to recreate the triumphal entry of Jesus into Jerusalem, but in the streets of the seaport of Bristol, England, instead. In October 1655 he rode into the city on a horse. In front and behind were a few men and women who were chanting, "Hosanna, Holy, Holy, Lord God of Sabaoth." As one would expect, one of them was Martha Simmons.[68] His followers spread their clothes in front of Nayler and his horse, as they had done repeatedly on the way to Bristol.[69] Nayler himself was passive, quiet, seemingly in a trance as his followers gloried in his presence and supernaturalness.[70] In keeping with his claims, he had adopted the hair and beard style depicted in contemporary images of Christ.[71] (In fairness to the man, however, it should be remembered that he had always struck people as having a surprising similarity to such pictures.[72])

Although this behavior attracted a large and boisterous crowd in spite of the inclement weather, what is of special interest is that Nayler attracted little or no support from the local Quaker community either at the moment or during his ensuing confinement. This could be either because they were appalled at the supernatural claim being made or because Fox's supporters had done their work well of neutralizing support for his rival.[73] This implicit repudiation had to be emotionally stunning; Bristol was one of the major centers of Quakerism, a place where meetings had an attendance of several thousands.[74]

Some have attempted to find an explanation of the procession that strips it of its Christocentric intentions. George Amoss, Jr., suggests it may have been "a bit of 'street theater' to demonstrate the fundamental Quaker experience that the same Spirit which was in Jesus and his disciples is available to us today...."[75] If so, it was an extraordinarily inflammatory way to make the point, and his supporters clearly declined to repudiate the "second Christ" implications of the act.

Others attempt to remove the stigma of Nayler being recognized as Christ by arguing that it was customary for individuals to make plain their religious commitments and enthusiasm by a dramatic overstatement of their core convictions in a form that was not intended to be taken literally.[76] However, we have here far more than mere rhetorical exaggeration in an event clearly designed to imitate Jesus' triumphal entry into Jerusalem and with similar language used of Jesus being applied to Nayler. Why, then, would observers have any reason to take the language as anything but literal?

The strange procession attracted a crowd, and the city magistrates sent a messenger to call the group to a meeting before them. By now his spirit had revived and he candidly conceded that he was both James Nayler and God's Son; the two were one and the same.[77]

For the time being, they were thrown in jail. Being there must have almost been a relief from the pressures he faced from his followers. Fox was also in jail in another place at the same time and Martha was able to talk her way into his cell. She laid it on the line: "Your heart is rotten. You must yield up your command to James Nayler."[78] Fox's sharp response went ignored.[79]

She then marched to the jail where Nayler was held. She brought with her various letters from friends and associates addressing him as if he were Christ or God. He read and meditated on the letters and wondered whether so many people, all supposedly guided by the divine inner light, could possibly be wrong.[80] When a female Quaker in another cell had drifted into unconsciousness and nothing could awaken her, Nayler was permitted to see if he could be of assistance. When he touched her, she immediately revived. To those already so inclined, this was miraculous external proof that he was, indeed, the Christ returned.[81]

Fox's first goal after being released from his latest imprisonment was to visit Nayler. As much as he wished a full reconciliation, so far as he was

10. Gentile Messiahs During the European Colonization 175

concerned the man had disgraced himself and could never again be considered on a par with him. A less friendly interpretation would have it a case of wounded pride; that Nayler had been all too clearly opposing Fox in intrachurch conflicts. Or, as R. A. Knox describes the broader conflict of the two men, "It was not that he was attempting to make himself equal with the Savior of the world, but that he was attempting to make himself equal with George Fox."[82]

When the two met, it would have been normal to exchange a friendly kiss either before or after the meeting. As Fox recorded the meeting, Nayler was not receptive to what he had to say, "yet he would have come and kissed me. But I said that since he had turned against the power of God, I could not receive his show of kindness. The Lord moved me to slight him, and to set the power of God over him."[83]

A less friendly interpretation would make it a case of wounded pride, since Fox offered him a boot to kiss instead of a cheek.[84] Such self-humiliation was beyond Nayler, and the meeting quickly ended.[85] The breach with Fox now was set in concrete and it is perhaps not surprising that Nayler now embraced the enthusiastic excess appraisal that others had bestowed upon him. After all, the alternative was a degree of self-abnegation few could have summoned themselves to give.

Meanwhile, the local government still had to decide what to do with Nayler. Their interrogation of him and other participants did nothing to reassure them. Sometimes it was not what the Quakers said but what they implied that shocked. Quakers refused to remove their hats even for government officials and only did so when praying. Timothy Wedlock had escorted Nayler into the city with the bare head that Quakers showed to deity and not to man. When pressed for his reason he responded, "I must do it if God command me; I did it as I was moved by the Spirit."[86] Perplexed and suspecting that they were out of their depths, the officials passed the problem to Parliament.

The bold imitation of Jesus' triumphal entry doubtless annoyed a good number of Parliamentarians, but of more concern was that he was both a Quaker (equated with radical irresponsibility) and that he was clearly gaining more supporters every week (which made him a potential source of civil unrest).[87] Standing trial before the Parliamentarians, Nayler impressed even these men who were predisposed to think the worst even while asserting his claims to be Christ.[88] Yet the grandiosity of his own words repeatedly undermined his sincerity and the good impression he made.

Admittedly, if one finds such reasoning congenial, one could argue that he did not mean that he was literally Christ but that it was the Christ *within* him that he referred to, but such fine distinctions seem to have been beyond his ability to articulate, and definitely were beyond that of his judges to take seriously.[89] Certainly, some of his remarks can be read in this manner,[90] yet this was far from the case with all of them. When he was asked, "Are you the everlasting Son of God?" the answer without hesitation or equivocation was, "Where God is manifest in the flesh, there is the everlasting Son, and I do witness God in the flesh; I am the Son of God, and the Son of God is but one," thereby seemingly obliterating any distinction between himself and the Christ within.[91]

His supporters, who were called to testify, made no attempt at rationalization: They bluntly and candidly held forth his role as Christ, and their very candor in proclaiming him as Savior made the judges even more determined that some severe punishment needed to be inflicted.[92] The letters he carried with him from his supporters were, upon occasion, equally blunt. Hannah Stranger had written to him, "Oh thou fairest of ten thousand, thou only begotten Son of God, how my heart panteth after thee...." John, her spouse, had added a note to the letter: "Remember my dear love to thy Master. Thy name is no more to be called James but Jesus."

It was a close call for Nayler; he escaped death by a margin of 14 votes: 96 to 82.[93] Yet many believed he deserved no punishment (beyond that of public opinion) or were convinced that any punishment would make a martyr and hero of the man.[94] Yet the punishment that was voted was still a severe one. He was to be publicly whipped in both London and Bristol, a hole burned through his tongue, and a "B" (for "blasphemer") burned into his skull. Afterwards he was to be displayed in the pillory and then imprisoned.[95]

Imprisonment (and the rejection by the bulk of Quakers) ultimately sobered Nayler's fantasies. He sent out a letter while in jail condemning "all those false worships with which any have idolized my person in the night of my temptation."[96] It was not quite an admission that he had accepted the claims being made of him, but certainly an acknowledgment of what his disciples' language intended and that he had been deeply tempted by the praise.

After Richard Cromwell abdicated on behalf of a new king, Nayler was freed from jail in 1659. He soon traveled to Bristol and confessed to Fox how profoundly wrong he had been. He was admitted once again into his fellowship and even given the opportunity to preach before his fellow Quakers, but he did not have much time left to live. He died in October 1660, while traveling from London to visit his family. His long-suffering wife, who had endured desertion, rejection, and the public humiliation of her husband's religious excesses, had accepted him back while he was in jail.[97]

Historical Context: Fifth Monarchy Men

This British movement was convinced that the return of Jesus was imminent and cited as evidence the grievous and bloody disturbances on the European mainland as prime evidence that their interpretation of scriptural prophecy was correct. Dates in the mid-1650s and mid-1660s were especially popular among them.[98] The year 1666 had a special resonance for some because of the last three digits being the number of the beast in the Book of Revelation. Indeed, of all the alternatives this was the one most widely accepted, and it was embraced by many with no involvement at all in the Fifth Monarchy movement itself.[99] Although there had been significant agitation on behalf of the date in earlier decades, the 1666 alternative reached its greatest popularity beginning in 1660. It remained in the forefront of public opinion until the date proved itself futile through nonfulfillment.[100]

Some individuals thought they could move along the prophetic program by attempting to raise insurrection.[101] The propriety even of rebellion to establish their understanding of God's truth grew, in part, out of the peculiar political circumstances in which they lived.[102] The English monarchy seemed so mired in sin and opposition to God's will that it must be equated with the corrupt Babylon of the Book of Revelation and doomed to receive divine wrath. From that premise, various incidents in the Apocalypse were interpreted as having been fulfilled in the recent history of the country.[103]

Combined with this was the conviction that they had not only the inherent right as freeborn Englishmen to strike out against tyranny but also the demand of Scripture itself compelling them to do so[104]:

> Major-General Harrison quoted Daniel 7:18 to a skeptic: "The saints … shall *take* the kingdom." Their favorite was Psalm 149:6–9, in which the saints were authorized to 'bind their kings with chains, and their nobles with fetters of iron." … Though God alone had the power to establish his kingdom, He had chosen to work through His saints on earth. This seemed to be the clear meaning of Jeremiah 51:20: "Thou art my battle axe and weapons of war: for with thee will I break in pieces the nations, and with thee will destroy kingdoms." … Tillinghast argued that every generation had a special divine duty. "The present work of God is, to bring down lofty men, to lay men low, and to throw down Antichrist."

This was, however, a two-edged political sword, exposing the Fifth Monarchy Men to censure from moderate radicals as well as those more conventional in their Anglican or Roman Catholic theologies: It raised the bloody spectacle of Munster. The Fifth Monarchists were repeatedly tarred individually and collectively by critics arguing that their theology was so extreme that the excesses found in Germany might be brought to England and plunge their nation into chaos.[105]

The Fifth Monarchists responded in three different ways to this accusation. Some vigorously repudiated the Munsterites as wrong in action and as not reflecting anything in their own theology. Another group stressed that the accounts came from those who hated the Munster revolution and that no one could be sure of what the real facts were. As for atrocities, if they occurred at all, they were certainly to be condemned. Yet another group tried to change the subject by arguing that the Lutheranism and Calvinism being opposed by Munster was just as evil as the "Romanism" condemned in England.[106]

The virtue of insurrection as a positive and constructive aspect of the Christian religion did not spring up overnight. It was the result of an intense reexamination of the Scriptures as spurred on by actual events. Without the specific course of opposition and attempted suppression that the religio-political establishment of the day attempted to impose upon dissenters, a revolutionary theology would have remained a fringe theory and lacking major support. Faced with what seemed a "do or die" situation that was reinforced by the political policies embraced by the government, men felt compelled to embrace actions and theory that even a generation or two before would have been regarded as abhorent.

The course of events in which this radicalization evolved developed along this line: Charles I (1625–1649) was faced with a series of problems, some of his own making, that drove grievous divisions into the country. The escalating prices of all products not only harmed the common man but meant a major increase in the basic costs of maintaining a monarchy. Parliament did not take kindly to the idea of making a challenging economic situation worse by increasing taxes.[107] The king's various attempts to overcome this opposition by finding methods to increase revenue that did not directly fall under Parliament's control did nothing but intensify their anger.[108]

The religious issues were equally volatile. Foreign policy overlapped reformation concerns when the English government tried to stay out of European conflicts that seemed to give the "Romanists" the opportunity to take back much of the Europe they had lost. Domestically, Charles accepted a French Roman Catholic as bride and this provided a convenient excuse to explain why Puritans were treated more repressively than the members of the Church of Rome. The antiliturgical wing of the Anglican Church represented a body of sentiment that grew during his reign and refused to be intimidated by the royally backed efforts in the opposite direction.[109] This shift likely would have occurred regardless of who the king had married, but the choice of marriage partner increased the alienation.

The king vastly overplayed his royal status when he followed Archbishop Laud's advice in attempting to apply his Laudian hierarchical and "ritualistic" church system to Scotland in the late 1630s. In effect, Presbyterian-dominated Scotland declared religious independence and, to make it viable, political separation as well.

Faced with the need to raise an army to subjugate the rebellious region — a vast expense — he called Parliament into session to negotiate with it for the best he could obtain. Having been humiliated in his reach for new power over the church, this put him in an extraordinarily difficult situation which only a political genius far superior to his could have altered to his own betterment.[110]

When Charles in January 1642 decisively repudiated striking a compromise with Parliament and began the civil war by attempting to arrest hostile Parliamentarians, two distinct but overlapping issues were fundamental. To the legally and Parliamentarian inclined, the paramount issue was the right of Parliament to speak for the nation and to keep the king — any king — from usurping his position by denying the people and their representatives their rights. To the Puritan idealists, the core issue was one of whether royalty would support papalism in England (of which Laudianism was regarded as but a thinly veiled variety) or whether the nation would maintain its loyalty to Christ. By equating Laudianism with papalism and the Antichrist, the emotional fervor of opposition was ratcheted even higher.[111]

Pivotal to success would be the power and ability of the Parliamentarian army and the reaction of the Scots. The army functioned well, and the Scots joined forces to crush the royalists. This created a new set of religious problems. The country was faced with the rival claims of the Calvinists, who wished to maintain a strong, centralized but non-hierarchical "purified" church, and a variety of religious dissenters, who saw in the new regime the opportunity for general religious freedom of choice, often in a far more decentralized form and varied content than the Calvinists desired. The Calvinists were horrified to discover after the formation in 1645 of the New Model Army that the worldview of the Baptists and other religious "independents" was gaining dominance in the new institution. Their own millennial dream had been effectively co-opted by those of a very different religious emphasis.[112]

After a period of peace, civil war broke out again in 1648 as the king attempt to regain the ascendancy. Although a significant number of

Calvinists had now shifted their loyalties to the regal side, they were successfully defeated by Cromwell's New Model Army. The army had had enough of Parliament's unsuccessful efforts to negotiate an understanding with the king and moved later in the same year to purge these unsuccessful compromisers so that a firm and consistent religio-political reform of the land could be executed. By this means the "Long Parliament" was transformed into "the Rump" composed of those willing to push on relentlessly toward their shared goals.[113]

Things moved at a swift pace in this period. The king was executed in January 1649. The army gained victory after victory in both Scotland and Ireland. Widespread amongst the army troops was the view that they were fighting on the side of Christ in the battles depicted in the Book of Revelation.[114]

Because they viewed Cromwell's government as a monumental step in preparing the world for the inauguration of the returned Christ's earthly kingdom, Fifth Monarchy men formed a major element of support for the new regime.[115] Indeed, messianic/redeemer style rhetoric was freely heaped upon him by enthusiastic supporters.[116] More moderate supporters warned against such verbal excesses, pointing to the unresolved impurities and failures in the land as a whole.[117] (For what it is worth, the pro-restoration writers who came afterwards used even more enthusiastic messianic or millennial language to describe Charles II being returned to power after Cromwell.[118])

Even those Puritans unwilling to bestow a messianic "crown" on Cromwell still saw the dramatic changes before, during, and after the English Civil War as part of the effort to create a truly godly society and as part of the human preparation for the imminent earthly triumph of God's kingdom.[119] So intense was this that Puritans in the new world discovered that those of a similar mindset in England — the overwhelmingly dominant element in those willing to undertake the potentially dangerous journey to New England — were no longer willing to take the risk of immigration. As John Winthrop wrote at the time, the anticipation of this made "all men to stay in England in expectation of a new world."[120] Those moved to millennial expectations did not do so out of desperation or despair; they did so because they saw the kind of positive and constructive revolutionary changes in the world around them that seemed ready to transform the humble earthly soil into an idyllic, heavenly earthly millennium.[121]

Yet however glowing an interpretation they preferred to put on Cromwell and the *potential* for creating a truly pious government in the land, it did not take long for the ever-present human imperfections and human disagreements to enter the picture. As the result, a major faction came to view even the Rump Parliament as too little enthused for the perfectionist/millenialists' aspirations of the day. Some of these men supported Cromwell; others were suspicious even of him. The latter found in Major-General Harrison — the highest-ranking officer clearly in their camp — an individual more visibly and clearly in tune with their millennial aspirations. His supporters came in a variety of forms and included those who believed that private property could be abolished, all hierarchy eliminated, and everyone enjoy exactly the same liberties.[122]

One thing they could all agree on, though, was that the Rump had not gone far enough. In 1651 the Fifth Monarchists crystallized into a distinct movement out of this determination to replace the Rump with a more enthusiastic group backing their hopes for a purified earthly kingdom of Christ.[123] To complicate the picture further, the hard core of the movement in Parliament consisted of only a one-twelfth of the entire body, but their actual support was subject to dramatic increase according to what specific legislative action was being discussed or voted upon.[124] In other words, ever-shifting coalitions formed over specific issues rather than, primarily, because of support of a clear-cut party. As the result of this and high absenteeism, the outcome of most votes could never be predicted, adding a further element of instability to the entire situation.[125]

Cromwell and such significant Independent religious leaders as Thomas Goodwin and John Owen vigorously opposed the Fifth Monarchists on their core earthly spiritual kingdom agenda.[126] Yet the growing public animosity against the Rump was so strong that even Cromwell was ultimately won over to act against Parliament, even though it ran the danger of increasing the power of his foes. As the result, in 1653 he staged a coup and dissolved the existing institution. He viewed the Rump as incapable of agreeing to a viable consensus that would reunite the country and as stubbornly refusing to embrace the social changes he believed essential for the welfare of the nation.[127] In short, he had to run the risks of acting against it.

Likely in large part to avoid confrontations over how the franchise for a new Parliament was to be determined, he opted for a different method of resolving the potential difficulty, but one which had already been bandied about: Through discussion with his most important officers, the members of the Barebones Parliament (also known as the Parliament of Saints) were selected.[128] Cromwell saw in this new group the potential to perfect God's plans for England: "Truly, you are called by God to rule with him and for him."[129]

In spite of the fact that these new representatives were not selected through the church as the Fifth Monarchists wanted, few of them broke with Cromwell over the matter.[130] A major reason was probably that the Fifth Monarchy Men themselves represented a larger percentage of Parliamentarians than before, though still not rising to the level of the controlling element in the Barebones. Even so, they energetically pushed a religious agenda that called for the formal abolishment of obligatory tithing and a political agenda that called for major changes in the British legal system.[131]

As in the Rump, the Barebones legislated through the combination and dissolution of an ever-shifting variety of factions that came together in temporary alliances over one issue or another, only to split and appear in rearranged alliances over the next matter on the legislative calendar.[132] When faced with the reality that no faction had sufficient support to enact its set of preferences, Cromwell became the target for vehement denunciation by supporters of the Fifth Monarchy. Efforts to reach a general compromise were unavailing, and the anti–Fifth Monarchists agreed with Cromwell that social chaos would be the result if that element gained their way. Hence in December 1653 these men collectively resigned, denying Parliament a working majority. This left only Fifth Monarchists, and they were forcibly compelled to leave the Parliament building as well.[133] Thereafter they were Cromwell's bitter rivals and undying in their opposition.[134]

Cromwell had had a major problem removed but he still did not have what was obviously needed — a stable means of governing the land. With a Parliamentary government unable to be obtained, this left Cromwell to rule alone, and he did so under the title of "Protector." The army could have posed a problem, but the chronic unrest and the inability to arrive at a consensus had fatally undermined the willingness of most to push matters to the level of confrontation (not to mention that a large number held significantly different views of the ideal millennial state than did the Fifth Monarchists). Though there was much muttering in the ranks and various resignations, no mutiny ensued, and the army felt compelled to put confidence in Cromwell to achieve success since Parliament had repeatedly failed.[135]

Even most of the religious radicals of the day (and many who simply wanted a government capable of governing) backed the new regime as the best approach to an impossible situation. The sole holdouts were the Fifth Monarchists.[136] They propagandized loudly and at length but found that they could not broaden their base of support; their opportunity to decisively shake up the political structure had passed.[137] As they bluntly pointed out, many individuals who had previously worked with them to remove insufficiently pious and just Parliaments now refused to back a continuation of the effort. On the other hand, their former allies were now more concerned with societal stability than with fulfillment of their one time joint hopes.[138]

Oliver Cromwell died in 1658. His son Richard succeeded him, but was unable to retain the loyalty of the military. In 1659 the Parliament that had been under Protectorate control was dissolved after pressure from the army. A restoration of the old Rump Parliament seemed the most generally accepted alternative, so those who had been members of that group were restored to their old seats and offices.[139] Internal divisions were profound, and the army refused to obey this Parliament. It was dissolved but, after it was clear that the military was deeply divided over the issue, was allowed to resume office. Bitter division within the military and among those inside Parliament left the situation chaotic.[140]

In February 1660 General Monk seized London and replaced the Rump with the members who had constituted the Long Parliament. Its members supported giving the throne to Charles II, which occurred in May of that year. In spite of much effort to bring about the rejection of this choice and, failing that, another military intervention, it was all for naught. The revolutionary political and religious enthusiasm had run its course and too few now believed it to be a viable alternative.[141]

In 1661 a desperate Fifth Monarchist revolt was launched to abort these changes. It was done out of the conviction that since they were doing God's will, He would give them the triumph over the royalists. It turned out to be not faith (which is based on evidence) but desperation (which is driven by the lack of alternative paths to success) that was being manifested: The revolt was decisively crushed.[142]

Thomas Tany (c. 1654–1655)

The idea of living and abiding in Jerusalem was not merely a dream cherished by Jews, but one which enticed certain Protestant radicals of the day as well. One Thomas Tany discovered by divine revelation in 1649 that he was actually a Jew and had been ordained to lead Jews and Gentile supporters to Palestine.[143] Indeed, his own role in the divine plan was even greater, for he had been designated by God to rule over them as king when they arrived.[144]

He announced this to the world in a tract entitled *I Proclaime from the Lord of Hosts The Returne of the Jewes*, which appeared in 1650, quite possibly printed in part at the expense of Robert Norwood of the High Court of Justice.[145] Unquestionably, Norwood felt so closely aligned to

Tany that he provided an essay to go with Tany's remarks in a pamphlet issued the following year.[146]

A London goldsmith by trade, as Tany told it, he was a descendant of Aaron, the first Jewish high priest. From this lineage, he claimed the right to be high priest over God's people as well.[147] More recently, he was also the descendant of Henry VII. As such, he felt he rightly deserved to rule over not only Palestine but also England as well — not to mention France and parts of Italy, which had been under the control of his purported ancestors.[148]

The impact that even such an outspoken advocate as Tany could have on the very respectable elements of seventeenth century society can be demonstrated through his ability to gain such well-respected supporters as John Pordage and Robert Norwood and how their lives became legally and ecclesiastically intertwined — to the detriment of his followers.

John Pordage was rector of Bradfield in Berkshire and was widely suspected of having meetings in which he and his family communicated with angelic beings. He was initially acquitted on such charges in 1651, but these charges were revived in late 1654, with an abundance of many additional accusations thrown in for good measure, including that of providing Tany with food and lodging. Enough of the charges were believed that he was stripped of his ministerial post.[149] Cynics suspect that a major motive of the prosecution lay not in Pordage's support for a delusional heretic but in the desire to free up his parish and the substantial financial stipend that went with it for a more "deserving" individual.[150]

As for Norwood, in April 1651 Tany began to give a series of well-attended speeches at his home. Challenged in private about embracing Tany's teachings, Norwood appeared in church in April to publicly affirm them. The retaliation came quickly in the form of excommunication. He was then called to appear before Oliver Cromwell and refused to heed the admonitions he received from Cromwell's councilors.[151]

In June he was charged, along with Tany, with the two blasphemies of denying the existence of hell and of arguing that the human soul represents the essence of the Deity. In light of the seriousness of the charges, it is not surprising that the two pleaded not guilty. In the same month, Parliament judged him unfit to be serve on the High Court and removed him from office.[152]

When tried in August, Tany refused to back away from his expressed convictions, while Norwood seemed to waver as if on the verge of repudiation of them. Regardless of any wavering, the two men were sentenced to six months jail time in Newgate Prison as punishment for these opinions.[153] While imprisoned, Norwood challenged the convictions on grounds which would have gotten both men released: He argued that it was improper to try them jointly rather than separately. Furthermore, the law only condemned those who denied the existence of both heaven and hell, while their challenged convictions only related to the latter. Finally, he contended that the connotations the judge and jury placed on the mutual beliefs of Norwood and Tany concerning the soul were their deductions from the convictions and not the convictions themselves.[154]

The court refused to accept the arguments, and the two men had to serve out their full term in confinement.[155] When it was completed, a condition of their release was the providing of a cash bond to assure their proper behavior for the following year.[156]

Norwood's crusade against the convictions did not end with their release, however. In June 1652 Norwood managed to have the convictions thrown out on narrow technicalities.[157] Nevertheless, the time in jail drastically cooled Norwood's enthusiasm for the prophet.[158] Even so, as time passed he reconsidered and decided that his fundamental embracal of Tany as legitimate ruler had been quite sound and proper. Hence in June 1654 he again went on record as backing the man's claim to several thrones, including those of England and France.[159]

However enthusiastic Norwood might be about Tany, Tany's convictions were immensely out of step with anything that might be considered within the normal range of contemporary English religious convictions. As it developed, his theology included the rejecting of any final judgment on the behavior of mankind.[160] Hell did not exist as a place but was a mere "state"—the state of alienation from God.[161] He despised contemporary organized religion with a passion. It was all, he insisted, "a lie, a cheat, a deceit, for there is but one truth, and that is love."[162] The Scriptures were worthless as a moral or spiritual guide. During December 1654 he went to St. George's Field and publicly burned a Bible. He had to, he insisted, "because the people say it is the Word of God, and it is not."[163]

For that matter, even the traditional conceptions of God were totally erroneous. Rather than existing as an external being, God dwelt in any and all things found in the world.[164] Attempting to sum up his convictions, J. C. Davis concludes, "His strange language comes close to a pantheist universalism, but he never entirely rejects the notion of sin—indeed, his greatest vehemence is reserved for hypocrisy, which he saw as a kind of knowing and willful sinning."[165]

How seriously did Tany take all this? At one point, in 1651, he publicly proclaimed, "Know that I am a madman."[166] But was that the astute self-diagnosis of a man only partially under his own control or that of a street-smart dissident who recognizes that the best way to protect himself against legal retribution is to deny his own culpability for his claims?[167]

In 1655 he received a revelation that Parliament must be assaulted and its members killed.[168] In obedience to the vision, he attempted to do exactly that. Oddly enough, he did this single-handedly (did he dream that he was a modern-day Samson?) and for armament he carried but one sword — and a rusty one at that. All he ended up doing was wounding the Parliamentarian doorkeeper and being arrested and sentenced to jail.[169]

Upon his release, he attempted to revive the redemptive dream by traveling to Holland. There he disappears into the mists of history after visiting Antoinette Bourignon, a prominent mystic of the age.[170] Some at the time were convinced that he had drowned at sea.[171]

Mary Adams: Mother of the New Messiah

Mary Adams appeared on the public stage in Essex, England, when she announced in 1652 that she was the new Virgin Mary. Just as the original Mary had miraculously conceived by the action of the Holy Spirit, so also Adams claimed to be carrying a child by supernatural means. Again duplicating the New Testament pattern, when the child was born he was to be savior of the human race.[172]

The pregnancy part was certainly true. Reports at the time indicate the child was born severely malformed. While she served out a prison term the child died, and both she and her dreams were heard of no more.[173]

Mother Ann and the Shakers: The Wife of Christ (1736–1784)

Born in Manchester, England, in February 1735, Ann Lee was the daughter of a blacksmith. More exactly she was born "Ann Lees," though she ultimately abandoned the final letter just as she did the name of her husband, Abraham Standerin, when she turned against the institution of marriage.[174]

Shakerism came into existence in 1747 as an offshoot of Quakerism due to the work of John and Jane Wardley, residents of a community near Manchester. The "shaking" part was meant literally: Under the claimed direct influence of the Holy Spirit, members would suddenly start shaking in guilt at their own sin and that of the world. In their view, their physical tribulation was a manifestation of the divine anger at human sin.[175] If we make the reaction purely from within, then guilt over their sin would be the motivating factor: Members would feel so emotionally agitated by it that they would rush around the meeting place as if to run off the spiritual anxiety that overwhelmed them. Since any sin in any degree is theoretically equal, and since no one can exist without a recognition of having fallen short of his or her own standards (much less God's), then hypersensitive guilt could produce extreme reactions even among those who had done little or nothing to justify such guilt.

It was to this worldview that Lee was converted at age 22. Four years later she married, an action which unintentionally made her own life that much more miserable. The fundamental problem was that she had developed a strong distaste for human sexuality as a youth, an aversion so strong that she informed her mother that even in marriage conjugal relations should be avoided. This did not amuse her father, who responded with a whipping.[176] Even so, she lived up to the normal sexual expectations of marriage, but the death of all four of her offspring reinforced her objections to even married sexuality.[177] Not to mention her evolving religious perceptions on the matter.

She was 31 when she made the pivotal spiritual breakthroughs that changed her opinion of herself and her world. The preceding nine preparatory years were ones of severe self-denial, described by one early Shaker record as "watchings, fastings, tears, and incessant prayer."[178] As one account has it, these were so intense that they "caused the blood to perspire through the pores of her skin. Sometimes for whole nights together, her cries, screeches and groans were such as to fill every soul around her with fear and trembling."[179] The critic might well cite this as proof of incipient and growing insanity; a friendlier interpretation might well attribute much of it to unusually severe postpartum depression.[180]

Soon after her conversion, she became convinced that the "two witnesses" spoken of in Revelation 12 were Jesus Christ and Ann Lee. That chapter refers to a period of 42 months during which God's city would be oppressed. That, Shakers interpreted, translated into 1,278 "prophetic days" (which means that number of human years). Add 1,278 to the year the papacy triumphed in A.D. 457 and we have 1735, the year before Lee's birth. Hence scriptural "substantiation" of her place in God's scheme of things.[181]

Even more dramatically, she was the equivalent of the male Christ; this time the Christ came in the form of a woman.[182] In 1859 F. W. Evans published a work on behalf of the Shakers in order to explain the movement to outsiders. One of the matters he discusses is the need for a female deityship, including the biblical texts believed to point in that direction, and alluding to the theoretical assumptions underlying that interpretation of the texts. Although he implies unmistakably the divinity of Mother

Ann, he avoids making it so explicit as to anger the religious sensitivities of the age.[183]

> 25. An all-important, sublime, and foundational doctrine of the Shakers is the Existence of an Eternal Father and an Eternal Mother in Deity — the Heavenly Parents of all angelical and human beings. They claim that the *knowledge of God* has been *progressive* from age to age, and from Dispensation to Dispensation.
>
> 28. In the fourth cycle [of Divine revelation], when spirituality is becoming as a deep and broad expanse of waters, "that can not be measured" (see Ezekiel xlvii.), God is also revealed in the character of *Mother* — an Eternal Mother — the bearing spirit of all the creation of God, to whom the Shakers think reference is made in the Scriptures, particularly in the following extracts from the book of "Proverbs," under the appellation of *Wisdom*:
>
> 32. But, as *Mother*, "God is love" and tenderness! If all the *maternal* affections of all the female or bearing spirits in animated nature were combined together, and then concentered in *one individual human female*, that person would be but as a type or image of our Eternal Heavenly *Mother*.
>
> 33. The *duality* of God is expressed in the book of "Genesis" as follows: "Let us make man in our image, after our likeness. So God created man in his own image; male and female created He them; and called their name Adam."
>
> 38. The Shakers believe that the distinction of sex is eternal; that it inheres in the soul itself; and that no angels or spirits exist who are not male and female.
>
> 41. Jesus, being a male, could only reveal and manifest the *Father* in Christ and God. But when the *second* Adam appeared to Ann, and became her spiritual Parents, she, being a female, revealed and manifested the *Mother Spirit* in Christ and in Deity [emphasis in original].

Mother Ann also claimed a unique relationship with the Christ of the first century. She lived with Him "as with a lover.... I am married to the Lord Jesus Christ. He is my head and my husband, and I have no other."[184] As later Shakers interpreted it, Christ appeared to her in 1770 and entered into this special relationship. To use biblical language, this constituted the promised "second coming" mentioned in the gospels.[185]

In a vision of a burning tree, Ann heard the command for her and her followers to move across the Atlantic. The three-month crossing was emotionally and physically traumatic due to encountering a major storm en route. So extreme were the conditions that the Shakers were convinced that only miraculous intervention had made their safe arrival possible.[186]

After arriving in New York in 1774, the group temporarily broke up and resided in different places so that they might be able to support themselves financially. Two years later, they were able to reunite outside Albany.[187]

In spite of Ann's cutting off all sexual relations, her husband traveled to America with her, but eventually he washed his hands of her and took up with a different woman.[188] Although married couples could join the movement without dissolving their marital relationship legally, new nonsexual group relationships were designed to constitute new families in place of what had previously existed.

Mother Ann (as she was commonly known) maintained her bodily strength and charisma until the end,[189] when she perished of unknown causes.[190] By the time of her death in 1784, the group had expanded to around 1,000 adherents. These were scattered among a number of groups in both New York and the broader New England area.[191] By 1803 the group had expanded with another few hundred members and it reached its maximum size between 1840 and 1850 with a peak membership of at least 5,500.[192]

The group went into a gradual decline and was back to its 1784 membership level by 1910.[193] In light of its rigid asceticism, rejection not just of extramarital sexuality but even of marriage and its sexual aspects, it is not surprising that the group could never become a mass movement. It was a doctrinal stance alien to the surrounding world and, to its critics, human nature, and nullified the possibility of the movement perpetuating itself through the children and grandchildren of members.

"Luckie" Buchan: The Holy Spirit in Fleshly Female Form (c. 1738–1791)

Elspeth Simson was born the daughter of a small innkeeper and lost her mother by death when she was only two. Although her father remarried, Elspeth was raised in a relative's household. She met Robert Buchan, a potter, and their marriage produced a number of children, but only three were still alive when the marriage broke up in 1781. The publicly stated reasons were her "licentious conduct" (according to those viewing it from the husband's standpoint) and his leaving his wife behind while he searched elsewhere for the employment he could not find locally (an appealing scenario for those viewing the events from the wife's side).[194]

Either way, these were more the immediate provocations for the breakup than an indication of the underlying problem. In either case, her drift into religious radicalism, which began in 1774, was the underlying factor.[195] God began to work miraculously within her, she reported. She wandered from one sect to another seeking an atmosphere congenial to her religious experience and her extremely unorthodox explanations of

Scripture.[196] On the personal level, she once nearly starved herself to death, being convinced that she was acting under a divine necessity.[197]

In 1782 she heard Reverend Hugh White preach and was thoroughly intrigued by him. After a four-month correspondence, he invited her to take up residence in his home. As they discussed religious matters, his awe and respect for her quickly grew. As they discussed spiritual and biblical matters, he began to interpret the Scriptures in light of her claims. To him, she was the dispeller of the darkness of the Antichrist and the woman "clothed" with the sun in Revelation 12. To her, he was the "man child" brought forth by that woman, her own spiritual child, and he would ultimately be God's regent over the entire world.[198]

If her claim to be described in the Apocalypse were not radical enough, she also claimed to be the Holy Spirit. She could also convey the gift of that spirit, but it was not given by the laying on of hands or by direct action upon the individual from heaven. Instead, it occurred by her breathing on a person.[199] In light of her claim to be one of the members of the Christian Trinity, she certainly did not appear arrogant in taking for herself the title "Friend Mother," a terminology that was adopted by other members of her growing company of supporters.[200]

One might naturally seek some supernatural proof of such claims in the form of miracles. These weren't needed, she insisted. After all, when the apostles first followed Jesus' call to discipleship there had been no miracles involved. Neither must there be any before becoming her disciple.[201]

Although the British were far from reluctant to embrace the idea of their king ruling the world, the idea of a little-known clergyman doing so struck White's congregation as ludicrous. Although the church had been happy to have Buchan join their group, these teachings caused a congregational mutiny in which the majority demanded that White eject her from membership. After he refused to do so, the issue was taken to the presbytery, which solved the difficulty by ousting her clerical defender from the pulpit during the summer of 1783.[202]

A minority of the congregation left with Buchan and White and met in the homes of the minister and one of the members. These followers were now known as the Buchanites. The relationship between White and Buchan was widely assumed to be sexually immoral and this, as well as the exotic beliefs of the group, led to loss of jobs and ridicule.[203] Even so, the group had attracted a cross-section of different types of people, running the gamut from common laborers to tradesmen.[204]

On one occasion a mob assaulted her and drove her out of town, and she had to make her way back bruised, bloodied, and almost naked. Facing a situation that gave every indication of degenerating further, the local magistrates ordered her permanently out of their community.[205]

In May 1784, convinced that God was about to wipe their town off of the map in retribution for the treatment meted out to them and their two leaders, the entire group took up residence at a farm in Dumfriesshire.[206] The only building was a barn that consisted of one main floor room and a loft above.[207]

Here Buchan whipped up the congregation's hopes for an imminent return of Jesus. To prepare for it, a 40-day period of fasting was announced. They locked their meeting place and screened and nailed the windows. After 40 days during which they existed on only a little water, the physically exhausted but emotionally sure congregation made their way to a hill where they would await their Lord's appearance.[208]

When nothing happened, Buchan placed the responsibility not on herself for being a self-deceived false prophet, but upon their lack of adequate faith.[209]

Beginning with 46 people, the group grew to 60. All of their limited funds were placed in a common treasury and they lived during this period on that money alone. When this was exhausted, they sought local farm work to bring in the funds they needed for essentials.[210]

Renamed "Buchan Ha" by their critics, the church property was attacked during the winter, but the fleeing members soon returned to reestablish their group.[211] Things did not always go so well for Buchan's more violent critics. On one occasion, the sheriff aborted an attempted attack on her for witchcraft and prosecuted 42 of the people involved.[212]

Local rumor had it that she vigorously suppressed the slightest hint that anyone might wish to leave the group. Any members thought to be considering such a step were confined and plunged into cold water daily to bring them to their senses.[213] Even if this is true, it is unlikely that many contemplated such a step, since the group was so small to begin with. Yet for the same reason, even the loss of those few individuals who did leave must have been a major blow to the group's spirits.[214]

In March 1787 the group finally pulled out because the county magistrates were thoroughly distrustful of their ability to economically survive and demanded a bond to protect the community against any costs created by their members seeking poor relief.[215] They then took up residence at another farm, in Kirkcudbrightshire, where they attempted to establish more secure roots for their community by farming the property themselves rather than hiring out as laborers for others. In addition, some sought outside work in such areas as spinning yarn. As the result of these efforts, the group found sound financial footing.[216] Slowly, good relations with outsiders were established as they got to know the members and the group's skill in herbal medicine further enhanced their status.[217]

Among the Buchanites, marriage was held to be nonessential, though acceptable. Deep suspicions existed as to whether their "community of property" extended to sexual matters as well.[218] The practice of the two leaders, Buchan and White, who slept together in the same bed (though White kept his wife and children on the premises), was not the type of behavior to reassure those with suspicious minds.[219]

To the extent that the group comes to the attention of moderns, it is likely to be through study of Robert Burns, the poet. In 1784 he wrote a letter condemning the sexual immorality of the group, denouncing them as lazy.[220] The latter was a fear clearly in the minds of the county leadership in forcing the group to leave. There may have been more to this criticism than meets the eye, since Burns admitted to knowing many of the members. One individual who spent five years researching the subject came away with the conclusion that Burns had fallen in love with one member and that his vigorous criticism grew out of a desire to hide his once close association with the group.[221]

In their new location, the group enjoyed sufficient societal tolerance and internal stability that it was able to remain in the same place until Buchan died in 1791. Knowing that she was dying, she assured her disciples that she would conquer death through a swift bodily resurrection. However, there was a catch to this promise: It all hinged upon the completeness and purity of their faith. If they faltered, it would not happen, and they would be punished by an unknown number of years having to intervene before she ultimately returned.[222]

They accepted the truth of her resurrection promise and took care not to nail her coffin or to bury it. Yet time passed and no resurrection occurred. Avoiding public attention, they then clandestinely buried her.[223]

Some 30 members moved to America the following year and the 14 who remained lingered on in a dying sect that came to an end when the last member was buried in 1845.[224]

11

Messianic Movements During the Birth of the Technological Age (1800–1900)

Jemima Wilkinson (1752–1819)

Born into a Quaker household in November 1752 in Rhode Island, Wilkinson grew up with an intense interest in spiritual matters.[1] Her willingness to seek any and all outlets for this concern was manifested when she began to read the printed sermons of the powerful contemporary evangelist George Whitefield.[2] After doing so for a while, in 1776 she began to attend a local Baptist congregation. This Baptist attendance, however, resulted in her being rejected by the Quakers,[3] though her attendance elsewhere argues that she had already made the break with her past in her mind even if not openly saying so in her words.

It was in September of that year that her life changed forever. At that time, she was stricken with a vicious fever that left her unconscious and unmoving for a prolonged period. According to one version of the event, she gave every indication of having died. Only after being placed in a coffin preparatory to final rites and burial did she snap out of it.[4] As she told the story, it was during this period that she had a vision of how she had died and been commissioned by God to return to earth to share His redemptive message.[5] The description she gave has reminded some of how "near death experiences" are often recalled: a blinding light, a review of one's life, and a sense that one is now blessed with a spirituality that must be further developed because one has survived the brush with death.[6]

Wilkinson promptly adopted a new name to go with this new mission and refused to go by her old family name. Now it was the unwieldy "Public Universal Friend,"[7] or, if one preferred, the much easier "the Friend."[8] She firmly rejected gender descriptions of herself: She insisted that the feminine words "her" and "she" were to be avoided in speaking of her. In addition, she regularly wore a black robe to give her a male clergyman's appearance.[9] This was supplemented by a masculine hat that was wide-brimmed.[10]

Her social message had a clear appeal for many contemporaries. Wilkinson emphasized plain, nonostentatious apparel, the rejection of the violence inherent in warfare, and the need to abolish slavery.[11] Her sexual doctrine also stood out from the traditional in that she enjoined celibacy rather than marriage[12] and, of course, had no room in her theology for extramarital or premarital sexual relationships.

She had a powerful preaching style that impressed her listeners.[13] This was enhanced by her physical appearance, which was described by a contemporary as being one of "a tall and graceful woman with dark hair and dark eyes."[14] Her preaching journeys were not confined to her home area, but also took her into several New England states as well. Congregations formed under the name of "Universal Friends" in Connecticut, Rhode Island, and Philadelphia, Pennsylvania, as the result of these labors.[15]

Although a woman preacher was unconventional[16] and her claims of having a visionary call by God unlikely to gain a positive reception, what was guaranteed to outrage others was the claim that she was God's Messiah. Although she was careful to keep her own public teaching vague, she noticeably did not repudiate these claims.[17] This assured that the church membership would continue to make these claims and that they would be accepted by the general public as representing her true convictions.

The year 1788 brought some of her associates to the Seneca Lake, New York, region, where they formed the town of "Friend's Settlement." In two years this grew to 260 residents, including Wilkinson herself.[18] This growth was made possible not only by individuals moving there, but entire small congregations as well.[19]

At the time this town was created, that part of New York was wild country with minimal population. Because of this it was an appealing location for a group that literally was attempting to withdraw from a hostile world. Unknowingly and unintentionally, they discovered themselves to be part of the cutting edge of a massive population expansion into areas previously unavailable to Englishmen.[20] As the result of population growth and the informal circumstances of the initial settlement, in the following years repeated controversies arose over land ownership and title due to the uncertain legalities of frontier property possession that faced the first settlers.[21]

In 1794 these repeated title conflicts resulted in her taking a cadre of dedicated followers from the town. They moved a few miles to Crooked Lake (now known as Keuka Lake). This new community she christened "Jerusalem."[22]

Having faced public violence by stone throwers back east, in these years she shifted from an effort to convert others to one of building up her own people within the confines of their own settlements.[23] Without the spur of her proselytization, however, the groups in both towns failed to have any but a minimal growth in numbers.[24]

Outsiders gained the impression that Wilkinson ruled severely and with virtually no consideration for the opinions of others. Violators of her rules were severely punished.[25]

While residing in that area, locals reported, she once went with her followers to Seneca Lake. Stepping ankle deep into the water, she asked them if they believed that she could walk on the water. When receiving the response that she could, she responded that since they believed it that there was no need for her to do it.[26]

The community and the movement were held together by their shared loyalty to the founder. When she died on July 1, 1819, it rapidly evaporated as individuals went their separate ways.[27] By 1840 the group had totally dissipated.[28]

To those who believe in such things, the only remnant of her movement may be her ghost. Near the time of her death, she promised that she would appear dressed in gray at the lake near her home. This would be to comfort the broken-hearted and to give advice to those facing the death of loved ones.[29]

Richard Brothers (1757–1824): The "Nephew of God"

Born in Newfoundland, Canada, in 1757, he was sent by his father to England in his youth for an education and to prepare himself for a life of naval duty. He entered the navy at 14, rose to the rank of lieutenant, and pulled war duty against the French. He was, however, ultimately released from service in 1783 when the navy's size was reduced as part of the adjustment to peacetime conditions.[30]

Brothers came to the conclusion that he could not continue to make an oath of loyalty — a precondition for continuing to receiving his post-service half pay — and the Admiralty's rules canceled it as the result. Without this underlying financial support, he found himself destitute and was ordered into a workhouse in August of 1791.[31]

At this point, he had already begun to receive angelic revelations of the future, including one warning of London's imminent doom by fire.[32] His physical appearance, firmness in speech, and courtesy impressed even those who ran the workhouse where he lived and worked for the six months necessary to get his financial affairs in order. He seemed amiable and rational on every subject one could discuss, except for that of religion.[33] The administrators of the workhouse intensely lobbied the Admiralty for his back pay, received it, and used it to pay off those debts that they could not get him released from. Brothers' debt to society was thereby paid off and he was released from confinement.[34]

After he regained his freedom, the political aspects of his revelations became central to his thinking. He took to writing leading political dignitaries, including the prime minister and the king. In one such letter he warned that, based upon the revelations God had given him, "the Revolution in France proceeded from the judgment of God. Therefore all attempts to preserve the Monarchy there would be opposing God."[35]

Again he fell behind in his bills because he refused to sign the required oaths to collect his pay,[36] and this time he was sent to Newgate Prison in May 1792 for nonpayment of rent. Unlike his earlier confinement, this one was in the most extreme circumstances. He was provided with minimal food and, like other prisoners, crammed into small quarters shared by more than a dozen others, with neither blankets or beds provided. He remained jailed until November of 1792 and his treatment appears to have confirmed his belief that England deserved the divine wrath that was inevitably coming its way if it did not stop trying to quash the French Revolution.[37] It did nothing to increase his faith in the government that, though he signed the power of attorney for the prison in July so that they could collect his pension, it took until November to receive it and to be released.[38]

God had set him aside for a prophetic ministry, he reported in his *Revealed Knowledge* (see below), but he conceded that at this point he had had every intention of defying God on the matter. So embittered was he when he was released from Newgate that he started to walk to Bristol to seek passage abroad. He was determined "never to have anything to do with prophesying or the character of restoring the Hebrews to Jerusalem."[39] To stop him, God intervened miraculously. Part way to Bristol, all of "a sudden, God by His power stopped the action of every joint and limb, and turned me feelingly round with more ease than a strong man would a young child; commanding me, at the same instant to return and wait His proper time."[40]

In late 1794 and early 1795, he announced in print that God had ordained him to gather together all Jews for a return to Palestine. "Jews" included both those who recognized they were such and those who, like him, had not previously recognized their true nature and heritage.[41] Truth be told, by and large the English people were all Jews, the descendents of the proverbial ten lost tribes.[42] He would be "King of the Hebrews," ruling over them in the new land until Jesus appeared in his second coming.[43] (He had only discovered, due to his revelations, that he was actually one of David's descendants and, therefore biologically and genealogically entitled to rule in his place.)[44]

Hence he was not Jesus personally but simply a regal replacement for Him, so to speak, until He chose to personally exercise that authority. He became, in effect, a messianic redeemer preparing the way for the Messiah, something surely unconsciously bordering on a two-messiah doctrine. During the following decades, Brothers spent much of him time designing the paraphernalia that would be required — such things as uniforms for its soldiers and flags for the kingdom.[45]

In his *Revealed Knowledge* (which grew from a 60-page pamphlet in 1793 to a 168-page book in February 1795), God had revealed to him the true and accurate interpretation of both Daniel and the Apocalypse and how the predictions would be carried out in the contemporary world. God was behind the French Revolution, and English opposition would be divinely permitted only for the three and a half years predicted by Daniel. Then God would act against earthly monarchies, with all of them to perish by 1798. At some point before then, George III would deliver his crown over to Brothers, who rightly deserved it as God's agent. Of more immediate concern was the fact that June 1795 would bring a mammoth earthquake that would destroy not only London but gravely damage other places as well.[46] A prophet who speaks this precisely of the short term had best be right to preserve his credibility or have provided adequate "wiggle room" in his wording in order to justify his mistake.

Pivotal to the underlying interpretation (though not the timing he gave) was the identification of contemporary events and London in particular with events described in the text of the Apocalypse. As he wrote, "Be no longer astonished that London in one part of the Revelation is called under the name of the 'great city' ... ; in another she is called 'Sodom' and in a third, she is, as well as Rome, spiritually called 'Babylon the Great.'"[47]

Revealed Knowledge sold widely because the recent revolution in France was part and parcel of Brothers' scriptural interpretation. To those who embraced the idealism of the revolution, the work sparked their hopes; to those who feared it, the book stoked their dread.[48] From an author's standpoint, it met the most important criteria: It sold, sold well, and kept selling.[49]

Some accepted Brothers' claims about himself and what the Scriptures meant, a much larger body was intrigued by the interpretation, and critics mocked both his prophetic claims and his scriptural explanations. But even if Scripture seemed to contradict him on some point it was irrelevant, for Scripture was manifestly wrong in those matters. At one point, God graciously promised him that this was his unique privilege: "There is no [other] man under the whole Heaven that I discover the errors of the Bible to, and reveal a knowledge how to correct them."[50] He also provided information that He had denied to the Scripture writers. Of one prediction, Brothers was told by God, "I passed by this part with Daniel."[51]

So intimate was this special relation of Brothers that God once assured him that, "You may yourself [be] my Nephew."[52] *How* one could be God's nephew without holding a polytheist's conception of the supernatural world represented an obvious difficulty. Brothers' followers dodged this potential problem by insisting that their leader was the descendant of Jesus' brother James and therefore, quite rightly, could use the expression.[53]

The endorsement of Brothers' prophetic interpretations by the scholarly and respected Parliamentarian Nathaniel B. Halhed brought him to the attention of both Parliament and a wide range of opinion outside that body which had not previously paid him any attention.[54] Unfortunately, the politics of Brothers' interpretation were guaranteed to inflame the dominant political establishment of the time.

After a scathing editorial attack by the *London Times*,[55] the authorities finally summoned the will to formally arrest him. Although the political content of his biblical interpretations was clearly their main concern, the legal justification was a statue from the days of Elizabeth which made it a punishable offense to "unlawfully, maliciously, and wickedly [be guilty of] writing, printing, and publishing various fantastical prophecies, with intent to create dissensions, and other disturbances with this realm."[56]

Halhed publicly defended Brothers before a fascinated Parliament. He vigorously attacked the hypocrisy of arresting a man for alleged treason and then using his alleged insanity as an excuse to confine him.[57] The fact that it had been a secret trial before the Privy Council and that, even there, they found it impossible to convict him of sedition,[58] did not make it any easier for the critics to defend what had happened. The Privy Council's decision to bounce the issue over to a commission to judge his sanity (with its conclusion a foregone conclusion),[59] made the entire procedure even more clearly a matter of politics rather than subversion. Hence the controversy over the arrest and ultimate charges against Brothers became a matter of vigorous debate among many and interested discussion among others not tied to either side of the controversy.[60]

The earthquake prophecy worried not only those who were convinced that the city would be leveled on June 4, 1795, but also those who were merely concerned that at least on this point he might turn out to be right. Passing references in contemporary publications and diaries indicate that thousands decided to be cautious by temporarily leaving the city.[61] A vicious rainstorm of unusual intensity struck that night and more than a few who remained feared that they had erred in doing so.[62]

When dawn rose the next day, the city still stood. According to one contemporary who claimed to have visited him afterwards, Brothers defended his predictive lapse by arguing that one pivotal event had occurred that caused God to change his mind: Brothers explained "with all solemnity and placidity of manner, that the earthquake had, at his earnest and oft-repeated intercession, been by the Almighty postponed, and the destruction of London averted."[63]

To Brothers, this was not all that astounding. Had not his face-to-face confrontation with God in 1791 once before saved London from utter destruction?[64] Hence Brothers was tranquil, calm, quiet and confident that God's change of mind was fully consistent with what had happened back in 1791. Others were unconvinced. Even on His own terms, why would God — having spared London once from terrible destruction and giving it a second opportunity — why would He relent when that opportunity had not changed the city a whit in the things that mattered?

The failure of London to crumble burst the bubble of widespread interest in Brothers. When an earthquake finally occurred in England in November of the year, only the most dedicated follower was left to connect the event with Brothers' earlier prediction of London's fate.[65]

Even so, Brothers remained confined, the support essential to freeing him having vanished. Penniless, having automatically lost his pension when judged insane, he should have been sent to one of the abhorent public insane asylums of the day. The fact that he was in a privately run institution — where his treatment and standard of living was immeasurably better — argues that the government had decided to pick up the much higher costs of such confinement[66] either out of a guilty conscience or to calm potential protest.

Although he was eventually freed in 1806, King George III insisted that the legal judgment of lunacy not be revoked; he would tolerate the man's freedom but nothing that might even remotely hint that he was to be regarded as credible on any subject he spoke about.[67] Having lost his dominance in his movement to Joanna Southcott (see below), Brothers continued active in it until his death in the mid 1820s.

Joanna Southcott: Mother of the Messiah (1750–1814)

The earlier prophetess Catherine Therot (at her most influential c. 1788–1791), pictured herself lavishly as the new Eve who would give birth to Jesus Christ. She insisted to her listeners, "God has announced a New Eve who will deliver us from the iniquity into which the first Eve led us by her disobedience."[68] On the other hand, however, her followers insisted that this was to be a "spiritual" rather than a literal birth.[69] In vivid contrast, Joanna Southcott took her own claim of being mother to the redeemer as quite literal.[70]

Southcott worked for her first two decades of life on the family farm and then moved to Exeter, where she took up employment as a household servant. Since she worked for several upholsterers, she not unnaturally developed a competency in their line of work as well.[71] In spite of her modest social stature or, perhaps, encouraged by it, she developed a passionate interest in spiritual matters far different than the typical contemporary, as manifested in her embracing the claims of Brothers (see above).[72]

Pivotal in expanding her basis of support within Brothers' movement was her reassurance to those who had been convinced by him that Jesus' millennial kingdom was imminent in the 1790s, but had, to their horror, seen their hopes evaporate. To these people she brought the reassurance that the event had only tarried rather than been abandoned: Now, she insisted, it was finally imminent — and the hope was kindled afresh among many in the dispirited movement.[73]

Most prophets of the time claimed that God (or Jesus or the Holy Spirit) had given them their message. Southcott added to this traditional claim her own special twist: God's power overcame her and by a kind of "automatic writing"— more often associated with spiritualism — she was given her message in the form of rough poetic verse.[74] Some were impressed, but others reacted like Dr. John Lettsom. This Quaker physician bought one of two tracts out of curiosity and dismissed it as not wrong or erroneous but outright "unintelligible," a far severer judgment.[75]

When faced with reputed new revelations, the traditionalist naturally asked whether they were intended to replace the Scriptures. She insisted that was definitely not the case: "I have not added to the Scriptures nor taken from them but explained their meaning," she wrote to one challenger.[76]

In 1792, at the age of 42, the first messages began to come to her. These initial revelations concerned the horrible domestic side effects that would occur because of the French Revolution. She warned that though English prices were currently low, they would skyrocket to unheard-of heights.[77]

In 1801 she brought out the first of her 65 published tracts, *The Strange Effects of Faith*. This was published through combining her own savings with loans.[78] Learning the names of various individuals scattered around the country who might be interested in her, she began writing to them and including copies of her pamphlet. She stirred up sufficient interest that a seven-man delegation came to visit her in Exeter and became convinced of the validity of her revelations. This marked a pivotal movement upwards, from being merely an isolated prophetess standing alone into a prophetess with a distinct group, howbeit small, rallied around her.[79]

In May 1802 she moved her base of operations to London. Residing in Paddington, she released large printings of her individual revelations as inexpensive pamphlets, and they enjoyed a wide circulation.[80] Her base of support still consisted primarily not of new adherents but of the followers of Richard Brothers. In the years from 1802 to 1806 she was content to build up her own recognition as prophetess and kept a certain public distance from him, declining to even read his newer predictions and teachings, claiming that all she needed was being directly revealed by God.[81] In the year when it became clear that Brothers would probably be released from confinement, she made the public break: True, his work of 1791–1792 had been vindicated by the fulfillment of his predictions, but afterwards the divine gift had been withdrawn from him.[82] His pride had simply gotten the best of him, and she could no longer honor him as leader of the movement.[83]

The political implications of Southcott's message were basically irrelevant to her, while such matters had been a major emphasis of Brothers' own teachings.[84] For example, when we read of the Beast in the book of Revelation, we should not look for its fulfillment in the papacy or a regal monarchy or in any other system of religious or political organization; rather, it was sin in all its forms that constituted the true Beast that endangered all believers.[85] To the extent that she directly touched on the matter at all, she repudiated Brothers' positive view of the French Revolution and denounced vigorously the excess of such "extreme" democratic theorists as Thomas Paine, who, she was convinced, had done much to demoralize and divide the English people.[86]

She made enough accurate predictions to impress many individuals not bound up in her movement. Predictions of a navy mutiny came true in 1797; predictions of war with France came true; predictions that the bishop of Exeter would die were confirmed in actual events; horrendously bad crop failures did, indeed, occur in 1794, 1795, and 1797, as did her dire warnings of the effects of heavy rains in 1799.[87] Some were right as to the event, but not the timing: The Irish Rebellion that she thought would break out in 1795 did not erupt until three years later.[88] It was still close enough to impress many, though the cynical would have viewed it as merely decent insight into the depths of Irish resentment.

To herself, she was the woman of Revelation 12 who plays a pivotal role in human redemption and whom Satan attempts to destroy.[89] She was also the second Eve who was to be at enmity with Satan in fulfillment of Genesis 3's prediction of hostility between Eve's descendant and Satan.[90] The promised "seed" of that text, however, consisted not of Southcott's physical children but of her loyal followers,[91] allowing them a sense of shared glory and personal involvement in the consummation of the divine purpose.

In 1802, in imitation of those mentioned in Revelation 7:3, she was instructed to begin "sealing" those believers who wished to escape danger and death. In contrast with that passage—where the sealing was done on the foreheads—she accomplished it through a piece of paper with a large circle on it, verifying that a person was one of that supernaturally protected number. The recipient's name was placed above this and Southcott signed it below. This document was then folded and literally sealed shut with a seal that Southcott had found while housekeeping. The impression carried a star on both sides and initials that she said stood for "Jesus Christ."[92]

To accomplish their protective work, these had to be continually carried about on one's person. The talisman-like nature of the object appealed to the superstitious, and reports of the success of the seals that she issued further enhanced their popularity.[93] By 1804, 8,144 had been granted; this number grew by September 1807 to about 14,000.[94] Cynics accused her of making money in the guise of benefiting others and in 1807, even she had to admit that "there are thousands sealed who know not for what they are sealed."[95] At that point, she began to demand at least a modest acquaintance with her published revelations in order to obtain the documents.[96]

At age 65 she predicted that she would conceive and bear the mysterious "Shiloh" predicted in the Book of Genesis.[97] Some suspect that it was a subconscious effort to revitalize a movement whose growth had dramatically decreased in recent years.[98]

She submitted to a medical examination by no less than 21 doctors, and all but four agreed that she was definitely pregnant. The birth, she predicted, would be during the autumn of 1814.[99] Her body grew as if she were indeed as pregnant as she thought.[100] The disciples prepared a golden crib and a small pair of slippers made out of satin. Such touches were appropriate because of the mother's advanced age and because the child would be no less than the Messiah.[101] Although, as with Jesus' mother, the child was to be virgin born, Southcott privately married,[102] presumably to further the parallel with the life of Jesus and to protect against any rumors that she was, indeed, pregnant, though by non-marital human means.

Although some left in disgust at her claim, they were amply replaced by new followers.[103] To the bulk of her supporters, the pregnancy was the supreme physical proof of the legitimacy of her spiritual claims. As one of her disciples had written on March 16, "Now let the Mockers be silent for if she is [a] deceiver herself or is deceived she has now completely committed herself. So let them wait the issue of the event."[104]

By November the birth had not occurred. In December Southcott died. Only a few days before her demise, she whispered to an attendant, "I am not afraid to appear before my God, as I have done nothing but what I believed to be in true obedience to my Lord."[105] Oddly confident words from a woman whose death was about to disprove her own most famous prophecy.

Although the dead body was kept warm for a few days by means of hot water bottles, the group then agreed to an autopsy. This was performed in front of a large number of her followers, who were convinced that the new Jesus would be produced, quite alive, from the apparently dead corpse.[106] The examination indicated that there was no child present,[107] but was unable to establish a specific cause of death.[108] A friendly interpretation would suggest that her age had caught up with her; a less friendly one that she died of guilt produced by the recognition that her prediction was false: An attending doctor claimed that she had begun to fear that the pregnancy hopes were delusional, but her followers denied that she ever admitted any such thing.[109]

The disciples dealt with this embarrassment in several ways. Some said she died because of the unbelief and opposition of Anglican Church officials, which left unresolved what happened to the alleged child she was carrying. Others insisted that a "spiritual" rather than a literal childbirth was intended, which was markedly inconsistent with her emphasis on proving her pregnancy. Finally, there were those who claimed that the infant was immediately taken to heaven upon its birth, which at least solved the problem of why there was no child in the womb.[110]

Her following as of 1815 was estimated as including at least 100,000 in London alone. Retrospectively, these figures give every indication of being vastly exaggerated, but a band of disciples in the range of 20,000 nationwide seems quite reasonable.[111] After her death, whatever fragile unity existed among her supporters perished as they divided into a variety of new, small sects that, in spite of their disagreements, all gave their religious loyalty to her and her claims.[112]

The Panacea Society (Bedford, England) is perhaps the most important because it maintained physical possession of her "Box of Sealed Writings," revelations which were never released to the public.[113] According to Southcott, the day would come when two dozen Anglican bishops would attend the opening of the box, and at that point the writings would be made available to the world.[114]

The society was formed more than a century after Southcott's death, after the conclusion of the First World War, by the wife of an Anglican vicar. To perpetuate memory of the important messages in the box, she recruited 12 "apostles," all female. They began a long-running and well-known advertising campaign with the message "Crime and Banditry, Distress and Perplexity will increase in England until the bishops open Joanna Southcott's box."[115] Throughout the decades and even into the 21st century, the group pleaded with various Anglican bishops to yield to their wish. None agreed. In fact, "some replies are quite rude," noted Ruth Klein, the chairwoman of the group, in 2003.[116]

As a sign of their confidence that Jesus would be returning to Bedford to live — the site of the Garden of Eden in their eyes— they purchased a home for His residence. This brought considerable amusement to the cynical press when they were permitted to tour it in 2003. The fact that the group had discussed the desirability of adding a shower for the Lord's use seemed particularly amusing and incongruous to these unsympathetic outsiders.[117]

John (Zion) Ward (1781–1837)

After moving to Bristol from Ireland in 1790, Ward was apprenticed out to learn the trade of shipwright. Before completing this apprenticeship, he joined his father in London and started learning how to make shoes under the tutelage of his brother. Shifting back to being a shipwright, he was then admitted to the navy, saw battle, and decided this was not the lifetime occupation he had thought it might be. He left the service in 1803 and in the same year he married and began to practice shoemaking as his trade.[118]

As a child he had been raised as a Presbyterian, but in adulthood he tried out several very different alternatives. From the Methodists, he went to the Baptists and from the Baptists he joined the Sandemanians. In each case he found himself ultimately locked in conflict with the traditional teachings and power structure of the respective bodies.[119]

He came under the influence of Joanna Southcott's writings after her death and, in particular, of George Turner, who was the dominant force among her supporters in the north of England after her demise.[120] From 1825 to 1828 Ward endured a serious of mentally wrenching dreams and he began to wonder about his own true identity. Finally he came to the conclusion that the Shiloh prediction had come true, but not in the fashion that Turner and others had anticipated. Shiloh had not only returned but was John Ward himself.[121]

As time passed by, his spiritual aspirations increased. He became God. But, in an extremely odd twist, he was to be regarded as Satan as well.[122] The date of Ward's birth linked this all into one neat package, for he had been born on December 25, the traditional birthdate of Christ. Then one must factor in the fact that his mother's name was Mary. Putting all this together, he concluded, "This is the great mystery of the Scriptures, that Satan became Christ."[123]

Furthermore there never was a true, historically unique "Jesus Christ" who once walked the dusty roads of Galilee and Judea. Instead there was a Christ principle, a supernatural light that transformed Ward into Christ and had the potential for transforming anyone else who sought it diligently enough.[124] In that transformation, one also became sinless.[125]

In spite of the radicalness of such teachings, he seems to have gained at least several thousand adherents.[126] In light of the degree of his support and his enthusiasm for his claims, he abandoned his secular trade and depended upon the generosity of others for a livelihood. This came chiefly through Charles Bradley, a successful tobacconist in Birmingham,[127] and his family.

In the process of teaching his doctrines, Ward was estranged from the bulk of Southcottians.[128] He also gained the ongoing attention of the Society for the Suppression of Vice because of the potential of his teachings to encourage sexual misbehavior. He attracted the even more dangerous attention of the government for his increasing support of radical social and political reform, which was viewed as potentially encouraging revolt and revolution.[129]

In 1832 the government used the accusation of blasphemy to jail him for 18 months, though it was clear from their accusations that his political apocalypticism was of primary concern to them.[130] Upon his release, he continued to advocate his religio-political convictions with his previous enthusiasm and dedication. He also instituted the practice of marrying women to Christ, with him conducting the ceremony and acting as surrogate for their new "husband."[131] In the two years prior to his death in 1837, strokes limited his abilities to proselytize. The movement quickly dissipated after his death, although a loyal cadre was dedicated enough to have his works reprinted after his death.[132]

Judah Jehiel Safrin (1806–1874)[133]

If Safrin's account is trustworthy, his father encouraged him to believe that God had marked him out for special importance. As he tells it, it had visions from ages two to five, and when Safrin was seven Elijah appeared in bodily form as a peasant. He concedes that he was so spiritually immature that he did not recognize who it was until the identity was pointed out by his father. At least in retrospect, he interpreted this and various actions by others as implying his greatness and spiritual importance to his age.[134] The father died when the boy was twelve and three years later he underwent a major a crisis of spiritual confidence that was resolved in a manner that he considered as advancing his spirituality to a new level.[135]

Safrin was an important leader of the Hasidic movement, and as part of his teaching ministry he poured out many studies presenting and advocating his spiritual agenda.[136] Vital had been so egocentric that he resented the success and praise given others, and even his mentor Luria he regarded as of importance only because of his influence on his disciple and not so much in his own right. In contrast, Safrin had no difficulty in acknowledging the value of the work of his contemporaries.[137]

Safrin's *Megillat Setarim* ("Book of Secrets") is of special interest because the first section, "Book of Visions," contains a partial autobiography interwoven with mystical experiences and convictions in the style of Vital's writings. These contain a record of his key dreams from 1845 to 1857, though why he chose those beginning and ending dates is unknown.[138]

Much as this reveals the man himself, equally significant is the "Deeds of the Lord" section, in which he preserves the firsthand account of the life of the Besht, who created the Hasidic movement. These anecdotes were collected from both his own father-in-law and others who were contemporaries of the events and had personally known the man.[139]

Safrin was convinced that he was the reincarnation of several past messianic claimants and those who were accepted as such by many followers. More recently these included the Besht and, at an earlier date, Isaac

Luria.[140] Indeed, he also regarded himself as the beneficiary of a transmigration of the soul of a younger brother who had died at one year of age.[141]

The world's salvation would only occur when Safrin had managed to purge himself from all mortal taints of the flesh and spirit.[142] The reconciliation of the inner being of mortals with the infinity that exists beyond human perception could only occur through his messianic success.[143] One of the key evidences that he was the "Messiah of Joseph" was that of applying gematria (the "science" of number interpretation) to his birth year of 1806: By doing so, one derived that designation, he insisted.[144]

Shukr Kuhayl I[145]

This Yemenite's public career encompassed the brief period of the four years from 1861 to 1865. In the beginning he presented himself in a John the Baptist type role: He was the man who would prepare the world for the Messiah. In this period he put away his spouse (a biblical phrase for divorce), traveled widely pleading for personal moral reformation, and intentionally lived in poverty. Throughout this stage he received repeated visions of earthly catastrophe and disaster.[146]

In the next stage, he announced that he was the Messiah Himself. As biblical proof, he appealed to Isaiah 45:1. Though that text speaks of the Messiah as *koresh*, he insisted that the text had been corrupted and that its original reading was *shukr*, which, of course, just happened to be his own name.[147] He felt free to similarly "correct" other texts in the Scriptures and even from the mystic *Zohar*.[148] He claimed a kind of omniscience in the interpretation both of the scriptural text and in the motivations and intentions of those he dealt with.[149]

If this were not enough to convince others, he claimed that even the great ancient magicians of Egypt did not exercise the degree of magical power available to him.[150] Such powers were exhibited in his reported miracles that impressed many onlookers and increased the number of his supporters.[151]

Some of these were even Muslim and, in Muslim-dominated Yemen, this created considerable annoyance and resentment.[152] The Islamic rulers considered him of sufficient concern that they ultimately ordered his execution.[153] His followers suggested a variety of explanations to explain this away. Some believed he was indeed dead but God would bring him back.[154] (He had predicted his resurrection if his death were to occur.)[155] Others preferred to deny the death had even happened and insisted that he was still alive but dwelling somewhere in secret.[156]

Shukr Kuhayl II

Taking advantage of the resurrection and temporary disappearance scenarios to explain the fate of Kuhayl, three years later another individual appeared claiming to be the wished-for Messiah who had earlier worked among the people. He avoided as much as humanly possible those who had known the first Kuhayl well and those he could not avoid dismissed him as an imposter.[157]

His two highest priorities were money and good living. He demanded that everyone provide him with a tithe of their income and spent the proceeds on luxuries for himself and his guests.[158]

At some point this con man (for no other epithet seems appropriate) appears to have begun believing the mythology he had built up around himself.[159] In spite of disavowals from those who had known the genuine Kuhayl and efforts to rally opposition to the man as a fraud,[160] positive word about him spread not only into Egypt and Aden but even to India. In all three places, supporting movements sprung up.[161] When a scathing exposé of him was published, the good times began to disappear. Sinking deep into poverty, he died about 1877.[162]

Yusuf Abdallah (Yosef Eved-El)

This Yemenite messianic claimant came from a lower-class background.[163] He preached a message of repentance, which, for women, meant the abandoning of the jewelry and clothing styles that were popular at the time.[164] For all individuals, the changed lifestyle included totally abandoning all alcoholic beverages.[165]

He was not one to overlook his own financial needs and insisted that individuals provide him with generous financial assistance.[166] The financial ethics of the man was sometimes highly questionable not only because of this but also because he was known to "roll over" his debt by using borrowed money from one person to pay off an earlier debt.[167]

He was imprisoned upon a number of occasions, including 1893, when he spent Passover in jail.[168] In each of the cases he was able to convince the authorities and those accusing him to relent and permit him to be released.[169]

Henry Prince

The Agapemone or Abode of Love was a creation of one Henry Prince. Coming to the town of Stoke, England, to preach near the end of the 1840s, he attracted the devotion and undying attention of the five daughters of Josias Nottidge. In spite of all their family could do to discourage their feelings and adoration — even up to banning the man from their home — the father could do nothing to quell their enthusiasm.[170]

Prince's powerful and effective rhetoric produced disciples in several other towns as well. These he brought together in Spaxton, the small village where he had earlier occupied the pulpit as minister for the Church of England. (Even at that earlier "orthodox" stage of his preaching, the overwhelming commitment a minority felt toward him unnerved the other members of the congregation and he had been ousted.)[171] Although his appeal was more to women than men — especially those never married or to widows[172] — there were a significant number of male converts brought into the movement as well. Chief and most important among them was Samuel Starky, who provided access to the most important families of the area and who coordinated the raising of the funds so that Prince could have his longed-for church.[173] Altogether they raised at least 20,000 pounds sterling to construct the facility,[174] an immense figure in that day and age.

The worship facility went with a piece of property encompassing some 200 acres, and the 60-some members attempted to transform it into it a self-sufficient farm,[175] although the upper-middle-class roots of most of the members meant that their own personal participation in any serious manual labor was likely to be minimal because it was beneath their societal status. The fact that a number had brought significant sums of money with them provided the necessary start-up funds that made the job of creating an economically independent community far easier, however.[176] In addition to those with direct loyalty to Prince, a number of individual members' servants also resided on the property.[177] As the community set down roots, it became a de facto assumption that those who joined would "voluntarily" give up all their economic resources for the survival and prosperity of the group.[178]

Even before this localization of his ministry, Prince had slowly begun to make his messianic claims more explicit. He began with a mysticism in which the distinction between man and God virtually disappeared. As he put it on one occasion, "I am utterly absorbed and swallowed up in God."[179] He took this quite seriously. As he insisted to his followers, "In me you behold the Love of God. Look on me. I am one in the flesh with Christ. I died to God, and was renewed in the spirit to do His work. By me, and in me, God has redeemed all flesh from death, and brought the bodies of breathing men into the resurrection state."[180]

Soon his followers were beginning each of their prayer meetings with the biblical admonition that hitherefore had been reserved for Deity: "Lo!

He cometh!"[181] These words were now considered applicable to Prince because he was the divine comforter of fallen mankind.

He advocated a nonsexual permanent relationship that was called "spiritual" marriage: Though members were to go through the outward forms of matrimony, there were to be no sexual relationships within the relationship.[182] That was the theory and most probably lived by it, but definitely not all. One wife who was influencing her husband to leave became pregnant and was literally thrown out of the enclave. A nasty court case was required for her to keep their child.[183] Not that all the underhanded behavior was on one side: One young woman desired to convert and was thrown into an asylum by her family. One of the commissioners running the asylum was convinced that it had been an abuse of family privilege. She was released — and she moved herself into the Agapemonite community and remained there until she died.[184]

Prince himself was married but he began to teach that he was to take an additional woman — "the Bride of the Lamb" — so that the community might be fully purged of its sin. This young woman was the 16-year-old orphan "Sister Zoe."[185] One of the high points of his ministry was when he solemnly promised his followers that in the marriage he was about to undertake, the two of them would cease to be flesh-and-blood creatures and become beings of pure spirit and therefore free of the power of human sexuality. It was perplexing to the members when it was proved that this had not happened. Indeed, it became a public scandal, attended by the loss of a number of members, when the new wife became pregnant and the disgruntled ex-members spread their stories of the sect to enquiring newsmen. As enthusiastically reported to indignant readers, the group was a cesspool of sexual excess.[186]

The couple kept their child, but the nickname "Satan's offspring" stuck, and even the mother gave no indication of being upset by it. The name was justified on the ground that it was the parting indication of Satan's defeat at the hands of Prince, the final opportunity for the devil to inflict pain upon their leader.[187]

One tenet of Prince was that the members of his group would never physically die. When a visitor enquired about those who had, the response was, "They have erred."[188] Prince himself fell into that ultimate "error" when he died in 1899. He had, though, lived to a quite respectable 88. He was buried, local citizens reported, in a standing posture so as to make his resurrection that much easier.[189]

Notes

Introduction

1. Dan Cohn-Sherbok, *A Dictionary of Judaism and Christianity* (Philadelphia, Pennsylvania: Trinity Press International, 1991), 99.
2. Ibid.
3. Ibid.
4. For example, Harris Lenowitz, *The Jewish Messiahs: From the Galilee to Crown Heights* (New York: Oxford University Press, 1998), 98–99, uses Ines of Herrera in the early 1500s as an example of this. We have omitted her from discussion because her "prophetic precursor" role had no specific individual in mind as the promised Messiah nor was the appearance necessarily viewed as imminent.
5. On Communism as a secular messianic/millenarian movement, see Ernest L. Tuveson, "The Millenarian Structure of *The Communist Manifesto*," in *The Apocalypse in English Renaissance Thought and Literature: Patterns, Antecedents and Repercussions*, ed. C. A. Patrides and Joseph Wittreich (Ithaca, New York: Cornell University Press, 1984), 323–341. For a consideration of Marx in particular as advocating a messianic vision see Alistair Kee, "Marx's Messianic Faith," in *Messianism through History*, ed. Wim Beuken, Sean Freyne, and Anton Weiler (Maryknoll, New York: Orbis Books, 1993), 101–113.

Stephen Sharot, *Messianism, Mysticism, and Magic: A Sociological Analysis of Jewish Religious Movements* (Chapel Hill, North Carolina: University of North Carolina Press, 1982), observes that "a number of historians" have argued that the large amount of Jewish involvement in Bolshevism and related movements was caused "in part at least, by the influence of traditional messianism" (213). He contends, however, that the more prominent individuals were secularized Jews and, therefore, the argument will not hold (213–214). A better judgment would seem to be that for secularists, Communism became a nonreligious and substitute form of messianism. For other factors encouraging Jewish support of communism, see 214–217. For a discussion of whether Zionism should be considered a secular form of messianism, see 218–224.

Chapter 1

1. San. 99a, as quoted by Abba H. Silver, *A History of Messianic Speculation in Israel—From the First through the Seventeenth Centuries* (New York: Macmillan Company, 1927), 14.
2. As quoted by M. Avi-Yonah, *The Jews of Palestine: A Political History from the Bar Kokhba War to the Arab Conquest* (New York: Schocken Books, 1976), 169.
3. San. 98b, 99a, as quoted by Raphael Patai, *The Messiah Texts* (Detroit, Michigan: Wayne State University Press, 1979), 26. Parenthetical comment in quote is commentary provided by the translator.
4. San. 99a, as quoted by Silver, 14.
5. Joseph Sarachek, *The Doctrine of the Messiah in Medieval Jewish Literature* (New York: Jewish Theological Seminary of America, 1932), 215, probably has this or similar texts in mind when he vaguely refers to an ancient tradition of this nature that explained why Hezekiah was not made Messiah.
6. San. 94b, as cited by Silver, 13.
7. For a summary of the view, see Rex Mason, "The Messiah in the Postexilic Old Testament Literature," in *King and Messiah in Israel and the Ancient Near East — Proceedings of the Oxford Old Testament Seminar*, ed. John Day, *Journal for the Study of the Old Testament* Supplement Series 270 (Sheffield, England: Sheffield Academic Press, 1998), 343–349.

8. Stewart Perowne, *The Life and Times of Herod the Great* (London: Hodder and Stoughton, 1956), 75.
9. *Ibid.* 70–71. For examples of her efforts to undermine him, see E. Mary Smallwood, *The Jews under Roman Rule — From Pompey to Diocletian*, Studies in Judaism in Late Antiquity Volume 20 (Leiden, Netherlands: E. J. Brill, 1976), 62, 65–67.
10. *Ibid.* 69.
11. Perowne, 80.
12. Smallwood, 69.
13. Perowne, 72.
14. *Ibid.*, 86.
15. For an analysis of the military construction projects of his reign, see Smallwood, 75–80, and Yoram Tzafir, "The Desert Fortresses of Judaea in the Second Temple Period," in *The Jerusalem Cathedra: Studies in the History, Archaeology, Geography and Ethnography of the Land of Israel*, volume 2, ed. Lee I. Levine (Jerusalem: Yad Izhak Ben-Zvi Institute/Wayne State University Press, 1981), 120–145.
16. Doron Mendels, *The Rise and Fall of Jewish Nationalism* (New York: Doubleday, 1992), 286.
17. Richard Fenn, *The Death of Herod: An Essay in the Sociology of Religion* (Cambridge, England: Cambridge University Press, 1992), 95–96.
18. Gerard Israel and Jacques Lebar, *When Jerusalem Burned*, translated from the French by Alan Kendall (New York: William Morrow & Company, Inc., 1973), 33–34.
19. For a description, see Perowne, 119–121.
20. *Ibid.*, 124–125.
21. Sean Freyne, *Galilee and Gospel: Collected Essays* (Tubingen, Germany: Mohr Siebeck, 2000), 93, 95.
22. Aryeh Kasher, *Jews and Hellenistic Cities in Eretz-Israel: Relations of the Jews in Eretz-Israel with the Hellenistic Cities during the Second Temple Period (332 BCE–70 CE)* (Tubingen, Germany: J. C. B. Mohr, 1990), 199. For a description, see Perowne, 125–126.
23. Perowne, 152.
24. For an overview see *Ibid.*, 153–157.
25. Solomon Zeitlin, *Studies in the Early History of Judaism*, Volume 1 (New York: KTAV Publishing House, Inc., 1973), 357.
26. Freyne, *Essays*, 238.
27. Steven M. Bryan, *Jesus and Israel's Traditions of Judgement and Restoration* (Cambridge, England: Cambridge University Press, 2002), 197.
28. *Ibid.*
29. Josephus, *Antiquities* 15.62–65, as quoted by *Ibid.* There are two ways of citing texts in Josephus and, therefore, the style will vary according to which particular source is being utilized.

30. *San.* 97b, as quoted by Albert I. Baumgarten, *The Flourishing of Jewish Sects in the Maccabean Era: An Interpretation*, Supplements to the Journal for the Study of Judaism, volume 55 (Leiden, Netherlands; Brill, 1997), 186. Italicized text is as in Baumgarten's translation to distinguish the scriptural text from the comments. Bracketed remarks are his commentary-explanation.
31. Gaalyahu Cornfeld, *Daniel to Paul: Jews in Conflict with Graeco-Roman Civilization — Historical Background to the Hasmoneans, Dead Sea Scrolls, the New Testament World, Early Christianity, and the Bar-Kochba War* (New York: Macmillan Company, 1962), 139. The subtitle is actually a far better reflection of what is in the book than the title.
32. Martin Sicker, *Between Rome and Jerusalem: 300 Years of Roman-Judaean Relations* (Westport, Connecticut: Praeger, 2001), 106.
33. Sean Freyne, *Galilee: From Alexander the Great to Hadrian, 323 B.C.E. to 135 C.E. — A Study of Second Temple Judaism* (Wilmington, Delaware: Michael Galzier, Inc., and University of Notre Dame Press, 1980), 215.
34. Sicker, 106.
35. R. A. Horsley, "'Messianic' Figures and Movements in First-Century Palestine," in *The Messiah: Developments in Earliest Judaism and Christianity*, ed. James H. Charlesworth, the First Princeton Symposium on Judaism and Christian Origins (Minneapolis, Minnesota: Fortress Press, 1992), 286. Cf. Richard A. Horsley, *Galilee: History, Politics, People* (Valley Forge, Pennsylvania: Trinity Press International, 1995), 269.
36. Josephus, *Antiquities of the Jews* (William Whiston translation), part of the Gutenberg Project, available: http://www.gutenberg.net/etext01/taofj10.txt May 2004, XVII.10.6. Cf. the description of the insurrection in Josephus, *Wars of the Jews* (William Whiston translation), part of the Gutenberg Project, available: http://www.gutenberg.net/etext01/warje10.txt May 2004, II.4.2. Except when a translation is specified as coming from a different source, all quotations from Josephus come from the Whiston translation.
37. Josephus, *Antiquities*, XVII.10.6.
38. The evaluation of whether Simon was regarded as or claimed to be a Messiah varies. Some believe he definitely did, such as Robert Furneaux, *The Roman Siege of Jerusalem* (New York: David McKay Company, Inc., 1972), 15; Jack Gratus, *The False Messiahs* (New York: Taplinger Publishing Company, 1975), 25; Richard Horsley, "Palestinian Jewish Groups and Their Messiahs in Late Second Temple Times," in *Messianism through History*, ed. Wim Beuken, Sean Freyne, and Anton Weiler (Maryknoll, New York: Orbis Books, 1993),

27; and Benedikt Otzen, *Judaism in Antiquity: Political Development and Religious Currents from Alexander to Hadrian*, translated from the Danish by Frederick H. Cryer (Sheffield, England: JSOT Press, 1990). 133.

Others prefer to think in terms of it being possible rather than certain: Jonathan J. Price, *Jerusalem under Siege: The Collapse of the Jewish State, 66–70 C.E* (Leiden: E. J. Brill, 1992), 12, and Menahem Stern, "The Reign of Herod and the Herodian Dynasty," in *The Jewish People in the First Century: Historical Geography, Political History, Social, Cultural and Religious Life and Institutions*, volume 1, edited by S. Safrai and M. Stern (Assen, Netherlands: Van Gorcum & Company, B.V., 1974), 280–281.

Some are skeptical: John J. Collins, *The Scepter and the Star: The Messiahs of the Dead Sea Scrolls and Other Ancient Literature* (New York: Doubleday, 1995), 199.

Others reject the possibility entirely: Jonah Lindering, "Simon of Peraea (4 BCE)," available: http://www.livius.org/men-mh/messiah/messianic_claimants02.html September 2004.

39. Price, 12.
40. Cf. Smallwood, 111.
41. Horsley, "Movements," 287.
42. Israel and Lebar, 50.
43. *Ibid.*
44. Price, 12.
45. Israel and Lebar, 50.
46. Smallwood, 112.
47. *Ibid.*, 112.
48. Jonah Lindering, "Athronges, the Shepherd (4 BCE)," available: http://www.livius.org/men-mh/messiah/messianic_claimants03.html September 2004.
49. The evaluation of whether Athronges should be counted as a messiah varies. That he should be is the position taken by Horsley, "Messiahs," 27, and Otzen, 133. That it is possible but not certain is the stance taken by Lindering, "Athronges" Price, 12; and Stern, "Reign," 280–281. Skeptical is the stance of Collins, *Messiahs*, 199, and outright rejecting (though the explicit term "messianic" is not used) are Richard Gottheil and Kaufmann Koher, "Atthronges," part of *JewishEncyclopedia.com*, available: http://www.jewishencyclopedia.com/view.jsp?artid=2088&letter=A September 2004.
50. Lindering, "Athronges."
51. *Ibid.*
52. For example, Freyne, *Galilee*, 215, 218.
53. Horsley, *Galilee* 269–270.
54. *Ibid.*, 270.
55. Josephus, *Antiquities*, XVII.10.5.
56. Smallwood, 112.
57. Josephus, *Antiquities*, XVII.10.5.
58. Eric M. Meyers, "Sepphoris on the Eve of the Great Revolt (67–68 C.E.): Archaeology and Josephus," in *Galilee through the Centuries: Confluence of Cultures*, ed. Eric M. Meyers (Winona Lake, Indiana: Eisenbrauns, 1999), 114.
59. *Ibid.*
60. Horsley, *Galilee*, 270, who only argues for this as a possibility rather than probability.
61. *Ibid.*, 270–271.
62. In favor of recognizing Judas as a Messiah are Gratus, page 26; Horsley, "Messiahs," 27; Lenowitz, 26–27; and David M. Rhoads, *Israel in Revolution: 6–74 C.E.: A Political History Based on the Writings of Josephus* (Philadelphia, Pennsylvania: Fortress Press, 1976), 51. Stern, "Reign," 280–281, regards it as a mere possibility. Collins, *Messiahs*, 199 is skeptical and it is rejected by Jonah Lindering, "Judas, son of Hezekiah (4 BCE)," available: http://www.livius.org/men-mh/messiah/messianic_claimants01.html September 2004.
63. As quoted by Israel Knohl, *The Messiah before Jesus: The Suffering Servant of the Dead Sea Scrolls*, translated from the Hebrew by David Maisel (Berkeley, California: University of California Press, 2000), 54.
64. As quoted by *Ibid.*, 53.
65. *Ibid.*, 55.
66. *Ibid.*, 60–61.
67. As quoted by *Ibid.*, 62.
68. *Ibid.*
69. As quoted by *Ibid.*, 58.
70. As quoted by *Ibid.*, 59. On the meaning of this word properly being "armor," see n. 26, 126.
71. *Ibid.*, 68.
72. *Ibid.*, 67.
73. *Ibid.*
74. Rebecca Gray, *Prophetic Figures in Late Second Temple Jewish Palestine: The Evidence from Josephus* (New York: Oxford University Press, 1993), 97. For Herod's efforts to neutralize or overcome that Hasmonean opposition, see 97–98.
75. *Ibid.*, 98.
76. *Ibid.*
77. Smallwood, 112.
78. *Ibid.*
79. *Ibid.*
80. *Ibid.*, 112–113.
81. *Ibid.*, 113.
82. *Ibid.*
83. *Ibid.*
84. *Ibid.*

Chapter 2

1. Josephus, *Wars*, II.8.1.
2. For example, Otzen, 133, concurs in this judgment by placing the man's actions

near the time of Jesus' birth. Robert L. Cate, *A History of the Bible Lands in the Interbiblical Period* (Nashville, Tennessee: Broadman Press, 1989), 134, argues that it is "probably the same" man.

3. For a concise but detailed argument, see Rhoads, 50–51.
4. Josephus, *Antiquities*, 18.1.1.
5. Rhoads, 48.
6. Josephus, *Wars*, 2:568, as cited by Rhoads, 48.
7. Rhoads, 50.
8. *Ibid.*, 48.
9. *Ibid.*
10. *Ibid.*, 49.
11. Cf. *Ibid.*, 48.
12. *Ibid.*, 49.
13. *Ibid.*, 53.
14. *Ibid.*, 53.
15. Josephus, *Antiquities*, XVIII.1.1.
16. *Ibid.*, XVIII.10.5.
17. Collins, *Messiahs*, 197.
18. Robert T. Anderson and Terry Giles, *The Keepers: An Introduction to the History and Culture of the Samaritans* (Peabody, Massachusetts: Hendrickson Publishers, Inc., 2002), 38.
19. Cf. Jonah Lindering, "The Samaritan Prophet (36 CE)," available: http://www.livius.org/men-mh/messiah/messianic_claimants06.html September 2004.
20. Josephus, *Antiquities*, XX.8.6.
21. Josephus, *Wars*, II.13.6.
22. Gray, 118.
23. Collins, *Messiahs*, 198.
24. Josephus, *Antiquities*, XX.5.1.
25. Most scholars accept the messianic pretender status of this prophet. For example, Baumgarten, 181; Cate, 142–143; Cornfeld, 322; and Gratus, 26; Lenowitz, 27; Patai, xli; Silver, 6; Smallwood, page 259; and Wilhelm Bacher and Schulim Ochser, "Theudas"; part of *JewishEncyclopedia.com* website, available: http://www.jewishencyclopedia.com/view.jsp?artid=188&letter=T "Theudas." September 2004.Otzen, 133, reduces the evaluation to a probability while Collins, *Messiahs*, 199, is skeptical. Horsley ("Movements," 28) uses Josephus' emphasis on the man claiming to be a prophet to exclude his claiming messianic status.
26. Those who believe that the Jordan image is uppermost in mind include Collins, *Messiahs*, 196. Supporting the idea that both crossings are in mind is Gray, 115.
27. Smallwood, 260.
28. Kasher, *Cities*, 248.
29. Gray, 116.
30. For this common approach, see among others, Usman Sheikh and Mohd Elfie Nieshaem Juferi, "Gamaliel and the Revolt of Theudas;" copyright 2004; available: http://bismikaallahuma.org/Bible/Contra/External/gamaliel-error.htm September 2004.
31. Smallwood, 260.
32. Glen Miller, "Two Historical Issues in Acts: Theudas and the Sanhedrin," available: http://www.christian-thinktank.com/qtheudy.html September 2004.
33. Cate, 143.
34. Gray, 116–117.
35. Suggested as a possibility by Gray, 117.
36. Suggested as a possibility by *Ibid.*, 117–118.
37. *Ibid.*, 117.
38. Josephus, *Antiquities*, XX.8.6.
39. Josephus, *Wars*, II.13.5:6.
40. The Egyptian has been regarded as a messianic aspirant by such individuals as Cornfeld, 323; Gratus, 26; and Smallwood, 275, 276. In contrast, as in the case of Theudas, Horsley ("Movements," 282), uses Josephus' emphasis on the man claiming to be a prophet to exclude his claiming messianic status.
41. Lindering, "Egyptian."
42. *Ibid.*
43. Gray, 118.
44. Josephus, *Wars*, II.22.2.
45. Martin Goodman, *The Ruling Class of Judaea: The Origins of the Jewish Revolt against Rome, A.D. 66–70* (Cambridge: Cambridge University Press, 1987), 163, 205.
46. *Ibid.*, 205.
47. *Ibid.*, 205–206.
48. Horsley, "Movements," 288.
49. Josephus, *Wars*, IV.9.10.
50. Horsley, "Movements," 289.
51. Cf. Jonah Lindering, "Simon bar Giora (69–70 CE)," available: http://www.livius.org/men-mh/messiah/messianic_claimants14.html September 2004.
52. Cf. *Ibid.*, who edges up to this argument without directly expressing it.
53. Martin Goodman, *Judaea*, 205.
54. Gerbern S. Oegema, *The Anointed and His People: Messianic Expectations from the Maccabees to Bar Kochba*, Journal for the Study of the Pseudepigrapha Supplement Series 27 (Sheffield, England: Sheffield Academic Press, 1998), 196.
55. Josephus, *Wars*, 4.504 and 7.118, as cited by Martin Goodman, *Judaea*, 203.
56. Martin Goodman, *Judaea*, 203.
57. Oegema, 196.
58. Jonah Lindering, "John of Gischala (67–70 CE)," available: http://www.livius.org/men-mh/messiah/messianic_claimants12.html September 2004.
59. *Ibid.*
60. Josephus, *Wars*, II.21.1.
61. *Ibid.*

62. *Ibid.*, IV.7.1.
63. Furneaux, 3.
64. *Ibid.*
65. Israel and Lebar, 75.
66. *Ibid.*
67. *Ibid.*
68. *Ibid.*, 76.
69. Collins, *Messiahs*, 200.
70. Rhoads, 9–10.
71. Josephus, *Wars*, III.8.3.
72. *Ibid.*, III.8.9.
73. *Ibid.*, VI.5.4.
74. Tacitus, *Histories*, 5.13, translated by Alfred John Church and William Jackson Brodribb, available: http://classics.mit.edu/Tacitus/histories.html September 2004.
75. Suetonius, in the *Lives of the Caesars*, the *Life of Vespasian* 4.5, J. C. Rolf translation, available: http://www.fordham.edu/halsall/ancient/suetonius-index.html September 2004.
76. For a discussion of the skepticism, see Tessa Rajak, *Josephus: The Historian and His Society*, Second Edition (London: Duckworth, 1983, 2002), 187–188.
77. *Ibid.*, 188.
78. Jonah Lindering, "Vespasian (67 CE)," available: http://www.livius.org/men-mh/messiah/messianic_claimants13.html September 2004.
79. *Ibid.*
80. Cf. *Ibid.*

Chapter 3

1. Oegema, 197. For a concise review of the rationale for the suggested dates for each of the rebellions, see Shimon Applebaum, *Jews and Greeks in Ancient Cyrene*, Studies in Judaism in Late Antiquity, Volume 28 (Leiden, Netherlands: E. J. Brill, 1979), 265–269.
2. The view of Anthony R. Birley, *Hadrian: The Restless Emperor* (London: Routledge, 1997), 73, among others.
3. Smallwood, 397–399.
4. Cornfeld, 346.
5. *Ibid.*
6. Applebaum, *Cyrene*, 294–295; Gedaliah Alon, *The Jews in Their Land in the Talmudic Age (70–640 C.E.)*, translated and edited by Gershon Levi, Volume 2 (Jerusalem: Mangnes Press, the Hebrew University, 1980), 399–400; and John M. G. Barclay, *Jews in the Mediterranean Diaspora: From Alexander to Trajan (323 B.C.E.–117 C.E.)* (Edinburgh: T & T Clark, 1996), 80.
7. Cf. Applebaum, *Cyrene*, 339. For possible evidence that the exports were temporarily disrupted, see 339–340.
8. Alon, 2:407.

9. Dio Cassius only mentions the fact of the rebellion, while it is Eusebius who points out the major Jewish role in the events: Cf. Smallwood, 418–419.
10. Barclay, 78.
11. Cassius Dio, *History*, LXVIII, 32.1–2, as cited by Menahem Stern, *Greek and Latin Authors on Jews and Judaism;* volume 2: *From Tacitus to Simplicius* (Jerusalem: Israel Academy of Sciences and Humanities, 1980), 385.
12. Applebaum, *Cyrene*, 303. For possible archaeological evidence, see Alon, 2:417–418 and n. 14, 417. For possible evidence from the Talmud, see Alon, 2:420–425.
13. Lenowitz, 51.
14. Julius H. Greenstone, *The Messiah Idea in Jewish History* (Philadelphia, Pennsylvania: Jewish Publication Society of America, 1906), 89–90.
15. Cornfeld, 350.
16. For a summary of his reported journeys, see Peter Schafer, "Rabbi Aqiva and Bar Kokhba," in *Approaches to Ancient Judaism*, volume 2, ed. William Scott Green, in the Brown University Judaic Studies number 9 (Chico, California: Scholars Press, 1980), 114–117.
17. As quoted by Yigael Yadin, *Bar-Kokhba: The Rediscovery of the Legendary Hero of the Second Jewish Revolt against Rome* (New York: Random House, 1971), 18.
18. As quoted by *Ibid.*, 18–19.
19. Eusebius, *Ecclesiastical History*, 4.6, 2, as quoted by Joseph A. Fitzmyer, "The Bar Cochba Period," in *The Bible in Current Catholic Thought*, ed. John L. McKenzie (New York: Herder and Herder, 1962), n. 26, 140.
20. Dan Cohn-Sherbok, *The Jewish Messiah* (Edinburgh, Scotland: T & T Clark, 1997), 83.
21. Greenstone, 90, 91; and Henk Jagersma, *A History of Israel from Alexander the Great to Bar Kochba*, translated from the Dutch by John Bowden (Philadelphia, Pennsylvania: Fortress Press, 1986), 158.
22. Greenstone, 91.
23. As quoted by *Ibid.*, 90.
24. Joseph Klausner, *The Messianic Idea in Israel — From Its Beginning to the Completion of the Mishnah*, translated from the third Hebrew edition by W. F. Stinespring (New York: Macmillan Company, 1955), 395.
25. *Ibid.*
26. For a form of this idea, see *Ibid.*
27. *Ibid.*, 394–395. Birley (270), estimates he would have been in his eighties.
28. Cf. Robert N. Levine, *There Is No Messiah and You're It: The Stunning Transformation of Judaism's Most Provocative Idea* (Woodstock, Vermont: Jewish Lights Publishing, 2003), 30.

29. For this line of reasoning and the quotation, see Robert N. Levine, 30.
30. Greenstone, 90.
31. Sarachek, 12.
32. As quoted by A. Cohen, *The Teachings of Maimonides* (New York: KTAV Publishing House, Inc., 1968), 223. For a different translation of this, in the broader original context, see Maimonides, "Maimonides— the Messiah: The Laws Concerning Mashiach; Chapters 11 & 12 of Hilchos Melachim from the Mishneh Torah of the Rambam." available: *http://chebar0.tripod.com/id109.htm* May 2004.
33. As quoted by Nahumn N. Glatzer, *The Judaic Tradition* (Boston, Massachusetts: Beacon Press, 1969), 489. See 488–491 for both statements in their broader context.
34. Eusebius, *Church History* iv, 6, 2, as quoted by Smallwood, 439.
35. Smallwood, n. 44, 439.
36. All the quotations about this incident come from the *Yerushalmi Taanit* 4:5, as quoted by Jacob Neusner, "Bringing the Messiah: The Torah and Responsive Grace," in *Jewish-Christian Debates: God, Kingdom, Messiah*, ed. Jacob Neusner and Bruce Chilton (Minneapolis, Minnesota: Augsburg Fortress Publishers, 1998), 180. For a discussion of differences between the Jerusalem Talmud and the Babylonian Talmud in their treatment of this revolt and why the Jerusalem version is more credible, see Joshua Efron, *Studies on the Hasmonean Period*, Studies in Judaism in Late Antiquity, volume 39 (Leiden: E. J. Brill, 1987), 145–147.
37. *Yerushalmi Taanit* 4:5, as quoted by Neusner, "Torah," 180.
38. Collins, *Messiahs*, 203.
39. As quoted by Yadin, 125.
40. As quoted by *Ibid.*, 126.
41. As quoted by *Ibid.*, 137.
42. *Ibid.* 137. For a discussion of who these "Galileans" might have been and why it is unlikely that the term was an euphemism for Christians, see 138.
43. For the account of this killing, see Neusner, "Torah," page 181.
44. Robert N. Levine, 29.
45. *Ibid.*
46. For a discussion of the Talmudic texts touching on his death, see Schafer, 121–124, which notes that there is a later tradition that refers to his execution but does not mention the torture and abuse.
47. Jacob Neusner, *A History of the Jews in Babylonia: The Parthian Period*, Brown University Judaic Studies Number 62 (Chico, California: Scholars Press, 1969, 1984), 86.
48. As quoted by Avi-Yonah, 77.
49. Smallwood, 467–468.
50. Neusner, *Babylonia*, 86, and Smallwood, 468.
51. Neusner, *Babylonia*, 86.
52. As quoted by Avi-Yonah, 77.
53. *Ibid.*
54. *Ibid.*, 78.
55. As quoted by *Ibid.*, 79.
56. *Ibid.*, 79.

Chapter 4

1. Jacob Neusner, *Israel and Iran in Talmudic Times: A Political History* (Lanham, Maryland: University Press of America, 1986), 121.
2. As quoted by *Ibid.*, 120–121.
3. *Ibid.*, 122.
4. Silver, 27–28.
5. Such as Cyril of Jerusalem in the fourth century. See Silver, 35.
6. Silver, 28.
7. *Ibid.*, 29.
8. *Ibid.*
9. Cohn-Sherbok, *Messiah*, 84.
10. *Sanhedrin* 99a, as quoted by *Ibid.*
11. *Sanhedrin* 99a, as quoted by *Ibid.*
12. *Mid. R. Ekah* 1.13, as quoted by Silver, 29. For assorted other quotations, see 28–29.
13. The translator of Klausner (unnumbered note, 423), argues that, for computational purposes, this can just as appropriately be rounded down to 3760 B.C.
14. *Abodah Zarah* 9b, as quoted by Klausner, 422.
15. *Sanhedrin* 97b, as quoted by *Ibid.*
16. For example, *Ibid.*, 423.
17. Silver, 30.
18. For quotations, see Silver, 30.
19. *Pesahim* 54b, as quoted by Klausner, 423. Klausner notes (n. 18, 423–424) that certain manuscripts subject to non-Jewish review substituted the kingdom of "Persia" or "Macedonia" in the final words of the quote.
20. *Sanhedrin* 97b, as quoted by *Ibid.*, 424.
21. Silver, 29.
22. Socrates, *The Ecclesiastical History of Socrates*, translated from the Greek (London: Henry G. Bohn, 1853), Book 7, Chapter 8.
23. For example, by Gratus, 55;Patai, xli; and Sharot, 53.
24. Sharot, 55.
25. Socrates, Book 7, Chapter 8.
26. *Ibid.*

Chapter 5

1. Avi-Yonah, 260.
2. *Ibid.*
3. *Ibid.*
4. *Ibid.*

5. *Ibid.*, 266.
6. *Ibid.*
7. *Ibid.*, 268.
8. *Ibid.*, 269.
9. As quoted by *Ibid.*
10. *Ibid.*
11. *Ibid.*
12. For a detailed analysis of the evidence from both midrashes and contemporary apocalypses that the Arabs were now pictured in this role, see the extensive collection of summaries and quotations in Silver, 37–54.
13. Avi-Yonah, 271–272.
14. *Ibid.*, 272–273.
15. Silver, 36–37.
16. As quoted by George W. Buchanan, *Revelation and Redemption: Jewish Documents of Deliverance from the Fall of Jerusalem to the Death of Nahmanides* (Dillsboro, North Carolina: Western North Carolina Press, 1978), 177.
17. Lenowitz, 64.
18. The name is variously spelled Serenus, Saur, Zonoria, and Sari'a.
19. The fragment of which this is part is found in some copies of the *Espana Sagrada*, Trat. 27, Apend. 2, 53, as quoted by Buchanan, 176–177.
20. Buchanan, 177.
21. Lenowitz, 77.
22. As quoted by *Ibid.*
23. Cohn-Sherbok, *Messiah*, 94, and Silver, 56.
24. Cohn-Sherbok, *Messiah*, 94, and Silver, 56.
25. Silver, 56.
26. Gratus, 56.
27. For two specific examples, see Silver, 45, 46.
28. *Ibid.*, 55.
29. Sharot, 53.
30. Buchanan, 178, and Cohn-Sherbok, *Messiah*, 94.
31. Silver, 55.
32. *Ibid.*, 55–56.
33. Jonah Lindering, "Abu Isa'," available: http://www.livius.org/men-mh/messiah/messiah_med02.html September 2004.
34. Haim Beinart, *Atlas of Medieval Jewish History* (New York: Simon & Schuster, 1992), 29, and Sharot, 54.
35. As quoted by Buchanan, 178.
36. Cohn-Sherbok, *Messiah*, 93–94.
37. Sharot, 53.
38. Cohn-Sherbok, *Messiah*, 94, and Silver, 56.
39. Sharot, 54.
40. Cohn-Sherbok, *Messiah*, 94.
41. Sharot, 54.
42. Silver, 56.
43. Beinart, *Atlas*, 29.
44. *Ibid.*
45. Silver, 56.
46. As quoted by Cohn-Sherbok, *Messiah*, 95.
47. Sharot, 54.
48. Cohn-Sherbok, *Messiah*, 95.
49. Silver, 57.
50. *Ibid.*
51. *Ibid.* notes only two documentable dissenters, one in the twelfth and one in the thirteenth century.
52. *Ibid.*
53. *Ibid.*, 48–54.
54. *Ibid.*, 52.
55. *Ibid.*, 52–53.
56. *Ibid.*, 53–55.

Chapter 6

1. Marjorie Reeves, "The Development of Apocalyptic Thought: Medieval Attitudes," in *The Apocalypse in English Renaissance Thought and Literature: Patterns, Antecedents and Repercussions*, ed. C. A. Patrides and Joseph Wittreich (Ithaca, New York: Cornell University Press, 1984), 45–46.
2. Bernard McGinn, *Visions of the End: Apocalyptic Traditions in the Middle Ages* (New York: Columbia University Press, 1979), 88.
3. Sharot, n. 13, 259.
4. *Ibid.*, 55, and Lenowitz, 65.
5. Silver, 79. On the rival dates, see Sharot, 58.
6. As quoted by Silver, 79.
7. Sharot, 55.
8. *Ibid.*
9. Guibert of Nogent, *The Deeds of God through the Franks*, Book 2: 86, 90–91, translated by Robert Levine; copyright 1997 (part of Project Gutenberg). Available: http://www.gutenberg.net/etext03/7deed10.txt May 2004.
10. For an analysis that concludes that the armies resulting from the pope's plea were far different than what he had been hoping for, see Robert Chazan, *In the Year 1096: The First Crusade and the Jews* (Philadelphia: Jewish Publication Society, 1996), 19–21.
11. For a summary of specific individuals referring to this year see Silver, 58–60.
12. *Ibid.*, 77.
13. For contemporary quotations on the subject, see Adrian J. Boas, *Jerusalem in the Time of the Crusades: Society, Landscape and Art in the Holy City under Frankish Rule* (London: Routledge, 2001), 40, 165.
14. Silver, 59.
15. For a book-length development of this theme, see Allan H. Cutler and Helen Elmquist Cutler, *The Jew as Ally of the Muslim:*

Medieval Roots of Anti-Semitism (Notre Dame, Indiana: University of Notre Dame Press, 1986), 92–94.

16. As quoted by Guibert of Nogent, *The Memoirs of Abbot Guibert of Nogent — Self and Society in Medieval France* (Toronto, Ontario: University of Toronto Press, 1970; 1984 reprint), 134–135.

17. As quoted by Beinart, *Atlas*, 38. Bracketed interjections are the remarks of the translator. On efforts of Catholics to abort such extremism, see page 39. For four accounts by Jews as to how the Crusades affected their community, see the texts reprinted in Shlomo Eidelberg, *The Jews and the Crusaders: The Hebrew Chronicles of the First and Second Crusades*, texts translated and edited by Shlomo Eidelberg (Madison, Wisconsin: University of Wisconsin Press, 1977). On whether the persecutions of 1096 should be regarded as a turning point in Jewish history in the Middle Ages, see the discussion of Jeremy Cohen, "A 1096 Complex? Constructing the First Crusade in Jewish Historical Memory, Medieval and Modern," in *Jews and Christians in Twelfth-Century Europe*, ed. Michael A. Signer and John Van Engen, Notre Dame Conferences in Medieval Studies Number X (Notre Dame, Indiana: University of Notre Dame Press, 2001), 9–26.

18. Chazan, *1096*, 24, and Robert Chazan, "From the First Crusade to the Second: Evolving Perceptions of the Christian-Jewish Conflict," in *Jews and Christians in Twelfth-Century Europe*, ed. Michael A. Signer and John Van Engen, Notre Dame Conferences in Medieval Studies Number X (Notre Dame, Indiana: University of Notre Dame Press, 2001), 47.

19. For quotations see Silver, 60–61.
20. See the quotations in *Ibid.*, 61–63.
21. Eidelberg, 13.
22. *Ibid.*
23. Silver., 74.
24. Eidelberg, n. 19, 140.
25. The exact data is uncertain: Silver, 78, 80.
26. *Ibid.*, 78.
27. *Ibid.*, page 78.
28. Lenowitz, 66.
29. *Ibid.*
30. *Ibid.*
31. *Ibid.*
32. *Ibid.*
33. *Ibid.*
34. Gratus, 60.
35. *Ibid.*
36. *Ibid.*, 61.
37. *Ibid.*
38. *Ibid.*
39. Philip Schaff, Chapter 10, "History and Its Suppression," in *History of the Christian Church* (1910 edition), available: http://www.bible.ca/history/philip-schaff/5_ch10.htm October 2004.
40. *Ibid.*
41. Dana C. Munro, *The Middle Ages, 395–1272* (New York: The Century Company, 1921), 354–365, as available at: http://www.shsu.edu/~his_ncp/Munro25.html October 2004.
42. Gratus, 61.
43. Munro, n.p.
44. *Ibid.*
45. Some date this individual in the first decade of the twelfth century (Sharot, 55), while others choose the second (Silver, 79).
46. As quoted by Silver, 79.
47. *Ibid.*
48. Sharot, 55.
49. Lenowitz, 65.
50. Azriel Eisenberg, Hannah G. Goodman, and Alvin Kass, *Eyewitnesses to Jewish History: From 586 B.C.E. to 1967* (New York: Union of American Hebrew Congregations, 1973), 55.
51. For the view that the Karaites' recognition of him as their founder actually vastly overstated his influence — since they relied on his teachings quite selectively — see Robert Brody, *The Geonim of Babylonia and the Shaping of Medieval Jewish Culture* (New Haven: Yale University Press, 1998), 85–91. For a collection of representative Karaite writings, see Leon Nemoy, *Karaite Anthology: Excerpts from the Early Literature* (New Haven: Yale University Press, 1952).
52. Reuben Kaufman, . *Great Sects and Schisms in Judaism* (New York: Jonathan David, Publishers, 1967), 38.
53. *Ibid.*, 39.
54. Beinart, *Atlas*, 29.
55. Kaufman, 39.
56. *Ibid.*, 40.
57. Silver, 77.
58. Kaufman, 39.
59. Silver, 77.
60. Lenowitz, 67.
61. Moshe Idel, *Messianic Mystics* (New Haven: Yale University Press, 1998), 263.
62. *Ibid.*
63. Lenowitz, 68.
64. *Ibid.*, 67.
65. Sharot, 259.
66. Idel, 263.
67. Silver, 79.
68. *Ibid.*, 48, 79.
69. Cf. *Ibid.*, 75.
70. *Ibid.*, 212.
71. *Ibid.*, 212.
72. *Ibid.*, 75.
73. Cf. *Ibid.*, 80–81.

74. Lenowitz, 81.
75. *Ibid.*
76. *Ibid.*, 82–83.
77. *Ibid.*, 82.
78. *Ibid.*, 82–83.
79. Cohn-Sherbok, *Messiah*, 108.
80. As quoted by *Ibid.*
81. *Ibid.*
82. Sharot, 56.
83. Cohn-Sherbok, *Messiah*, 108.
84. For accounts and denials see Lenowitz, 84–86.
85. For accounts, see *Ibid.*, 84, 86.
86. *Ibid.*, 83.
87. *Ibid.*
88. *Ibid.*
89. Cohn-Sherbok, *Messiah*, 108.
90. *Ibid.*
91. Lenowitz, 83.
92. As quoted by *Ibid.*, 87.
93. *Ibid.*, 83.
94. Sharot, 56.
95. Silver, 80.
96. *Ibid.*
97. For the account, see Jacob R. Marcus, *The Jew in the Medieval World: A Source Book, 315–1791* (Cincinnati, Ohio: Sinai Press, 1938), 148.
98. As quoted by *Ibid.*, 249. For a detailed account of his life, see 247–250. Cf. Eisenberg, Goodman, and Kass, 85.
99. Silver, 74–75.
100. As quoted by A. Cohen, 229.
101. Silver, 75.
102. Cohen, 230.
103. Marcel Poorthuis, "Messianism between Reason and Delusion: Maimonides and the Messiah," in *Messianism through History*, ed. Wim Beuken, Sean Freyne, and Anton Weiler (Maryknoll, New York: Orbis Books, 1993), 64.
104. *Ibid.*
105. Maimonides, *Letters of Maimonides*, translated and edited with introductions and notes by Leon D. Stitskin (New York: Yeshiva University Press, 1977), 128–129.
106. *Ibid.*, 128.
107. *Ibid.*, 128–129.
108. Silver, 88.
109. *Ibid.*
110. *Ibid.*
111. *Ibid.*, 82.
112. *Ibid.*
113. Jonah Lindering, "Abulafia," available: http://www.livius.org/men-mh/messiah/messiah_med06.html September 2004.
114. Idel, 58.
115. *Ibid.*
116. *Ibid.*, and Cohn-Sherbok, *Messiah*, 113.
117. Idel, 58–59.
118. *Ibid.*
119. Cohn-Sherbok, *Messiah*, 113.
120. Lindering, "Abulafia."
121. Lenowitz, 94.
122. As quoted by Abraham Burger, "The Messianic Self-Consciousness of Abraham Abulafia: A Tentative Evaluation," in *Essays on Jewish Life and Thought — Presented in Honor of Salo W. Baron*, ed. Joseph L. Blau (New York: Columbia University Press, 1959), 55. For various ways in which the messianic claim was expressed by Abulafia, see 56–57.
123. *Ibid.*, 57.
124. As quoted by *Ibid.*, 69.
125. Idel, 59. On doubts as to the accuracy of his chronology, see page 59.
126. As quoted by *Ibid.*, 98.
127. Cohn-Sherbok, *Messiah*, 113.
128. Idel, 61.
129. *Ibid.*, 99.
130. The view of Gratus, 45, Lindering, "Abulafia," and Abraham A. Neuman, *The Jews in Spain: Their Social, Political and Cultural Life during the Middle Ages*, Volume 2 (Philadelphia, Pennsylvania: Jewish Publication Society of America, 1942; 1944 printing), 114.
131. Idel, 98.
132. *Ibid.*
133. *Ibid.*, 99.
134. *Ibid.* For possible evidence that this event had a direct impact upon the composition of the *Zohar*, see 122–123.
135. Cohn-Sherbok, 113.
136. Idel, 59.
137. *Ibid.*, 60.
138. *Ibid.*
139. *Ibid.*
140. Neuman, 115.
141. Idel, 60.
142. Yitzhak Baer, *A History of the Jews in Christian Spain*, volume 1: *From the Age of Reconquest to the Fourteenth Century*, translated from the Hebrew by Louis Schoffman (Philadelphia, Pennsylvania: Jewish Publication Society of America, 1961), 278.
143. Idel, 109.
144. Neuman, 113–114.
145. Baer, 1:278.
146. *Ibid.*
147. Neuman, 114.
148. *Ibid.*
149. *Ibid.*
150. *Ibid.*
151. Silver, 100.
152. Baer, 1:278.
153. As quoted by *Ibid.*, 279.
154. As quoted by *Ibid.*, 278–279.
155. *Ibid.*
156. *Ibid.*, 279.
157. Silver, 90.

Chapter 7

1. Silver, 102.
2. *Ibid*. For a discussion of how they arrived at their dates see 104–108.
3. Paul Goodman, "Introduction," in *Isaac Abravanel: Six Lectures*, ed. J. B. Trend and H. Loewe (Cambridge, England: Cambridge University Press, 1937), 3.
4. M. Gaster, Abravanel's Literary Work," in *Isaac Abravanel: Six Lectures*, ed. J. B. Trend and H. Loewe (Cambridge, England: Cambridge University Press, 1937), 57.
5. As quoted by L. Rabinowitz, "Abravanel as Exegete," in *Isaac Abravanel: Six Lectures*, ed. J. B. Trend and H. Loewe (Cambridge: At the University Press, 1937), 87.
6. *Ibid*.
7. *Ibid*.
8. As quoted by Marc Saperstein, *Jewish Preaching: 1200–1800 — An Anthology* (New Haven, Connecticut: Yale University Press, 1989), 183.
9. As quoted by *Ibid*., 13.
10. Silver, 111.
11. *Ibid*., 110.
12. See the testimony of Jehiel ben Samuel of Pisa, Italy, in 1539: Silver, 111.
13. For an evaluation that accepts the number of secret Jews between 1480 and 1492 as some 13,000, see Yitzhak Baer, *A History of the Jews in Christian Spain; volume 2: From the Fourteenth Century to the Expulsion*, translated from the Hebrew by Louis Schoffman (Philadelphia, Pennsylvania: Jewish Publication Society of America, 1961), 424. For the argument that the number of *conversos* secretly practicing Judaism was actually declining precipitously before the Inquisition was created in 1480, see Benzion Netanyahu, *Toward the Inquisition: Essays on Jewish and Converso History in Late Medieval Spain* (Ithaca, New York: Cornell University Press, 1997), 194–195. For a wide selection of Inquisition-gained testimony as to how Portuguese and Spanish covert Jews pictured the coming Messiah during the 1400s and 1500s, see David M. Gitlitz, *Secrecy and Deceit: The Religion of the Crypto-Jews* (Philadelphia Pennsylvania: Jewish Publication Society, 1996), 103–110.
14. Renee L. Melammed, *Heretics or Daughters of Israel? The Crypto-Jewish Women of Castile* (New York: Oxford University Press, 1999), 45, 169.
15. *Ibid*., 65, 72.
16. *Ibid*., 45. For a detailed study of Ines of Herrera, see Haim Beinart, "Inez of Herrera del Duque: The Prophetess of Extremadura," in *Women in the Inquisition: Spain and the New World*, ed. Mary E. Giles (Baltimore Maryland: Johns Hopkins University Press, 1999), 42–52.
17. Silver, 110–111.
18. Joseph Dan, "Introduction," in *The Early Kabbalah*, ed. Joseph Dan (Mahwah, New Jersey: Paulist Press, 1986), 1.
19. *Ibid*., 4.
20. For an analysis of the evidence, see *Ibid*., 4–5.
21. *Ibid*., 5–6.
22. *Ibid*., 6.
23. David J. Halperin, *Abraham Miguel Cardozo: Selected Writings*, in the series Classics of Western Spirituality (Mahwah, New Jersey: Paulist Press, 2001), 22.
24. Cf. *Ibid*.
25. Dan, 9.
26. *Ibid*.
27. Lawrence Fine, *Safed Spirituality: Rules of Mystical Piety, the Beginning of Wisdom*, in the series Classics of Western Spirituality (New York: Paulist Press, 1984), 3.
28. Idel, 164.
29. Lenowitz, 126.
30. Fine, 2.
31. *Ibid*., and Lenowitz, 126.
32. Silver, 113.
33. Cf. *Ibid*.
34. *Ibid*., 101.
35. Joseph Jacobs and Jacob Z. Lauterbach, "Moses Botarel," part of *JewishEncyclopedia.com*, available: 36. http://www.jewishencyclopedia.com/view.jsp?artid=848&letter=M September 2004.
37. As quoted by Silver, 108.
38. No attribution, *Sefer Yetzirah*, translated from the Hebrew by William W. Westcott (1887), available: http://www.houseofthehorizon.org/public/documents.php?id=123 October 2004.
39. Silver, 109.
40. *Ibid*. Cf. Jacobs and Lauterbach.
41. Heinrich Gratez, Chapter 6, "Jewish Apostates and the Disputation at Tortosa," in the *History of the Jews* (Philadelphia Pennsylvania: Jewish Publication Society of America, 189?), available: http://216.239.41.104/search?q=cache:7vLCHkMfR80J:www.saltshakers.com/lm/GraetB.rtf+Moses%2BBotarel&hl=en October 2004.
42. Silver, 109.
43. *Ibid*.
44. Lenowitz, 99, and Silver, 143.
45. Ruth Ellen Gruber and Samuel D. Gruber, "*Jewish Monuments in Slovenia*," *Jewish Heritage Report*, Vol. II, Nos. 1–2/Spring–Summer 1998, Slovenia.
46. Silver, 143.
47. Idel, 140.
48. Cecil Roth, *The History of the Jews of Italy* (Philadelphia, Pennsylvania: Jewish Publication Society of America, 1946), 191.
49. Silver, 144.

Notes—Chapter 7

50. *Ibid.*
51. *Ibid.*, 144–145.
52. As quoted by Lenowitz, 101.
53. As quoted by *Ibid.*
54. *Ibid.*, 100.
55. The view, for example, of Silver, 144, and Morris M. Faierstein, *Jewish Mystical Autobiographies: "Book of Visions" and "Book of Secrets,"* in the series Classics of Western Spirituality (Mahwah, New Jersey: Paulist Press, 1999), 5.
56. For example, Lenowitz, 100.
57. For example, Idel, 140.
58. Roth, *Italy*, 191.
59. *Ibid.*
60. Silver, 145.
61. Lenowitz, 100.
62. Silver, 145–146.
63. Cf. n. 144, p. 145, 145, on the apparent covert propaganda of the movement.
64. *Ibid.*, 146–147.
65. Cohn-Sherbok, *Messiah*, 126.
66. Sharot, 64.
67. Patai, xlv.
68. Lenowitz, 103.
69. *Ibid.*, 103.
70. As quoted by B. Halper, *Post-Biblical Hebrew Literature: An Anthology* (Philadelphia, Pennsylvania: Jewish Publication Society of America, 1921), 234.
71. Silver, 146.
72. Roth, *Italy*, 191.
73. Silver, 146.
74. Leon Poliakov, *Jewish Bankers and the Holy See—From the Thirteenth to the Seventeenth Century,* translated from the French by Miriam Kochan (London, England: Routledge & Kegan Paul, 1977), 125.
75. Sam Waagenaar, *The Pope's Jews* (La Salle, Illinois: Open Court Publishers, 1974), 148.
76. *Ibid.*, 148–149.
77. Cf. *Ibid.*, 149.
78. *Ibid.*
79. *Ibid.*, 150.
80. Cohn-Sherbok, *Messiah*, 127.
81. Beinart, *History*, 97.
82. *Ibid.*
83. *Ibid.*
84. Abraham B. Mordecai Ferizon as quoted by Halper, 233.
85. Abraham B. Mordecai Ferizon as quoted by *Ibid.*, 234.
86. Waagenaar, 151.
87. *Ibid.*
88. Poliakov, 125.
89. As quoted by Gratus, 81.
90. *Ibid.*, 81–82.
91. Waagenaar, 146.
92. *Ibid.*
93. *Ibid.*, 147.
94. Poliakov, 125.
95. Cohn-Sherbok, *Messiah*, 127.
96. Beinart, *History*, 98.
97. *Ibid.*
98. Waagenaar, 151.
99. *Ibid.*, 152.
100. *Ibid.*
101. Cf. *Ibid.*
102. Silver, 146.
103. Waagenaar, 152.
104. Cohn-Sherbok, *Messiah*, 128.
105. Waagenaar, 153.
106. *Ibid.*, 154–155.
107. Beinart, *History*, 98.
108. Cf. *Ibid.*
109. *Ibid.*, 156.
110. Beinart, *History*, 98.
111. Silver, 147.
112. Cohn-Sherbok, *Messiah*, 128. In light of their conviction that a major cause of medieval anti-Semitism was the widespread conviction that Jews were implicit and even explicit allies of the Islamic foe, Cutler and Cutler (n. 68, 417), speculate that the two men were "probably arrested because he considered them Turkish double agents who pretended to want to help the Christians but who in reality were attempting to gain the confidence of the Christians in order to betray them to the Turks at a decisive moment later in time."
113. Waagenar, 138.
114. Lenowitz, 107.
115. *Ibid.*
116. Waagenaar, 138.
117. Silver, 147.
118. *Ibid.*, 107.
119. *Ibid.*
120. Cohn-Sherbok, *Messiah*, 128.
121. Silver, 149.
122. Lenowitz, 104.
123. Silver, 149.
124. Waagenaar, 152.
125. Silver, 149.
126. Waagenaar, 152–153.
127. *Ibid.*, 153.
128. *Ibid.*, 152.
129. Silver, 148.
130. Waagenaar, 153.
131. *Ibid.*
132. Cf. Idel, 144.
133. *Ibid.*, 145.
134. Lenowitz, 93.
135. As quoted by Idel, 149. For the entire, lengthy quotation of which this is part, see 148–149.
136. As quoted by *Ibid.*, 145–146.
137. As quoted by Marcus, 253.
138. Silver, 149.
139. Idel, 145.
140. Silver, 149.
141. As quoted by Gratus, 86–87.

142. Waagenaar, 153.
143. Silver, 149.
144. Waagenaar, 154–155.
145. Lenowitz, 107; Roth, *Italy*, 192; and Sharot, 65.
146. Waagenaar, 154.
147. For the inferential reasoning that leads to this conclusion, see Idel, 146.
148. *Ibid.*, 147.
149. Waagenaar, 154–155.
150. *Ibid.*, 155.
151. *Ibid.*, 156.
152. Roth, *Italy*, 192, and Silver, 149.
153. *Ibid.*, 150.
154. *Ibid.*, 156.
155. Sharot, 65.
156. *Ibid.*
157. Waagenaar, 156.
158. *Ibid.*, 157.
159. *Ibid.*, 156–157.
160. Gratus, 87.
161. Idel, 146.
162. Gratus, 87, and Roth, 192.
163. Waagenaar, 157.
164. As quoted by Gratus, 87.
165. Waagenaar, 157.
166. Silver, 149.
167. *Ibid.*, 150.
168. Sharot, 78.
169. *Ibid.*
170. *Ibid.*
171. *Ibid.*
172. Lenowitz, 98.
173. Sharot, 79.
174. Cf. the comments on this report in Lenowitz, 98.
175. *Ibid.*
176. Sharot, 79.
177. Fine, 61.
178. Lenowitz, 127.
179. *Ibid.* On where to place it in his lifetime, see Gershom Scholem, *Kabbalah* (New York: New York Times Book Company, 1974), 421.
180. Fine, 30.
181. *Ibid.*, 61.
182. Lenowitz, 127.
183. Fine, 61.
184. *Ibid.*
185. Cf. *Ibid.*, 61–62.
186. Idel, 165.
187. Faierstein, 10. For a discussion of the other individuals, see Scholem, *Kabbalah*, 424–426.
188. Faierstein, 6.
189. Idel, 165.
190. *Ibid.*
191. Lenowitz, 126.
192. *Rules of Mystical Piety*, 15, as quoted by Fine, 69.
193. *Ibid.*, 127.

194. *Ibid.*
195. *Ibid.*
196. *Ibid.*, 137.
197. *Ibid.*
198. *Ibid.*, 136.
199. Faierstein, 7.
200. *Ibid.*, 13.
201. Lenowitz, 137.
202. *Ibid.*
203. Faierstein, 7.
204. *Ibid.*
205. *Ibid.*
206. *Ibid.*
207. *Ibid.*, 8.
208. *Ibid.*, 7.
209. *Ibid.*
210. *Ibid.*
211. *Ibid.*, 8.
212. *Ibid.*
213. *Ibid.*, 9.
214. *Ibid.*, 8.
215. *Ibid.*, 8.
216. See the account of his various dreams proving that he was superior to Karo in *Ibid.*, 16–17.
217. *Ibid.*, 8.
218. *Ibid.*
219. *Ibid.*, 9.
220. *Ibid.*
221. *Ibid.*, 21.
222. *Ibid.*, 21–22.
223. *Ibid.*, 9.
224. *Ibid.*, 9–10.
225. *Ibid.*, 22–23.
226. *Ibid.*, 10.
227. As quoted by Idel, 166. For three examples of such dreams, see the texts in Patai, 267–269, and the one by his son, Samuel Vital (269–270). Also see the discussion of his varying types of messianic claims in Faierstein, 15–16.
228. Idel, 166.
229. See the two examples in Patai, 268–269.
230. *Shivhe R. Hayyim Vital*, 2b–3a, as quoted by Patai, 30.
231. For others in the broader kabbalistic movement in Safed who made messianic allusions without quite fully embracing their personal application, see Idel, 166.
232. *Ibid.*, 167.
233. *Ibid.*
234. *Ibid.*
235. Faierstein, 17.
236. *Ibid.*

Chapter 8

1. For his account of the vision, see Sara T. Nalle, *Mad for God: Bartolome Sanchez, the*

Secret Messiah of Cardenete (Charlottesville, Virginia: University Press of Virginia, 2001), 16–17.

2. *Ibid.*, 17.
3. As quoted by *Ibid.*, 28.
4. As quoted by *Ibid.*, 38.
5. *Ibid.*, 101.
6. *Ibid.*, 107–109.
7. For a detailed discussion of the actions, see *Ibid.*, 110–119.
8. As quoted by *Ibid.*, 120.
9. *Ibid.*, 121–122.
10. *Ibid.*, 128–137.
11. For a description of the facility, see *Ibid.*, 159–160.
12. *Ibid.*, 161–162.
13. Gratus, 92, and Eric W. Gritsch, *A Tragedy of Errors: Thomas Muntzer* (Minneapolis, Minnesota: Fortress Press, 1989), 4. For collections of his writings, see Michael G. Baylor, editor and translator, *Revelation and Revolution: Basic Writings of Thomas Muntzer* (Bethlehem Pennsylvania: Lehigh University Press, 1993), and Peter Matheson, editor and translator, *The Collected Works of Thomas Muntzer* (Edinburgh Scotland: T. & T. Clark, 1988).
14. Gratus, 92.
15. *Ibid.*, 93.
16. As quoted by Baylor, 200. Baylor observes (45) that though this was part of his post-capture interrogation and extracted under torture, there seems no reason to question the basic accuracy of the claims attributed to him in it.
17. *Ibid.*, 199.
18. *Ibid.*, 22.
19. Gratus, 94, and Gritsch, 75.
20. Gritsch, 75, 93.
21. Gratus, 94–95.
22. *Ibid.*, 95.
23. Gritsch, 99–100.
24. Norman Cohn, *The Pursuit of the Millennium* (London: Secker & Warburg, 1957), 265.
25. As quoted by Gritsch, 100.
26. Baylor, 39.
27. Cohn, 269–270.
28. *Ibid.*, 270.
29. As quoted by Gratus, 95.
30. *Ibid.*, 261.
31. *Ibid.*, 270, and Gratus, 95–96.
32. Gratus, 96.
33. *Ibid.*, 97–98.
34. For example, Gratus, 99.
35. *Ibid.*
36. *Ibid.* provides the lower figure. Michael Barkun, *Crucible of the Millennium: The Burned-over District of New York in the 1840s* (Syracuse, New York: Syracuse University Press, 1986), 140, places it at less than 20,000.

37. Anthony Arthur, *The Tailor-King: The Rise and Fall of the Anabaptist Kingdom of Munster* (New York: Thomas Dunne Books/St. Martin's Press, 1999), 48.
38. Gratus, 99.
39. Gratus, 100.
40. *Ibid.*, 99–100.
41. *Ibid.*, 100.
42. *Ibid.*
43. *Ibid.*, 100–101.
44. *Ibid.*, 101.
45. Bernard. S. Capp, *The Fifth Monarchy Men: A Study in Seventeenth-Century English Millenarianism* (London: Faber and Faber, 1972), 27.
46. Gratus, 101–102.
47. *Ibid.*, 102.
48. *Ibid.*, 104.
49. *Ibid.*, 104.
50. *Ibid.*, 104–105.
51. As quoted by *Ibid.*, 105.
52. *Ibid.*
53. As quoted by *Ibid.*, 106.
54. As quoted by Cohn, 296.
55. As quoted by Gratus, 106.
56. Cohn, 296.
57. As quoted by Gunter Volger, "The Anabaptist Kingdom of Munster in the Tension between Anabaptism and Imperial Policy," in *Radical Tendencies in the Reformation: Divergent Perspectives*, ed. by Hans J. Hillerbrand (Kirksville, Missouri: Sixteenth Century Journal Publishers, 1988), 109–110.
58. Eugen Weber, *Apocalypses: Prophecies, Cults, and Millennial Beliefs through the Ages* (Cambridge, Massachusetts: Harvard University Press, 1999), 27.
59. James M. Stayer, "Christianity in One City: Anabaptist Munster, 1534–1535," in *Radical Tendencies in the Reformation: Divergent Perspectives*, ed. Hans J. Hillerbrand (Kirksville, Missouri: Sixteenth Century Journal Publishers, 1988), 127.
60. As quoted by *Ibid.*
61. As quoted by *Ibid.*, 129.
62. Cohn, 287.
63. Weber, 27.
64. Arthur, 113, and Gratus, 106.
65. *Ibid.*, 94–96.
66. Gratus, 107.
67. *Ibid.*, 108.
68. *Ibid.*
69. Weber, 28.
70. *Ibid.*
71. For examples from the long siege, see Arthur, 78–81, 106–109.
72. Cohn, 301.
73. Gratus, 109.
74. *Ibid.*, 109–110.
75. *Ibid.*, 111.
76. Cohn, 304–305.

Notes — Chapter 8

77. For example, Arthur, 96–102.
78. *Ibid.*, 150–155.
79. Gratus, 112.
80. *Ibid.*
81. Peter Toon, "Introduction," in *Puritans, the Millennium and the Future of Israel: Puritan Eschatology, 1600 to 1660*, ed. Peter Toon (Cambridge, England: James Clarke & Company, Ltd., 1970), 19.
82. As quoted by *Ibid.*
83. No attribution, "David Joris," *Encyclopaedia Britannica* (11th edition, 1911), as reprinted at LoveToKnow 1911 Online Encyclopedia. © 2003, 2004 LoveToKnow, available: http://35.1911encyclopedia.org/J/JO/JORIS_DAVID.htm October 2004.
84. *Ibid.*
85. Helgler and K. Holl, "Joris Jan David," *The New Schaff-Herzog Encyclopedia of Religious Knowledge*, Vol. VI: Innocents–Liudger, ed. Philip Schaff, CCEL (Internet) Edition v0.1, available: http://www.ccel.org/s/schaff/encyc/encyc06/htm/iii.lvii.cxvii.htm October 2004.
86. No attribution, "David Joris," *Encyclopaedia Britannica*.
87. Helgler and K. Holl.
88. *Ibid.*
89. *Ibid.*
90. No attribution, "David Joris," *Encyclopaedia Britannica*.
91. Helgler and K. Holl, "Joris Jan David."
92. Gratus, 116.
93. *Ibid.*
94. *Ibid.*
95. No attribution, "David Joris," *Encyclopaedia Britannica*.
96. *Ibid.*
97. Gratus, 116.
98. *Ibid.*, 115.
99. *Ibid.*, 114.
100. *Ibid.*
101. *Ibid.*
102. *Ibid.*, 115.
103. *Ibid.*
104. *Ibid.*
105. Cf. No attribution, "Familists," *Encyclopaedia Britannica* (11th edition, 1911), as reprinted at LoveToKnow 1911 Online Encyclopedia. © 2003, 2004 LoveToKnow, available: http://18.1911encyclopedia.org/F/FA/FAMILISTS.htm October 2004.
106. *Ibid.*
107. *Ibid.*
108. As quoted by Gratus, 116.
109. Barbara Meyers, "Textiles and the Reformation," *Unitarian Universalist History*, Part I (Fall, 2001), available: http://www.online.sksm.edu/ce/papers/p-meyers~textilesreformation.htm October 2004.
110. No attribution, "Familists."
111. F. N. Lee, "The Anabaptists and Their Stepchildren," available: http://www.reformedreader.org/history/step.htm October 2004.
112. *Ibid.*
113. Gratus, 70.
114. *Ibid.*
115. *Ibid.*
116. *Ibid.*
117. *Ibid.*
118. *Ibid.*, 71.
119. *Ibid.*
120. *Ibid.*
121. *Ibid.*, 118.
122. *Ibid.*, and Keith Thomas, *Religion and the Decline of Magic* (New York: Charles Scribner's Sons, 1971), 133.
123. *Ibid.*
124. *Ibid.*
125. Unidentified Author, "Henry Arthington and Richard Cosin," part of *Redefining the Sacred in Early Modern England*, available: http://www.folger.edu/institute/sacred/image15.html September 2004.
126. Walter A. Copinger. "Edward Copinger the Prophet." (Internet).
127. Gratus, 118.
128. Walter A. Copinger. "Edward Copinger the Prophet." (Internet).
129. Thomas, 134.
130. Gratus, 118.
131. As quoted by Thomas, 134.
132. As quoted by Walter A. Copinger, "Edward Copinger the Prophet," Chapter 18 of *History of the Copingers or Coppingers of the Country of Cork, Ireland, and the Counties of Suffolk and Kent England*, Second Edition, available: 42. http://www.copinger.org.uk/4Edmund18.html September 2004.
133. Thomas, 134.
134. Gratus, 118–119.
135. *Ibid.*, 119.
136. Copinger.
137. As quoted by *Ibid.*
138. Gratus, 119.
139. *Ibid.*
140. *Ibid.*
141. *Ibid.*
142. As quoted by *Ibid.*
143. As quoted by Gratus, 120.
144. *Ibid.*, 119–120.
145. Thomas, 134.
146. Gratus, 120.
147. Thomas, 134.
148. Unidentified Author, "Henry Arthington and Richard Cosin."
149. Thomas, 134.
150. As quoted by Bernard S. Capp, "The Political Dimension of Apocalyptic Thought," in *The Apocalypse in English Renaissance Thought and Literature: Patterns, Antecedents and Repercussions*, ed. C. A. Patrides and

Joseph Wittreich (Ithaca, New York: Cornell University Press, 1984), 96.
151. As quoted by *Ibid.*
152. As quoted by *Ibid.*
153. As quoted by Capp, *Monarchy,* 34.

Chapter 9

1. Silver, 153.
2. *Ibid.*
3. *Ibid.,* 153–154.
4. For examples, see *Ibid.,* 154.
5. For examples, see *Ibid.,* 151–152.
6. Robert N. Levine, 102.
7. Silver, 157.
8. Robert N. Levine, 157.
9. As quoted by Beinart, *History,* 112.
10. Nathan Nata Hanover, *Yeven Metzula* (Venice, 1653), as quoted by *Ibid.,* 112.
11. Silver, 156–157.
12. *Ibid.,* 172, 174.
13. *Ibid.,* 179.
14. Pepys, *Diary and Correspondence of Samuel Pepys, F.R.S,* Volume 2 (London: Bell & Daldy, 1867), 352.
15. *Ibid.,* 2:359.
16. *Ibid.,* 2:353.
17. *Ibid.,* n. 1, 2:353.
18. Samuel Pepys, *The Diary of Samuel Pepys,* edited with additions by Henry B. Wheatley, electronic edition of 1666 diary prepared by David Widger as part of the Gutenberg Project, Available: http://www.gutenberg.net/etext03/sp56g10.txt May 2004.
19. Capp, *Monarchy,* 193–194, 214.
20. Lenowitz, 102.
21. *Ibid.,* 101–102.
22. *Ibid.,* 102.
23. As quoted by *Ibid.,* 102. Lenowitz argues that in Mexico such women became de facto messiahs—at least until and if the real one appeared.
24. Gitlitz, 58.
25. Alternative spellings of his name include Shabbati Zevi, Shabbetai Zebi, Sabbathai Zwi, and Sabbatai Zvi.
26. Harry C. Schnur, *Mystic Rebels* (New York: Beechhurst Press, 1949), 160–161, 163–164.
27. Gratus, 147.
28. Idel, page 185, and Schnur, 165.
29. Schnur, 166–167.
30. Lenowitz, 149.
31. Cohn-Sherbok, *Messiah,* 134.
32. Waagenaar, 217.
33. Lenowitz, 150.
34. Cohn-Sherbok, *Messiah,* 134.
35. Sharot, 91.
36. As quoted by Gershom G. Scholem, *Major Trends in Jewish Mysticism* (New York: Schocken Books, 1946, 1954), 290–291.
37. As quoted by Robert N. Levine, 102.
38. *Ibid.,* 103.
39. Jacob Katz, *Tradition and Crisis: Jewish Society at the End of the Middle Ages,* translated from the Hebrew (New York: Schocken Books, 1961; 1971 reprint), 86.
40. Barkun, 126.
41. *Ibid.*
42. Silver, 181, and Waagenaar, 215–216.
43. Kaufman, 53.
44. As quoted by Robert N. Levine, 102.
45. Silver, 181.
46. The approach of Marcus, 261, and Sharot, 92.
47. Lenowitz, 151.
48. Eisenberg, Goodman, and Kass, 145, and Philip Sigal, *The Emergence of Contemporary Judaism;* Volume 2: *Survey of Judaism from the 7th to the 17th Centuries* (Pittsburgh, Pennsylvania: Pickwick Press, 1977), 304.
49. As quoted by *Ibid.,* 305.
50. Halperin, 43.
51. As quoted by Sigal, 2:305.
52. Cf. *Ibid.*
53. Sharot, 92.
54. Gershom Scholem, *The Messianic Idea in Judaism* (New York: Schocken Books, 1971), 60.
55. Gratus, 148.
56. *Ibid.*
57. Lenowitz, 150.
58. *Ibid.*
59. Cohn-Sherbok, *Messiah,* 134.
60. Lenowitz, 150.
61. Cohn-Sherbok, *Messiah,* 135.
62. Sharot, 198.
63. Kaufman, 54.
64. *Ibid.*
65. Cohn-Sherbok, *Messiah,* 135.
66. Sigal, 2:306.
67. Cohn-Sherbok, *Messiah,* 134, and Patai, xlv.
68. Waagenaar, 217–218.
69. Patai, xlv.
70. Lenowitz, 151.
71. Waagenaar, 217.
72. *Ibid.*
73. Robert H. Levine, 105.
74. *Ibid.*
75. Marcus van Loopik, "The Messianism of Shabbetai Zevi and Jewish Mysticism," in *Messianism through History,* ed. Wim Beuken, Sean Freyne, and Anton Weiler (Maryknoll, New York: Orbis Books, 1993), 76.
76. *Ibid.*
77. Ruth Gay, *The Jews of Germany: A Historical Portrait* (New Haven, Connecticut: Yale University Press, 1992), 81.
78. *Ibid.*

79. *Ibid.*
80. Kaufman, 53.
81. *Ibid.*
82. Robert N. Levine, 109.
83. *Ibid.*
84. Katz, 215, and Robert N. Levine, 112.
85. Brody, 193.
86. Marcus, 261. For a detailed account of the reception his claims had in various European countries, see Gershom Scholem, *Sabbatai Sevi: The Mystical Messiah, 1626–1676* (Princeton, New Jersey: Princeton University Press, 1973), 461–463.
87. Robert N. Levine, 112.
88. Pepys, 2:353–354.
89. As quoted by Ceil Roth, *Anglo-Jewish Letters (1158–1917)* (London: Soncino Press, 1938), 70–71. The legitimacy of the attribution is implicitly accepted by both Roth and Bernard Glassman, *Anti-Semitic Stereotypes without Jews: Images of the Jews in England, 1290–1700* (Detroit, Michigan: Wayne State University Press, 1975), 148.
90. Sharot, 93.
91. On Germany in particular, see Gay, 81. For a survey of the popular correlation between adversity and injustice and millennialism, see Baumgarten, 153–159.
92. For a summary of this approach, see Baumgarten, 160–181, especially 165–166.
93. Cf. Kaufman, 55.
94. See the discussion in Idel, 188–197.
95. *Ibid.*, 184, 185, 188, argues that Lurianic thought had little impact on either Zevi personally or the wider Jewish community. Sharot, 95–101 is also highly skeptical of it having much influence.
96. See the analysis of Sharot, 101–104.
97. *Ibid.*, 104.
98. Katz, 217–218.
99. *Ibid.*, 218.
100. Cf. Kaufman, 55.
101. Robert N. Levine, 113–114.
102. Sharot, 115.
103. *Ibid.*
104. Kaufman, 55.
105. *Ibid.*
106. *Ibid.*
107. Waagenaar, 219.
108. Yehuda Liebes, *Studies in Jewish Myth and Jewish Messianism*, translated from the Hebrew by Batya Stein (Albany, New York: State University of New York Press, 1993), 96–97.
109. *Ibid.*, 96.
110. *Ibid.*
111. As quoted by Gay, 82.
112. Idel, 206.
113. As quoted by Liebes, 100.
114. *Ibid.*, 96.
115. *Ibid.*
116. Robert N. Levine, 107.
117. Kaufman, 56.
118. *Ibid.*
119. Lenowitz, 149.
120. *Ibid.*
121. Scholem, *Idea*, 99–101.
122. Scholem, *Kabbalah*, 396.
123. Sharot, 115.
124. Kaufman, 55.
125. Robert N. Levine, 117–118.
126. *Ibid.*, 118.
127. Sharot, 115.
128. Kaufman, 53.
129. Sharot, 88.
130. *Ibid.*
131. *Ibid.*
132. *Ibid.*
133. Robert N. Levine, 105.
134. Sharot, 86.
135. Idel, 198.
136. Robert N. Levine, 106.
137. *Ibid.*
138. Robert N. Levine, 116.
139. Robert N. Levine, 116, and Lenowitz, 150.
140. Robert N. Levine, 119.
141. As quoted by Idel, 197.
142. As quoted by *Ibid.*, 198.
143. *Ibid.*, 202–203.
144. *Ibid.*, 198.
145. Lenowitz, 168.
146. *Ibid.*
147. As quoted by Halperin, 4.
148. As quoted by *Ibid.*, 7.
149. *Ibid.*, 9.
150. *Ibid.*, 13.
151. *Ibid.*, 44–45.
152. *Ibid.*, 45. Halperin believes that Cardozo was putting an extravagantly optimistic spin on his recounting of this period; he argues that this must have been the case because of the size of Cardozo's household (multiple wives and relatives) and because there seem to have been virtually constant medical difficulties of one type or another in his extended family.
153. Lenowitz, 168.
154. Halperin, 43.
155. As quoted by *Ibid.*, 46.
156. *Ibid.*
157. Liebes, 104.
158. Halperin, 54, for example.
159. *Ibid.*, 58–59.
160. *Ibid.*, 59.
161. *Ibid.*
162. *Ibid.*, 72–73.
163. *Ibid.*, 73–74.
164. *Ibid.*, 81.
165. *Ibid.*, 71, 81, 83.
166. *Ibid.*, 83.
167. *Ibid.*, 88, 90, 96.

168. *Ibid.*, 90, 96.
169. As quoted by Halperin, 96.
170. As quoted by *Ibid.*, 97–98.
171. *Ibid.*, 98.
172. *Ibid.*, 99.
173. Liebes, 104.
174. *Ibid.*
175. *Ibid.*
176. As quoted by *Ibid.*, 105.
177. Lenowitz, 168.
178. Halperin, 56–57.
179. As quoted by *Ibid.*, 49.
180. *Ibid.*, 76, 77, and n. 21, 332–333.
181. Lenowitz, 168.
182. Halperin, 87.
183. *Ibid.*
184. No attribution, "Messiah," available: http://www.wordiq.com/definition/Messiah October 2004.
185. Halperin, 168.
186. No attribution, "Messiah."
187. Lenowitz, 169.
188. *Ibid.*
189. For example, *Ibid.*
190. Roth, *Italy*, 405.
191. No attribution, "Messiah."
192. *Ibid.*
193. Roth, *Italy*, 405.
194. No attribution, "Messiah."
195. Alternative spellings of his name include Leibele Prossnitz and Prostitz.
196. Lenowitz, 169.
197. *Ibid.*
198. Gotthard Deutsch and Henry Malter, "Lobele Prossnitz," *Jewish Encyclopedia*, available: http://www.jewishencyclopedia.com/view.jsp?artid=560&letter=P October 2004.
199. *Ibid.*
200. Lenowitz, 169–170.
201. *Ibid.*, 170.
202. *Ibid.*
203. *Ibid.*
204. *Ibid.*
205. *Ibid.*
206. *Ibid.*
207. Yakov haKohain, "Rabbi Moshe Chiam Luzzatt," available: http://www.kheper.net/topics/Kabbalah/Luzzatto.htm October 2004.
208. Tzvi H. Adelman, "Jewish Ethics: Are They Ethical? Are They Jewish?," in *Cultural History of the Jews*, available: http://www.jafi.org.il/education/juice/history1/week8.html October 2004.
209. Lenowitz, 170–171.
210. Alexandr Kraushar, *Jacob Frank: The End to the Sabbataian Heresy*, translated from the Polish by Stanley Bergman and Alexandr Kraushar (Lanham, Maryland: University Press of America, Inc., 2001), 67–68.
211. Cohn-Sherbok, *Messiah*, 144.
212. Cf. Lenowitz, 171.
213. Cohn-Sherbok, *Messiah*, 144.
214. *Ibid.*, 145.
215. Lenowitz, 171.
216. Cohn-Sherbok, *Messiah*, 145.
217. Cohn-Sherbok, *Messiah*, 145.
218. Simon Bunow, "The Rabbinic-Mystical Period, or the Hegemony of the German-Polish Jews (1492–1789)," Chapter 10 of *Jewish History: An Essay in the Philosophy of History*, available: http://www.lithead.com/show_section/Dubnow,-Simon/Jewish-History-:-an-essay-in-the-philosophy-of-history/Chapter-10/ November 2004.
219. Lenowitz, 171.
220. Kaufman, 58.
221. Cohn-Sherbok, *Messiah*, 145.
222. Kraushar, 102.
223. Cohn-Sherbok, *Messiah*, 145.
224. Kraushar, 103–104.
225. Cohn-Sherbok, *Messiah*, 145.
226. *Ibid.*, 146.
227. Lenowitz, 171.
228. Kraushar, 124–125.
229. As quoted by *Ibid.*, 127.
230. *Ibid.*, 139.
231. Cohn-Sherbok, *Messiah*, 146.
232. *Ibid.*, 125, 146.
233. Sharot, 136.
234. *Ibid.*, 137, and Lenowitz, 172.
235. Lenowitz, 171–172.
236. *Ibid.*, 172. For the text of the interrogation, see Kraushar, 162–176.
237. *Ibid.*, 189.
238. Cohn-Sherbok, *Messiah*, 146–147.
239. Kraushar, 220–221.
240. As quoted by *Ibid.*, 223.
241. Lenowitz, 172.
242. Kaufman, 59.
243. Cohn-Sherbok, *Messiah*, 147.
244. Sharot, 130.
245. 59.
246. *Ibid.*
247. Lenowitz, 167.
248. *Ibid.*, 167–168.
249. Kaufman, 58.
250. *Ibid.*
251. As quoted by Scholem, *Idea*, 130.
252. As quoted by *Ibid.*
253. Robert N. Levine, 124.
254. Sharot, 137.
255. Robert N. Levine, 125.
256. *Ibid.*
257. Sharot, 137–138.
258. *Ibid.*, 137.
259. *Ibid.*, and Lenowitz, 172.
260. Lenowitz, 172–173.
261. Robert N. Levine, 124.
262. *Ibid.*
263. Cohn-Sherbok, *Messiah*, 147.
264. *Ibid.*, 148.

265. *Ibid.*
266. Cf. Lenowitz, 196.
267. Cohn-Sherbok, *Messiah*, 148.
268. *Ibid.*
269. Sharot, 130.
270. Cohn-Sherbok, *Messiah*, 148–149.
271. *Ibid.*, 130.
272. *Ibid.*
273. Yrachmiel Tilles, "A Mystic Story: Master Kabbalists, Chasidic Rebbes, and Remarkable Jews," adapted from an article in *Kfar Chabad Magazine*, available: http://www.kabbalaonline.org/Holydays/ellul/A_Lesson_in_Talmud.asp October 2004.
274. *Ibid.*
275. *Ibid.*, 131.
276. For interpretations of how much historicity to read into stories of the Besht's youth and life, see Louis Jacobs, "The Founder of Hasidism Is Shrouded in Legend and Mystery," from *The Jewish Religion: A Companion* (Oxford University Press, 1995), available: http://www.myjewishlearning.com/ideas_belief/Kabbalah_and_Mysticism/Overview_Kabbalah_And_Hasidism/Hasidic_Mysticism/Mysticism_Besht_Jacobs.htm October 2004. On this theme also see Moshe Rosman, "Life Stories: Shivhei Ha-Besht," an extract from *Founder of Hasidism: A Quest for the Historical Ba'al Shem Tov*, available: http://www.storypower.com/hasidic/Articles/Background_and_Sources/rosman1.html October 2004.
277. Sharot, 138.
278. Jeff Hadden, "Hasidism," part of the Religious Movements Project at the University of Virginia, available: http://religiousmovements.lib.virginia.edu/nrms/hasid.html October 2004.
279. Lenowitz, 202.
280. Gerhard Falk, "Baal Shem Tov," available: http://www.jbuff.com/c012501.htm October 2004.
281. Jeff Hadden, "Hasidism."
282. Joseph Telushkin, "Hasidim and Mitnagdim," extract from *Jewish Literacy: The Most Important Things to Know About the Jewish Religion, Its People and Its History* (New York: William Morrow and Co., 1991), available: http://www.jewishvirtuallibrary.org/jsource/Judaism/hasidim_&_mitnagdim.html October 2004.
283. *Ibid.*
284. Falk, "Baal Shem Tov."
285. No attribution., "Ba'al Shem Tov," *Jewish Heritage Online Magazine*, available: http://www.jhom.com/personalities/nahman_bratslav/baalshem.htm October 2004. For a collection of these stories in audio form, see Israel Baal Shem Tov (the Besht), *Readings of Stories of the Besht*, read by Sholom Dov Ber Wineberg, available: http://www.sichosinenglish.org/audio/stories/ October 2004.
286. Sharot, 138.
287. Hadden, "Hasidism."
288. Sharot, 138–139.
289. *Ibid.*, 141.
290. *Ibid.*, 139.
291. *Ibid.*
292. *Ibid.*
293. *Ibid.*
294. On the emphasis on honorable joy in his thought, see Robert Ellsberg, "Baal Shem Tov: Founder of Hasidism (1700–1760)," extract from *All Saints: Daily Reflections on Saints, Prophets, and Witnesses From Our Time*, available: http://www.gratefulness.org/giftpeople/BaalShemTov.htm October 2004.
295. Telushkin, "Hasidim and Mitnagdim."
296. *Ibid.*
297. As quoted by Robert Ellsberg, "Baal Shem Tov."
298. As quoted by Joseph Telushkin, "Hasidim and Mitnagdim." On possible pantheistic implications of Besht's insistence that a spark of divinity is found in all of creation, see Manfred Gerstenfeld and Netanel Lederberg, "Nature and the Environment in Hasidic Sources," *Jewish Environmental Perspectives*, no. 5 (October 2002), available: http://www.jcpa.org/art/jep5.htm October2004.
299. Sharot, 140.
300. *Ibid.*, 141.
301. For a concise discussion of the two sides of the coin and why the millenarian aspects of messianism might be wished to be downplayed, see Sharot, 150. Cf. Lenowitz, 202–204.
302. As quoted by Sharot, 149–150. For the full text of the revelation, see Patai, 270–272.
303. Sharot, 150.
304. No attribution, "Nahman of Bratslav: Master of Tales," *Jewish Heritage Online Magazine*, available: http://www.jhom.com/personalities/nahman_bratslav/index.htm September 2004.
305. *Ibid.* On the tendency among many twentieth century Jews to sanitize the Besht into a kind of vague folk hero, ignoring his actual life and teachings in the process, see Tzi Freeman, "Happy Birthday, Baal Shem Tov!," available: http://www.sichosinenglish.org/holiday/shavuos/besht.html September 2004.
306. Sharot, 179.
307. *Ibid.*
308. *Ibid.*
309. No attribution, "Israel ben Eliezer." part of the *Wikipedia* Internet encyclopedia, as reprinted from the 1906 *Encyclopedia Judaica*, available: http://en.wikipedia.org/wiki/Israel_ben_Eliezer September 2004.

310. *Ibid.*
311. *Ibid.*
312. *Ibid.*
313. Sharot, 179.
314. Arthur Green, *Tormented Master: A Life of Rabbi Nahman of Bratslav* (University, Alabama: University of Alabama Press, 1979), 182.
315. As quoted by *Ibid.*, 183, the parenthesis material being in the original recorded version of the remarks.
316. For an example, see the text in *Ibid.*, 190. For a summary of the evidence pointing to a correlation of himself and the messiah, see 192–197. "Most historians" believe that Nahman considered himself the Messiah, notes Eliezer Segal in "Rabbi Nahman, Napoleon and Other Messiahs," part of the website *From the Sources,* available: http://www.acs.ucalgary.ca/~elsegal/Shokel/940630_Napoleon.html September 2004.
317. Liebes, 115.
318. Green, 185–186. He also notes (209, for example) that even when partial texts have survived, "etc." is often inserted at the point where one would have anticipated a clear explanation of the ambiguous remarks.
319. Sharot, 180.
320. *Ibid.*
321. *Ibid.*
322. Green, 211–212.
323. *Ibid.*, 189.
324. Sharot, 180.
325. Segal, "Rabbi Nahman."
326. *Ibid.*
327. No attribution, "Nahman of Bratslav." For an examination of the differences in the folk tales of Nahman and his contemporaries the Grimm brothers, see Arnold J. Band, "The Bratslav Theory of the Sacred Tale," available: http://www.hasidicstories.com/Articles/Hasidic_Theories/bratslav.html September 2004.
328. Cf. Band "Bratslav Theory."

Chapter 10

1. No attribution, "Edward Wightman," part of *Wikiverse: A World of Knowledge.* Available: http://edward-wightman.wikiverse.org/ September 2004.
2. *Ibid.*
3. *Ibid.*
4. Champlin Burrage, *The Early English Dissenters in the Light of Recent Research (1550–1641);* volume 1: *History and Criticism* (Cambridge: At the University Press, 1912), 218.
5. As quoted by *Ibid.*, 218–219.
6. Thomas, 135.
7. *Ibid.*
8. *Ibid.*
9. Burrage, 2:219.
10. No attribution. "Edward Wightman."
11. Stephen A. Coston, Sr., " 'Guilty Until Proven Innocent:" The Desperation of King James' Critics" (copyright 1996), available: http://www.jesus-is-lord.com/guilty.htm September 2004.
12. Thomas, 135.
13. No attribution. "Edward Wightman."
14. *Ibid.*, and Burrage, 2:220.
15. Stephen Whitman, "The Death-Bed Soliloquy of Stephen Whitman, May 6, 1866," posted by Roy Whitman, descendant of Edward Whitman, available: *http://www.whitmania.com/pdpdpd/deathbed.htm* September 2004.
16. No attribution, "Church Succession to the Twentieth Century," part of *Reformed Baptist Reader,* available: http://www.reformedreader.org/history/ivey/ch10.htm September 2004.
17. See the extended argument of Coston. Also see the agreements and disagreements between Whitman and the Anabaptist heritage discussed in Burrage, 2:65–66.
18. No attribution. "Edward Wightman."
19. Gratus, 122.
20. *Ibid.*
21. *Ibid.*, 122–123.
22. *Ibid.*, 123.
23. *Ibid.*
24. *Ibid.*
25. Thomas, 136.
26. Christopher Hill, *The World Turned Upside Down: Radical Ideas during the English Revolution* (New York: Viking Press, 1972), 40.
27. As quoted by J.C. Davis, *Fear, Myth, and History: The Ranters and the Historians* (Cambridge, England: Cambridge University Press, 1986), 26.
28. *Ibid.*
29. Hill, *World,* 137.
30. Gratus, 123–124.
31. *Ibid.*, 124.
32. *Ibid.*
33. *Ibid.*
34. *Ibid.*
35. *Ibid.*, 124–125.
36. J. F. McGregor, "Seekers and Ranters," in *Radical Religion in the English Revolution,* edited by J. F. McGregor and B. Reay (New York: Oxford University Press, 1984), 133.
37. For examples of specific individuals, see *Ibid.*, 133–134.
38. Thomas, 136.
39. *Ibid.*
40. As quoted by *Ibid.*
41. Glassman, 109.
42. Christopher Hill, *Antichrist in Seventeenth-Century England* (London: Oxford University Press, 1971), 115.

43. Hill, *World*, 253–254.
44. Glassman, 109.
45. Leo Damrosch, *The Sorrows of the Quaker Jesus: James Nayler and the Puritan Crackdown on the Free Spirit* (Cambridge, Massachusetts: Harvard University Press, 1996), 196, and Hillel Schwartz, *The French Prophets: The History of a Millenarian Group in Eighteenth-Century England* (Berkeley, California: University of California Press, 1980), 51.
46. Thomas, 136.
47. Gratus, 129.
48. McGregor, 133.
49. Gratus, 129.
50. C.E. Whiting, *Studies in English Puritanism from the Restoration to the Revolution, 1660–1688* (London: Society for Promoting Christian Knowledge, 1931), 243.
51. As quoted by Schwartz, 51.
52. For example, by Damrosch, 196.
53. On the relation of Robins and the broader movement, see A.L. Morton, *The World of the Ranters: Religious Radicalism in the English Revolution* (London: Lawrence & Wishart, 1970), 92–93.
54. For a collection of his writings, see James Nayler, Unidentified compiler, "James Nayler's Spiritual Writings," available: http://www.strecorsoc.org/jnayler/ September 2004.
55. Gratus, 133, and T.L. Underwood, "Early Quaker Eschatology," in *Puritans, the Millennium and the Future of Israel: Puritan Eschatology, 1600 to 1660*, ed. Peter Toon (Cambridge, England: James Clarke & Company, Ltd., 1970), 92.
56. Gratus, 133.
57. *Ibid.*
58. *Ibid.*
59. *Ibid.*
60. Underwood, 92.
61. Gratus, 132.
62. *Ibid.*, 134.
63. *Ibid.*
64. *Ibid.*, 135.
65. Barry Reay, "Quakerism and Society," in *Radical Religion in the English Revolution*, ed. J.F. McGregor and B. Reay (New York: Oxford University Press, 1984), 147.
66. Gratus, 135–136.
67. Reay, "Quakerism," 158.
68. Gratus, 137–138, and Silver, 175.
69. William G. Bittle, *James Nayler, 1618–1660: The Quaker Indicted by Parliament* (York, England: William Sessions, Ltd., 1986), 103.
70. Gratus, 137. For contemporary accounts, see Damrosch, 148–149.
71. Barry Reay, *The Quakers and the English Revolution* (New York: St. Martin's Press, 1985), 54.
72. R.A. Knox, *Enthusiasm: A Chapter in the History of Religion, with Special Reference to the XVII and XVIII Centuries* (New York: Oxford University Press, 1950), 160.
73. Bittle, 104.
74. Damrosch, 147.
75. George Amoss, Jr., "The Power of Suffering Love: James Nayler and Robert Rich" (copyright 1996, 2002), available: http://www.qis.net/~daruma/naylor2.html September 2004.
76. George F. Nuttall, *The Holy Spirit in Puritan Faith and Experience* (Oxford, England: Basil Blackwell, 1946), 184. In his *Studies in Christian Enthusiasm — Illustrated from Early Quakerism* (Wallingford, Pennsylvania: Pendle Hill, 1948), 76–77, he backs off a bit from this by conceding that Nayler had drifted down "a mistaken path" due to his "tender, delicate, ethereal nature" and that what happened at Bristol represented his "spiritual collapse."
77. Gratus, 138.
78. As quoted by Gratus, 136.
79. *Ibid.*
80. *Ibid.*
81. *Ibid.*, 137.
82. Knox, 161.
83. George Fox, *George Fox: An Autobiography*, edited with introduction and notes by Rufus M. Jones (Philadelphia, Pennsylvania: Ferris & Leach, 1903; 1919 reprint), 271.
84. Amoss, "Love."
85. Gratus, 137.
86. As quoted by Damrosch, 149.
87. Gratus, 139.
88. *Ibid.*, 139–140.
89. Knox, 163.
90. For possible examples, see *Ibid.*, 165. Quakers were inclined to language that blurred the distinction between themselves and Deity. For language applied to Foxe — and accepted by him — that could easily bear a messianic interpretation, see Damrosch, 119, 169.
91. As quoted by Knox, 166, who prefers this version of Nayler's words to an even clearer cut version of the same remarks. Knox interprets the words not as equating Nayler with Christ but equating the "Christ" that was within Nayler with the "Christ" that was within Jesus. Such fine distinctions were hardly likely to jump into the minds of those hearing the words, however.
92. Gratus, 140.
93. Reay, "Quakerism," 159.
94. *Ibid.*, *Revolution*, 54–55.
95. Gratus, 140–142.
96. As quoted by Meic Pearse, *The Great Restoration: The Religious Radicals of the 16th and 17th Centuries* (Cumbria, England: Paternoster Press, 1998), 273.

97. Gratus, 142.
98. For a discussion of their dating theories, see Silver, 175–177. Cf. Paul J. Korshin, "Queuing and Waiting: The Apocalypse in England, 1660–1750," in *The Apocalypse in English Renaissance Thought and Literature: Patterns, Antecedents and Repercussions*, ed. C.A. Patrides and Joseph Wittreich (Ithaca, New York: Cornell University Press, 1984), 250.
99. Bernard S. Capp, "Extreme Millenarianism," in *Puritans, the Millennium and the Future of Israel: Puritan Eschatology, 1600 to 1660*, ed. Peter Toon (Cambridge, England: James Clarke & Company, Ltd., 1970), 71.
100. Korshin, 252.
101. Silver, 177.
102. Capp, "Millenarianism," 68.
103. For examples, see *Ibid.*, 77–78.
104. *Ibid.*, 68.
105. Capp, *Monarchy*, 145.
106. *Ibid.*, 145–146.
107. Gerhard Rempel, "Oliver Cromwell: Constitutional Crisis in England," available: http://mars.acnet.wnec.edu/~grempel/courses/wc2/lectures/cromwell.html September 2004.
108. *Ibid.*
109. *Ibid.*
110. Cf. Capp, "Political," 109.
111. *Ibid.*, 111–112.
112. *Ibid.*, 112–113.
113. *Ibid.*, 113.
114. *Ibid.*, 113–114.
115. Greenstone, 208.
116. Korshin, 250–251.
117. *Ibid.*, 251.
118. For a discussion, see *Ibid.*, 251–252.
119. For a discussion of this theme, see Baumgarten, 201–207.
120. As quoted by *Ibid.*, 163.
121. *Ibid.*
122. Capp, "Political," 114.
123. *Ibid.*, and Capp, "Millenarianism," 79.
124. Capp, *Monarchy*, 69.
125. *Ibid.*
126. Capp, "Political," 114.
127. Capp, "Millenarianism," 80.
128. Capp, "Political," 114–115.
129. *Ibid.*
130. Capp, "Millenarianism," 80.
131. Capp, "Political," 115.
132. Capp, "Millenarianism," 80.
133. Capp, "Political," 115.
134. Capp, *Monarchy*, 75.
135. Capp, "Political," 115.
136. Capp, "Millenarianism," 81.
137. Capp, "Political," 115–116.
138. Capp, "Millenarianism," 81. For Fifth Monarchists critiques of the new one-man regime and their efforts to remove it, see pages 82–84.
139. *Ibid.*, 85.
140. *Ibid.*
141. *Ibid.*, 88.
142. Capp, "Political," 117.
143. Gratus, 127.
144. Clarke Garrett, *Respectable Folly: Millenarians and the French Revolution in England and France* (Baltimore, Maryland: Johns Hopkins University Press, 1975), 184.
145. Ariel Hessayon, "Provisional Entry of 'Robert Norwood (1610–1654)' for the New Dictionary of National Biography," available: http://www.geocities.com/Heartland/Estates/4805/robtnrwd.html September 2004.
146. *Ibid.*
147. Capp, *Monarchy*, 191.
148. Garrett, 43.
149. David N. Ford, "Rev. Dr. John Pordage (1607–1681)" (copyright 2003), available: http://www.berkshirehistory.com/bios/jpordage.html September 2004.
150. Davis, 27–28.
151. Hessayon, "Norwood."
152. *Ibid.*
153. *Ibid.*
154. *Ibid.*
155. *Ibid.*
156. *Ibid.*
157. *Ibid.*
158. *Ibid.*
159. *Ibid.*
160. Davis, 27.
161. *Ibid.*
162. As quoted by Hill, *World*, 181.
163. As quoted by *Ibid.*
164. *Ibid.*
165. Davis, 27.
166. As quoted by Hill, *World*, 227.
167. *Ibid.*
168. Garrett, 184.
169. Capp, *Monarchy*, 43.
170. Garrett, 184.
171. Whiting, 243.
172. No attribution, "English Dissenters: Ranters," available: http://www.exlibris.org/nonconform/engdis/ranters.html September 2004.
173. *Ibid.*, and Davis, n. 39, p. 26.
174. Richard Francis, *Ann the Word: The Story of Ann Lee, Female Messiah, Mother of the Shakers, the Woman Clothed with the Sun* (New York: Arcade Publishing, 2000), 3.
175. *Ibid.*, 25.
176. Harrison, 167.
177. *Ibid.*
178. As quoted by Nardi R. Campion, *Mother Ann Lee: Morning Star of the Shakers* (Hanover, New Hampshire: University Press of New England, 1976, 1990), 21.
179. *Ibid.*
180. Cf. the comments of Francis, 42–44.

181. *Ibid.*, 46–47.
182. Campion, 33.
183. F.W. Evans, *Compendium of the Origin, History, Principles and Regulations, Government, and Doctrines of the Principles of the United Society of Believers in Christ's Second Appearing* (1859), full text reprint available: http://www.bible.ca/cr-shakers.htm November 2004.
184. As quoted by Harrison, 166.
185. *Ibid.*
186. Robert Peters, "Ann Lee," *The Reader's Companion to American History*, available: http://college.hmco.com/history/readerscomp/rcah/html/ah_052200_leeann.htm November 2004.
187. Harrison, 164.
188. *Ibid.*, 168.
189. Francis, 317.
190. See the description of her symptoms in *Ibid.*, 317–318.
191. Harrison, 164.
192. *Ibid.*, 165.
193. *Ibid.*
194. *Ibid.*, 32.
195. *Ibid.*
196. *Ibid.*
197. *Ibid.*
198. *Ibid.*, 33.
199. *Ibid.*, 34.
200. *Ibid.*, 35.
201. *Ibid.*, 34.
202. *Ibid.*, 33.
203. *Ibid.*
204. No attribution, "Elspeth Buchan," available: http://21.1911encyclopedia.org/B/BU/BUCHAN_ELSPETH.htm September 2004, and Harrison, 33.
205. Harrison, 33.
206. *Ibid.*
207. No attribution, "Buchan," and Sandy Stevenson (?), "Elspeth Buchan (1738–1791)," part of *Tour Scotland*, available: http://www.fife.50megs.com/elspeth-buchan.htm September 2004.
208. Harrison, 34–35.
209. *Ibid.*, 35.
210. *Ibid.*
211. *Ibid.*, 33.
212. Francis H. Groome, "Closeburn," in *Ordnance Gazetteer of Scotland: A Survey of Scottish Topography, Statistical, Biographical and Historical* (Edinburgh, Scotland: published in parts by Thomas C. Jack, Grange Publishing Works, 1882–1885), available: http://www.geo.ed.ac.uk/scotgaz/towns/townhistory2991.html September 2004.
213. No attribution, "Elspith Buchan," part of *Electric Scotland*.com, available: http://www.electricscotland.com/history/other/buchan_elspith.htm September 2004.
214. *Ibid.*
215. Harrison, 34.
216. *Ibid.*, 34, 35.
217. *Ibid.*, 36.
218. *Ibid.*
219. *Ibid.*
220. Stevenson, "Buchan."
221. Annabel House, "Robert Burns Was Member of Scandalous Religious Sect," *Scotsman* of January 19, 2003, available: http://news.scotsman.com/topics.cfm?tid=162&id=70662003 September 2004. For the text of Burns' remarks, see No attribution, "The Buchanites," part of *The Burns Encyclopedia*, available: http://www.robertburns.org/encyclopedia/BuchanitesThe.135.shtml September 2004.
222. Harrison, 34.
223. *Ibid.*
224. *Ibid.*

Chapter 11

1. No attribution, "Jemima Wilkinson," part of *Women in American History* (copyright 1999), available: http://search.eb.com/women/articles/Wilkinson_Jemima.html September 2004.
2. James Henretta, "Unruly Women: Jemima Wilkinson and Deborah Sampson Gannett," part of *Biographies from Early America*, available: *http://earlyamerica.com/review/fall96/biography.html* September 2004.
3. No attribution, "Wilkinson" (*Women* website). The material in parenthesis here and in later entries is used to distinguish this from an identically titled internet source.
4. Dan Pietrafesa, "Chodikee Lake: A Great Place for Paddling," *Poughkeepsie Journal*, August 15, 2002, available: http://www.poughkeepsiejournal.com/sportsextra/thegreateight/sp081502s3.shtml#jump September 2004.
5. No attribution, "Wilkinson" (*Women* website).
6. See the description in Roxanne Peters, "Jemima Wilkinson," available: http://www.rootsweb.com/~nwa/jemima.html September 2004.
7. No attribution, "Wilkinson," (*Women* website).
8. Henretta, "Unruly."
9. *Ibid.*
10. No attribution, "The Universal Friend," part of the website of The Yates County Office of Public History, available: http://www.yatescounty.org/upload/12/historian/friend.html September 2004.
11. Henretta, "Unruly."
12. *Ibid.*

Notes—Chapter 11

13. Roxanne Peters, "Wilkinson."
14. As quoted by *Ibid.*
15. No attribution, "Wilkinson," (*Women* website).
16. No attribution, "Friend."
17. No attribution, "Wilkinson" (*Women* website).
18. *Ibid.*
19. For an example, see John W. Barber, "Town of New Milford, Litchfield County, Connecticut," *Connecticut Historical Collections ... History and Antiquities of Every Town in Connecticut* (Second Edition, 1837), available: http://www.rockvillemama.com/nmhistor.htm September 2004.
20. No attribution, "Friend."
21. No attribution, "Wilkinson" (*Women* website).
22. No attribution, "Wilkinson" (*Women* website), and No attribution, "Friend."
23. Henretta, "Unruly."
24. *Ibid.*
25. No attribution, "Wilkinson" (*Women* website).
26. No attribution, "Jemima Wilkinson," *Western Palladium* of New Lisbon, Ohio, September 5, 1829, as reprinted by Dale R. Broadhurst as part of his *Readings in Early Mormon History,* available: http://www.lavazone2.com/dbroadhu/OH/miscohio.htm September 2004. This incident interested this Mormonism website because of a parallel story told of Joseph Smith, which it then describes in detail as well.
27. No attribution, "Wilkinson" (*Women* website).
28. Henretta, "Unruly."
29. Pietrafesa, "Chodikee Lake."
30. Garrett, 179, and J.F.C. Harrison, *The Second Coming: Popular Millenarianism, 1780–1850* (New Brunswick, New Jersey: Rutgers University Press, 1979), 58.
31. Garrett, 180.
32. *Ibid.,* 180–181.
33. *Ibid.,* 181–182.
34. E. M. Chamberlin, *Antichrist and the Millennium* (New York: Saturday Review Press/E.P. Dutton & Company, Inc., 1975), 114.
35. As quoted by Garrett, 182.
36. Chamberlin, 114.
37. Garrett, 182–183.
38. Harrison, 59.
39. As quoted by Garrett, 184.
40. As quoted by Harrison, 60–61.
41. Garrett, 183.
42. Harrison, 62, 80–82.
43. Garrett, 183, 209, 217.
44. *Ibid.,* 187.
45. *Ibid.,* 183.
46. Garrett, 189.
47. As quoted by Chamberlin, 115.
48. *Ibid.*
49. *Ibid.*
50. As quoted by *Ibid.,* 116.
51. As quoted by *Ibid.*
52. As quoted by *Ibid.*
53. *Ibid.*
54. Garrett, 191–194.
55. For text, see Chamberlin, 119.
56. As quoted by Garrett, 197.
57. *Ibid.,* 197–198.
58. Chamberlin, 124.
59. *Ibid.,* 125.
60. For details, see Garrett, 198–203.
61. For quotations, see *Ibid.,* 203–206.
62. *Ibid.,* 206.
63. As quoted by *Ibid.*
64. For his description of that encounter, see Chamberlin, 111.
65. Garrett, 207.
66. Chamberlin, 125.
67. Garrett, 209.
68. As quoted by Garrett, 90.
69. *Ibid.,* 89–90.
70. *Ibid.,* 90.
71. No attribution, "Joanna Southcott (1750–1814): Domestic Servant and Upholsterer," part of *The Apocalypse in English Romantic Literature,* Anne Zanzucchi, General Editor, available: http://www.rochester.edu/College/ENG/eng529/aeza/southcott.htm September 2004.
72. We discuss him first even though Southcott's birth preceded his because her importance grew in large part out of her role in his movement and because her own dominance became blatant as his went into decline.
73. Garrett, 216.
74. *Ibid.,* and James K. Hopkins, *A Woman to Deliver Her People: Joanna Southcott and English Millenarianism in an Era of Revolution* (Austin, Texas: University of Texas Press, 1982), 35.
75. As quoted by Garrett, 217.
76. As quoted by Hopkins, 112.
77. No attribution, "Southcott."
78. *Ibid.*
79. Garrett, 216.
80. *Ibid.,* 216–217.
81. *Ibid.,* 217.
82. *Ibid.*
83. *Ibid.,* 221.
84. *Ibid.,* 220, 223.
85. *Ibid.,* 223.
86. No attribution, "Southcott."
87. *Ibid.*
88. Harrison, 104.
89. Garrett, 221.
90. Hopkins, 113.
91. *Ibid.,* 113–114.
92. Harrison, 93.
93. *Ibid.*

94. *Ibid.*
95. As quoted by *Ibid.*, 93.
96. *Ibid.*, 93–94.
97. *Ibid.*, 97.
98. Hopkins, 199.
99. *Ibid.*, 200.
100. *Ibid.*
101. Nancy Banks-Smith, "Second Homecoming: Maidens of the Lost Ark/Gods in the Sky," television program reviews in *The Guardian* (Great Britain), August 18, 2003. Available: http://www.guardian.co.uk/arts/critic/feature/0,1169,1160457,00.html September 2004. For other gifts, see Hopkins, 203–204.
102. Harrison, 97.
103. Hopkins, 201–202.
104. As quoted by Hopkins, 206.
105. As quoted by Hopkins, 209.
106. Harrison, 98.
107. Hopkins, 210.
108. Harrison, 98.
109. *Ibid.*
110. No attribution, "Southcott."
111. *Ibid.*
112. Garrett, 210.
113. No attribution, "Southcott."
114. *Ibid.*
115. Banks-Smith. "Homecoming."
116. *Ibid.*
117. No attribution, "Weird Cult Waits in House of God: Venue for Christ's Second Coming Will Be an English Town," *Evening Times,* Glasgow (United Kingdom), August 16, 2003, available: http://www.rickross.com/reference/general/general573.html September 2004.
118. Harrison, 153, and Henry Boylan, editor, *A Dictionary of Irish Biography* (Dublin, Ireland: Gill & Macmillan, 1998), available http://www.rte.ie/culture/millennia/people/wardjohn.html December 2004.
119. *Ibid.*
120. Harrison, 136.
121. *Ibid.*, 154.
122. *Ibid.*
123. As quoted by *Ibid.*, 155.
124. *Ibid.*
125. *Ibid.*
126. *Ibid.*, 158, and Boylan, *Irish* (Internet).
127. Jackie E.M. Latham, "The Bradleys of Birmingham: The Unorthodox Family of 'Micahel Field,' " *History Workshop Journal,* Spring 2003, available: http://www3.oup.co.uk/hiwork/hdb/Volume_55/Issue_01/550189.sgm.abs.html September 2004.
128. Harrison, 158.
129. *Ibid.*, 158–159.
130. *Ibid.*, 121, 159.
131. *Ibid.*, 121.
132. *Ibid.*, 159–160.

133. Also known as Yizhak Isaac Yehiel Safrin.
134. Faierstein, 268–269.
135. Faierstein, 269.
136. *Ibid.*, 267.
137. *Ibid.*, 270.
138. *Ibid.*, 268.
139. *Ibid.*, 267.
140. Sharot, 179, and Dan Karr, *Notes on the Study of Later Kabbalah in English: The Safed Period and Lurianic Kabbalah* (copyright 1985, 1995, 2004), available: http://www.digital-brilliance.com/kab/karr/lkie.pdf December 2004.
141. Gedalyah Nigal, "Transmigration of Souls," an excerpt from *Magic, Mysticism, and Hasidism,* available: http://www.storypower.com/hasidic/Articles/Themes_In_Hasidic_Stories/nigal_1transf.html December 2004.
142. Sharot, 179.
143. S. Giora Shoham, "Antonin Artaud: Noah's Ark Outside Time," *Journal of Criminal Justice and Popular Culture* 8(3) (2001), available: http://www.albany.edu/scj/jcjpc/vol8is3/shoham.html December 2004.
144. Faierstein, 267.
145. Also known as Judah ben Sholom.
146. Lenowitz, 235.
147. *Ibid.*
148. *Ibid.*
149. *Ibid.*
150. *Ibid.*
151. Abraham J. Karp, *From the Ends of the Earth: Judaic Treasures of the Library of Congress* (Washington, D.C.: Library of Congress, 1991) (extract part of the "Jewish Virtual Library"), available: http://www.jewishvirtuallibrary.org/jsource/loc/False.html December 2004.
152. *Ibid.*
153. Lenowitz, 235.
154. *Ibid.*
155. Karp, *Treasures* (Internet).
156. Lenowitz, 235.
157. *Ibid.*, 240.
158. *Ibid.*
159. *Ibid.*, 240–241.
160. Karp, *Treasures* (Internet).
161. Lenowitz, 241.
162. *Ibid.*
163. *Ibid.*, 257.
164. *Ibid.*, 256.
165. *Ibid.*, 257.
166. *Ibid.*, 256.
167. *Ibid.*, 257.
168. *Ibid.*
169. *Ibid.*, 256.
170. Gratus, 193–194.
171. *Ibid.*, 194.
172. Anne Beech, "The Clapton Messiah," *N16 Internet Magazine,* available: http://www.

n16mag.com/issue14/p28i14.htm September 2004.

173. Gratus, 194.

174. Richard Canvendish, editor, "Agapemonites," extract from volume 13 of *Man, Myth & Magic: An Illustrated Encyclopedia of the Supernatural* (New York: Marshall Cavendish Corp., 1970), available: http://www.dgbdgb.btinternet.co.uk/clapton/agapemon.htm September 2004.

175. Malcolm Rigby, "The Abode of Love," undated article from *The Somerset Gateway* (Great Britain), available: http://www.dgb-dgb.btinternet.co.uk/clapton/agapemon.htm September 2004.

176. Beech, "Messiah."
177. Canvendish, "Agapemonites."
178. Rigby, "Love."
179. As quoted by Gratus, 194.
180. As quoted by *Ibid.*, 195.
181. As quoted by *Ibid.*, 194.
182. *Ibid.*, 195.
183. *Ibid.*
184. *Ibid.*, 196.
185. Rigby, "Love."
186. Gratus, 196–197.
187. *Ibid.*, 197–198.
188. *Ibid.*, 199.
189. Rigby, "Love."

Bibliography

Books and Articles

Alon, Gedaliah. *The Jews in Their Land in the Talmudic Age (70–640 C.E.).* Translated and edited by Gershon Levi. Volume 1. Jerusalem: Mangnes Press, the Hebrew University, 1980.

———. *The Jews in Their Land in the Talmudic Age (70–640 C.E.).* Translated and edited by Gershon Levi. Volume 2. Jerusalem: Mangnes Press, the Hebrew University, 1984.

Anderson, Robert T., and Terry Giles. *The Keepers: An Introduction to the History and Culture of the Samaritans.* Peabody, Massachusetts: Hendrickson Publishers, Inc., 2002.

Applebaum, Shimon. *Jews and Greeks in Ancient Cyrene.* Studies in Judaism in Late Antiquity, Volume 28. Leiden, Netherlands: E. J. Brill, 1979.

Arthur, Anthony. *The Tailor-King: The Rise and Fall of the Anabaptist Kingdom of Munster.* New York: Thomas Dunne Books/St. Martin's Press, 1999.

Avi-Yonah, M. *The Jews of Palestine: A Political History from the Bar Kokhba War to the Arab Conquest.* New York: Schocken Books, 1976.

Baer, Yitzhak. *A History of the Jews in Christian Spain;* volume 1: *From the Age of Reconquest to the Fourteenth Century.* Translated from the Hebrew by Louis Schoffman. Philadelphia, Pennsylvania: Jewish Publication Society of America, 1961.

———. *A History of the Jews in Christian Spain;* volume 2: *From the Fourteenth Century to the Expulsion.* Translated from the Hebrew by Louis Schoffman. Philadelphia, Pennsylvania: Jewish Publication Society of America, 1961.

Barclay, John M. G. *Jews in the Mediterranean Diaspora: From Alexander to Trajan (323 B.C.E.–117 C.E.).* Edinburgh, Scotland: T & T Clark, 1996.

Barkun, Michael. *Crucible of the Millennium: The Burned-over District of New York in the 1840s.* Syracuse, New York: Syracuse University Press, 1986.

Baumgarten, Albert L. *The Flourishing of Jewish Sects in the Maccabean Era: An Interpretation.* Supplements to the *Journal for the Study of Judaism,* volume 55. Leiden, Netherlands: Brill, 1997.

Baylor, Michael G., editor and translator. *Revelation and Revolution: Basic Writings of Thomas Muntzer.* Bethlehem, Pennsylvania: Lehigh University Press, 1993.

Beinart, Haim. *Atlas of Medieval Jewish History.* New York: Simon & Schuster, 1992.

———. "Inez of Herrera del Duque: The Prophetess of Extremadura." In *Women in the Inquisition: Spain and the New World,* edited by Mary E. Giles, 42–52. Baltimore, Maryland: Johns Hopkins University Press, 1999.

Birley, Anthony R. *Hadrian: The Restless Emperor.* London: Routledge, 1997.

Bittle, William G. *James Nayler, 1618–1660: The Quaker Indicted by Parliament*. York, England: William Sessions Ltd., 1986.
Boas, Adrian J. *Jerusalem in the Time of the Crusades: Society, Landscape and Art in the Holy City under Frankish Rule*. London: Routledge, 2001.
Brody, Robert. *The Geonim of Babylonia and the Shaping of Medieval Jewish Culture*. New Haven, Connecticut: Yale University Press, 1998.
Bryan, Steven M. *Jesus and Israel's Traditions of Judgement and Restoration*. Cambridge, England: Cambridge University Press, 2002.
Buchanan, George W. *Revelation and Redemption: Jewish Documents of Deliverance from the Fall of Jerusalem to the Death of Nahmanides*. Dillsboro, North Carolina: Western North Carolina Press, 1978.
Burger, Abraham. "The Messianic Self-Consciousness of Abraham Abulafia: A Tentative Evaluation." In *Essays on Jewish Life and Thought — Presented in Honor of Salo W. Baron*, edited by Joseph L. Blau, et al., 55–61. New York: Columbia University Press, 1959.
Burrage, Champlin. *The Early English Dissenters in the Light of Recent Research (1550–1641); volume 1: History and Criticism*. Cambridge: At the University Press, 1912.
Campion, Nardi R. *Mother Ann Lee: Morning Star of the Shakers*. Hanover, New Hampshire: University Press of New England, 1976, 1990.
Capp, Bernard S. "Extreme Millenarianism." In *Puritans, the Millennium and the Future of Israel: Puritan Eschatology, 1600 to 1660*, edited by Peter Toon, 66–90. Cambridge, England: James Clarke & Company, Ltd., 1970.
_____. *The Fifth Monarchy Men: A Study in Seventeenth-Century English Millenarianism*. London: Faber and Faber, 1972.
_____. "The Political Dimension of Apocalyptic Thought." In *The Apocalypse in English Renaissance Thought and Literature: Patterns, Antecedents and Repercussions*, edited by C. A. Patrides and Joseph Wittreich, 93–146. Ithaca, New York: Cornell University Press, 1984.
Cate, Robert L. *A History of the Bible Lands in the Interbiblical Period*. Nashville, Tennessee: Broadman Press, 1989.
Chamberlin, E. R. *Antichrist and the Millennium*. New York: Saturday Review Press/E. P. Dutton & Company, Inc., 1975.
Chazan, Robert. "From the First Crusade to the Second: Evolving Perceptions of the Christian-Jewish Conflict." In *Jews and Christians in Twelfth-Century Europe*, edited by Michael A. Signer and John Van Engen, 46–62. Notre Dame Conferences in Medieval Studies Number X. Notre Dame, Indiana: University of Notre Dame Press, 2001.
_____. *In the Year 1096: The First Crusade and the Jews*. Philadelphia, Pennsylvania: Jewish Publication Society, 1996.
Cohen, A. *The Teachings of Maimonides*. New York: KTAV Publishing House, Inc., 1968.
Cohen, Jeremy. "A 1096 Complex? Constructing the First Crusade in Jewish Historical Memory, Medieval and Modern." In *Jews and Christians in Twelfth-Century Europe*, edited by Michael A. Signer and John Van Engen, 9–26. Notre Dame Conferences in Medieval Studies Number X. Notre Dame, Indiana: University of Notre Dame Press, 2001.
Cohn, Norman. *The Pursuit of the Millennium*. London: Secker & Warburg, 1957.
Cohn-Sherbok, Dan. *A Dictionary of Judaism and Christianity*. Philadelphia, Pennsylvania: Trinity Press International, 1991.
_____. *The Jewish Messiah*. Edinburgh, Scotland: T & T Clark, 1997.
Collins, John J. *The Scepter and the Star: The Messiahs of the Dead Sea Scrolls and Other Ancient Literature*. New York: Doubleday, 1995.
Cornfeld, Gaalyahu. *Daniel to Paul: Jews in Conflict with Graeco-Roman Civilization —*

Historical Background to the Hasmoneans, Dead Sea Scrolls, the New Testament World, Early Christianity, and the Bar-Kochba War. New York: Macmillan Company, 1962.

Cutler, Allan H., and Helen E. Cutler. *The Jew as Ally of the Muslim: Medieval Roots of Anti-Semitism.* Notre Dame, Indiana: University of Notre Dame Press, 1986.

Damrosch, Leo. *The Sorrows of the Quaker Jesus: James Nayler and the Puritan Crackdown on the Free Spirit.* Cambridge, Massachusetts: Harvard University Press, 1996.

Dan, Joseph. "Introduction." In *The Early Kabbalah,* edited by Joseph Dan, 1–41. Mahwah, New Jersey: Paulist Press, 1986.

Davis, J. C. *Fear, Myth and History: The Ranters and the Historians.* Cambridge, England: Cambridge University Press, 1986.

Efron, Joshua. *Studies on the Hasmonean Period.* Studies in Judaism in Late Antiquity volume 39. Leiden, Netherlands: E. J. Brill, 1987.

Eidelberg, Shlomo. *The Jews and the Crusaders: The Hebrew Chronicles of the First and Second Crusades.* Texts translated and edited by Shlomo Eidelberg. Madison, Wisconsin: University of Wisconsin Press, 1977.

Eisenberg, Azriel, Hannah G. Goodman, and Alvin Kass. *Eyewitnesses to Jewish History: From 586 B.C.E. to 1967.* New York: Union of American Hebrew Congregations, 1973.

Faierstein, Morris M. *Jewish Mystical Autobiographies: "Book of Visions" and "Book of Secrets."* In the series Classics of Western Spirituality. Mahwah, New Jersey: Paulist Press, 1999.

Fenn, Richard. *The Death of Herod: An Essay in the Sociology of Religion.* Cambridge, England: Cambridge University Press, 1992.

Fine, Lawrence. *Safed Spirituality: Rules of Mystical Piety, the Beginning of Wisdom.* In the series Classics of Western Spirituality. New York: Paulist Press, 1984.

Fitzmyer, Joseph A. "The Bar Cochba Period." In *The Bible in Current Catholic Thought,* edited by John L. McKenzie, 133–168. New York: Herder and Herder, 1962.

Fox, George *George Fox: An Autobiography.* Edited with introduction and notes by Rufus M. Jones. Philadelphia, Pennsylvania: Ferris & Leach, 1903; 1919 reprint.

Francis, Richard. *Ann the Word: The Story of Ann Lee, Female Messiah, Mother of the Shakers, the Woman Clothed with the Sun.* New York: Arcade Publishing, 2000.

Freyne, Sean. *Galilee and Gospel: Collected Essays.* Tubingen, Germany: Mohr Siebeck, 2000.

_____. *Galilee: From Alexander the Great to Hadrian, 323 B.C.E. to 135 C.E.—A Study of Second Temple Judaism.* Wilmington, Delaware: Michgael Galzier, Inc., and University of Notre Dame Press, 1980.

Furneaux, Rupert. *The Roman Siege of Jerusalem.* New York: David McKay Company, Inc., 1972.

Garrett, Clarke. *Respectable Folly: Millenarians and the French Revolution in England and France.* Baltimore, Maryland: Johns Hopkins University Press, 1975.

Gaster, M. "Abravanel's Literary Work." In *Isaac Abravanel: Six Lectures,* edited by J. B. Trend and H. Loewe, 39–73. Cambridge: At the University Press, 1937.

Gay, Ruth. *The Jews of Germany: A Historical Portrait.* New Haven, Connetcticut: Yale University Press, 1992.

Gitlitz, David M. *Secrecy and Deceit: The Religion of the Crypto-Jews.* Philadelphia, Pennsylvania: Jewish Publication Society, 1996.

Glassman, Bernard. *Anti-Semitic Stereotypes without Jews: Images of the Jews in England, 1290–1700.* Detroit, Michigan: Wayne State University Press, 1975.

Glatzer, Nahum N. *The Judaic Tradition.* Boston, Massachusetts: Beacon Press, 1969.

Goodman, Martin. *The Ruling Class of Judaea: The Origins of the Jewish Revolt against Rome, A.D. 66–70.* Cambridge, England: Cambridge University Press, 1987.

Goodman, Paul. "Introduction." In *Isaac Abravanel: Six Lectures,* edited by J. B. Trend and H. Loewe, 1–16. Cambridge: At the University Press, 1937.
Gratus, Jack. *The False Messiahs.* New York: Taplinger Publishing Company, 1975.
Gray, Rebecca. *Prophetic Figures in Late Second Temple Jewish Palestine: The Evidence from Josephus.* New York: Oxford University Press, 1993.
Green, Arthur. *Tormented Master: A Life of Rabbi Nahman of Bratslav.* University, Alabama: University of Alabama Press, 1979.
Greenstone, Julius H. *The Messiah Idea in Jewish History.* Philadelphia, Pennsylvania Jewish Publication Society of America, 1906.
Gritsch, Eric W. *A Tragedy of Errors: Thomas Muntzer.* Minneapolis, Minnesota: Fortress Press, 1989.
Guibert of Nogent. *The Memoirs of Abbot Guibert of Nogent—Self and Society in Medieval France.* Toronto, Ontario: University of Toronto Press, 1970; 1984 reprint.
Halper, B. *Post-biblical Hebrew Literature: An Anthology.* Philadelphia, Pennsylvania: Jewish Publication Society of America, 1921.
Halperin, David J. *Abraham Miguel Cardozo: Selected Writings.* In the series Classics of Western Spirituality. Mahwah, New Jersey: Paulist Press, 2001.
Harrison, J. F. C. *The Second Coming: Popular Millenarianism, 1780–1850.* New Brunswick, New Jersey: Rutgers University Press, 1979.
Hill, Christopher. *Antichrist in Seventeenth-Century England.* London: Oxford University Press, 1971.
_____. *The World Turned Upside Down: Radical Ideas during the English Revolution.* New York: Viking Press, 1972.
Hopkins, James K. *A Woman to Deliver Her People: Joanna Southcott and English Millenarianism in an Era of Revolution.* Austin, Texas: University of Texas Press, 1982.
Horsley, Richard A. *Galilee: History, Politics, People.* Valley Forge, Pennsylvania: Trinity Press International, 1995.
_____. "'Messianic' Figures and Movements in First-Century Palestine." In *The Messiah: Developments in Earliest Judaism and Christianity,* edited by James H. Charlesworth, 276–295. (The First Princeton Symposium on Judaism and Christian Origins.) Minneapolis, Minnesota: Fortress Press, 1992.
_____. "Palestinian Jewish Groups and Their Messiahs in Late Second Temple Times." In *Messianism through History,* edited by Wim Beuken, Sean Freyne, and Anton Weiler, 14–29. Maryknoll, New York: Orbis Books, 1993.
Idel, Moshe. *Messianic Mystics.* New Haven, Connecticut: Yale University Press, 1998 pages.
Israel, Gerard, and Jacques Lebar. *When Jerusalem Burned.* Translated from the French by Alan Kendall. New York: William Morrow & Company, Inc., 1973.
Jagersma, Henk. *A History of Israel from Alexander the Great to Bar Kochba.* Translated from the Dutch by John Bowden. Philadelphia, Pennsylvania: Fortress Press, 1986.
Kasher, Aryeh. *Jews and Hellenistic Cities in Eretz-Israel: Relations of the Jews in Eretz-Israel with the Hellenistic Cities during the Second Temple Period (332 BCE–70 CE).* Tubingen, Germany: J. C. B. Mohr, 1990.
Katz, Jacob. *Tradition and Crisis: Jewish Society at the End of the Middle Ages.* Translated from the Hebrew. New York: Shocken Books, 1961; 1971 reprint.
Kaufman, Reuben. *Great Sects and Schisms in Judaism.* New York: Jonathan David, Publishers, 1967.
Kee, Alistair. "Marx's Messianic Faith." In *Messianism through History,* edited by Wim Beuken, Sean Freyne, and Anton Weiler, 101–113. Maryknoll, New York: Orbis Books, 1993.
Klausner, Joseph. *The Messianic Idea in Israel—From Its Beginning to the Completion*

of the Mishnah. Translated from the third Hebrew edition by W. F. Stinespring. New York: Macmillan Company, 1955.

Knohl, Israel. *The Messiah before Jesus: The Suffering Servant of the Dead Sea Scrolls.* Translated from the Hebrew by David Maisel. Berkeley, California: University of California Press, 2000.

Knox, Ronald A. *Enthusiasm: A Chapter in the History of Religion, with Special Reference to the XVII and XVIII Centuries.* New York: Oxford University Press, 1950.

Korshin, Paul J. "Queuing and Waiting: the Apocalypse in England, 1660–1750." In *The Apocalypse in English Renaissance Thought and Literature: Patterns, Antecedents and Repercussions,* edited by C. A. Patrides and Joseph Wittreich, 240–265. Ithaca, New York: Cornell University Press, 1984.

Kraushar, Alexandr. *Jacob Frank: The End to the Sabbataian Heresy.* Translated from the Polish by Stanley Bergman and Alexandr Kraushar. Lanham, Maryland: University Press of America, Inc., 2001.

Lenowitz, Harris. *The Jewish Messiahs: From the Galilee to Crown Heights.* New York: Oxford University Press, 1998.

Levine, Robert N. *There Is No Messiah and You're It: The Stunning Transformation of Judaism's Most Provocative Idea.* Woodstock, Vermont: Jewish Lights Publishing, 2003.

Liebes, Yehuda. *Studies in Jewish Myth and Jewish Messianism.* Translated from the Hebrew by Batya Stein. Albany, New York: State University of New York Press, 1993.

Loopik, Marcus van. "The Messianism of Shabbetai Zevi and Jewish Mysticism." In *Messianism through History,* edited by Wim Beuken, Sean Freyne, and Anton Weiler, 69–82. Maryknoll, New York: Orbis Books, 1993.

Maimonides. *Letters of Maimonides.* Translated and edited with introductions and notes by Leon D. Stitskin. New York: Yeshiva University Press, 1977.

Marcus, Jacob R. *The Jew in the Medieval World: A Source Book, 315–1791.* Cincinnati, Ohio: Sinai Press, 1938.

Mason, Rex. "The Messiah in the Postexilic Old Testament Literature." In *King and Messiah in Israel and the Ancient Near East— Proceedings of the Oxford Old Testament Seminar,* edited by John Day, 338 – 364. *Journal for the Study of the Old Testament* Supplement Series 270. Sheffield, England: Sheffield Academic Press, 1998.

Muntzer, Thomas. *The Collected Works of Thomas Muntzer.* Edited and translated by Peter Matheson. Edinburgh, Scotland: T. & T. Clark, 1988.

McGinn, Bernard. *Visions of the End: Apocalyptic Traditions in the Middle Ages.* New York: Columbia University Press, 1979.

McGregor, J.F. "Seekers and Ranters." In *Radical Religion in the English Revolution,* edited by J.F. McGregor and B. Reay, 121–139. New York: Oxford University Press, 1984.

Melammed, Renee L. *Heretics or Daughters of Israel? The Crypto-Jewish Women of Castile.* New York: Oxford University Press, 1999.

Mendels, Doron. *The Rise and Fall of Jewish Nationalism.* New York: Doubleday, 1992.

Meyers, Eric M. "Sepphoris on the Eve of the Great Revolt (67–68 C.E.): Archaeology and Josephus." In *Galilee through the Centuries: Confluence of Cultures,* edited by Eric M. Meyers, 109–122. Winona Lake, Indiana: Eisenbrauns, 1999.

Miller, Stuart S. "New Perspectives on the History of Sepphoris." In *Galilee through the Centuries: Confluence of Cultures,* edited by Eric M. Meyers, 145–159. Winona Lake, Indiana: Eisenbrauns, 1999.

Morton, A. L. *The World of the Ranters: Religious Radicalism in the English Revolution.* London: Lawrence & Wishart, 1970.

Nalle, Sara T. *Mad for God: Bartolome Sanchez, the Secret Messiah of Cardenete.* Charlottesville, Virginia: University Press of Virginia, 2001.

Nemoy, Leon. *Karaite Anthology: Excerpts from the Early Literature.* New Haven, Connecticut: Yale University Press, 1952.
Netanyahu, Benzion. *Toward the Inquisition: Essays on Jewish and Converso History in Late Medieval Spain.* Ithaca, New York: Cornell University Press, 1997.
Neuman, Abraham A. *The Jews in Spain: Their Social, Political and Cultural Life during the Middle Ages.* Volume 2. Philadelphia, Pennsylvania: Jewish Publication Society of America, 1942; 1944 printing.
Neusner, Jacob. "Bringing the Messiah: The Torah and Responsive Grace." In *Jewish-Christian Debates: God, Kingdom, Messiah*, edited by Jacob Neusner and Bruce Chilton, 159–187. Minneapolis, Minnesota: Augsburg Fortress Publishers, 1998.
____. *Israel and Iran in Talmudic Times: A Political History.* Lanham, Maryland: University Press of America, 1986.
____. *A History of the Jews in Babylonia: The Parthian Period.* Brown University Judaic Studies Number 62. Chico, California: Scholars Press, 1969, 1984.
Nuttall, Geoffrey F. *The Holy Spirit in Puritan Faith and Experience.* Oxford, England: Basil Blackwell, 1946.
____. *Studies in Christian Enthusiasm — Illustrated from Early Quakerism.* Wallingford, Pennsylvania: Pendle Hill, 1948.
Oegema, Gerbern S. *The Anointed and His People: Messianic Expectations from the Maccabees to Bar Kochba. Journal for the Study of the Pseudepigrapha* Supplement Series 27. Sheffield, England: Sheffield Academic Press, 1998.
Otzen, Benedikt. *Judaism in Antiquity: Political Development and Religious Currents from Alexander to Hadrian.* Translated from the Danish by Frederick H. Cryer. Sheffield, England: JSOT Press, 1990.
Patai, Raphael. *The Messiah Texts.* Detroit, Michigan: Wayne State University Press, 1979.
Pearse, Meic. *The Great Restoration: The Religious Radicals of the 16th and 17th Centuries.* Cumbria, Great Britain: Paternoster Press, 1998.
Pepys, Samuel. *Diary and Correspondence of Samuel Pepys, F.R.S.* Volume 2. London: Bell & Daldy, 1867.
Perowne, Stewart. *The Life and Times of Herod the Great.* London: Hodder and Stoughton, 1956.
Poliakov, Leon. *Jewish Bankers and the Holy See — From the Thirteenth to the Seventeenth Century.* Translated from the French by Miriam Kochan. London: Routledge & Kegan Paul, 1977.
Poorthuis, Marcel. "Messianism between Reason and Delusion: Maimonides and the Messiah." In *Messianism through History,* edited by Wim Beuken, Sean Freyne, and Anton Weiler, 57–68. Maryknoll, New York: Orbis Books, 1993.
Price, Jonathan J. *Jerusalem under Siege: The Collapse of the Jewish State, 66–70 C.E.* Leiden, Netherlands: E. J. Brill, 1992.
Rabinowitz, L. "Abravanel as Exegete." In *Isaac Abravanel: Six Lectures,* edited by J. B. Trend and H. Loewe, 75–92. Cambridge: At the University Press, 1937.
Rajak, Tessa. *Josephus: The Historian and His Society.* Second Edition. London: Duckworth, 1983, 2002.
Reay, Barry. "Quakerism and Society." In *Radical Religion in the English Revolution,* edited by J. F. McGregor and B. Reay, 141–164. New York: Oxford University Press, 1984.
____. *The Quakers and the English Revolution.* New York: St. Martin's Press, 1985.
Reeves, Marjorie. "The Development of Apocalyptic Thought: Medieval Attitudes." In *The Apocalypse in English Renaissance Thought and Literature: Patterns, Antecedents and Repercussions,* edited by C. A. Patrides and Joseph Wittreich, 40–73. Ithaca, New York: Cornell University Press, 1984.

Rhoads, David M. *Israel in Revolution: 6–74 C.E.: A Political History Based on the Writings of Josephus.* Philadelphia, Pennsylvania: Fortress Press, 1976.
Roth, Cecil. *Anglo-Jewish Letters (1158–1917).* London: Soncino Press, 1938.
_____. *The History of the Jews of Italy.* Philadelphia, Pennsylvania: Jewish Publication Society of America, 1946.
Saperstein, Marc. *Jewish Preaching: 1200–1800— An Anthology.* New Haven, Connecticut: Yale University Press, 1989.
Sarachek, Joseph. *The Doctrine of the Messiah in Medieval Jewish Literature.* New York: Jewish Theological Seminary of America, 1932.
Schafer, Peter. "Rabbi Aqiva and Bar Kokhba." In *Approaches to Ancient Judaism,* volume 2, edited by William Scott Green, 113–130. In the Brown University Judaic Studies number 9. Chico, California: Scholars Press, 1980.
Schnur, Harry C. *Mystic Rebels.* New York: Beechhurst Press, 1949.
Scholem, Gershom. *Kabbalah.* New York: New York Times Book Company, 1974.
_____. *Major Trends in Jewish Mysticism.* New York: Schocken Books, 1946, 1954.
_____. *The Messianic Idea in Judaism.* New York: Schocken Books, 1971.
_____. *Sabbatai Sevi: The Mystical Messiah, 1626–1676.* Princeton, New Jersey: Princeton University Press, 1973.
Schwartz, Hillel. *The French Prophets: The History of a Millenarian Group in Eighteenth-Century England.* Berkeley, California: University of California Press, 1980.
Sharot, Stephen. *Messianism, Mysticism, and Magic: A Sociological Analysis of Jewish Religious Movements.* Chapel Hill, North Carolina: University of North Carolina Press, 1982.
Sicker, Martin. *Between Rome and Jerusalem: 300 Years of Roman-Judaean Relations.* Westport, Connecticut: Praeger, 2001.
Sigal, Phillip. The Emergence of Contemporary Judaism; volume 2: *Survey of Judaism from the 7th to the 17th Centuries.* Pittsburgh, Pennsylvania: Pickwick Press, 1977.
Silver, Abba H. *A History of Messianic Speculation in Israel— From the First through the Seventeenth Centuries.* New York: Macmillan Company, 1927.
Smallwood, E. Mary. *The Jews under Roman Rule— From Pompey to Diocletian.* Studies in Judaism in Late Antiquity volume 20. Leiden, Netherlands: E. J. Brill, 1976.
Socrates. *The Ecclesiastical History of Socrates.* Translated from the Greek. London: Henry G. Bohn, 1853.
Stayer, James M. "Christianity in One City: Anabaptist Munster, 1534–1535." In *Radical Tendencies in the Reformation: Divergent Perspectives,* edited by Hans J. Hillerbrand, 117–134. Kirksville, Missouri: Sixteenth Century Journal Publishers, 1988.
Stern, Menahem. *Greek and Latin Authors on Jews and Judaism;* volume 2: *From Tacitus to Simplicius.* Jerusalem: Israel Academy of Sciences and Humanities, 1980.
_____. "The Reign of Herod and the Herodian Dynasty." In *The Jewish People in the First Century: Historical Geography, Political History, Social, Cultural and Religious Life and Institutions,* edited by S. Safrai and M. Stern, 216–307. Assen, Netherlands: Van Gorcum & Company, B.V., 1974.
Thomas, Keith. *Religion and the Decline of Magic.* New York: Charles Scribner's Sons, 1971.
Toon, Peter. "Introduction." In *Puritans, the Millennium and the Future of Israel: Puritan Eschatology, 1600 to 1660,* edited by Peter Toon, 8–22. Cambridge, England: James Clarke & Company, Ltd., 1970.
Tzafir, Yoram. "The Desert Fortresses of Judaea in the Second Temple Period." In *The Jerusalem Cathedra: Studies in the History, Archaeology, Geography and Ethnography of the Land of Israel,* volume 2, edited by Lee I. Levine, 120–145. Jerusalem: Yad Izhak Ben-Zvi Institute/Wayne State University Press, 1981.

Underwood, T. L. "Early Quaker Eschatology." In *Puritans, the Millennium and the Future of Israel: Puritan Eschatology, 1600 to 1660,* edited by Peter Toon, 91–103. Cambridge, England: James Clarke & Company, Ltd., 1970.

Volger, Gunter. "The Anabaptist Kingdom of Munster in the Tension between Anabaptism and Imperial Policy." In *Radical Tendencies in the Reformation: Divergent Perspectives,* edited by Hans J. Hillerbrand, 99–116. Kirksville, Missouri: Sixteenth Century Journal Publishers, 1988.

Yadin, Yigael. *Bar-Kokhba: The Rediscovery of the Legendary Hero of the Second Jewish Revolt against Rome.* New York: Random House, 1971.

Waagenaar, Sam. *The Pope's Jews.* La Salle, Illinois: Open Court Publishers, 1974.

Weber, Eugen. *Apocalypses: Prophecies, Cults, and Millennial Beliefs through the Ages.* Cambridge, Massachusetts: Harvard University Press, 1999.

Whiting, C. E. *Studies in English Puritanism from the Restoration to the Revolution, 1660–1688.* London: Society for Promoting Christian Knowledge, 1931.

Zeitlin, Solomon. *Studies in the Early History of Judaism.* Volume 1. New York: KTAV Publishing House, Inc., 1973.

Internet Resources: Attributed Material

Adelman, Tzvi H. "Jewish Ethics: Are They Ethical? Are They Jewish?" in *Cultural History of the Jews.* Available: ttp://www.jafi.org.il/education/juice/history1/week8.html October 2004.

Amoss, Jr., George. "The Power of Suffering Love: James Nayler and Robert Rich." Copyright 1996, 2002. Available: http://www.qis.net/~daruma/naylor2.html September 2004.

Bacher, Wilhelm, and Schulim Ochser. "Theudas." Part of JewishEncyclopedia.com. Available: http://www.jewishencyclopedia.com/view.jsp?artid=188&letter=T September 2004.

Band, Arnold J. "The Bratslav Theory of the Sacred Tale." Available: http://www.hasidicstories.com/Articles/Hasidic_Theories/bratslav.html September 2004.

Banks-Smith, Nancy. "Second Homecoming: Maidens of the Lost Ark/Gods in the Sky." Television program reviews in *The Guardian* (Great Britain), August 18, 2003. Available: http://www.guardian.co.uk/arts/critic/feature/0,1169,1160457,00.html September 2004.

Barber, John W. "Town of New Milford, Litchfield County, Connecticut," *Connecticut Historical Collections ... History and Antiquities of Every Town in Connecticut* (Second Edition, 1837). Available: http://www.rockvillemama.com/nmhistor.htm September 2004.

Beech, Anne. "The Clapton Messiah." *N16 Internet Magazine.* Available: http://www.n16mag.com/issue14/p28i14.htm September 2004.

Boylan, Henry. *A Dictionary of Irish Biography* (Dublin: Gill & Macmillan, Dublin, 1998), as reprinted at http://www.rte.ie/culture/millennia/people/wardjohn.html December 2004.

Bunow, Simon. "The Rabbinic-Mystical Period, or the Hegemony of the German-Polish Jews (1492–1789)." Chapter 10 of *Jewish History: An Essay in the Philosophy of History.* Available: http://www.lithead.com/show_section/Dubnow,-Simon/Jewish-History-:-an-essay-in-the philosophy-of-history/Chapter-10/ November 2004.

Cavendish, Richard, editor. "Agapemonites," extract from volume 13 of *Man, Myth & Magic: An Illustrated Encyclopedia of the Supernatural* (New York: Marshall Cavendish Corp., 1970). Available: http://www.dgbdgb.btinternet.co.uk/clapton/agapemon.htm September 2004.

Copinger, Walter A. "Edward Copinger the Prophet." Chapter 18 of *History of the Copingers or Coppingers of the Country of Cork, Ireland, and the Counties of Suffolk and Kent England.* Second Edition. Available: http://www.copinger.org.uk/4 Edmund18.html September 2004.

Coston, Stephen A. Sr. "'Guilty until Proven Innocent": The Desperation of King James' Critics." Copyright 1996. Available: http://www.jesus-is-lord.com/guilty.htm September 2004.

Deutsch, Gotthard, and Henry Malter. "Lobele Prossnitz." Jewish Encyclopedia. Available: http://www.jewishencyclopedia.com/view.jsp?artid=560&letter=P October 2004.

Ellsberg, Robert. "Baal Shem Tov: Founder of Hasidism (1700–1760)." Extract from *All Saints: Daily Reflections on Saints, Prophets, and Witnesses From Our Time.* Available: http://www.gratefulness.org/giftpeople/BaalShemTov.htm October 2004.

Evans, F. W. *Compendium of the Origin, History, Principles and Regulations, Government, and Doctrines of the Principles of the United Society of Believers in Christ's Second Appearing* (1859). Full text reprint. Available: http://www.bible.ca/cr-shakers.htm November 2004.

Falk, Gerhard. "Baal Shem Tov." Available: http://www.jbuff.com/c012501.htm October 2004.

Ford, David N. "Rev. Dr. John Pordage (1607–1681)." Copyright 2003. Available: http://www.berkshirehistory.com/bios/jpordage.html September 2004.

Freeman, Tzi. "Happy Birthday, Baal Shem Tov!" Available: http://www.sichosinenglish.org/holiday/shavuos/besht.html September 2004.

Gerstenfeld, Manfred, and Netanel Lederberg. "Nature and the Environment in Hasidic Sources." *Jewish Environmental Perspectives*, no. 5 (October 2002). Available: http://www.jcpa.org/art/jep5.htm October 2004.

Gottheil, Richard, and Kaufmann Koher. "Atthronges." Part of JewishEncyclopedia.com. Available: http://www.jewishencyclopedia.com/view.jsp?artid=2088&letter=A September 2004.

Graetz, Heinrich, Chapter 6, "Jewish Apostates and the Disputatioy at Tortosa," *History of the Jews.* (Philadelphia, Pennsylvania: Jewish Publication Society of America, 189?). Available: http://216.239.41.104/search?q=cache:7vLCHkMfR80J:www.saltshakers.com/lm/GraetzB.rtf+Moses%2BBotarel&hl=en October 2004.

Groome, Francis H. "Closeburn." In *Ordnance Gazetteer of Scotland: A Survey of Scottish Topography, Statistical, Biographical and Historical* (Edinburgh, Scotland: published in parts by Thomas C. Jack, Grange Publishing Works, 1882–1885). Available: http://www.geo.ed.ac.uk/scotgaz/towns/townhistory2991.html September 2004.

Gruber, Ruth E., and Samuel D. Gruber, "Jewish Monuments in Slovenia," *Jewish Heritage Report,* Vol. II, Nos. 1–2 / Spring–Summer 1998, Slovenia. Available: http://www.istrianet.org/istria/religion/history/hebrews-sloistria.htm October 2004.

Guibert of Nogent. *The Deeds of God through the Franks.* Translated by Robert Levine; copyright 1997. Part of Project Gutenberg. Available: http://www.gutenberg.net/etext03/7deed10.txt May 2004.

Hadden, Jeff. "Hasidism." Part of the Religious Movements Project at the University of Virginia. Available: http://religiousmovements.lib.virginia.edu/nrms/hasid.html October 2004.

haKohain, Yakov L. "Rabbi Moshe Chiam Luzzatto." Available: http://www.kheper.net/topics/Kabbalah/Luzzatto.htm October 2004.

Helgler, A., and K. Holl, "Joris Jan David." *The New Schaff-Herzog Encyclopedia of Religious Knowledge,* Vol. VI: Innocents—Liudger, edited by Philip Schaff. CCEL

(Internet) Edition v0.1. Available: At: http://www.ccel.org/s/schaff/encyc/encyc06/htm/iii.lvii.cxvii.htm October 2004.

Henretta, James. "Unruly Women: Jemima Wilkinson and Deborah Sampson Gannett." Part of Biographies from Early America. Available: http://earlyamerica.com/review/fall96/biography.html September 2004.

Hessayon, Ariel. "Provisional Entry of 'Robert Norwood (1610–1654)' for the New Dictionary of National Biography." Available: http://www.geocities.com/Heartland/Estates/4805/robtnrwd.html September 2004.

House, Annabel. "Robert Burns Was Member of Scandalous Religious Sect." *Scotsman* of January 19, 2003. Available: http://news.scotsman.com/topics.cfm?tid=162&id=70662003 September 2004.

Jacobs, Joseph, and Jacob Z. Lauterbach. "Moses Botarel." Part of JewishEncyclopedia.com. Available: http://www.jewishencyclopedia.com/view.jsp?artid=848&letter=M September 2004.

Jacobs, Louis. "The Founder of Hasidism Is Shrouded in Legend and Mystery." From *The Jewish Religion: A Companion* (Oxford University Press, 1995). Available: http://www.myjewishlearning.com/ideas_belief/Kabbalah_and_Mysticism/Overview_Kabbalah_And_Hasidism/Hasidic_Mysticism/Mysticism_Besht_Jacobs.htm October 2004.

Josephus. *The Antiquities of the Jews.* William Whiston translation. Part of the Gutenberg Project. Available: http://www.gutenberg.net/etext01/taofj10.txt May 2004.

———. *The Wars of the Jews.* William Whiston translation. Part of the Gutenberg Project. Available: http://www.gutenberg.net/etext01/warje10.txt May 2004.

Karp, Abraham J. *From the Ends of the Earth: Judaic Treasures of the Library of Congress* (Washington, D.C.: Library of Congress, 1991). (Part of the Jewish Virtual Library). Aavailable: http://www.jewishvirtuallibrary.org/jsource/loc/False.html December 2004.

Karr, Dan. *Notes on the Study of Later Kabbalah in English: The Safed Period and Lurianic Kabbalah* (copyright 1985, 1995, 2004). Available: http://www.digital brilliance.com/kab/karr/lkie.pdf December 2004.

Latham, Jackie E. M. "The Bradleys of Birmingham: The Unorthodox Family of 'Micahel Field.' " *History Workshop Journal*, Spring 2003. Available: http://www3.oup.co.uk/hiwork/hdb/Volume_55/Issue_01/550189.sgm.abs.html September 2004.

Lee, F. N. "The Anabaptists and Their Stepchildren." Available: http://www.reformedreader.org/history/step.htm October 2004.

Lindering, Jonah. "Abu Isa'." Available: http://www.livius.org/men mh/messiah/messiah_med02.html September 2004.

———. "Abulafia." Available: http://www.livius.org/men mh/messiah/messiah_med06.html September 2004.

———. "Athronges, the Shepherd (4 BCE)." Available: http://www.livius.org/men-mh/messiah/messianic_claimants03.html September 2004.

———. "The Egyptian Prophet (between 52 and 58 CE)." Available: http://www.livius.org/men-mh/messiah/messianic_claimants09.html September 2004.

———. "John of Gischala (67–70 CE)." Available: http://www.livius.org/men-mh/messiah/messianic_claimants12.html September 2004.

———. "Judas, son of Hezekiah (4 BCE)." Available: http://www.livius.org/men-mh/messiah/messianic_claimants01.html September 2004.

———. "Simon of Peraea (4 BCE)." Available: http://www.livius.org/men mh/messiah/messianic_claimants02.html September 2004.

———. "The Samaritan Prophet (36 CE)." Available: http://www.livius.org/men-mh/messiah/messianic_claimants06.html September 2004.

_____. "Simon bar Giora (69–70 CE)." Available: http://www.livius.org/men-mh/messiah/messianic_claimants14.html September 2004.

_____. "Vespasian (67 CE)." Available: http://www.livius.org/men mh/messiah/messianic_claimants13.html September 2004.

Maimonides. "Maimonides—the Messiah: The Laws Concerning Mashiach; Chapters 11 & 12 of *Hilchos Melachim* from the *Mishneh Torah* of the Rambam." Available: http://chebar0.tripod.com/id109.htm May 2004.

Meyers, Barbara. "Textiles and the Reformation." *Unitarian Universalist History*, Part I (Fall, 2001). Available: http://www.online.sksm.edu/ce/papers/p meyers~textilesreformation.htm October 2004.

Miller, Glen. "Two Historical Issues in Acts: Theudas and the Sanhedrin." Available: http://www.christian-thinktank.com/qtheudy.html September 2004.

Munro, Dana C. *The Middle Ages, 395–1272* (New York: The Century Company, 1921), 354–365, as Available: http://www.shsu.edu/~his_ncp/Munro25.html October 2004.

Nayler, James. Unidentified compiler. "James Nayler's Spiritual Writings." Available: http://www.strecorsoc.org/jnayler/ September 2004.

Nigal, Gedalyah. "Transmigration of Souls," an excerpt from *Magic, Mysticism, and Hasidism*. Available: http://www.storypower.com/hasidic/Articles/Themes_In_Hasidic_Stories/nigal_1transf. html December 2004.

Pepys, Samuel. *The Diary of Samuel Pepys*. Edited with additions by Henry B. Wheatley. Electronic edition of 1666 diary prepared by David Widger as part of the Gutenberg Project. No date, publisher, or location provided for print edition utilized. Available: http://www.gutenberg.net/etext03/sp56g10.txt May 2004.

Peters, Robert. "Ann Lee." *The Reader's Companion to American History*. Available: http://college.hmco.com/history/readerscomp/rcah/html/ah_052200_leeann.htm November 2004.

Peters, Roxanne. "Jemima Wilkinson." Available: http://www.rootsweb.com/~nwa/jemima.html September 2004.

Pietrafesa, Dan. "Chodikee Lake: A Great Place for Paddling." *Poughkeepsie Journal*, August 15, 2002. Available: http://www.poughkeepsiejournal.com/sportsextra/thegreateight/sp081502s3.shtml#jump September 2004.

Rempel, Gerhard. "Oliver Cromwell: Constitutional Crisis in England." Available: http://mars.acnet.wnec.edu/~grempel/courses/wc2/lectures/cromwell.html September 2004.

Rigby, Malcolm. "The Abode of Love." Undated article from *The Somerset Gateway* (Great Britain). Available: http://www.dgbdgb.btinternet.co.uk/clapton/agapemon.htm September 2004.

Rosman, Moshe. "Life Stories: Shivhei Ha-Besht." An extract from *Founder of Hasidism: A Quest for the Historical Ba'al Shem Tov*. Available: http://www.storypower.com/hasidic/Articles/Background_and_Sources/rosman1.html October 2004.

Schaff, Philip. Chapter 10, "History and Its Suppression," *History of the Christian Church*, 1910 edition. Available: http://www.bible.ca/history/philip-schaff/5_ch10.htm October 2004.

Segal, Eliezer. "Rabbi Nahman, Napoleon and Other Messiahs." Part of From the Sources. Available: http://www.acs.ucalgary.ca/~elsegal/Shokel/940630_Napoleon.html September 2004.

Sheikh, Usman, and Mohd Elfie Nieshaem Juferi. "Gamaliel and the Revolt of Theudas." Copyright 2004. Available: http://bismikaallahuma.org/Bible/Contra/External/gamaliel-error.htm September 2004.

Shoham, S. Giora. "Antonin Artaud: Noah's Ark Outside Time," *Journal of Criminal*

Justice and Popular Culture 8(3) (2001). Available: http://www.albany.edu/scj/jcjpc/vol8is3/shoham.html December 2004.

Stevenson, Sandy (?). "Elspeth Buchan (1738–1791)." Part of Tour Scotland_website. Available: http://www.fife.50megs.com/elspeth-buchan.htm September 2004.

Suetonius. *Lives of the Caesars*. J. C. Rolf translation. Available: http://www.fordham.edu/halsall/ancient/suetonius-index.html September 2004.

Tacitus. *Histories*. Translated by Alfred John Church and William Jackson Brodribb. Available: http://classics.mit.edu/Tacitus/histories.html September 2004.

Telushkin, Joseph. "Hasidim and Mitnagdim." Extract from *Jewish Literacy: The Most Important Things to Know About the Jewish Religion, Its People and Its History* (New York: William Morrow and Co., 1991). Available: http://www.jewishvirtuallibrary.org/jsource/Judaism/hasidim_&_mitnagdim.html October 2004.

Tilles, Yrachmiel. "A Mystic Story: Master Kabbalists, Chasidic Rebbes, and Remarkable Jews." Adapted from an article in *Kfar Chabad Magazine*. Available: http://www.kabbalaonline.org/Holydays/ellul/A_Lesson_in_Talmud.asp October 2004.

Tov, Israel Baal Shem (the Besht). *Readings of Stories of the Besht*. Read by Sholom Dov Ber Wineberg. Available: http://www.sichosinenglish.org/audio/stories/ October 2004.

Whitman, Stephen. "The Death-Bed Soliloquy of Stephen Whitman, May 6, 1866." Posted by Roy Whitman, descendent of Edward Whitman. Available: http://www.whitmania.com/pdpdpd/deathbed.htm September 2004.

Internet Resources: Unattributed Material

"Ba'al Shem Tov." *Jewish Heritage Online Magazine*. Available: http://www.jhom.com/personalities/nahman_bratslav/baalshem.htm October 2004

"Church Succession to the Twentieth Century." Part of Reformed Baptist Reader. Available: http://www.reformedreader.org/history/ivey/ch10.htm September 2004.

"David Joris," *Encyclopaedia Britanica* (11th edition, 1911), as reprinted at LoveToKnow 1911 Online Encyclopedia. © 2003, 2004 LoveToKnow. Available: http://35.1911encyclopedia.org/J/JO/JORIS_DAVID.htm October 2004.

"Elspeith Buchan." Available: http://21.1911encyclopedia.org/B/BU/BUCHAN_ELSPETH.htm September 2004.

"Elspeith Buchan." Part of Electric Scotland.com. Available: http://www.electricscotland.com/history/other/buchan_elspith.htm September 2004.

"English Dissenters: Ranters." Available: http://www.exlibris.org/nonconform/engdis/ranters.html September 2004.

"Edward Wightman." Part of Wikiverse: A World of Knowledge. Available: http://edward-wightman.wikiverse.org/ September 2004.

"Familists." *Encyclopaedia Britannica* (11th edition, 1911), as reprinted at LoveToKnow 1911 Online Encyclopedia. © 2003, 2004 LoveToKnow. Available: http://18.1911encyclopedia.org/F/FA/FAMILISTS.htm October 2004.

"Henry Arthington and Richard Cosin." Part of Redefining the Sacred in Early Modern England. Available: http://www.folger.edu/institute/sacred/image15.html September 2004.

"Israel ben Eliezer." Part of Wikipedia, as reprinted from the 1906 *Encyclopedia Judaica*. Available: http://en.wikipedia.org/wiki/Israel_ben_Eliezer September 2004.

"Jemima Wilkinson," *Western Palladium* of New Lisbon, Ohio, September 5, 1829, as reprinted by Dale R. Broadhurst as part of his *Readings in Early Mormon History*. Available: http://www.lavazone2.com/dbroadhu/OH/miscohio.htm September 2004.

"Jemima Wilkinson." Part of Women in American History. Copyright 1999. Available: http://search.eb.com/women/articles/Wilkinson_Jemima.html September 2004.

"Joanna Southcott (1750–1814): Domestic Servant and Upholsterer." Part of the website, The Apocalypse in English Romantic Literature, Anne Zanzucchi, General Editor. Available: http://www.rochester.edu/College/ENG/eng529/aeza/southcott.htm September 2004.

"Messiah." WorldIQ. Available: http://www.wordiq.com/definition/Messiah October 2004.

"Nahman of Bratslav: Master of Tales." *Jewish Heritage Online Magazine.* Available: http://www.jhom.com/personalities/nahman_bratslav/index.htm September 2004.

"The Buchanites." Part of *The Burns Encyclopedia.* Available: http://www.robertburns.org/encyclopedia/BuchanitesThe.135.shtml September 2004.

"The Universal Friend." Part of The Yates County Office of Public History. Available: http://www.yatescounty.org/upload/12/historian/friend.html September 2004.

Sefer Yetzirah, translated from the Hebrew by William W. Westcott (1887). Available: http://www.houseofthehorizon.org/public/documents.php?id=123 October 2004.

"Weird Cult Waits in House of God: Venue for Christ's Second Coming Will Be an English Town." *Evening Times,* Glasgow (United Kingdom), August 16, 2003. Available: http://www.rickross.com/reference/general/general573.html September 2004.

Index

Abbas, Ibn Samuel 74, 75
Abdallah, Yusuf 208
Abode of Love 208
Abraham 15, 133
Abraham of Avila 81–82
Abraham of Granada 89
Abravanel, Isaac 83, 84
Abulafia, Abraham 78–80, 100, 108
Adams, Mary 186
Aden 208
Adonai 134
Adret, Solomon 79
Adrianople 98, 142, 148; trial of Zevi in 140–141
Africa 87
Agapemone 208
Agrippa 33
Akiba (Aqiba), Rabbi 39, 40, 41, 42; and oral law of Judaism 109; death 48
Albany, New York 188
Albigensians 86
alchemy 106
Alexandria, Egypt 38
Alfakar, Ibn 72
Allstedt, Germany 112
Almohades movement 71
Almyer, John 126
Alonso, Luis 85
Alroy, David 72–75
Alroy, Solomon 72, 73
Alshekh, Moses 107
amphitheaters 9
Amsterdam 68
Anabaptism/Anabaptists 113, 119, 121, 122
Anglicanism/Anglican Church 88, 129
Antichrist 52, 64–65, 77, 79, 84, 88, 172, 179, 190; conqueror of 125, 177
Antioch 56
anti–Semitism, rationale behind 66
Antonia (fortress) 33

Antony, Mark 9
Arabia 91, 93
Arabs 57
Arcabatene 29
Archelaus 18, 19, 20
Ardington, Henry 124, 125
Arye, Abn 69–70
Ashkenazi, Joseph 92
Asia Minor: Herod's trip to 11
astrology 75
atheists 170
Athronges 14–15
Augsburg Confession 120

Babylonia 50, 53, 62; anonymous messiah from 58; Jewish religious life in 53–54, 70
Baghdad 67, 72, 74
Balaam 75
Baptists 166, 167, 168, 179, 193, 205
"Barebones Parliament" 181, 182
bar Giora, Simon 29–31
bar-Kahana, Abba (Rabbi) 52–53
Bar Kappara of Sepphoris (Rabbi) 8
bar Kochba, Simeon: leadership policies and actions 43–49; as messiah 39–41; non–miracle-worker 41–43
bar Tahlifa, Rab Hanan 53
Bateman, Roland 170
Becon, Thomas 125
beggars 172
Ben Nehemiah, Natronai 58–59
Benjamin of Tudela 74
Berit Menuha 89
Betar (town) 47
Black Sea 72
Blasphemy Act 170
Bockelson, Jan 113–119
Bohemia 152
Book of Visions 108
Book of Wondrous Wisdom 81

250 Index

Book of Zerubbabel 57
Botarel, Moses 89
Bourignon, Antoinette 186
Bradley, Charles 205
Brazil 96
Bristol, England 173, 174, 176, 196
Brothers, Richard 195–200
Buchan, Elspeth ("Luckie") 189–192
Buchan, Robert 189
Buchanites 190–192
Bucharest 154
Burns, Robert 192
Byzantium 65, 66

Caesarea: building of 10
Caesarea of Cappadocia 56
Cairo, Egypt 135, 136
Calabrese, Hayyim Vital 104
Caligula 10
Calvinism 88, 179
Cardenete, Spain 110, 111
Cardozo, Abraham 145–150; as defender of Zevi's conversion to Islam 142
Cassius Dio 39
Cathars 86
Charles I (King of England) 170–171, 178–180
Charles II (King of England) 180
Charles V (Holy Roman Emperor) 93, 97, 99, 102
Cheapside (London) 124
Clement VII (Pope) 92, 93, 94, 95, 96, 99, 102
Cleopatra 9
Communism 6
Community of the Sacred 122
Connecticut 194
Constantine the Great 50
Constantinople 87, 135, 138, 139; Cardozo in 148
Copinger, Edmund 124
Cordova, Spain 69
Cordovero, Moshe 103–104
Cossacks 128
Cresscas, Hasdai 89
Crete: messianic claimant in 54–55; second century insurrection in 38
Crooked Lake 195
Crouch, Nathaniel 141
Cromwell, Oliver 176, 180, 181, 182, 183, 184
Cromwell, Richard 176, 183
crucifixion 19, 58
Crusade (First): attacks on Jews during 65–66; estimates during, of appearance of Anti-Christ 64–65; messianic appearance dates among Jews 65, 67
Crusade (Second) 67

Crusade (Third) 67
Cyprus, second century insurrection in 38
Cyrene, second century insurrection in 38, 39
Cyrus the Great 36

Damascus 60, 107, 108
Daniel (Bible prophet) 72, 75, 113, 129, 177, 197, 198
David (king) 8, 15, 41, 54, 72, 91, 113, 116, 119
"Davidists" 120
de Leon, Moses 86
Derech HaShem 153–154
Dias, Luis 102–103
Diaspora 39
Donmeh (sect) 151
Donzeille (Daniel ben Isaac) 94
Dosa (Rabbi) 52
Dubrovner, Isaac Leib 165
Dusentscheuer, Jan 115

Easter 115
Effendi, Mehmed 141
Egypt 62, 92, 108, 207, 208; messiahs from 27–29; second century insurrection in 38–39
Eisenstadt, Mordecai 152
Eleazar (Rabbi) of Modiin 46–48
Elijah (Bible prophet) 73, 111, 115, 143, 206
Elizabeth (Queen) 124, 125–126, 198
Emmaus 14, 19, 57
end of world: already arrived 121; date estimates centering about 1000 A.D. 63; end times thinking in mid-seventeenth century 127–130; in Fifth Monarchy Men thinking 177
England 119, 122, 123, 125, 129, 134, 184, 185, 195; propaganda for Zevi as messiah 137–138; traders from 131
Enoch 115
Enriquez, Dona Juana 130
Essenes 16, 17, 18, 21
Essex (England) 123, 186
Ethiopia 61, 92
Eucharist 122
Euphrates River 58
Eusebius 40, 43, 48
Ezekiel (Bible prophet) 112
Ezra, Abraham Ibn 72

Fadus, Cuspius 25, 26
"Familists" 122
"Family of Love" 121
Felix 24, 28
Ferizon, Abraham B. Mordecai 92
Fifth Monarchy Men 130, 172–183; reasons for popularity of 138

Index

Fox, George 172, 173, 174
France 64, 76, 77, 86, 184, 185, 195
Francis I (French king) 93
Francis of Assisi 77
Franciscan Spirituals 81, 82
Frank, Eva 159–160
Frank, Jacob Leibovicz 154–159
Frank, Josef 159
Frank, Rochus 159
Frankfort, Germany 157
Frankist Movement 154–159
Franklin, William 168–170
"French plague" 83
French Revolution 197, 201

Gadbury, Mary 168, 169
Galilee 19, 46, 87, 205; messiah to appear in 104, 108–109
Galimidi, Solomon 148
Gallipoli 140
Gamala 21
Gamaliel (Rabbi) 26, 27
Garden of Eden 204
Gaulanitis 21
gematria 65, 77–78, 142
Geneva Bible 125
Georg, David 119–120
George III (king of England) 197, 199–200
Germany 89, 157, 178; expulsion of Jews from 85; Gentile-Jewish tensions 128; migrants to Palestine 87
Gidel (Rabbi) 7
Gnosticism 86
Gog and Magog 53, 67
Gomez, Maria 85, 131
Goodwin, Thomas 181
Gratus 13
Greece 78
Greek 111
Gresbeck, Henry 118
Guibert (Abbot of Nogent) 64–65
Guide to the Perplexed 78

Hacket, William 123–125
Ha-Cohen, Joseph 90
Ha-Dani, Eldad 61–62
Hadrian 41, 47
Halfon, Elia 100
Halhed, Nathaniel B. 198
Halley's Comet 101
ha-Nasi, Judah (Rabbi) 52
Hanover, Nathan N. 128
Hasidism 160–163, 206
Hebrew 92, 98, 111
Henry VII 184
Henry VIII 88, 100
Heraclius 57

Herod the Great 14, 16–17; building projects 9–10; crushing of insurrectionary forces after his death 18–19; as Messianic claimant 10–12; palace 12; relatives punished by Rome 19; rise to political leadership 8–9
Hezekiah (king) 7–8, 133
high priest 30
Hillel (Rabbi) 7, 11
hippodromes 9
Historia Augusta 48, 49
Hitler, Adolf 6
Holland 135, 186; traders of 131
Holy Spirit 69, 167, 186
Hungary 87, 152
Huns 52
Hushil 56–57

Idumaea 19
Iggeret Teman 69
Ikriti, Shemariah ben Elijah 88
In Praise of the Besht 160–161
India 208
Ines of Herrera 85
Inquisition 85, 101, 102; injustices of 110; in Mexico 130
insanity 111, 124, 152, 168, 185, 199
Ireland 180, 202, 204
Isa, Abu 59–61
Isaiah (Bible prophet) 112, 162, 207
Islam 70, 71, 73, 141, 142, 147, 155
Italy 77, 78, 89, 95, 147, 151, 152, 153, 184; Nathan of Gaza in 142; restrictions on Jews 85
Izmir, Turkey 147

Jaffa, Palestine 149
Jeffrey, William 123
Jeremiah (Bible prophet) 112, 177
Jericho 13
Jerome 43, 64
Jerusalem 14, 19, 25, 27, 30, 33, 41, 56, 62, 65, 73, 90, 94, 107, 108–109, 112, 123, 135, 141, 171, 183, 196; Cardozo blocked from coming to 149; Jesus' entry into 173
Jesus of Nazareth 60, 69, 79, 87, 166–167, 168, 174; miracles of 145; re-appeared in form of Jacob Frank 158; triumphal entry into Jerusalem 173
Joachim of Floris 77
Job 133
John (gospel of) 116, 167
John, Prester 93
John of Giscala 31, 32
John the Baptist 163, 207
John III (king of Portugal) 95–96
Jordan River 25

Index

Joseph (Rabbi) 7
Josephus 5, 11, 13, 16, 20, 21, 22, 24, 25, 26, 28, 29, 30, 32, 34–35
Joshua 25
A Journey to Jerusalem 141
Juarez, Blanca 131
Judaea (Judea) 24, 25, 33, 49, 50, 205
Judas (son of Hezekiah) 15–16
Judas (the Galilean) 20–22, 26
Julian 50–51

Kabbalah 77, 78, 80, 85–86, 89, 106, 133, 134, 139, 144, 145, 153; the Bresht and 160, 161, 162–163; Cardozo and 146; Luria of Safed and 103–105; more authoritative than the Torah 155; relation of Molko and Reubeni to 98–99; Zevi and 131
Karaites 88; messiahs of 70–71
Karo, Joseph (Rabbi) 107
Keuka Lake 195
Knipperdolling, Bernard 114–115, 118
Kuhayl I, Shukr 207–208
Kuhayl II, Shukr 209
Kurdistan 72

Lamentations Rabbah 33
Laudianism 179
League of the Elect 112, 113
Lee, Ann *see* Mother Ann
Lemlein, Asher 89–91
lepers 147
Lettsom, John (Dr.) 200
levites 71
"Linon," messiah of 63–64
Lisbon, Portugal 102
Lithuania 151
Livorno, Italy 95, 135
London, England 123, 124, 168, 169, 171, 176, 196, 201, 204; earthquake in 199; George Fox in 173; plague in 129
London Times 198
"Long Parliament" 180
"lost tribes of Israel" 61–62, 78
Ludwig, Claus 122
Luria of Safed 103–105, 152, 206, 207
Luther, Martin 88, 114, 121, 126
Lutheranism 88
Luzzatto, Moshe Hayim 153–154
Lyons, France 63

Maimonides 42, 63, 64, 67, 68, 69–70, 75, 76, 78
Malachi (Bible book) 167
Manchester, England 186
Mantino, Jacob 100, 101
Marranos 94, 95, 97, 101; as supporters of Zevi 139

Marseilles, France 76
Masada 29–30, 33
Matthys, Jan 114–115
Mediterranean Sea 38
Megillat Setarim ("Book of Secrets") 206
Mein Kampf 6
Melchizedek 79
Menahem 33–34
Menahem of Chazaria 67
Menahem the Essene 16–18
Mendes, Francisco 103
Mesopotamia 50, 58; eleventh century messiah in 67; second century insurrection in 39
Messiah: hopes concerning in 400s 52–54; Jewish and Christian speculation concerning from 1300 to 1600 83–85, 87–88; meaning and application of term 3–6; mothers of 130–131, 159–160, 200–204; right to freedom from traditional religious and moral norms 132–133; speculation concerning in mid-seventeenth century 128; spiritual insight as proof of 145; successful triumph of temptation over him prepares him for messianic duties 142; two messiah concept 133, 149–150, 151, 152
Methodists 205
Mexico 127
Mickiewicz, Adam 158
Midlands Association of Baptists 168
midrash 17
Mishnah 17, 134
Modena, Italy 152
Mohammed 60, 71, 91, 93
Molko, Solomon 96, 97, 97–102
Moore, John 123
Moravia 152, 157
Morocco 71, 87
Moses 22, 23, 54, 164, 167
Moses of Crete 54–55
Moshe (Rabbi) of Fez 68
Mosul 74
Mother Ann 186–189
Mount Gerizzim 22
Mount of Olives 28, 64
Muggleton, Lodowick 172
Muhlhausen, Germany 113
Munster, Germany 113–119, 121, 124, 177–178
Munster, Sebastian 90
Muntzer, Thomas 111–113, 121
mysticism: Jewish and Christian in thirteenth century 77–78; and Kabbalah 78

Nahman of Bratslav 163–165
Nathan (Rabbi) 11
Nathan of Gaza 135, 136, 143–145, 149;

Index

explanation for Zevi's conversion to Islam 142; grave of 154; as propagandist 138, 139; second most important man in Zevi movement 147
Nayler, James 172–176
Nehemiah 56–57
Nero 34, 78
New England 180
New Model Army 179, 180
New York City 188
Newfoundland, Canada 195
Newgate Prison 184, 196
Nicholas III (Pope) 79–80
Niklaes (Nicholas), David 120, 121–122
Nile River 103
Norwood, Robert 183, 184, 185
Nottidge, Josias 209

Obadiah 59–61, 71
Octavian 9
Olivi, Pierre Jean 82
Owen, John 181

Pacensis, Isador 59
pacifism 113–114, 119
Paine, Thomas 201
Palestine 72, 81, 87, 90, 91, 92, 95, 96, 98, 104, 134, 140, 150, 159, 171, 184, 196; flight to 68; messianic hopes in mid-tenth century 62; Polish pilgrimage to 151; unrest in 110s 39
Panacea Society 204
Parliament (England) 170, 179, 184, 186, 198; opposition to higher taxes 178; trial of James Nayler 175–176
Parliament of the Saints 181
Parthia (wars with Rome) 48
Passover 12, 68, 90, 208; Israel to be redeemed during 148
Peasants' Revolt 113
Pentecost 143
Pepys, Samuel 129, 137
Peraea 13, 26
Pereira, Ines 130
Persia 3, 52, 53, 87; messiahs in 50–51, 59–61
Peter (apostle) 123
Pfefferkorn, Yosef 90
Pharisees 21
Philip of Hesse 120
philosophy 78
Pilate 23
Pisces 134
plague 122, 147
Podolia 154, 160
Poland 87, 129, 135, 138, 140, 151, 151, 152, 157; Frankist movement as still controversial in late 20th century 157–158; invasion of by Cossacks 128; Podolia district 154 polygamy 117; division of 17th century Jewish opinion on practice of 146
Pordage, John 184
Portugal: earthquake predicted in 100, 101; expulsion of Jews from 85; Reubeni and king of 95–96
Potter, Francis 130
Prince, Henry 208–210
prophets 108, 124, 136, 144, 148
Prossnitz, Yehuda Leib 152–153
Pseudochristus 170
Puritans 129, 178, 179; setback in influence of 125

Quakers 172, 173, 175, 176, 186, 193, 200; Bristol a center of 174
Querido, Yakov 150–151

Ranters 172
Rashba 80, 81
Red Sea 54
Reggio, Italy 152
Rembrandt 131
resurrection of dead 133, 209
Reubeni, David 91–97
Revealed Knowledge 196, 197, 198
Revelation (book of) 18, 88, 168, 177, 180, 187, 197, 201, 202
Rhode Island 193, 194
Robins, John 171–172
Rouen France 66
Rome 31, 32, 51, 52, 69, 94, 96, 100; bridges 100; flood of 99, 100–101; sack of 99
Rothmann, Bernard 114–115, 117, 119
"Rump Parliament" 180, 181, 183
Russia 129, 159
Russian Orthodox Church 157
Russo, Barukhia 153

Sabbath 61
Sabbath River 78
Sabinus 12
Sadducees 21
Safed, Palestine 87, 103, 104, 108
Safrin, Judah Jehiel 206–207
St. George's Field 185
Salonika, Greece 98, 99, 134, 151, 152
Samaria 10, 19; messiahs from 22–24
Samaritans 47, 70
Samson, Solomon b. (Rabbi) 66
Sanchez, Bartolome 110–111
Sandemanians 205
Sandford, James 126
Saxony (Germany) 112
Schapiro, Nathan 67

Index

Scotland 179, 180
scribes 106
Sea of Galilee 21, 87
seaports 10
Second Helvetic Confession 119
Sefer ha-Mefo'ar 99
Sefer ha-Zohar see *Zohar*
Segal, Jacob (Rabbi) 84
Seneca Lake, New York 194
Seor of Syria 57–58
Sepphoris 8, 16, 19
Serene 58–59
Severus 49
Sevilla, Simon Vaez 130
Shakers 186–189
Shalom, Abraham 108–109
Shammai (Rabbi) 17
Shaput 51
Shekinah 153
Shiloh 202, 205
Shlomo, Hayim ben 151–152
Sicarii 22, 29, 30
Silencing of the Jews and the Christians through Rational Argument 74
Simmons, Martha 173, 174
Simon 12–14
Simson, Elspeth 189–192
Sinai 24
Smyrna 131, 134, 135–136, 139; foreign merchants traveling to 154
Society for the Suppression of Vice 205
Society of the Pious 151
Socrates 54, 55
soul: passed on from one generation to another 105
South America 127
Southcott, Joanna 200–204, 205
Spain 52, 72, 78, 80, 81, 84, 86, 110; danger of Hebrew Bible study in 146; expulsion of Jews from 85
Spaxton, England 209
Stalin, Joseph 6
Standerin, Abraham 186, 189
Starky, Samuel 209
Stoke, England 208
Storch, Nicklas 112
Strange Effects of Faith 201
Stranger, Hannah 176
Stranger, John 176
Suetonius 35–36, 37
Sukkot 46
Sweden 129
Syria 36, 49, 50, 57–58; messiahs in 82; travel route through 87

Tacitus 35, 37
Taheb 23
Talmud 17, 39, 60, 70, 81, 86, 100, 107, 109, 131, 158, 164; destruction of copies 155
Tanchelm of Bruges 68–69
Tany, Thomas 183–186
Tartars 128
taxes 21
Tekoa 46
temple (Jerusalem) 9, 30, 33, 42, 50–51, 86, 90, 108, 133, 148
Tetragrammaton 134, 153
theaters 9
Therot, Catherine 200
Theudas 25–27
Thirty Years' War 127–128
Tiber (River) 100–101
Tiberias 56, 57
Titus 31, 34
Tob, Shem (Rabbi) 84
Tov, Israel Baal Shem ("the Bresht") 160–163
Treaty of Westphalia 128
Tribe of Judah 74
Tripoli 146; Cardozo's role in overthrow of ruler 147
tuberculosis 172
Tumart, Ibn 71
Tunis 147
Turkey 78, 131, 151
Turner, George 205
Tzoref, Yehoshua Heshel 151

Ukraine 128, 154
Urban (Pope) 64

Vandals 52
Vatican 100
veneral disease 83
Venice, Italy 85, 89, 100, 146; diplomats of 95; expulsion of Reubeni 96; rabbis of urge action against Cardozo 147
Vespasian 5, 34–37
Vienna, Austria 157, 159
Visigoths 52
Vital, Joseph (of Safed) 106–109, 206; on Luria's methodology of gaining insight into Kabbalah 104–105
Vitell, Christopher 122

War of Varus 19
Ward, John ("Zion") 204–206
Wardley, Jane 186
Wardley, John 186
Wedlock, Timothy 175
Weimar, Germany 112
White, Hugh 190
White, John 123
Whitefield, George 193

Wightman, Edward 166–168
Wilkinson, Jemima 193–195
Winchester, England 169
Winthrop, John 180
Wondrous Tale of Alroy 72
Woodward, William 169
Worms, Germany 62
Wycliffe 126

Yemen 69, 75–77, 207, 208
Yohanan (Rabbi) 43, 44
Yosef (Rabbi) 7
Yudghan of Hamadan 61

zaddik 163–164
Zealots 22, 33
Zechariah 8, 149
Zerubbabel 8
Zevi, Mordecai 131
Zevi, Sabbatai 129, 131–143, 152, 154; importance of Cardozo in movement 146–147
Zevi, Sarah 135–136
Zohar 89, 104, 105, 154, 158, 207; date for appearance of Messiah in 133
Zoharists 158
Zwickau, Germany 112